West Coast Australia

THIS EDITION WRITTEN AND RESEARCHED BY

Brett Atkinson

Kate Armstrong, Steve Waters

PLAN YOUR TRIP

ON THE ROAD

RACHEL LEWIS/GETTY IMAGES ©

HOUTMAN ABROLHOS ISLANDS P164

KATY CLEMMANS/GETTY IMAGES ©

QUOKKA P92

Contents

UNDERSTAND

SURVIVAL GUIDE

SPECIAL FEATURES

Welcome to West Coast Australia

If you subscribe to the 'life's a beach' school of thought, you'll fall in love with Western Australia and its 12,500km of spectacular coastline.

An Immense, Sparsely Populated Land

If the huge expanses of Western Australia (WA) were a separate nation, it would be the world's 10th-largest country. Most of the state's population clings to the coast – yet you can wander along a beach for hours without seeing another footprint, or be one of only a handful of campers stargazing in a national park.

The south is a playground of white-sand beaches, expanses of springtime wildflowers and lush green forests teeming with life. Up north in the Kimberley, you'll encounter wide open spaces that conceal striking gorges, waterfalls and ancient rock formations.

Action Stations

WA has plenty for the active traveller. Traverse the 963km Bibbulmun Track – or focus on a few spectacular day walks – or mountain bike the 1000km Munda Biddi Trail. Shorter but equally interesting walks include wandering amid the wildflowers of the Stirling Range National Park and negotiating Porongurup's granite formations. Dive and snorkel in stunning marine parks and around fascinating shipwrecks, surf around Margaret River, and kiteboard and windsurf off Lancelin's expansive beaches.

All Creatures Great & Small

WA's fauna includes kangaroos, emus and colourful parrots, but there are also chances to get acquainted with lesser-known local critters such as quokkas, bilbies and potoroos. The WA coast's lengthy dalliance with the Indian and Southern Oceans means opportunities to spot marine wildlife are also extraordinary. Each year about 30,000 whales cruise the coast-hugging 'Humpback Hwy'. At Ningaloo Marine Park you can dive with the world's largest fish, the whale shark; while at Rockingham, Bunbury and Monkey Mia you can interact with wild dolphins.

The Finer Things in Life

Perth and neighbouring Fremantle are cosmopolitan cities, yet both retain a laid-back feel courtesy of their fantastic beaches and parks. Bold infrastructure projects are transforming central Perth, while the inner neighbourhoods of Northbridge and Leederville are growing in culinary confidence. Elsewhere, earlier boom times have left grand architectural legacies in Fremantle, Albany, Guildford and York.

Around Margaret River and the southwest, vignerons and brewers craft world-class wines and beers, complemented by the inventive menus of the region's restaurants. Truffles are grown down south, and WA's seafood is consistently sublime.

Why I Love West Coast Australia

By Brett Atkinson, Writer

Perth's pride at being the world's most remote capital is reflected in the verve and independence of the locals, and I love exploring the state's culinary scene, which combines great wine, farmers markets and local produce. Fremantle's historic townscape – and excellent pubs serving great craft beer – are worth multiple leisurely explorations, and the state's elemental red-dirt outback expanses are compellingly beautiful. Edging the cobalt Indian Ocean, the cliff-studded coastline is best explored by hiking or in a small plane, while always keeping a keen eye out for migrating whales.

For more about our writers, see page 272.

Above: Greens Pool in William Bay National Park (p138)

West Coast Australia

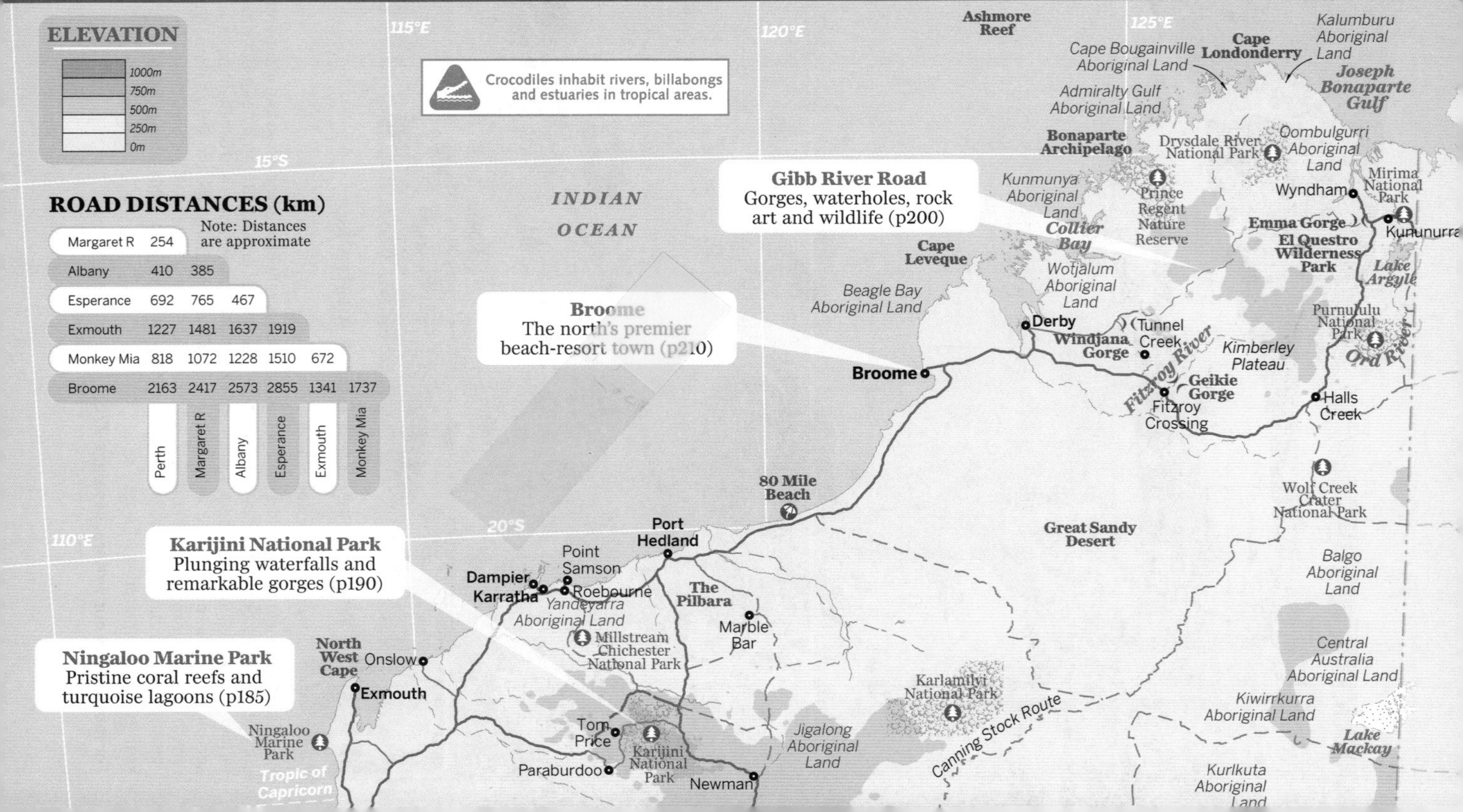

0 — 200 km
0 — 100 miles

ELEVATION

1000m
750m
500m
250m
0m

Crocodiles inhabit rivers, billabongs and estuaries in tropical areas.

ROAD DISTANCES (km)

Note: Distances are approximate

	Perth	Margaret R	Albany	Esperance	Exmouth	Monkey Mia
Margaret R	254					
Albany	410	385				
Esperance	692	765	467			
Exmouth	1227	1481	1637	1919		
Monkey Mia	818	1072	1228	1510	672	
Broome	2163	2417	2573	2855	1341	1737

Gibb River Road
Gorges, waterholes, rock art and wildlife (p200)

Broome
The north's premier beach-resort town (p210)

Karijini National Park
Plunging waterfalls and remarkable gorges (p190)

Ningaloo Marine Park
Pristine coral reefs and turquoise lagoons (p185)

115°E
120°E
125°E
110°E
15°S
20°S
INDIAN OCEAN
Ashmore Reef
Cape Bougainville Aboriginal Land
Cape Londonderry
Kalumburu Aboriginal Land
Joseph Bonaparte Gulf
Admiralty Gulf Aboriginal Land
Bonaparte Archipelago
Drysdale River National Park
Oombulgurri Aboriginal Land
Mirima National Park
Wyndham
Kununurra
Kunmunya Aboriginal Land
Prince Regent Nature Reserve
Collier Bay
Emma Gorge
El Questro Wilderness Park
Lake Argyle
Cape Leveque
Wotjalum Aboriginal Land
Beagle Bay Aboriginal Land
Purnululu National Park
Ord River
Derby
Tunnel Creek
Windjana Gorge
Kimberley Plateau
Fitzroy River
Geikie Gorge
Fitzroy Crossing
Halls Creek
Broome
80 Mile Beach
Wolf Creek Crater National Park
Great Sandy Desert
Port Hedland
Point Samson
Dampier
Karratha
Roebourne
The Pilbara
Yandeyarra Aboriginal Land
Marble Bar
Balgo Aboriginal Land
Millstream Chichester National Park
North West Cape
Onslow
Exmouth
Central Australia Aboriginal Land
Karlamilyi National Park
Kiwirrkurra Aboriginal Land
Tom Price
Karijini National Park
Jigalong Aboriginal Land
Canning Stock Route
Lake Mackay
Ningaloo Marine Park
Paraburdoo
Newman
Tropic of Capricorn
Kurlkuta Aboriginal Land

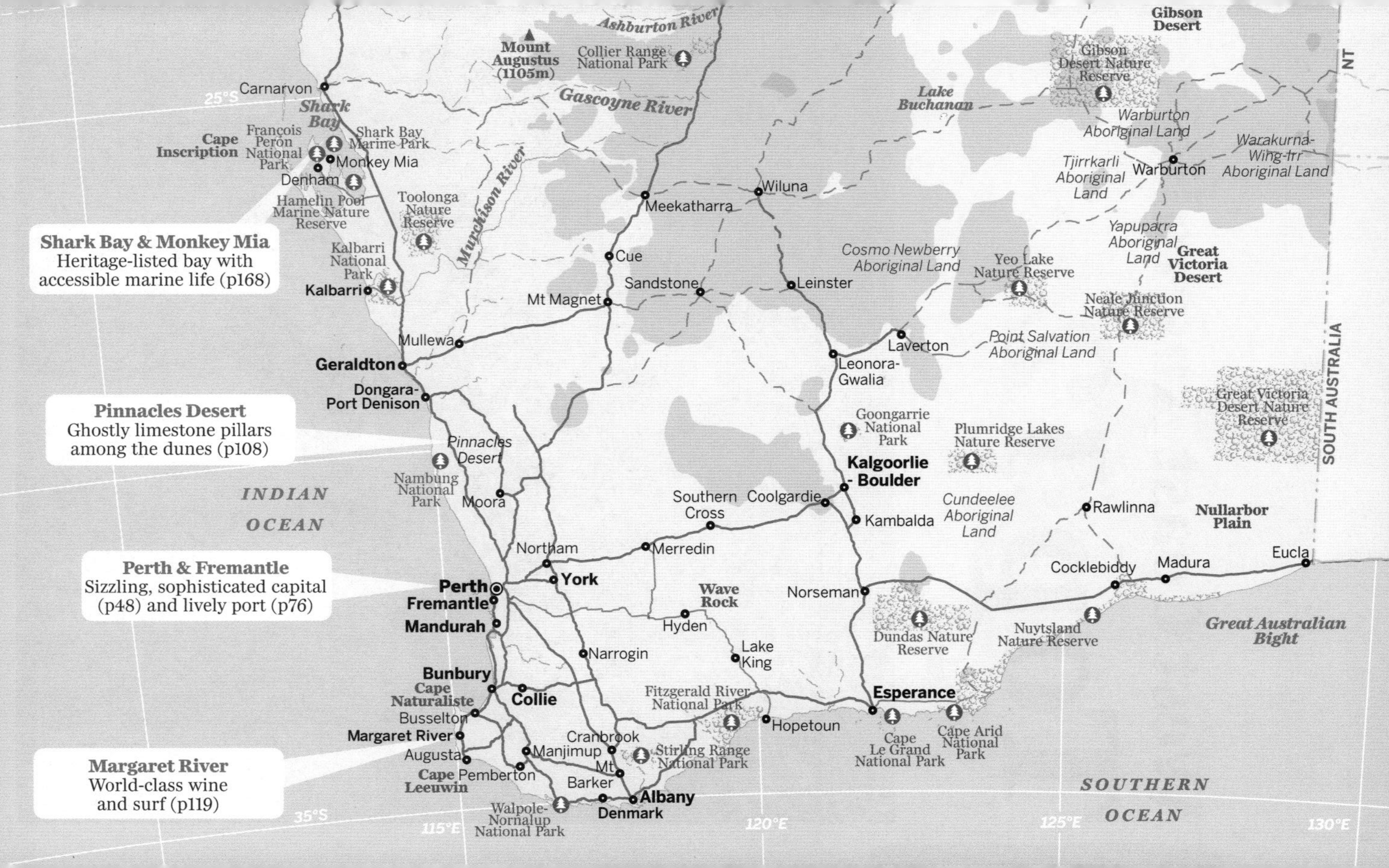

Shark Bay & Monkey Mia
Heritage-listed bay with accessible marine life (p168)
Pinnacles Desert
Ghostly limestone pillars among the dunes (p108)
Perth & Fremantle
Sizzling, sophisticated capital (p48) and lively port (p76)
Margaret River
World-class wine and surf (p119)
Ashburton River
Mount Augustus (1105m)
Collier Range National Park
Gascoyne River
Carnarvon
25°S
Shark Bay
Cape Inscription
François Peron National Park
Shark Bay Marine Park
Monkey Mia
Denham
Hamelin Pool Marine Nature Reserve
Toolonga Nature Reserve
Murchison River
Kalbarri National Park
Kalbarri
Mullewa
Geraldton
Dongara-Port Denison
Pinnacles Desert
Nambung National Park
Moora
INDIAN OCEAN
Perth
Fremantle
Mandurah
Bunbury
Cape Naturaliste
Busselton
Margaret River
Augusta
Cape Leeuwin
Pemberton
Manjimup
Collie
Walpole-Nornalup National Park
Denmark
Albany
Mt Barker
Cranbrook
Stirling Range National Park
Narrogin
Northam
York
Merredin
Southern Cross
Hyden
Wave Rock
Lake King
Fitzgerald River National Park
Hopetoun
Esperance
Cape Le Grand National Park
Cape Arid National Park
Norseman
Dundas Nature Reserve
Nuytsland Nature Reserve
Cocklebiddy
Madura
Eucla
Great Australian Bight
SOUTHERN OCEAN
35°S
115°E
120°E
125°E
130°E
Meekatharra
Cue
Mt Magnet
Sandstone
Wiluna
Leinster
Leonora-Gwalia
Laverton
Goongarrie National Park
Kalgoorlie-Boulder
Coolgardie
Kambalda
Cundeelee Aboriginal Land
Plumridge Lakes Nature Reserve
Rawlinna
Nullarbor Plain
Cosmo Newberry Aboriginal Land
Lake Buchanan
Yeo Lake Nature Reserve
Point Salvation Aboriginal Land
Neale Junction Nature Reserve
Great Victoria Desert
Yapuparra Aboriginal Land
Tjirrkarli Aboriginal Land
Warburton
Warburton Aboriginal Land
Warakurna-Wing-irr Aboriginal Land
Gibson Desert Nature Reserve
Gibson Desert
Great Victoria Desert Nature Reserve
SOUTH AUSTRALIA
NT

West Coast Australia's Top 12

Ningaloo Marine Park

1 Swim beside 'gentle giant' whale sharks, snorkel among pristine coral, surf off seldom-visited reefs and dive at one of the world's premier locations at this World Heritage–listed marine park (p185), which sits off the North West Cape on the Coral Coast. Rivalling the Great Barrier Reef for beauty, Ningaloo has much more accessible wonders: shallow, turquoise lagoons are entered straight from the beach for excellent snorkelling. Development is very low-key, so be prepared to camp, or take day trips from the access towns of Exmouth and Coral Bay.

Margaret River Wine Region

2 The joy of drifting from winery to craft brewery along country roads shaded by tall gum trees is just one of the delights of Australia's most beautiful wine region (p119). Right on its doorstep are the white sands of Geographe Bay, and even closer to the vines are the world-famous surf breaks of Yallingup and Margaret River Mouth. And then there are the caves – magical subterranean palaces of limestone, scattered along the main wine-tasting route. Sup, swim, surf, descend – the only difficulty is picking the order.

AUSCAPE/UIG/GETTY IMAGES ©

2

JANELLELUGGE/GETTY IMAGES ©

Shark Bay & Monkey Mia

3 The aquamarine waters of World Heritage–listed Shark Bay (p168) teem with an incredible diversity of marine life, from the world-famous dolphins of Monkey Mia to the ancient stromatolites of Hamelin Pool. National parks provide simple coastal camping, and excellent Indigenous cultural tours explain how to care for and understand Country. Explore remote, windblown Edel Land, Australia's westernmost tip, with towering limestone cliffs; cross over to historically rich Dirk Hartog Island; or relax and sail after the elusive, sea-grass-munching dugong. Below: Dolphins at Monkey Mia (p171)

Pinnacles Desert

4 It could be mistaken for the surface of Mars, but scattered among the dunes of Nambung National Park, thousands of ghostly limestone pillars rise from the surrounding plain like a vast, petrified alien army. One of the west's most bizarre landscapes, the Pinnacles (p108) attract thousands of visitors each year. Although it's easily enjoyed as a day trip from Perth, staying overnight in nearby Cervantes allows for multiple visits to experience the full spectrum of colour changes at dawn, sunset and full moon, when most tourists are back in their hotels.

DAVID WALL PHOTO/GETTY IMAGES ©

PETER PTSCHELINZEW/GETTY IMAGES ©

Perth & Fremantle

5 Perth may be isolated, but it's far from being a backwater. Scattered across the city (p48) are sophisticated restaurants showcasing modern Australian cuisine, while chic cocktail bars bubble away in unlikely lanes and restored heritage buildings. In contrast to the flashy face that Perth presents to the river, charmingly grungy inner suburbs echo with the hum of guitars and turntables, and the sizzle of woks. Just downstream, the lively port of Fremantle (p76) has a pub on just about every corner, most pouring craft brews from around Western Australia (WA) and the world. Above: Perth (p48) skyline

Broome

6 You can moan about the price of beer or how long your twice-cooked pork belly takes to arrive, but one thing is for certain: when that boiling crimson sun starts sinking slowly behind a conga line of camels into a languid Indian Ocean at Cable Beach, you'll realise there's no other place like it in the world. Broome (p210) is a melting pot of travellers, one of the world's great crossroads, and you'll find everything you need (though perhaps not everything you want) in the back streets, bars and markets, and on the noticeboards. Top right: Camel train, Cable Beach (p211)

Karijini National Park

7 Hidden deep in the heart of the Pilbara, the shady pools and plunging waterfalls of Karijini (p190) offer cool respite from the oppressive heat of the surrounding ironstone country. While most tourists are content to explore the open gorges, booking an adventure trip will take you beyond the public areas as you abseil, swim, dive, climb and paddle through deep water-worn passages. Up top, witness the amazing spring transformation as wildflowers carpet the plains, and get some altitude on the state's highest peaks, including the most excellent, Mt Bruce (1235m).

DOUGLAS PEARSON/GETTY IMAGES ©

Water Adventures

8 If you can't catch a wave on WA's 12,500km of coastline, mate, you're doing it wrong. In which case, head straight to one of the many surf schools and leave Margaret River (p124) and Gnaraloo (p173) to the pros, where breaks with nicknames such as 'Suicides' and 'Tombstones' beckon the fearless. Diving and snorkelling are excellent in many spots, and WA is the place to swim with your favourite marine animal. Windsurfers breeze off to gusty Lancelin (p107) and Gnaraloo, while paddlers splash their way along the many rivers. Above: Surfing at Margaret River (p124)

Bushwalking

9 Western Australia has 96 national parks, not counting the dozens of other nature reserves and regional parks. These special places present oodles of opportunities to go walkabout on the many waymarked trails, and camp in isolated spots. The Bibbulmun Track (p36), the mother of them all, starts on the outskirts of Perth and heads nearly 1000km to Albany on the south coast, sheltered by the cooling giant eucalypts of the southern forests. At the Valley of the Giants you can walk through the canopy on the 40m-high Tree Top Walk (p137). Top right: Tree Top Walk

Gibb River Road

10 Launch yourself into Australia's last frontier on a wild drive (p200) down this old cattle road into the heart of the Kimberley. This is not for the faint-hearted; you'll need a serious 4WD, good planning and plenty of fuel, spares, food and water. Bring big doses of self-reliance, flexibility and humour. The rewards are fantastic gorges, hidden waterholes, incredible rock art and amazing wildlife, and you'll gain a first-hand insight into life in the outback. Did we mention there are also flies, dust and relentless heat?

Wildlife

11 Welcome to a menagerie of wonderful species, many of which you may not have heard of. Visit the endangered numbats, woylies, bilbies and boodies of the Dryandra Woodland, the quokkas of Rottnest Island, or the freshwater crocodiles of Windjana Gorge National Park. Avian species include the shorebirds of Parry Lagoons Nature Reserve, and the red-tailed tropic birds of WA's southwest coast. Oceanic attractions include migrating humpback whales, the dolphins of Monkey Mia and the whale sharks of Ningaloo Reef. Below: Numbat

Indigenous Art

12 From urban galleries showcasing contemporary artists to centuries-old rock carvings (p242), the culture and spirit of Indigenous WA potently infuses this land. In Perth and Fremantle, visit the excellent Indigenart and Japingka galleries, while in the far northern reaches of the Kimberley visit local art cooperatives such as Waringarri or Mowanjum before looking back across the aeons at the Wandjina and Gwion Gwion rock-art sites. Bottom: Wandjina figures, Mitchell Plateau (p201)

11

12

Need to Know

For more information, see Survival Guide (p245)

Currency
Australian dollar ($)

Language
English

Visas
All visitors require a visa, although New Zealanders receive one on arrival. Residents of Canada, the US, many European countries and some Asian countries can apply online.

Money
ATMs widely available. Credit cards accepted in most hotels and restaurants.

Mobile Phones
Australia's network is compatible with most European phones, but generally not with the US or Japanese systems. The main service providers offer prepaid SIMs.

Time
Western Standard Time (GMT/UTC plus eight hours). Daylight saving does not operate in WA.

When to Go

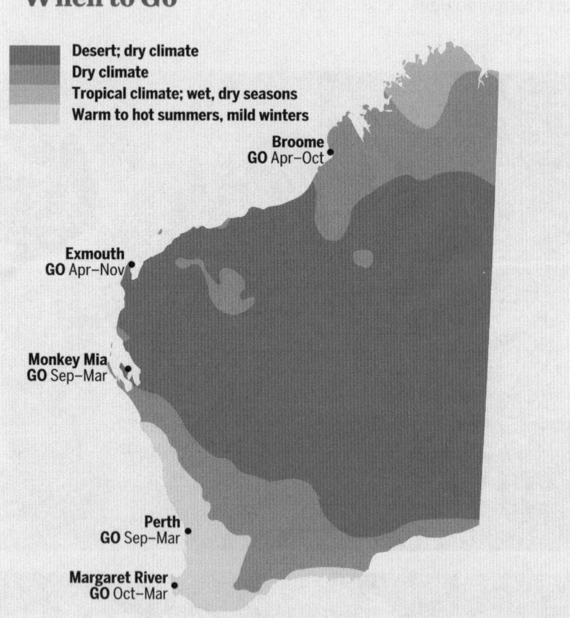

High Season (Dec–Mar)

- In the south the weather is at its hottest and driest.
- The season peaks from Christmas until the end of the school holidays in January.
- In the north, this is the wet (low) season.

Shoulder (Apr–May & Sep–Nov)

- Wildflowers are in bloom from September.
- The best months to visit the north.
- Humpback whales from September to November, whale sharks from April to June. Monkey Mia's dolphins are seen throughout the year.

Low Season (Jun–Aug)

- Wettest and coolest time in Perth and the south.
- Lows in the south are usually over 10°C.
- High season for the Coral Coast, the Pilbara, Broome and the Kimberley; dry and usually above 30°C.

Useful Websites

Lonely Planet (www.lonelyplanet.com/western-australia) Destination information, traveller forum and more.

Tourism Western Australia (www.westernaustralia.com) Official tourist site.

Tourism Australia (www.australia.com) Transport, event and destination information.

West Australian (www.thewest.com.au) Online version of the newspaper.

Department of Parks & Wildlife (www.parks.dpaw.wa.gov.au) Details on the state's national parks. Some camp sites can be prebooked.

Important Numbers

Drop the zero from the area code when calling from outside Australia (ie +61-8). If you're calling a WA number while in WA, you can drop the 08 prefix.

International access code	☎0011
Australia's country code	☎61
WA area code	☎08
Emergency (police, fire, ambulance)	☎000
Directory assistance	☎12455

Exchange Rates

Canada	C$1	$1.04
Euro	€1	$1.47
Japan	¥100	$1.09
New Zealand	NZ$1	$0.89
UK	£1	$2.11
USA	US$1	$1.36

For current exchange rates see www.xe.com.

Daily Costs

Budget: Less than $150

- Camp site (two people): $25–30
- Dorm bed: $30–50
- Private room in hostel: $80–120
- Mainly self-catering but having an occasional budget meal out: $30

Midrange: $150–300

- Double room in a midrange hotel: $150–220
- Lunch and dinner in cafes and pubs: $70
- Car hire: $40–50 per day

Top End: More than $300

- Mains in top restaurants: over $35
- Double room in a top hotel: from $250

Opening Hours

Outside Perth shops may not be open on weekends. Vineyard and craft brewery restaurants are usually only open for lunch, while many cafes also open later for dinner. Most central-city stores in Perth and major shopping malls are open seven days a week.

Banks 9.30am to 4pm Monday to Friday

Restaurants noon to midnight

Cafes 7am to 4pm

Pubs 11am to midnight

Shops 9am to 5pm Monday to Saturday, 11am to 5pm Sunday

Arriving in West Coast Australia

Perth Airport (p257) The Connect Shuttle runs every 50 minutes to five convenient and central locations in Perth ($15). A taxi is about $40 to central Perth and $60 to Fremantle. Buses ($4.40) run every 10 to 30 minutes to the city, hourly after 7pm; journey time is 40 minutes.

Getting Around

Rental Car The most flexible way to get around, especially in attraction-packed areas such as Margaret River. Distances are huge in other parts of the state, so a more time-efficient option can be to combine flying with local car rental.

Airlines A good option to cover WA's huge distances quickly. Consider flying from Perth to Esperance, Exmouth or Broome, and then renting a car locally if your focus is only around those areas.

Train A good option for day trips south of Perth to Mandurah and Rockingham. Regular trains make Fremantle a worthwhile base for exploring Perth.

Bus Extensive coverage and relatively good frequency between most traveller hot spots. Good links from Perth to Margaret River and the southwest, and north to Geraldton and Exmouth.

Public Transport Both Perth and Fremantle have excellent urban bus and train networks. Be sure to use the free CAT bus services.

For much more on **getting around**, see p258

What's New

Northbridge

Perth's grungiest inner suburb continues its hip resurrection with the addition of the cool Alex Hotel and funky eateries such as Pleased to Meet You and LOT 20. (p48)

Twilight Hawkers Market

Ethnic food stalls and food trucks promote culinary indecision on summer Friday nights in Forrest Chase in central Perth. (p64)

Fremantle

Perth's raffish southern sibling is further enlivened with pop-up galleries in the MANY6160 complex, summer night markets on Bathers Beach, and dining at Bread in Common. (p76)

Hougoumont Hotel

Centrally located, trimmed with cool decor, and helmed by an international crew, Fremantle's newest accommodation ticks all the boxes for a good-value stay in Western Australia's historic port town. (p82)

Homestead Brewery

Located in the Swan Valley alongside the award-winning Mandoon Estate winery, Homestead is lifting the craft-beer bar even higher in WA with its flavour-packed brews. (p101)

Wharncliffe Mill Bush Retreat

Concealed in forest near a former timber mill, this new accommodation near Margaret River township combines camping in safari tents, cosy wooden cabins and excellent mountain biking. (p124)

National Anzac Centre

Opened in November 2014 for Albany's Anzac centenary commemorations, this superb museum presents the poignant stories of the men and women who left from King George Sound for the Great War. (p141)

Ngurrangga Tours

Karratha-based Ngurrangga Tours run cultural expeditions to nearby sites including the petroglyphs of Murujuga National Park (Burrup Peninsula), and the waterholes of Millstream Chichester National Park. (p188)

Kimberley Indigenous Tours

Wundargoodie (p200) run women-only tours along Kalumburu Rd, while Bungoolee Tours (p203) introduce stories about the rebel Jandamarra. On the Fitzroy, Uptuyu (p199) know all about bushtucker, while Girloorloo (p204) explore the Mimbi Caves.

Purnululu National Park (Bungle Bungles)

New walks in the Bungle Bungles include a 10km (return) track to Whip Snake Gorge, a 4.4km (return) trail through Homestead Valley, and the Escarpment trail linking Echidna Chasm to the Bloodwoods. (p208)

Kayak-friendly Ningaloo

Moorings have been installed around Ningaloo Marine Park to facilitate snorkelling by kayakers, and an overnight kayak trail is being developed, with GPS markers on remote beaches designating approved camp sites for kayakers. (p186)

Cygnet Bay Pearl Farm

One of Australia's oldest pearl farms now features a cutting-edge eatery, luxury tents and cabins, and boat trips to experience the world's biggest tropical tides. (p220)

For more recommendations and reviews, see lonelyplanet.com/western-australia

If You Like...

Beaches

Western Australia (WA) has some of Australia's finest beaches, and you'll have many of them completely to yourself.

Cottesloe Perth's most iconic beach, with cafes and bars close at hand. (p52)

Bunker Bay Brilliant white sand edged by bushland; you'll have to look hard to spot the few houses scattered about. (p118)

Hellfire Bay Sand like talcum powder in the middle of Cape Le Grand National Park, which is precisely in the middle of nowhere. (p150)

Shark Bay 1500km of remote beaches and towering limestone cliffs. (p168)

Turquoise Bay A beautiful bay in Ningaloo Marine Park, with wonderful snorkelling. (p186)

80 Mile Beach You're guaranteed at least 79 miles of solitude on this remote, white-sand beach. (p210)

William Bay National Park Sheltered swimming around the granite boulders of Greens Pool and Elephant Rocks. (p138)

Cable Beach Surely the most famous, camel-strewn, sunset-photographed beach in WA. (p211)

Cape Leveque Red cliffs and superlative sunsets on the Dampier Peninsula. (p219)

Diving & Snorkelling

Reefs and wrecks are plentiful around WA and the marine life is lush, providing a smorgasbord of options for geared-up diving pros or gung-ho first-time snorkellers.

Mettams Pool Excellent snorkelling within Perth's city limits. (p53)

Rottnest Island Over a dozen wrecks and two underwater snorkelling trails make this an excellent option. (p91)

Busselton Lots to see around the southern hemisphere's longest timber jetty, plus the wreck of a decommissioned navy destroyer not far away. (p116)

Albany Look for sea dragons among the coral reefs and the wreck of the HMAS *Perth*. (p142)

Ningaloo Marine Park Australia's largest fringing reef, where you can snorkel and dive with the world's largest fish, the whale shark, along with turtles, dolphins and dugongs. (p185)

Houtman Abrolhos Islands Dive, snorkel, bushwalk or fish around these historic islands that rarely see tourists. (p164)

Surfing & Windsurfing

Wax the board and fire up the Kombi van: WA's surfing is legendary.

Trigg Beach Perth's surfers come here straight from work to catch a few waves. (p53)

Lancelin A mecca for windsurfers and kiteboarders; a great spot to learn to surf. (p107)

Yallingup/Margaret River 'Yals' and 'Margs' are the hub of the WA surf scene – with a major pro competition held there every year. (p119)

Ocean Beach, Denmark You might find yourself sharing this beautiful bay with whales. (p138)

Geraldton The surrounding beaches are thrilling for both wind- and wave-powered surfers. (p161)

IF YOU LIKE... FINE FOOD

Join a truffle hunt at the Truffle & Wine Co (p130) in Manjimup, or dine at the restaurant at the Cygnet Bay Pearl Farm (p220) near Broome.

Gnaraloo Surfers flock here in winter to try their luck at the famous Tombstones break; in summer the windsurfers take their place. (p174)

North West Cape Big swells hit the west of the cape from July to October. (p187)

Forests & Bushwalking

You might be forgiven for thinking that WA was all about white sand and red dirt. There is an awful lot of both, but the state's arboreal delights are also worthy of exploration.

Lesueur National Park A huge diversity of flora with many rare and endemic trees. (p108)

Karri Forest Explorer This shady circuit passes through three national parks surrounding Pemberton. (p133)

Valley of the Giants Tree Top Walk A wobbly walkway arches through the lofty canopy of the tingle forest. (p137)

Bibbulmun Track The big one – stretching nearly 1000km from the edge of Perth through the southern forests to Albany. (p36)

Cape to Cape Track Enjoy Indian Ocean views on this 135km trail from Cape Naturaliste to Cape Leeuwin. (p119)

Walyunga National Park Explore the trails in this beautiful park, where the Avon River cuts through the Darling Range. (p102)

Karijini National Park Rugged trails studded with gorges and waterfalls, and the tallest mountains in WA. (p190)

Stirling Range National Park This rugged range is known for its flora and chameleon-like ability to change colour. (p145)

Top: The bar at Little Creatures brewery (p84), Fremantle
Bottom: Kayaking at Mornington Wilderness Camp (p202)

Marine Mammals

It's extraordinarily easy to come close to the great creatures of the deep along WA's coast.

Perth & Fremantle Thirty thousand whales cruise past between mid-September and early December, and boat trips will take you out to cheer them on. (p56)

Rottnest Island The sharp-of-eye may spot New Zealand fur seals, dolphins and whales. (p89)

Rockingham Wild Encounters Cruise out to swim with dolphins and spot seals. (p58)

Sea Lion Charters, Green Head Splash with sea lions in the shallows. (p110)

Dampier Peninsula Excellent whale watching from a viewing platform. (p218)

Dolphin Discovery Centre, Bunbury Wade next to the wild dolphins that regularly drop by, or take a boat trip to swim with them. (p115)

Albany Between July and mid-October the bay turns into a whale nursery, with mothers and calves easily spotted from the beach, while cruises take you a little closer. (p142)

Monkey Mia Watch dolphins feeding in the shallows and take a dugong-spotting cruise. (p171)

Beer, Wine & Food

WA's wine industry is now being complemented by innovative craft breweries, while vineyard restaurants and provedores also abound.

Swan Valley Within Perth's eastern reaches, this semi-rural area's cosy wineries and bustling microbreweries are packed with city folk on weekends. (p99)

Fremantle The traditional home of WA craft beer, from mighty Little Creatures to the marvellous Sail & Anchor (27 taps and counting). (p84)

Margaret River Known for its Bordeaux-style varietals, chardonnay and sauvignon blanc, as well as a growing number of craft breweries. (p119)

Pemberton Another esteemed wine area, producing extremely good pinot noir, chardonnay and sauvignon blanc. (p131)

Denmark Notable wineries and craft breweries dot this picturesque area of the cool-climate Great Southern wine region. (p138)

Mt Barker & Porongurup Regarded as the most significant part of the Great Southern, with cool climes suiting riesling, pinot noir and cabernet sauvignon. (p144)

Aboriginal Art & Culture

Around 59,000 Aboriginal people call WA home, comprising many different Indigenous peoples, speaking many distinct languages.

Art Gallery of Western Australia A treasure trove of Indigenous art. (p49)

Kepa Kurl Eco Cultural Discovery Tours Day tours to visit rock art and waterholes, sample bush food and hear ancient stories. (p148)

Wula Guda Nyinda Aboriginal Cultural Tours Offers bushwalks and kayaking tours, and you'll learn some local Malgana language. (p171)

Dampier Peninsula Interact with remote communities and learn how to spear fish and catch mud crabs. (p218)

The Kimberley View artists' cooperatives, visit ancient rock art, and get to know 'Country' on a cultural tour. (p195)

Ngurrangga Tours Cultural and rock-art tours in Murujuga National Park in the Pilbara. (p188)

Uptuyu Personalised cultural tours taking in wetlands, rock art, fishing and Indigenous Kimberley communities. (p199)

Wundargoodie Offering a women-only Kimberley Spiritual Experience. (p200)

Off the Beaten Path

In a destination so varied and expansive, there are plenty of spectacular opportunities to craft your own journey of discovery.

Mornington Wilderness Camp The 95km stretch from the Gibb River Road to this riverside oasis is some of WA's most exquisite, lonely country. (p202)

Dryandra Woodland Less than two hours from Perth, but a world away, with endangered populations of endemic wildlife. (p99)

Gnaraloo Station Come for a night and stay for a month as your skills are put to work on this sustainable marvel. (p174)

Middle Lagoon Life doesn't get much more laid-back than at this Dampier Peninsula beachside campground far from anywhere. (p219)

Mt Augustus Uluru (Ayers Rock) is a mere pup compared to this art-adorned monolith five hours from the closest asphalt. (p172)

Duncan Road A real outback adventure without the masses, Duncan Rd is both a destination itself and a 'long-cut' to the Northern Territory. (p204)

Marble Bar Burnt into the Australian psyche by the sun's rays, the Ironclad Hotel is surrounded by incredibly scenic and empty landscapes. (p193)

Month by Month

TOP EVENTS

Southbound Festival, January

Perth International Arts Festival, February

West Coast Blues 'n' Roots Festival, April

Kings Park Festival, September

Margaret River Gourmet Escape, November

January

Summer school holidays sees families head to the beach en masse. Days are hot and dry, except in the far north, where the wet season is in full force.

Busselton's Southbound Festival

The Southbound Festival (www.southboundfestival.com.au) starts off the new year with three days of alternative music and camping in Busselton. Featuring big-name international artists, it's Western Australia's Glastonbury – but with less mud.

Lancelin's Windsurfing Challenge

In early January tiny Lancelin's renowned blustery conditions attract thousands for its world-famous windsurfing event, the Lancelin Ocean Classic (www.lancelinoceanclassic.com.au). Held over four days, the event starts with wave sailing on the Thursday and Friday, followed by the marathon on Saturday and the Sunday slalom.

February

The kids head back to school, freeing up some room at the beach and taking some of the pressure off coastal accommodation. It's still hot and dry in the south, and soggy in the north.

Laneway at Fremantle

Up-and-coming international bands with a boho indie vibe entice WA hipsters to Freo's West End at the annual Laneway festival. (p81)

Perth International Arts Festival

Held over 25 days from mid-February, Perth's festival attracts an international line-up, spanning theatre, classical music, jazz, visual arts, dance, film, literature – the whole gamut. It's worth scheduling your trip around. (p59)

Leeuwin Concert Series

Leeuwin Estate winery (www.leeuwinestate.com.au) in Margaret River hosts world-class performers of popular music, opera and the stage (Roxy Music, kd lang, Sting) during its annual event in mid-February; other concerts run from January to April.

March

It's still beach weather, but it's not quite as swelteringly hot in the south. It's hot and steamy in the north, however, as the rain is still bucketing down. Prices shoot up at Easter.

Nannup Music Festival

The sleepy forest town of Nannup comes alive with up to 30,000 fans of folk, blues and world music (www.nannupmusicfestival.org).

Margaret River Surfing Pro

Officially called the Drug Aware Pro (www.asp-worldtour.com), this World Qualifying Series (WQS) event, held over six days in mid-March, sees the world's best up-and-coming surfers battle it out in the epic surf at Margaret River.

April

A pleasant month in Perth, with temperatures dropping to the mid-20s and a little more rainfall. Up north they're finally starting to dry out and it's a great time for a Kimberley flyover.

West Coast Blues 'n' Roots Festival

Held in Fremantle Park, the West Coast Blues 'n' Roots Festival (www.westcoastbluesnroots.com.au) interprets its remit widely: the 2015 line-up featured Jurassic 5, Paolo Nutini and reggae icon Jimmy Cliff.

May

Temperatures creep down and Broome and Exmouth both finally drop below the 30s, making them particularly appealing – especially now the box jellyfish have retreated. Autumn showers are more common in the south.

Ord Valley Muster

For 10 days Kununurra hits overdrive during the annual Ord Valley Muster (www.ordvalleymuster.com), a collection of various sporting, charity and cultural events leading up to a large outdoor concert under the full moon on the banks of the Ord River.

June

Winter hits Perth with plenty of rain and possibly some snow on the Stirling Range further south. The warm, dry north, however, heads into peak season. Whale watching commences in Augusta.

Avon Valley Food & Wine

Gourmet food from around the world, tasty goodies from local producers, and the best of the expanding Avon Valley wine scene are all showcased at this welcome winter festival (www.avonvalleywa.com.au) in Northam.

Derby Boab Festival

Derby strings out its party season from late May to early July with concerts, mud footy, horse and mudcrab races, film festivals, poetry readings, art exhibitions, street parades and a dinner out on the mudflats (www.derbyboabfestival.org.au).

Denmark Festival of Voice

Rousing choruses blow away the cobwebs from the south-coast town of Denmark during the Festival of Voice (www.denmarkfestivalofvoice.com.au) held over the June long weekend. The town is flooded with soloists, duos, choristers and their admirers. It's accompanied by a workshop program.

July

It's wet and cold in the south and beautiful in the north – sparking a winter-break exodus from Perth. Whales congregate in the bays around Albany.

Indigenous Cultural Celebrations

Indigenous art exhibitions and performances take place throughout WA during NAIDOC (National Aboriginal & Islander Day Observance Committee) Week (www.naidoc.org.au), which celebrates the history, culture and achievements of Indigenous people.

August

Lovely in the north, but still wet and cold in the south, though temperatures do start to edge up. Manjimup truffles come into season, to the delight of Perth's chefs and their customers; whales continue to hang out on the south coast.

Avon River Festivities

Northam and Toodyay both turn on festivals the day before the Avon Descent (www.avondescent.com.au), a gruelling 133km white-water-rafting event for powerboats, kayaks and canoes between the two towns. Northam hosts the Avon River Festival, while Toodyay has an International Festival of Food.

CinéfestOZ

The sleepy southwest town of Busselton assumes a cinematic cosmopolitan sheen when this festival celebrating Australian and French cinema (www.cinefestoz.com) is held. Look forward to events and screenings in venues around town.

Broome Race Round

The local fillies and stallions frock up and get slaughtered as the Broome Race Round (www.broometurfclub.com.au) heads towards a frenzied climax with the Kimberley Cup, Ladies Day and the Broome Cup all held in early August. There's also some horse racing.

September

Spring brings a flurry of excitement, with wildflowers blooming and whales heading up the west coast. Broome pops back into the 30s and the tourists start to head south again.

Rottofest

Make the journey from Perth or Fremantle across to Rottnest Island for this annual weekend festival (www.rottofest.com.au) of live music, DJs, film and comedy.

Red Earth Arts Festival, Pilbara

Spread across the Pilbara's coastal mining towns during most of September, the Red Earth Arts Festival (www.reaf.com.au) is an eclectic mix of live music (all genres), theatre, comedy, visual arts (including film, photography and sculpture) and storytelling.

Festival of the Pearl

Starting either in late August or in early September, Broome's Shinju Matsuri (www.shinjumatsuri.com) celebrates the town's pearl industry and multicultural heritage with a carnival of nations, a film festival, art exhibitions, food, concerts, fireworks and dragon-boat races.

Kings Park Wildflower Festival

In September and early October, Perth's Kings Park and the Botanic Garden are filled with colourful wildflower displays in the annual Kings Park Festival (www.kingsparkfestival.com.au), which celebrates WA's unique and spectacular flora. Events include guided walks, talks and live music every Sunday.

October

The last of the whales depart the south coast and hit the west-coast leg of the Humpback Hwy. The weather is noticeably warmer and drier, and the wildflowers are wonderful.

Geraldton Greenough Sunshine Festival

It started in 1959 as a tomato festival, but now Geraldton's solar celebrations (www.sunshinefestival.com.au) include dragon-boat races, parades, sand sculptures and parties. It's held over nine days in early October. Sunshine guaranteed.

Perth Royal Show

The country comes to the city for the west's biggest agriculture, food and wine show (www.perthroyalshow.com.au) in late September. For Perth's kids it's a week of fun-fair rides, spun sugar and showbags full of plastic junk.

November

A great time to be in Fremantle, with temperatures in the mid-20s, very little rain and a convoy of whales passing by. In the far north, it's the start of the box-jellyfish season.

Margaret River Gourmet Escape

The culinary world's heavy hitters descend on Margaret River for four days of culinary inspiration (www.gourmetescape.com.au); Heston Blumenthal, Rick Stein and AA Gill attended the event in 2014. Australia's growing crew of celebrity chefs usually attend as well.

Fremantle Festival

Ten days of parades, performances, music, dance, comedy, visual arts, street theatre and workshops. Founded in 1905, it's Australia's longest-running festival (www.fremantle.wa.gov.au). Highlights include the Kite Extravaganza on South Beach and the Wardarnji Indigenous Festival.

Blues at Bridgetown

Now entering its third decade, one of WA's longest-running music festivals (www.bluesatbridgetown.com.au) fills the southwestern centre of Bridgetown with blues, folk and roots music annually on the second weekend of November.

Itineraries

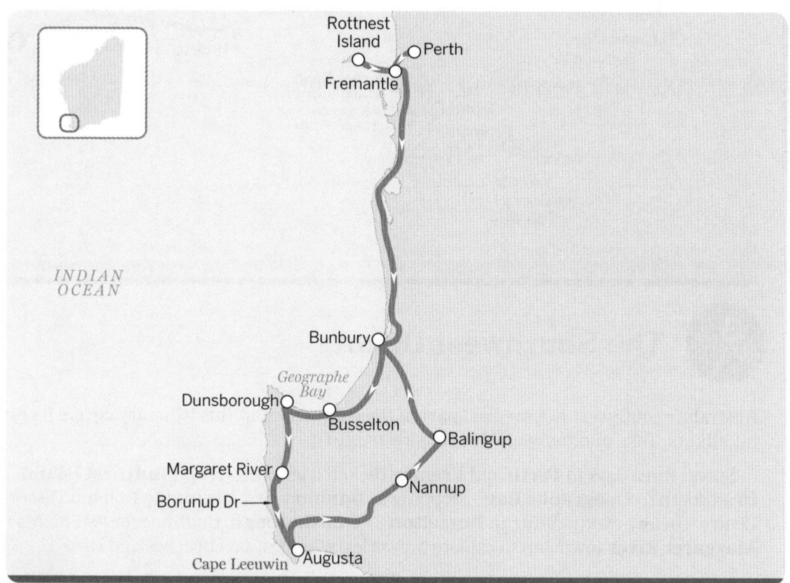

A Southwest Short Circuit

If you've got limited time, this itinerary offers a taste of the best of the state – city life, colonial history, beaches, wildlife, wine, forests and rural roads.

Base yourself in either **Perth** or **Fremantle** and spend three days exploring the conjoined cities and one day on **Rottnest Island**. Hire a car and head south, stopping first at **Bunbury** for lunch and a visit to the Dolphin Discovery Centre. Continue on to **Geographe Bay**, basing yourself in either **Busselton** or **Dunsborough**, and use the rest of the day to explore the beaches. Pick up a wine-region map and spend day six checking out the wineries, surf beaches and caves, all of which are close by. Base yourself in the **Margaret River** township that night and head to Settler's, the local pub. The next morning, head to **Augusta** via Caves Rd and take the scenic detour through the karri forest along unsealed **Borunup Drive**. Visit **Cape Leeuwin**, where the Indian and Southern Oceans meet, before heading back to Bunbury on a picturesque rural drive through **Nannup** and **Balingup**. From here it's a two-hour drive back to Perth.

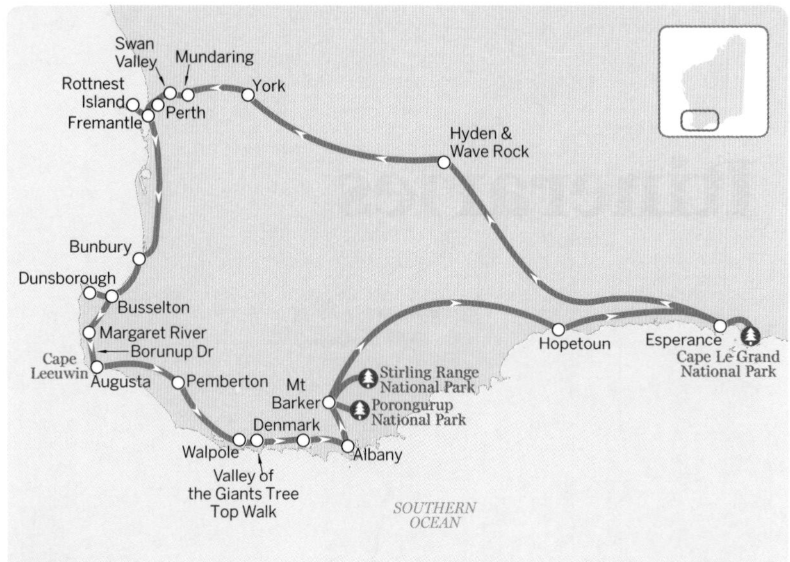

The Southwest Uncut

Australia's southwest is a magical part of the continent and this itinerary covers its main highlights. Take another week to really relax into it.

Spend three days in **Perth** and **Fremantle** and a leisurely day on **Rottnest Island**. Head south to **Geographe Bay** – stopping at **Bunbury** first to visit the Dolphin Discovery Centre – before overnighting in **Busselton** or **Dunsborough**. Continue for two nights in **Margaret River** township to explore breweries, wineries, surf beaches and caves.

The following morning head to **Augusta** via Caves Rd and detour through the karri forest along scenic **Borunup Drive**. Visit **Cape Leeuwin**, where the Indian and Southern Oceans meet, and continue to sleepy **Pemberton**. Highlights include more wineries, three national parks and the Karri Forest Explorer scenic drive. The next day, visit the **Valley of the Giants Tree Top Walk** near **Walpole** and overnight in **Denmark**. Check out beaches, wineries, breweries and restaurants before continuing to **Albany**. Spend two days there swimming (in summer), whale watching (in winter), and exploring coastal national parks and the poignant National Anzac Centre. Head north for more wineries at **Mt Barker** before tracking east to **Porongurup National Park**. Spend the next day (or two) tackling the mountainous tracks either here or at **Stirling Range National Park**.

Continue to the South Coast Hwy and at Ravensthorpe hop down to **Hopetoun**. This takes three hours from the Stirling Range, so spend the afternoon at the beach. The following day, head back to the South Coast Hwy and continue east to **Esperance** (around 2½ hours). Base yourself there two days, spending one of them exploring **Cape Le Grand National Park**. Head back on the South Coast Hwy and turn north just past Ravensthorpe for **Hyden** and **Wave Rock** (around four hours). The following day, head west to Brookton, turn north on the Great Southern Hwy, and follow the Avon Valley to quaintly colonial **York** (allow 3½ hours). For a leisurely final day back to Perth, travel via **Mundaring**, stopping at the **Swan Valley** en route for craft beer.

To make this itinerary shorter, head straight to Hyden from the Stirling Range, or take the Albany Hwy directly to Perth from Mt Barker.

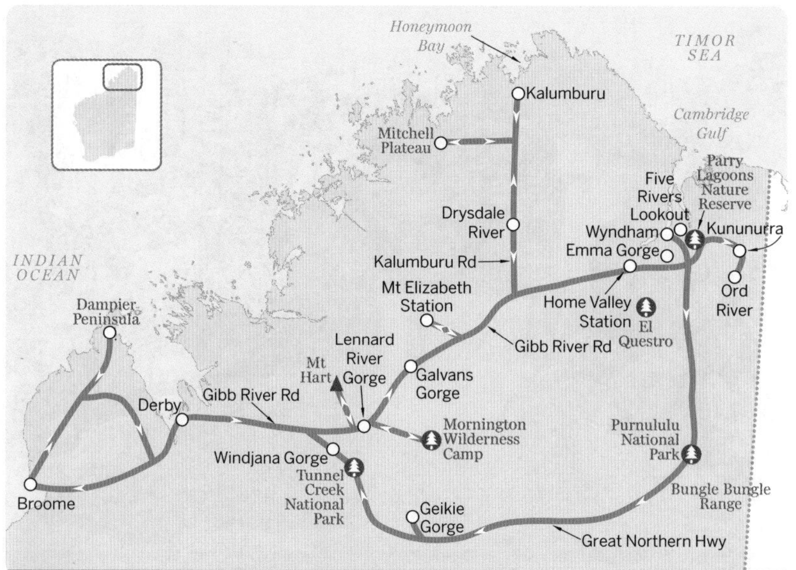

The Gibb River Road & Kimberley Outback

The biggest adventure in the west leaves **Broome** during the Dry and traverses the heart of the rugged Kimberley by 4WD.

First stop is the **Dampier Peninsula**, with its Aboriginal communities, beautiful beaches and mud crabs, and your last saltwater swim. Take the back road to **Derby** and its boabs, then on to the **Gibb River Road**, where **Lennard River** is the first of many inviting gorges. Explore wildlife and gorges at **Mt Hart** and remote **Mornington Wilderness Camp** and look for Wandjina at **Galvans Gorge** and **Mt Elizabeth Station**. Turn off onto the **Kalumburu Road**, check the road conditions at **Drysdale River** and drive on to the **Mitchell Plateau**, with its forests of *Livistona* and mind-blowing falls. Marvel at the area's rock art before hitting the northern coast and excellent fishing at **Honeymoon Bay**, just beyond the mission community of **Kalumburu**.

It's all downhill from here as you retrace your route back to the Gibb, then turn left for wonderful **Home Valley Station**, where someone else can do the cooking and the soft beds make a pleasant change from camping. Nearby **El Questro** has gorges aplenty, none more beautiful than **Emma Gorge**. Soon you're back on asphalt, but not for long as you take in the amazing bird life of **Parry Lagoons Nature Reserve**. Let **Wyndham's Five Rivers Lookout** blow your mind with its view of Cambridge Gulf, before heading for the civility of **Kununurra**, with its excellent food and supplies. You can look for fruit-picking work, ride a canoe down the mighty **Ord River**, or jump back behind the wheel for the wonders of **Purnululu**, the orange-domed **Bungle Bungle Range**.

Darwin and the Northern Territory are beckoning, or you can follow the Great Northern Hwy back to Broome, stopping in at beautiful **Geikie Gorge** for a relaxing boat cruise where you might spot freshwater crocs. If you don't see any, don't worry, as nearby **Windjana Gorge** has loads sunning themselves on the river banks. Grab your torch and head for a cold wade through the icy waters of **Tunnel Creek**, with its bats and rock art, before planting the pedal back to Broome, where you won't care how much that beer costs any more.

FRANCES ANDRIJICH/GETTY IMAGES ©

Above: Mitchell Falls (p201), the Kimberley

Left: Sailing boat, Perth (p48)

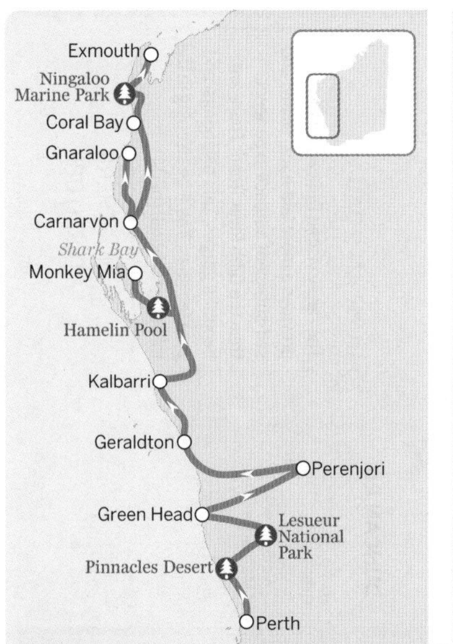

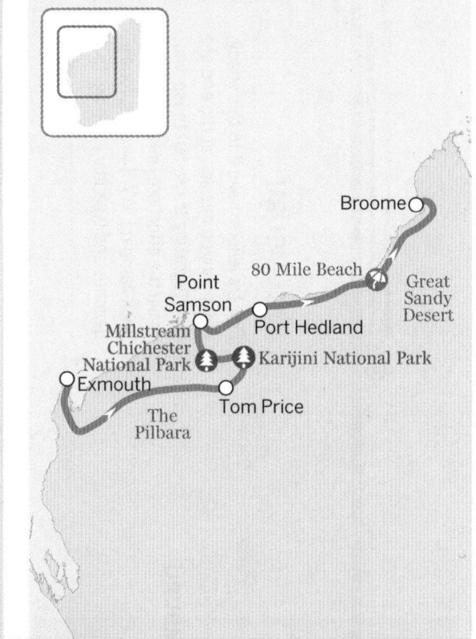

Indian Ocean Dreaming

Beautiful beaches, spectacular sunsets and wildlife are constants on this coastal cruise.

Take Indian Ocean Dr north from **Perth** to Cervantes for sunset on the otherwordly **Pinnacles Desert**. Cruise the wildflower-laden Kwongan back roads and marvel at the flora of **Lesueur National Park**'s flora before snorkelling with sea lions at **Green Head**. Follow the flowers out to **Perenjori**, then hit the cafes and museums of **Geraldton**. Have a surf on a kiteboard, then move on to the wonderful **Kalbarri** coastline. Enjoy a canoe in the gorges before sampling the outback on the long drive to World Heritage–listed **Shark Bay**. Watch dolphins at **Monkey Mia**, go sailing with dugongs, and learn about Country on an Indigenous cultural tour. Check out the stromatolites of **Hamelin Pool**, before putting in more road time on the stretch north to **Carnarvon**. Drop into **Gnaraloo** for world-class waves before arriving at tiny **Coral Bay** and **Exmouth**, where whale sharks, manta rays and turtles inhabit the exquisite **Ningaloo Marine Park**. You can fly out of Exmouth, drive back to Perth in two days (overnighting in historic Greenough), or push on to the gorges of Karijini.

Pilbara Jewels

You'll camp most of the way on this link between Ningaloo and Broome, with long empty beaches, shady pools and surprisingly good food.

From **Exmouth**, take Burkett Rd back to the highway, and head north, turning off at Nanutarra for the long, scenic haul up to **Tom Price**. After stocking up, spend the next few days camped in **Karijini National Park**, exploring the sublime gorges and indulging in a spot of peak bagging among the state's highest mountains. Don't miss a swim at Hamersley Gorge en route to the relaxing, shady pools in **Millstream Chichester National Park**. Admire the mesas and breakaways of the Chichester Range before dropping down to the coast, checking out the petroglyphs at Murujuga, then onto lovely **Point Samson** for snorkelling. Take the North West Coastal Hwy directly to **Port Hedland**, and scoff some wonderful coffee and cake in the Silver Star railcar, before camping at remote **80 Mile Beach**, where you might spot nesting turtles. Your last leg is a long stretch of nothing as you skirt the Great Sandy Desert to arrive in tropical **Broome**.

Off the Beaten Track - West Coast Australia

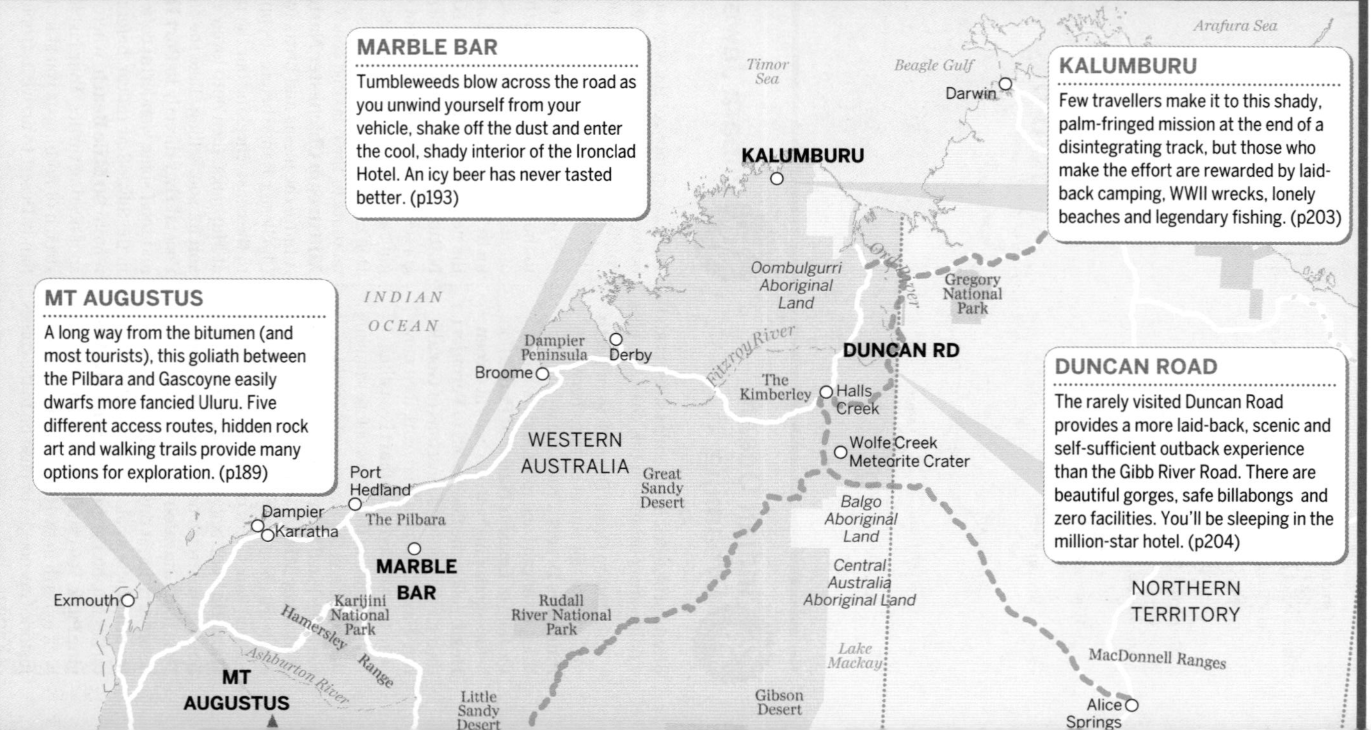

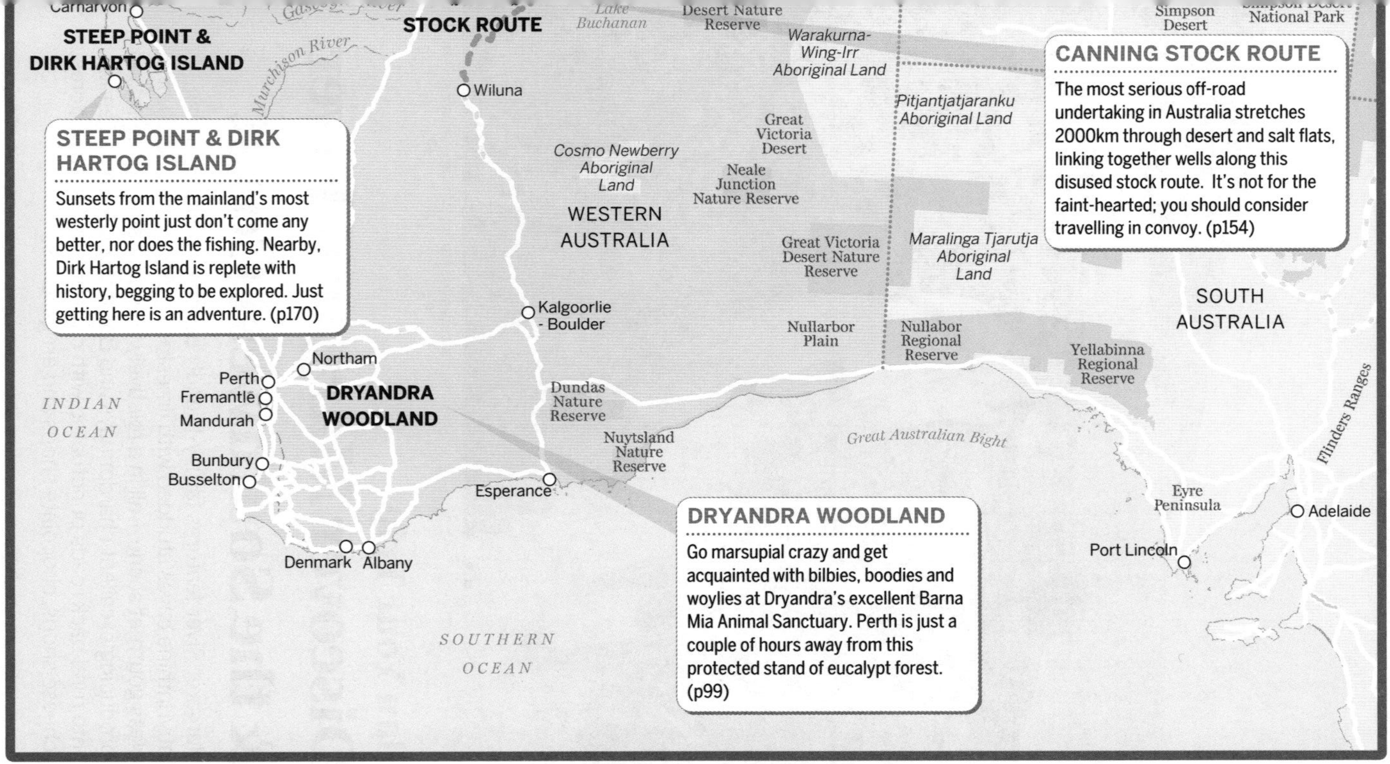
STEEP POINT & DIRK HARTOG ISLAND
STOCK ROUTE
DRYANDRA WOODLAND
Carnarvon
Murchison River
Lake Buchanan
Desert Nature Reserve
Warakurna-Wing-Irr Aboriginal Land
Simpson Desert
Simpson Desert National Park
Wiluna
Pitjantjatjaranku Aboriginal Land
Great Victoria Desert
Cosmo Newberry Aboriginal Land
Neale Junction Nature Reserve
WESTERN AUSTRALIA
Great Victoria Desert Nature Reserve
Maralinga Tjarutja Aboriginal Land
SOUTH AUSTRALIA
Kalgoorlie - Boulder
Nullarbor Plain
Nullabor Regional Reserve
Yellabinna Regional Reserve
Flinders Ranges
Northam
Perth
Fremantle
Mandurah
INDIAN OCEAN
Dundas Nature Reserve
Nuytsland Nature Reserve
Great Australian Bight
Bunbury
Busselton
Esperance
Eyre Peninsula
Adelaide
Port Lincoln
Denmark
Albany
SOUTHERN OCEAN
STEEP POINT & DIRK HARTOG ISLAND
Sunsets from the mainland's most westerly point just don't come any better, nor does the fishing. Nearby, Dirk Hartog Island is replete with history, begging to be explored. Just getting here is an adventure. (p170)
CANNING STOCK ROUTE
The most serious off-road undertaking in Australia stretches 2000km through desert and salt flats, linking together wells along this disused stock route. It's not for the faint-hearted; you should consider travelling in convoy. (p154)
DRYANDRA WOODLAND
Go marsupial crazy and get acquainted with bilbies, boodies and woylies at Dryandra's excellent Barna Mia Animal Sanctuary. Perth is just a couple of hours away from this protected stand of eucalypt forest. (p99)

Boogie boarders heading to the beach, Margaret River (p124)

Plan Your Trip

Discover Margaret River & the Southwest Coast

Margaret River features family-friendly beaches, brilliant surfing, labyrinthine caves studded with limestone formations, and a world-class gourmet scene – all in a relatively compact area. Vineyards producing excellent chardonnays and Bordeaux-style reds segue into rural back roads punctuated with craft breweries, provedores, cheese shops, chocolate shops and art galleries.

Best of the Region

Best Wineries

Vasse Felix (p123) Regional pioneer leading the way with its Heytesbury cabernet blend and Heytesbury chardonnay.

Cullen Wines (p124) Another Margaret River pioneer, with the 2009 Diana Madeline cabernet sauvignon merlot awarded Wine of the Year in the *Australian Wine Annual 2012*.

Leeuwin Estate (p128) Wonderful wines, especially its Art Series chardonnay and sauvignon blanc.

Watershed Premium Wines (p128) One of WA's best vineyard restaurants and renowned for its Awakening cabernet sauvignon.

Ashbrook (p124) Great quality, good value; try the cabernet merlot.

Four Things You Wouldn't Expect

- Artworks by Arthur Boyd and Sidney Nolan are hanging in the Bunbury Regional Art Gallery (p113).
- A highly rated French-Australian film festival, CinéfestOZ (p116), is held annually in beachy Busselton.
- A colony of red-tailed tropicbirds roosts off Cape Naturaliste.
- Most of the best restaurants aren't open in the evenings.

Where to Stay

- **For a beach holiday** Busselton or Dunsborough
- **For surfing** Yallingup, Prevelly or Margaret River
- **For wineries** Yallingup, Margaret River or anywhere in between
- **For caves** Anywhere between Yallingup and Augusta
- **For peace and quiet** Augusta

When to Go

- **For a beach holiday** December to March
- **For surfing** Any time, but the big surf pro is in March
- **For wineries, breweries and caves** All year
- **For whale watching** June to September from Augusta, September to December from Dunsborough
- **For French films** August

When to Avoid

- January in Busselton, unless you're going to the Southbound music festival or have booked well in advance.
- November in Dunsborough, when the place is overrun by end-of-school revellers.
- Weekends in Margaret River, accommodation prices are higher and there are always loads of people – but at least everything will be open.

Plan Your Attack

What's the Layout?

The sheltered white sands of Geographe Bay start south of Bunbury and arch along to Cape Naturaliste. Busselton and Dunsborough are the bay's main towns. At Cape Naturaliste the coastline pirouettes and runs nearly due south to Cape Leeuwin. The wine region runs parallel to this coast with the Margaret River itself cutting roughly east to west through the centre, passing through the town of the same name. Wineries are scattered all around, but the biggest concentration is found north of the river.

What to Do

Surfing the Wineries

The two main north–south routes are the Bussell Hwy (passing through Cowaramup, Margaret River and Augusta) and leafy Caves Rd (running south from Dunsborough). Numerous bucolic back roads link the two. Pick up one of the excellent free maps, squabble over who's going to be the nondrinking driver, and dive right in. The other alternative is to take a tour – public transport is not a workable option.

Most of the wineries offer tastings between 10am and 5pm daily. At busy times (this includes every weekend), consider booking ahead for lunch before you set out.

Above: Limestone formations inside Lake Cave (p127)

Left: Leeuwin Estate winery (p128)

Tasting the Waves

Known to surfers as 'Yals' (around Yallingup) and 'Margs' (around the mouth of the Margaret River), the beaches between Capes Naturaliste and Leeuwin offer powerful reef breaks, mainly left-handers (the direction you take after catching a wave). The surf at Margs has been described by surfing supremo Nat Young as 'epic', and by world surfing champ Mark Richards as 'one of the world's finest'.

As is the way with such hot spots, surfers can be quite territorial, so respect the etiquette and defer to locals if you're unsure. If you're planning on spending a lot of time on the breaks, call into the surf shops and get to know some locals.

Around Dunsborough, the better locations include Rocky Point (short left-hander) and the Farm and Bone Yards (right-handers), which are between Eagle and Bunker Bays. Near Yallingup there are the Three Bears (Papa, Mama and Baby, of course), Rabbits (a beach break towards the north of Yallingup Beach), Yallingup (reef with breaks left and right), and Injidup Car Park and Injidup Point (right-hand tube on a heavy swell; left-hander). You'll need a 4WD to access Guillotine/Gallows (right-hander), north of Gracetown. Also around Gracetown are Huzza's (an easy break within the beach), South Point (popular break) and Lefthanders (the name says it all). The annual surfer pro is held around Margaret River Mouth and Southside ('Suicides') in March.

Pick up a surfing map from one of the visitor centres.

Surfing is never without its risks. Three people have been killed by sharks in the vicinity of Gracetown in the last six years, and in 2014 a shark attacked an inflatable boat near Dunsborough.

Going Underground

The main cave complexes are spread, perhaps unsurprisingly, along Caves Rd. Ngilgi Cave sits by itself near Yallingup, but the other main complexes are between Margaret River township and Augusta, and are split between those run by the Department of Environment and Conservation (Calgardup Cave and Giants Cave) and the more commercialised CaveWorks caves (Lake Cave, Jewel Cave and Mammoth Cave). CaveWorks offers a combined ticket for its caves. If you're feeling adventurous, don overalls and a hard hat and explore the Moondyne Cave on a guided tour.

BEST FAMILY ACTIVITIES

- Dolphin Discovery Centre, Bunbury (p115)
- Bunbury Wildlife Park (p113)
- Busselton Jetty (p116)
- Margaret River Chocolate Company (p123)
- Mountain biking at Wharncliffe Mill Bush Retreat (p124)

Getting Crafty

The hoppy wave of craft beer that's sweeping many countries has also washed up on WA shores, and an innovative generation of brewers is proving there's more to beer than innocuous Euro lagers. Look forward to a global array of beer styles including India Pale Ales, Belgian Ales and Chocolate Porters, and decide on a designated driver or join a tour.

Other Attractions

- **Beaches** And lots of them; they're particularly beautiful between Dunsborough and Cape Naturaliste.
- **Walking** There are excellent tracks around Cape Naturaliste and between the capes.
- **Diving** Trips leave from Busselton and Dunsborough to explore local wrecks and reefs.
- **Whale watching** Cruises leave from Augusta (starting in June) and Dunsborough (starting in September).
- **Lighthouses** Both capes have them and both can be visited. From Cape Leeuwin you can watch the Indian and Southern Oceans collide.
- **Adventure sports** From mountain biking to climbing and kayaking.

Hawk's Head lookout, Kalbarri National Park (p165

Plan Your Trip

West Coast Australia Outdoors

With incredible landscapes and seascapes, intriguing wildlife, and all that brilliant sunshine, Western Australia (WA) is the perfect playground for outdoor enthusiasts, with numerous tracks to follow, waves to surf and reefs to explore.

Best Outdoors

Best for Daredevils

Scramble, abseil, slide and dive through the gorges of Karijini National Park, or ride the surge in a speedboat on the Horizontal Waterfalls near Derby.

Best Whale Watching

Whale-watching boats leave from Perth, Fremantle, Dunsborough, Augusta, Albany, Coral Bay, Exmouth, Kalbarri, Broome and the Dampier Peninsula.

Best Wildlife Encounters on Water

Swim with whale sharks and manta rays in Ningaloo Marine Park. For dolphins, head to Rockingham, Bunbury or Monkey Mia. Sea lions are best seen at Rockingham and Green Head, while seals can be spotted off Rottnest Island. Look out for dugongs at Monkey Mia.

Best Wildlife Encounters on Land

Seek out little marsupials on Rottnest Island or in the Dryandra Woodland, and huge lizards anywhere in the Kimberley. Emus are often spotted at Exmouth and Shark Bay, while kangaroos and parrots are everywhere!

Bushwalking

WA's excellent bushwalking terrain includes the southwest's cool forests, the expansive Bibbulmun Track and the north's rugged national parks.

See www.bushwalkingwa.org.au for details of local bushwalking clubs. To contact potential walking buddies, or to buy and sell gear, see the forums on www.bushwalk.com.

For responsible-bushwalking tips, see the camping and bushwalking guidelines online at www.parks.dpaw.wa.gov.au.

Perth & Surrounds

With hiking and camping facilities, John Forrest National Park (p99) has an easy 15km walk to waterfalls. The rugged Walyunga National Park (p102) has a medium-to-hard 18km walk that fords the Avon River and has excellent wildlife viewing. Yanchep National Park (p106) features short strolls and challenging full-day walks. The **Yaberoo Budjara Trail** (www.yellagonga.org) follows an Aboriginal walking trail.

Down South

Serious walkers gravitate to the ruggedly beautiful Stirling Range National Park (p145). Popular are the Bluff Knoll climb (6km, three to four hours), and the park's 1500 species of wildflower. Visit from September to November for the park's flowering glory, and be prepared for wind chill and rain (and sometimes snow) in winter.

North of Albany is the smaller Porongurup National Park (p144), with spectacular granite rocks and dense karri forest. Trails include the 10-minute Tree in the Rock stroll, the medium-grade Hayward and Nancy Peaks (three hours), and the challenging three-hour Marmabup Rock hike. Wildflowers and bird activity make springtime the peak season for Porongurup, but it can be visited year-round.

Spectacular coastal highlights are walks through Walpole, Fitzgerald River and Cape Le Grand National Parks. The Cape to Cape Track (p119) follows the coastline 135km from Cape Naturaliste to Cape Leeuwin, taking five to seven days, and featuring wild camp sites en-route.

Up North

Summer's no picnic in the sweltering, remote national parks of the north, and high season for many bushwalkers is from April to October. The arid terrain can be treacherous, so research carefully, be prepared with water and supplies, and check in with rangers before setting out.

Kalbarri National Park (p165) showcases scenic gorges, thick bushland and rugged coastal cliffs. The popular six-hour loop features dramatic seascapes, including spectacular Nature's Window.

Rugged, sometimes hazardous treks can be taken into the dramatic gorges of Karijini National Park (p190). The walk to the Mt

THE BIBBULMUN TRACK

Taking around eight weeks, the 963km **Bibbulmun Track** (www.bibbulmuntrack.org.au) goes from Kalamunda, 20km east of Perth, through mainly natural environment to Walpole and Albany.

Terrain includes jarrah and marri forests, wildflowers, granite outcrops, coastal heath country and spectacular coastlines.

Comfortable camp sites are spaced regularly along the track. The best time to do it is from August to October.

Bruce summit (9km, five hours) is popular with experienced bushwalkers.

Visitors to the Kimberley's Purnululu National Park (p208) come to see the striped beehive-shaped domes of the World Heritage–listed Bungle Bungles. Walks include the easy Cathedral Gorge walk, and the more difficult overnight trek to Piccaninny Gorge. The park is only open from April to November.

Surfing & Windsurfing

Beginners, intermediates, wannabe pros and adventure surfers will all find excellent conditions to suit their skill levels. WA gets huge swells (often over 3m), so it's critical to align the surf and the location with your ability. Look out for strong currents, sharks and territorial local surfers.

WA's traditional surfing home is the southwest, particularly from Yallingup to Margaret River (p124). This stretch has many different breaks to explore.

Around Perth the surf is smaller, but there are often good conditions at bodyboard-infested Trigg (p53) and Scarborough (p53). If the waves are small, head to Rottnest Island (p91) for (usually) bigger and better waves. Check out Strickland Bay.

Heading north, there are countless reef breaks waiting to be discovered (hint: take a 4WD). Best known are the left-hand point breaks of Jakes Point (p165) near Kalbarri; Gnaraloo Station (p174), 150km north of Carnarvon; and Surfers Beach (p187) at Exmouth. Buy the locals a beer and they might share a few secret world-class locations.

Windsurfers and kitesurfers have plenty of choice with excellent flat-water and wave sailing. Kitesurfers appreciate the long, empty beaches and offshore reefs.

After Perth's city beaches, head to Lancelin (p107), home to a large summertime population of surfers. Flat-water and wave sailing are excellent here. Further north, Geraldton (p160) has the renowned Coronation Beach. The Shark Bay (p168) area has excellent flat-water sailing and Gnaraloo Station is also a world-renowned wave-sailing spot.

Camping

It's very easy to 'get away from it all' in WA, and in the state's national parks, sleeping in a swag under the stars is almost obligatory. The weather is a factor, though: it can be uncomfortable in the north during summer due to heat and flash flooding, and cold down south during winter. School holidays can be very busy.

Wildlife Watching

Whales

Because so many southern right and humpback whales (upwards of 30,000) cruise along the WA coast, it has become known as the Humpback Hwy. From June onwards their annual pilgrimage begins from Antarctica to the warm tropical waters of the northwest coast; mothers with calves seek out the shallower bays and coves of King George Sound in Albany (p142) from July to October. In whale-watching season, whales can be spotted from coastal clifftops, and often from the beach as well.

Dolphins

Dolphins can be seen up close at the Dolphin Discovery Centre (p115) in Bunbury around Rockingham, and at Monkey Mia (p171). Monkey Mia also has 10% of the world's dugong population.

Boardwalk at Thomson Bay, Rottnest Island (p89)

Birds

The Broome Bird Observatory (p218) attracts a staggering 800,000 birds each year, and the Yalgorup National Park (p96) near Mandurah is another important waterbird habitat. The Lesueur National Park (p108) is home to the endangered Carnaby's cockatoo, while migratory shorebirds flock to Parry Lagoons Nature Reserve (p205) in the Kimberley. At the Mornington Wilderness Camp (p202), purple-crowned fairywrens and the endangered Gouldian finch are regular visitors.

Cycling

WA's southwest is good for cycle touring, and while there are thousands of kilometres of flat, virtually traffic-free roads elsewhere in the state, the distances between towns makes it difficult to plan.

Perth is a relatively bike-friendly city, with good recreational bike paths, including routes that run along the Swan River to Fremantle, and paths overlooking the city through Kings Park.

Cyclists rule on mostly car-free Rottnest Island (p93), with long stretches of empty roads circumnavigating the island and its beaches. Geraldton (p160) also has great cycle paths.

NATIONAL PARK PASSES

Thirty of WA's 96 national parks charge vehicle entry fees (per car/motorcycle $12/6), which are valid for any park visited that day. If you're camping within the park, the entry fee is only payable on the first day (camping fees are additional). If you plan to visit more than three WA parks with entry fees – quite likely if you're travelling outside Perth – get the four-week Holiday Pass ($44). All Department of Parks & Wildlife offices sell them, and if you've already paid a day-entry fee in the last week (and have the voucher to prove it), you can subtract it from the cost of the pass.

The most exciting route for mountain bikers is the **Munda Biddi Trail** (www.mundabiddi.org.au), meaning 'path through the forest' in the Noongar Aboriginal language. The 1000km mountain-biking equivalent of the Bibbulmun Track runs all the way from Mundaring on Perth's outskirts to Albany on the south coast. Camp sites are situated a day's easy ride apart, and maps are available online and at visitor centres.

Diving & Snorkelling

WA's fascinating diving and snorkelling locations include stunning marine parks and shipwrecks.

Close to Perth, divers can explore wrecks and marine life off the beaches of Rottnest Island (p91), or explore the submerged reefs and historic shipwrecks of the West Coast Dive Park (p94) within Shoalwater Islands Marine Park, near Rockingham. You can take a dive course in Geographe Bay with companies based in Dunsborough (p117) or Busselton (p116); the bay offers excellent dives under the Busselton jetty, on Four Mile Reef (a 40km limestone ledge about 6.5km off the coast) and at the scuttled HMAS *Swan*.

Other wrecks include the HMAS *Perth* (at 36m), deliberately sunk in 2001 in King George Sound (p144) near Albany; and the *Sanko Harvest,* near Esperance (p147). Both teem with marine life on the wrecks' artificial reefs.

Divers seeking warmer waters should head north. Staggering marine life can be found just 100m offshore within the Ningaloo Marine Park (p185), fantastic for both diving and snorkelling. In Turquoise Bay, underwater action is equally accessible, and one of the planet's most amazing underwater experiences is diving or snorkelling alongside the incredible whale shark, the world's largest fish. Tours leave from Exmouth (p180) and Coral Bay (p178).

There's also excellent diving and snorkelling around the Houtman Abrolhos Islands (p164).

REDUCING THE RISK OF SHARK ATTACK

This list of shark safety guidelines is from Western Australia's Department of Fisheries. After a spate of fatal shark attacks in 2012, the WA government announced a $20-million safety program, including a controversial system to track, catch and kill any sharks posing an imminent threat (p252).

A shark net was trialled at Dunsborough in late 2013, with an additional net planned for Busselton. Aerial shark-spotting patrols have also increased in frequency.

See www.sharksmart.com.au for more information.

- Swim between the flags at patrolled beaches.
- Swim close to shore.
- Swim, dive or surf with other people.
- Avoid areas close to bird rookeries or where there are large schools of fish, dolphins, seals or sea lions.
- Avoid areas where animal, human or fish waste enters the water.
- Avoid deep channels or areas with deep drop-offs nearby.
- Do not remain in the water with bleeding wounds.
- Look carefully before jumping into the water from a boat or jetty.
- If spearing fish, don't carry dead or bleeding fish attached to you and remove all speared fish from the water as quickly as possible.
- If schooling fish or other wildlife start to behave erratically or congregate in large numbers, leave the water.
- If you see a shark, leave the water as quickly and calmly as possible – avoid excessive splashing or noise.

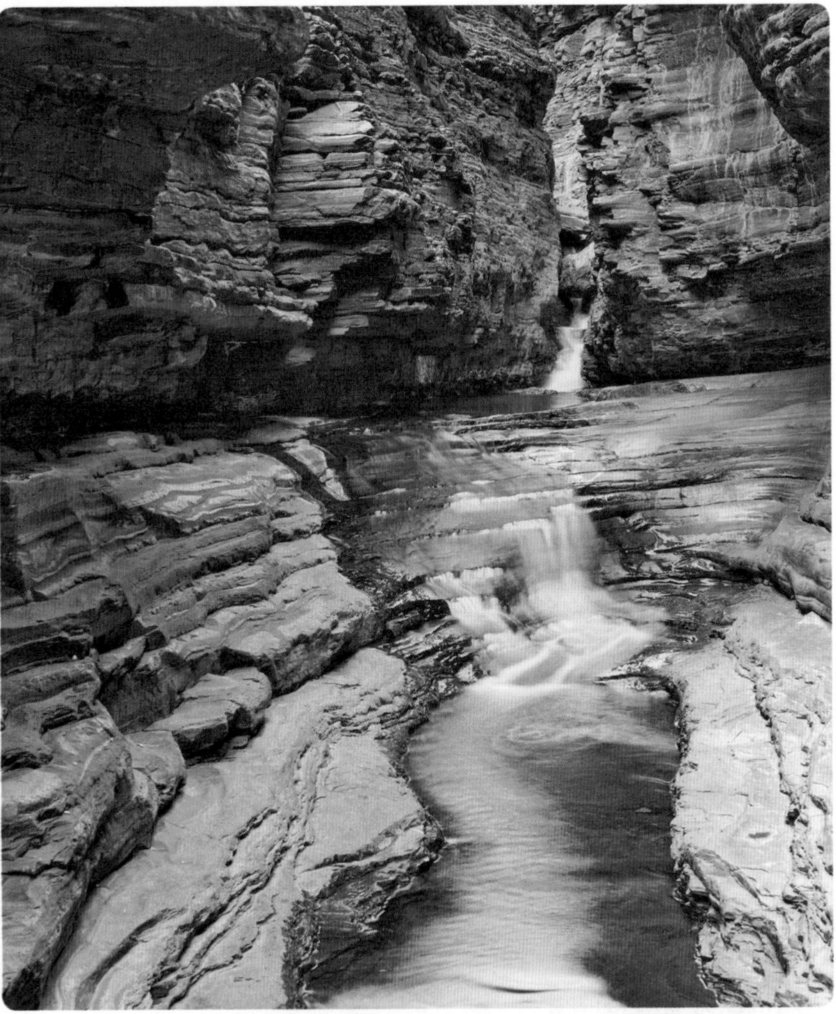

Above: Hancock Gorge (p191), Karijini National Park

Right: Thorny devil, Kalbarri National Park (p165)

CYRIL RUOSO/MINDEN PICTURES/GETTY IMAGES ©

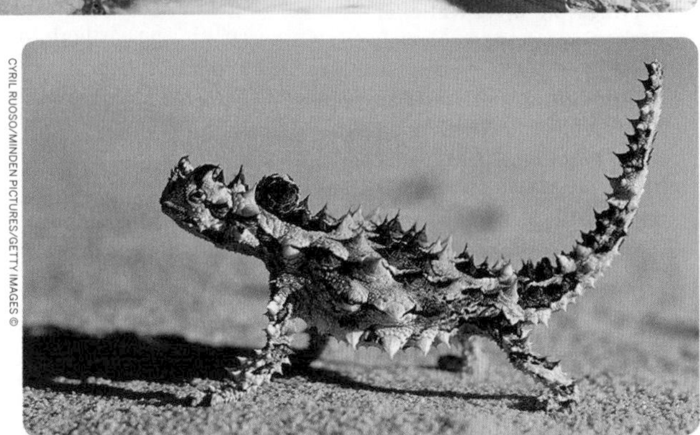

Banksia flowers, Fitzgerald River National Park (p146)

Fishing

From sailfish in the north to trout in the south, all types of fishing are on offer along WA's immense coastline. Fishing is the state's largest recreational activity, with many locals catching dinner nearly every time.

Close to Perth, Rottnest Island has plentiful schools of wrasse and Western Australian dhufish (previously called jewfish).

BEST WILDFLOWER SPOTS

- **Kings Park** (p51) In Perth, especially the Botanic Garden.
- **Fitzgerald River National Park** (p146) Between Albany and Esperance.
- **Porongurup National Park** (p144) North of Albany
- **Stirling Range National Park** (p145) Also north of Albany.
- **Mullewa** (p161) In the central midlands, especially at August's annual flower show.
- **Kalbarri National Park** (p165) On the Batavia Coast.
- **Wongan Hills and Morawa** (p161) In the central midlands.

South of Perth, popular fishing hot spots include Mandurah (p95), with options for deep-sea fishing, catching tailor from the beach or nabbing Mandurah's famed blue manna crabs and king prawns in the estuaries. In Augusta (p128) you can chase salmon in the Blackwood River or whiting in the bay, or drop a line from the Busselton Jetty (p116).Popular spots in sunny Geraldton (p160) include Sunset Beach and Drummond Cove, and fishing charters go to the nearby Houtman Abrolhos Islands (p164). There's great fishing all along the coast, and lots of charters in the hotter, steamier northwest. There's a good chance to hook a monster fish at Exmouth (p180), the Dampier Archipelago and the game-fishing nirvana of Broome (p210). The northern Kimberley is good for barramundi.

Buy a recreational fishing licence (RFL; $40) if you intend to catch marron (freshwater crayfish) or rock lobsters; if you use a fishing net; or if you're freshwater angling in the southwest. If you're fishing from a motorised boat, someone on the boat will need to have a Recreational Fishing from Boat Licence (RFBL; $30). Licences can be obtained online (www.fish.wa.gov.au) or from Australia Post offices. Note that there are strict licence, bag and size limits – see the Fisheries website for specific details.

Plan Your Trip

Travel with Children

With lots of sunshine, beaches and big open spaces, Western Australia (WA) is a wonderful destination for children of all ages. Australians are famously laid-back and their generally tolerant, 'no worries' attitude extends to children having a good time and perhaps being a little bit raucous.

West Coast Australia for Kids

Interacting with Australia's native fauna, either in the wild or in wildlife parks, will create lifetime memories for your kids. Australia's wildlife can be dangerous, but in reality you're extremely unlikely to strike any problems if you take sensible precautions.

The sun's harshness is more of a concern. Don't underestimate how quickly you and your kids can get sunburnt, even on overcast days. A standard routine for most Australian parents is to lather their kids in high-protection sunscreen (SPF 30-plus) before heading outside for the day. It's a habit worth adopting. Avoid going to the beach in the middle of the day. Head out in the morning or mid-afternoon instead.

On really hot days, dehydration can be a problem, especially for small children. Carry fluids with you, especially on long car journeys.

Many motels and larger caravan parks have playgrounds and swimming pools, and can supply cots and baby baths. Motels in touristy areas may have in-house children's videos and child-minding services. Top-end and midrange hotels usually welcome families with children, but some B&Bs market themselves as child-free havens.

Best Regions for Kids

Perth & Fremantle

Open spaces, beaches, kid-friendly museums, bike paths, playgrounds and festivals – Perth and Fremantle are great places to visit with the kids. Many major attractions – including the Aquarium of Western Australia, Perth Zoo, Art Gallery of Western Australia and Maritime Museum – have hands-on, kid-friendly exhibits.

Margaret River & the Southwest Coast

Geographe Bay features family-friendly beaches, Yallingup has a surf school, and Bunbury has the Dolphin Discovery Centre and Bunbury Wildlife Park. The region also features whale watching.

Monkey Mia & the Central West

Visit the world-famous dolphins of Monkey Mia, feed the pelicans at Kalbarri or learn about Indigenous culture and Country on a guided tour.

Babies & Toddlers

Perth and most major towns have public rooms where parents can nurse their baby or change nappies; check with the local visitor centre. While many Australians are relaxed about public breastfeeding or nappy changing, some aren't.

Many eateries lack a specialised children's menu, but others do have kids' meals or will provide smaller servings. Some supply high chairs.

Medical services and facilities are of a high standard, and baby food, formula and disposable nappies are widely available. Major car-hire companies will supply and fit booster seats for a fee.

School-Age Kids

The biggest challenge is a sudden attack of the 'are-we-there-yets?'. Adults – let alone kids – find the long drives tedious. Bring along books, computer games, iPads and child-friendly CDs. Consider hiring a car with a back-seat screen for playing DVDs.

Snacks are essential for journeys where shops might be 200km or further apart, and toilet paper is also a blessing.

Have a word to the kids about insects, snakes and spiders, stressing the need to keep their distance. This is particularly important for kids who like to prod things with sticks. While bushwalking, make sure they wear socks with shoes or boots.

Children's Highlights

Beaches

Beaches are a big part of the WA experience. Ensure kids swim between the flags, and ask locals about the safer beaches.

Wildlife Parks & Zoos

There are wildlife parks throughout WA, especially in tourist areas. Many have walk-in aviaries, so prepare for a freak-out when an over-friendly parrot lands on little Jimmy's shoulder. Watch out for emus: those beady eyes and pointy beaks are even more intimidating when they're attached to something that's double your height.

Whale Watching

If you're in the right part of the coast at the right time of year, you'll definitely see whales from the shore. Organised whale-watching boat trips depart from Perth, Fremantle, Dunsborough, Augusta, Albany, Coral Bay, Broome, Kalbarri, Exmouth and the Dampier Peninsula.

Other Marine Mammals

- **Rockingham Wild Encounters** (p58) An opportunity for the over fives to swim with wild dolphins.
- **Dolphin Discovery Centre, Bunbury** (p115) Wade into the shallows alongside the dolphins.
- **Monkey Mia** (p171) Watch dolphins being fed in the bay or head out on a cruise to spot dolphins and dugongs.
- **Sea Lion Charters** (p110) Splash about with sea lions in the shallows.

Surfing

- **Surfschool, Perth** (p57) Lessons for kids aged 11 and over.
- **Yallingup Surf School** (p121) 'Microgrom' lessons for the under 10s.

Amusement Parks & Rides

- **Adventure World, Perth** (p53) White-knuckle rides such as 'Bounty's Revenge', pools and water rides.
- **Perth Royal Show** (p59) Fun-fair rides, show bags and farm animals.

Planning

When booking accommodation and hire cars in advance, specify whether you need equipment such as cots, high chairs and car booster seats. If you're travelling with an infant, bring a mosquito net to drape over the cot. Bring rash tops for the beach and warm clothes if you're travelling south in winter. Anything you forget can be easily purchased when you arrive.

Regions at a Glance

Perth & Fremantle

Beaches
Culture
Architecture

Beaches

They may not offer the solitude and pristine surroundings of elsewhere in Western Australia (WA), but Perth and Fremantle's beaches are popular playgrounds for city dwellers. Surfers, snorkellers and swimmers can all find a stretch of sand to suit.

Museums & Galleries

Perth's public institutions include the Art Gallery of Western Australia, housing traditional and contemporary art; the edgy Perth Institute of Contemporary Arts; and the Western Australian Museum. Fremantle boasts the superb Maritime Museum and Shipwreck Galleries.

Historic Buildings

Relics of the colonial era and early gold rushes abound. Fremantle has a frozen-in-time streetscape with a wonderful historic ambience. The big drawcard is the convict-built prison, its murky stories brought to life through fascinating guided tours.

p46

Around Perth

Beaches
Wildlife
Day Trips

Beautiful Beaches

Rottnest Island is ringed by gorgeous beaches that are often deserted midweek. Mandurah, Rockingham and Yanchep are built-up beach burbs bustling with cafes and marinas. Guilderton sits on a picturesque lagoon, while Lancelin is windsurfing heaven.

Native Wildlife

Whales, dolphins, sea lions, seals, penguins, kangaroos, possums, quokkas, bilbies, boodies, woylies – it's quite amazing how much wildlife lives in such close proximity to the city.

Heritage Towns

The quaint townships in the forests, hills and river valleys surrounding Perth make perfect day trips. York has contiguous rows of historic buildings, preserving a gold-rush atmosphere.

p87

Margaret River & the Southwest Coast

Beaches
Food & Wine
Nature

Geographe Bay

The sandy beaches of Geographe Bay are perfect for a family holiday. The most beautiful spots are near Cape Naturaliste. The state's primo surf breaks also roll ashore to the south.

Margaret River Wine Region

Australia's most beautiful wine region also produces some of the country's best wine. The cool-climate vineyards around Pemberton are worth exploring, too.

Towering Forests

Studded with tuart and karri, WA's forests of tall trees are an impressive sight. Some of the larger specimens are rigged with spikes, allowing the fit and fearless to climb up to 68m into the canopy.

p111

Southern WA

Beaches
Wineries
Outdoors

Isolated Beaches

Glorious, isolated bays of powdery white sand are spread all along this stretch of coast. On many you'll be more likely to spot a whale than another person.

Great Southern Wine Region

The wineries of the Great Southern region are growing in stature. Sup your way from Denmark to Mt Barker and on to Porongurup.

National Parks

This region's parks encompass the dramatic Tree Top Walk in Walpole-Nornalup and the silky sands of Cape Arid. Don't miss the rugged Porongurup and Stirling Range National Parks, or the vast wild heath of Fitzgerald River.

p135

Monkey Mia & the Central West

Beaches
Adventure
History

Epic Coastline

The white-shell beaches of Shark Bay – with famous visitors, the Monkey Mia dolphins – are just part of a turquoise coastline stretching from family-friendly Port Denison to the wilds of Gnaraloo Station.

Outdoor Adventures

Surfers and windsurfers flock to Geraldton and Gnaraloo for winter swells and summer winds, while fisherfolk and explorers head west to Edel Land. Bushwalkers prefer Kalbarri in winter.

Shipwrecks & Settlements

Shipwrecks and 19th-century buildings stud this coastline. Highlights include Greenough's pioneer settlement and the 1629 wreck of the *Batavia* off the Houtman Abrolhos Islands.

p157

Coral Coast & the Pilbara

Beaches
Adventure
Wildlife

Ningaloo Marine Park

Superb isolated beaches lead down to shallow lagoons hemmed by World Heritage–listed Ningaloo Marine Park. World-class snorkelling and diving are only a short wade from shore, and camping is right behind the dunes.

Karijini National Park

Karijini National Park is the Pilbara's adventure playground, with deep, gorges inviting exploration, and the state's highest peaks begging to be climbed.

Native Wildlife

Whale sharks, manta rays, turtles and migrating whales all visit Ningaloo, while inland birds flock to the oasis pools of Millstream Chichester National Park, and pythons and rock wallabies hide in the shadows of Karijini.

p175

Broome & the Kimberley

Beaches
Culture
Adventure

Iconic Beaches

Don't miss the sunset camel trains of iconic Cable Beach. Equally spectacular are the seldom-visited beaches of the Dampier Peninsula.

Indigenous Culture

Learn traditional practices from the Aboriginal communities of the Dampier Peninsula. Follow Broome's Lurujarri Dreaming Trail, before exploring the Kimberley's amazing Wandjina and Gwion Gwion images.

Gibb River Road

Drive the bone-shaking Gibb River Road, detouring to Mitchell Falls and remote Kalumburu. Zip on a speedboat to the Horizontal Waterfalls, or negotiate a canoe down the mighty Ord River.

p195

On the Road

Perth & Fremantle

Includes ➡

Best Places to Eat

➡ Duende (p68)
➡ Brika (p66)
➡ Restaurant Amusé (p64)
➡ Pleased to Meet You (p66)
➡ Bread in Common (p83)

Best Places to Stay

➡ Durack House (p63)
➡ Above Bored (p62)
➡ Witch's Hat (p62)
➡ Alex Hotel (p62)
➡ Hougoumont Hotel (p82)

Why Go?

Planted by a river beneath an almost permanent canopy of blue sky, the city of Perth is a modern-day boom town, stoking Australia's economy from its glitzy central business district. Yet it remains as relaxed as the sleepy Swan River – black swans bobbing atop – which winds past the skyscrapers and out to the Indian Ocean.

Even in its boardrooms, Perth's heart is down at the beach, tossing around in clear ocean surf and stretching out on the sand. The city's beaches trace the western edge of Australia for some 40km, and you can have one to yourself on any given day – for a city of this size, Perth is sparsely populated.

Perth has sprawled to enfold Fremantle within its suburbs, yet the port city maintains its own distinct personality – proud of its nautical ties, working-class roots, bohemian reputation and, especially, its football team.

When to Go

Perth

°C/°F **Temp** — **Rainfall** inches/mm

40/104 — 30/86 — 20/68 — 10/50 — 0/32

20/500 — 16/400 — 12/300 — 8/200 — 4/100 — 0

J F M A M J J A S O N D

Feb Perth's Arts Festival is on and school starts, so the beaches are less crowded.

Mar Warm and dry, so great weather for the beach, and not as swelteringly hot.

Sep Kings Park wildflowers, the Perth Royal Show and the Listen Out festival.

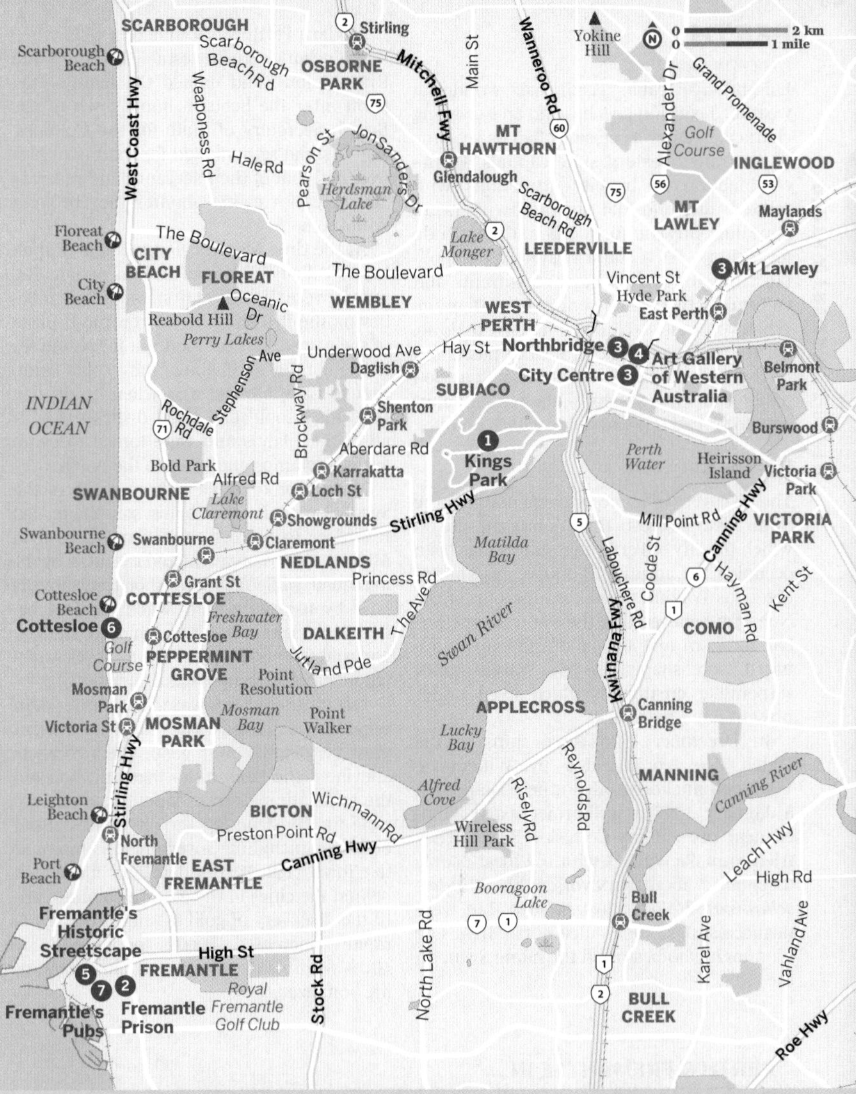

Perth & Fremantle Highlights

1 Stretching out on the lawn in **Kings Park** (p51) with the glittering river and city spread out below you.

2 Doing time with the ghosts of convicts past in World Heritage–listed **Fremantle Prison** (p77).

3 Experiencing Perth's emerging restaurant scene in the eateries of **Mt Lawley** (p66), **Northbridge** (p65) and the **city centre** (p64).

4 Exploring a wealth of local art, Indigenous and otherwise, at the **Art Gallery of Western Australia** (p49).

5 Soaking up the decaying gold-rush grandeur of **Fremantle's historic streetscape** (p76).

6 Enjoying the sunset with a sundowner in hand after a hard day's beaching at **Cottesloe** (p52).

7 Hitting **Fremantle's pubs** (p84) and letting the bands of Bon Scott's home town shake you all night long.

PERTH

POP 1.75 MILLION

Laid-back, liveable Perth has wonderful weather, beautiful beaches and an easygoing character. About as close to Bali as to some of Australia's eastern state capitals, Perth's combination of big-city attractions with relaxed and informal surrounds offers an appealing lifestyle for locals and lots to do for visitors. It's a sophisticated, cosmopolitan city with myriad bars, restaurants and cultural activities all vying for attention. When you want to chill out, it's easy to do so. Perth's pristine parkland, nearby bush, and river and ocean beaches – along with a good public transport system – allow its inhabitants to spread out and enjoy what's on offer.

History

The discovery of stone implements near the Swan River suggests that Mooro, the site on which the city of Perth now stands, has been occupied for around 40,000 years. The indigenous Wadjuk people, a subgroup of the Noongar, believed that the Swan River (Derbal Yaragan) and the landforms surrounding it were shaped by two Wargal (giant serpentlike creatures), which lived under present-day Kings Park.

In December 1696 three ships in the Dutch fleet commanded by Willem de Vlamingh anchored off Rottnest Island. On 5 January 1697 a well-armed party landed near present-day Cottesloe Beach. They tried to make contact with the local people to enquire about survivors of the *Ridderschap van Hollant,* lost in 1694, but were unsuccessful, so they sailed north. It was de Vlamingh who bestowed the name Swan on the river.

Modern Perth was founded in 1829 when Captain James Stirling established the Swan River Colony, and named the main settlement after the Scottish home town of the British Secretary of State for the Colonies. The original settlers paid for their own passage and that of their servants, and received 200 acres for every labourer they brought with them.

At the time Mooro belonged to a Wadjuk leader called Yellagonga and his people. Relations were friendly at first, the Noongar believing the British to be the returned spirits of their dead, but competition for resources led to conflict. Yellagonga moved his camp first to Lake Monger and when he died in 1843 his people had been dispossessed of all of their lands and were forced to camp around swamps and lakes to the north.

Midgegooroo, an elder from south of the Swan River, along with his son Yagan, led resistance to the British settlement. In 1833 Midgegooroo was caught and executed by firing squad, while Yagan was shot a few months later by teenage settlers whom he had befriended. Yagan's head was removed, smoked and sent to London where it was publicly displayed as an anthropological curiosity.

Life for the settlers was much harder than they had expected. The early settlement grew very slowly until 1850, when convicts alleviated the labour shortage and boosted the population. Convict labour was responsible for constructing the city's substantial buildings including Government House and the Town Hall. Perth's development lagged behind the cities in the eastern colonies, until the discovery of gold inland in the 1890s rapidly increased Perth's population by 400% within a decade and initiated a building bonanza.

PERTH & FREMANTLE IN...

Two Days

Have a leisurely dinner in **Highgate** or **Mt Lawley** and then spend your first morning in the art galleries and museum of the **Perth Cultural Centre**. Grab lunch in **Subiaco** or **Leederville** before exploring verdant and view-friendly **Kings Park**. For your second day, catch the train to **Fremantle** and spend the whole day there, prioritising the world-heritage prison, maritime museum and Shipwreck Galleries. Grab a bite in up-and-coming **South Fremantle** and then head to a **pub** to catch a band or drink a craft beer.

Four Days

Take the two-day itinerary but stretch it to a comfortable pace. Head to **Rottnest Island** for a day trip and spend any time left over on Perth's beaches. Allocate a night each to **Northbridge** and the city's best new bars and restaurants.

The mineral wealth of Western Australia (WA) has continued to drive Perth's growth. In the 1980s and '90s, though, the city's clean-cut, nouveau-riche image was tainted by a series of financial and political scandals.

Western Australia's 21st-century mining boom has cooled slightly in recent years, but there are still plenty of Aussie dollars awash in the state's economy, and Perth continues to blossom like WA's wildflowers in spring. Major civic works include a new football stadium, and visitors to Perth can witness ongoing work on two major reboots of the central city's urban landscape.

The Perth City Link project will transform the area between Northbridge and the CBD. At the opposite end of the CBD, the Elizabeth Quay development is adding parks and retail and hospitality precincts to the riverfront land between Barrack and William Sts. After the city turned its back on the river for many decades, downtown Perth will once again link with the silvery waters of the Swan. See www.getthebiggerpicture.com.au for information on these developments.

Largely excluded from this race to riches have been the Noongar people. In 2006 the Perth Federal Court recognised native title over the city of Perth and its surrounds, but this was appealed by the WA and Commonwealth governments. In December 2009 an agreement was signed in WA's parliament, setting out a time frame for negotiating settlement of native-title claims across the southwest. In mid-2015 a $1.3 billion native-title deal was settled by the WA government recognising the Noongar people as the traditional owners of the southwest. Covering over 200,000 sq km, the settlement area stretches from Jurien Bay to Ravensthorpe, and includes the Perth metropolitan area.

Sights

Many of Perth's main attractions are within walking distance of the inner city, and several are in the Perth Cultural Centre precinct past the railway station in Northbridge. Easy day trips include the Swan Valley.

City Centre

Bell Tower LANDMARK

(Map p54; www.thebelltower.com.au; adult/child $14/9; 10am-4pm, ringing noon-1pm Sat-Mon & Thu) This pointy glass spire fronted by copper sails contains the royal bells of London's St Martin's-in-the-Fields, the oldest of which dates to 1550. They were given to WA by the British government in 1988, and are the only set known to have left England. Clamber to the top for 360-degree views of Perth by the river.

The tower sits on land that was reclaimed in the 1920s and 1930s, and now forms a green strip between the river and the city. Long, thin Langley Park is still occasionally used as an airstrip for light aircraft demonstrations. Stirling Gardens and Supreme Court Gardens have lawns and formal gardens that fill up with city workers at lunchtime.

Perth Mint HISTORIC BUILDING

(Map p54; www.perthmint.com.au; 310 Hay St; adult/child $25/8; 9am-5pm) Dating from 1899, the compelling Mint displays a collection of coins, nuggets and gold bars. You can fondle a bar worth over $200,000, mint your own coins and watch gold pours (on the half-hour, from 9.30am to 3.30pm). The Mint's Gold Exhibition features a massive one-tonne gold coin worth a staggering $50 million.

Northbridge

★**Art Gallery of Western Australia** GALLERY

(Map p54; www.artgallery.wa.gov.au; Perth Cultural Centre; 10am-5pm Wed-Mon) FREE Founded in 1895, this excellent gallery houses the state's pre-eminent art collection. It contains important post-WWII works by Australian luminaries such as Arthur Boyd, Albert Tucker, Grace Cossington Smith, Russell Drysdale, Arthur Streeton and Sidney Nolan. Check the website for a changing array of free tours run most days at 11am and 1pm. The gallery's Indigenous galleries are also very well regarded.

Indigenous work ranges from canvases to bark paintings and sculpture, and artists include Rover Thomas, Angilya Mitchell, Christopher Pease and Phyllis Thomas. The annual WA Indigenous Art Awards entries are displayed here from August to December.

★**Western Australian Museum – Perth** MUSEUM

(Map p54; www.museum.wa.gov.au; Perth Cultural Centre; 9.30am-5pm) FREE The state's museum is a six-headed beast, with branches also in Fremantle, Albany, Geraldton and Kalgoorlie. This one includes dinosaur, mammal, butterfly and bird galleries, a **children's discovery centre**, and excellent displays covering Indigenous and colonial history.

Greater Perth

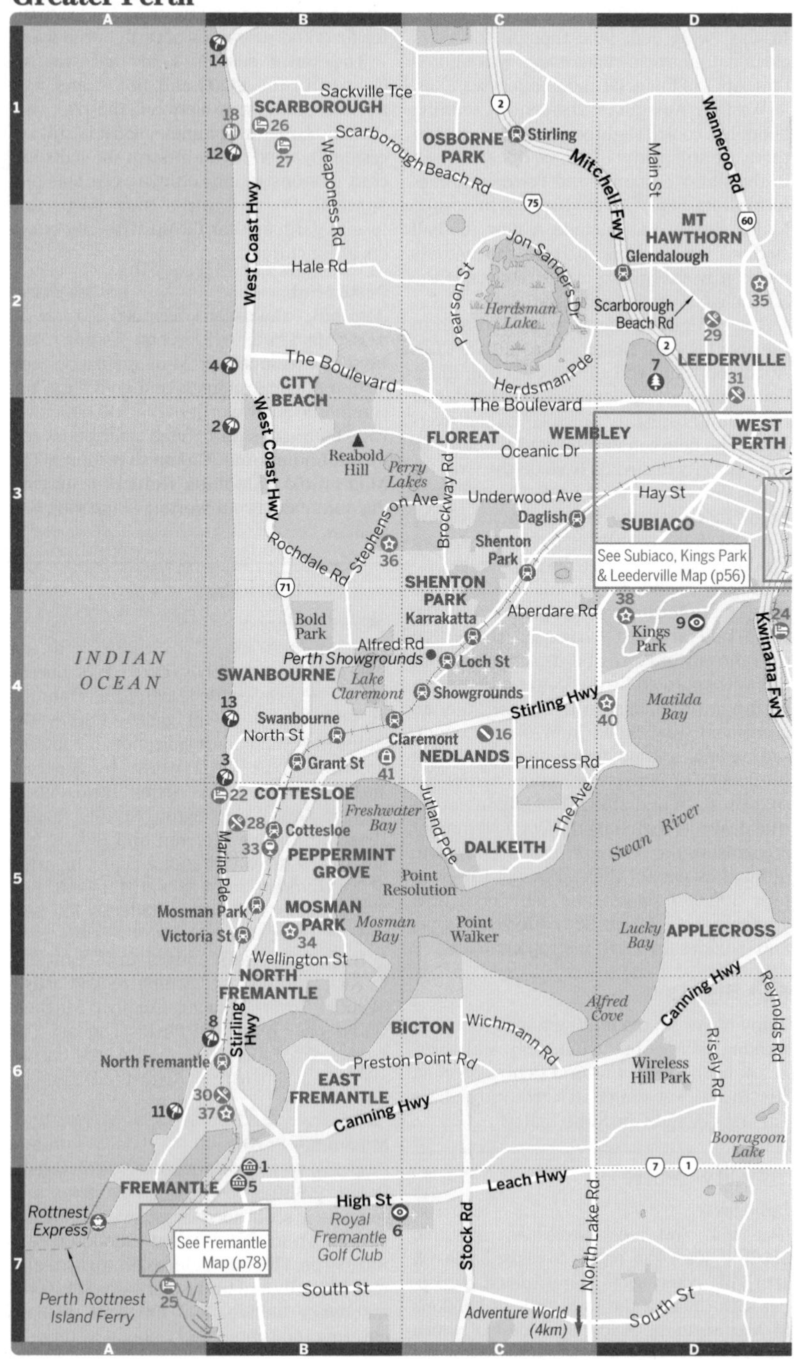

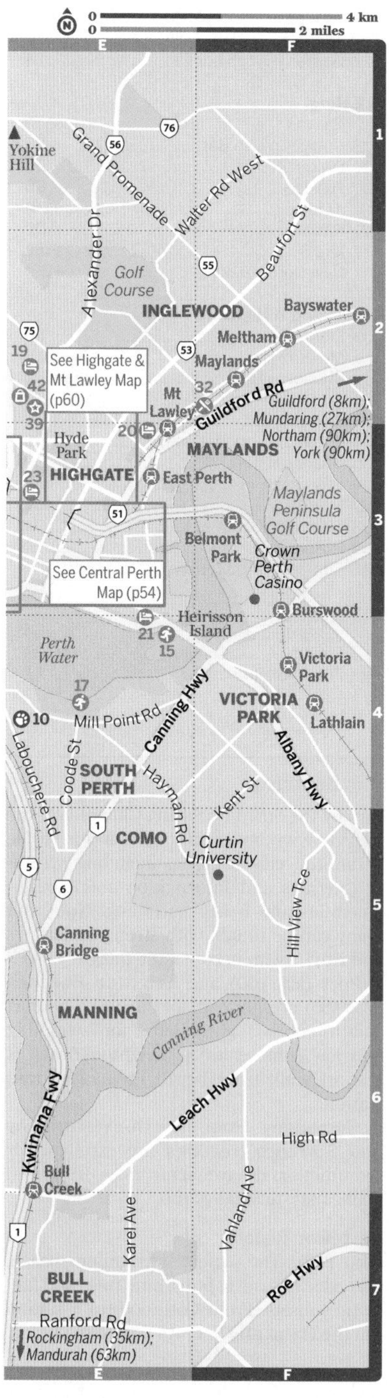

In the courtyard, set in its own preservative bath, is Megamouth, a curious-looking species of shark with a soft, rounded head. Only about five of these benign creatures have ever been found; this one beached itself near Mandurah, south of Perth.

The museum complex includes Perth's original gaol, built in 1856 and used until 1888 – the site of many hangings.

Perth Institute of Contemporary Arts GALLERY

(PICA; Map p54; www.pica.org.au; Perth Cultural Centre; ⏲10am-5pm) FREE PICA (pee-kah) may look traditional – it's housed in an elegant 1896 red-brick former school – but inside it's one of Australia's principal platforms for contemporary art including installations, performance, sculpture and video. PICA actively promotes new and experimental art, and exhibits graduate works annually. From 10am from Tuesday to Sunday, the PICA Bar is a top spot for a coffee or cocktail, and has occasional live music.

Hyde Park PARK

(Map p60; William St) One of Perth's most beautiful parks, suburban Hyde Park is a top spot for a picnic or lazy book-reading session on the lawn. A path traces the small lake, and mature palms, firs and Moreton Bay figs provide plenty of shade. It's within walking distance of Northbridge; continue northeast along William St.

Subiaco & Kings Park

★Kings Park & Botanic Garden PARK

(Map p56; www.bgpa.wa.gov.au; ⏲guided walks 10am, noon & 2pm) FREE Rising above the Swan River on the city's western flank, the 400-hectare bush-filled expanse of Kings Park is Perth's pride and joy. At the park's heart is the 17-hectare Botanic Garden, containing over 2000 plant species indigenous to WA. In spring there's an impressive display of the state's famed wildflowers. A year-round highlight is the **Lotterywest Federation Walkway** (Map p50; ⏲9am-5pm), a 620m path including a 222m-long, glass-and-steel bridge that passes through the canopy of a stand of eucalypts.

The main road leading into the park, Fraser Ave, is lined with towering lemon-scented gums that are dramatically lit at night. At its culmination are the State War Memorial, a cafe, a gift shop, Fraser's

Greater Perth

Sights

1 Army Museum of WA B6
2 City Beach B3
3 Cottesloe Beach B4
4 Floreat Beach B2
5 Fremantle Arts Centre B7
6 Fremantle Cemetery B7
7 Lake Monger D2
8 Leighton Beach B6
9 Lotterywest Federation Walkway D4
10 Perth Zoo E4
11 Port Beach A6
12 Scarborough Beach B1
13 Swanbourne Beach B4
14 Trigg Beach B1

Activities, Courses & Tours

15 About Bike Hire E4
16 Australasian Diving Academy C4
17 Funcats E4
18 Surfschool B1

Sleeping

19 Above Bored E2
20 Durack House E3
21 Fraser Suites E4
22 Ocean Beach Backpackers B5
23 One World Backpackers E3
24 Peninsula D4
25 Quest Harbour Village A7
26 Sunmoon Boutique Resort B1
27 Western Beach Lodge B1

Eating

Canvas .... (see 5)
28 Cott & Co Fish Bar B5
29 Divido D2
30 Flipside B6
Il Lido .... (see 28)
31 Kitsch D2
32 Mrs S F2
New Norcia Bakery .... (see 29)

Drinking & Nightlife

33 Elba B5
Mrs Browns .... (see 30)
Swallow .... (see 32)

Entertainment

34 Camelot Outdoor Cinema B5
35 Charles Hotel D2
36 HBF Stadium B3
37 Mojo's B6
38 Moonlight Cinema D4
39 Rosemount Hotel E2
40 Somerville Auditorium D4

Shopping

41 æ'lkemi B4
Found .... (see 5)
42 Future Shelter E2

restaurant (p68) and the Kings Park Visitor Centre. Free guided walks leave from here.

It's a good spot for a picnic or to let the kids off the leash in one of the playgrounds. Its numerous tracks are popular with walkers and joggers all year round, with an ascent of the steep stairs from the river rewarded with wonderful views from the top.

The Noongar people knew this area as Kaarta Gar-up and used it for thousands of years for hunting, food gathering, ceremonies, teaching and tool-making. A freshwater spring at the base of the escarpment, now known as Kennedy Fountain but before that as Goonininup, was a home of the Wargal, mystical snakelike creatures that created the Swan River and other waterways.

To get here take bus 37 (39 on weekends), heading west along St Georges Tce (S-stand), to the visitor centre. You can also walk up (steep) Mount St from the city or climb Jacob's Ladder from Mounts Bay Rd, near the Adelphi Hotel.

Beaches

Run by the Surf Life Saving Club of WA, the website www.mybeach.com.au has a profile of all the city beaches, including weather forecasts and information about buses, amenities and beach patrolling. Note that many can be rough, with strong undertows and rips – swim between the flags.

Port (Map p50) and **Leighton Beaches** (Map p50) are popular for surfing. The Port (south) end is slightly better for swimming and has some eateries. Leighton Beach is a short walk from North Fremantle train station.

Hamersley Pool, **North**, **Watermans and Sorrento Beaches** are excellent for swimming and have picnic areas, BBQs and a bike path through scrub.

Cottesloe Beach BEACH

(Map p50) The safest swimming beach, Cottesloe has cafes, pubs, pine trees and fantastic sunsets. From Cottesloe train station (on the Fremantle line) it's 1km to the beach.

Bus 102 from Wellington St station goes straight to the beach.

Swanbourne Beach BEACH
(Map p50) Safe swimming, and an unofficial nude and gay beach. From Grant St train station it's a 1.5km walk to the beach (2km from Swanbourne station). Catch bus 102 from Wellington St station and get off at Marine Pde.

City Beach BEACH
(Map p50) Swimming, surfing, lawn and amenities. Take bus 84 (85 on weekends) from the Roe St bus station.

Floreat Beach BEACH
(Map p50) A generally uncrowded beach, but it can sometimes be windy. There's good swimming, surfing, cafes and a playground. Catch bus 84 (85 on weekends) from the Roe St bus station to City Beach and walk north 800m.

Scarborough Beach BEACH
(Map p50) Popular young surfers' spot, so be sure to swim between flags as it can be dangerous. There are also lots of shops and eateries. Catch a Joondalup line train from Esplanade to Stirling, and then bus 421 to the beach.

Trigg Beach BEACH
(Map p50) Good surf with a hardcore group of locals who come out when the surf's up; dangerous when rough and prone to rips – always swim between the flags.

Mettams Pool BEACH
Like a turquoise paddle pool with good snorkelling.

Aquarium of Western Australia AQUARIUM
(AQWA; ☎08-9447 7500; www.aqwa.com.au; Hillarys Boat Harbour; adult/child $29/17; ⊙10am-5pm) Dividing WA's vast coastline into five distinct zones (Far North, Coral Coast, Shipwreck Coast, Perth and Great Southern), AQWA features a 98m underwater tunnel showcasing stingrays, turtles, fish and sharks. On weekdays, take the Joondalup train to Warwick station and then transfer to bus 423. By car, take the Mitchell Fwy north and exit at Hepburn Ave. The daring can snorkel or dive with the sharks with the aquarium's in-house dive master.

Diving costs $159 with your own gear (to hire snorkel/dive gear add $20/40). Another interactive option from Friday to Sunday is donning a wetsuit and breathing tube and negotiating an underwater seascape as a Reefwalker ($20).

Other Areas

Perth Zoo ZOO
(Map p50; www.perthzoo.wa.gov.au; 20 Labouchere Rd; adult/child $27/13; ⊙9am-5pm) Part of the fun of a day at the zoo is getting there – taking the ferry across the Swan River from Barrack St Jetty to Mends St Jetty (every half-hour) and walking up the hill. Zones include Reptile Encounter, African Savannah (with rhinos, cheetahs,

PERTH FOR CHILDREN

With a usually clement climate and plenty of open spaces and beaches to run around in, Perth is a great place to bring children. Of the beaches, Cottesloe is the safest and a family favourite. With older kids, arrange two-wheeled family expeditions along Perth's riverside and coastal bike paths. Kings Park has playgrounds and walking tracks.

The **Perth Royal Show** (p59), held late September, is an ever-popular family outing – sideshow rides, showbags and proudly displayed poultry. Many of Perth's big attractions cater well for young audiences, especially the **Aquarium of Western Australia** (p53), **Perth Zoo** (p53), the **Western Australian Museum – Perth** (p49) and the **Art Gallery of Western Australia** (p49).

Scitech (Map p56; www.scitech.org.au; Sutherland St, City West Centre; adult/child $17/11; ⊙9.30am-4pm Mon-Fri, 10am-5pm Sat & Sun) is a good rainy-day option, with over 160 hands-on, large-scale science and technology exhibits.

Adventure World has exciting rides such as the 'Black Widow', a G-Force defying spinning wonder, as well as pools, water slides and a castle. For real daredevils, the new 'Abyss' roller coaster is the ultimate exciting challenge. From Perth, come off the Kwinana Fwy at Farrington Rd, turn right and follow the signs. Buy tickets online to avoid weekend queues.

Central Perth

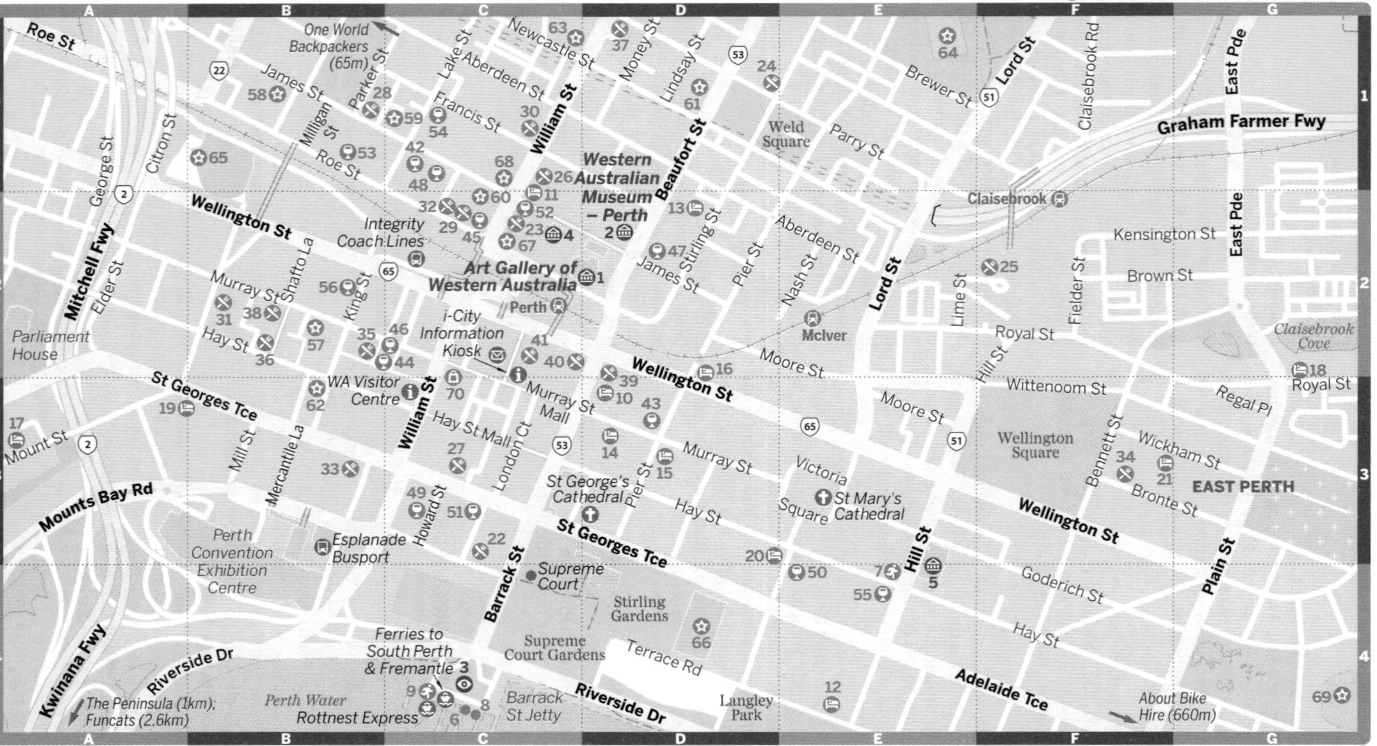

Central Perth

Top Sights
1 Art Gallery of Western Australia D2
2 Western Australian Museum – Perth .. D2

Sights
3 Bell Tower C4
4 Perth Institute of Contemporary Arts C2
5 Perth Mint E4

Activities, Courses & Tours
6 Captain Cook Cruises C4
7 Cycle Centre E4
Gecko Bike Hire .... (see 13)
8 Golden Sun Cruises C4
9 Oceanic Cruises C4
Swan Jet .... (see 6)

Sleeping
10 Adina Apartment Hotel Barrack Plaza D3
11 Alex Hotel C2
12 City Waters E4
13 Emperor's Crown D2
14 Kangaroo Inn D3
15 Pensione Hotel D3
16 Perth City YHA D2
17 Riverview 42 Mt St Hotel A3
18 Sebel East Perth G2
19 Terrace Hotel A3
20 Travelodge Perth D3
21 Wickham Retreat F3

Eating
22 Balthazar C3
23 Bivouac Canteen & Bar C2
24 Brika D1
25 City Farm Organic Growers Market F2
26 Flipside C1
27 Greenhouse C3
28 Izakaya Sakura B1
29 Kakulas Bros C2
30 Little Willy's C1
31 Mama Tran B2
32 Pleased to Meet You C2
33 Print Hall B3
34 Restaurant Amusé F3
35 Secret Garden B2
36 Stables Bar B2
37 Tak Chee House D1
38 Taka B2
39 Taka D2
40 Toastface Grillah C2
41 Twilight Hawkers Market C2
Viet Hoa .... (see 63)

Drinking & Nightlife
42 Air C1
43 Ambar D3
44 Bar Halcyon B2
45 Bird C2
46 Cheeky Sparrow C2
47 Court D2
Ezra Pound .... (see 29)
48 Geisha C1
Greenhouse .... (see 27)
49 Helvetica C3
50 Hula Bula Bar E4
51 Lalla Rookh C3
52 LOT 20 .... C2
Mechanics Institute .... (see 26)
53 Metro City B1
54 Northbridge Brewing Company C1
55 The Grosvenor E4
56 Varnish on King B2
Wolf Lane .... (see 35)

Entertainment
57 Amplifier B2
58 Bakery B1
59 Cinema Paradiso C1
60 Connections C2
61 Ellington Jazz Club D1
62 His Majesty's Theatre B3
63 Moon C1
64 NIB Stadium E1
65 Perth Arena B1
66 Perth Concert Hall D4
67 State Theatre Centre C2
68 Universal C1
69 WACA G4

Shopping
70 78 Records C3
Pigeonhole .... (see 38)

zebras, giraffes and lions), Asian Rainforest (with elephants, tigers, sun bears and orangutans) and Australian Bushwalk (with kangaroos, emus, koalas and dingos). Another transport option is bus 30 or 31 from the Wellington St bus station or Esplanade train station.

Lake Monger PARK
(Map p50; Lake Monger Dr) In spring black swans and their cygnets plod about the grounds – something of a meeting place for the local bird life – nonplussed by the joggers circling the lake on the flat 3.5km path. There's plenty of grass for cricket, football and picnics. It's walking distance from Leederville train station; exit on the side opposite the shops, turn right onto Southport St and veer left onto Lake Monger Dr.

Subiaco, Kings Park & Leederville

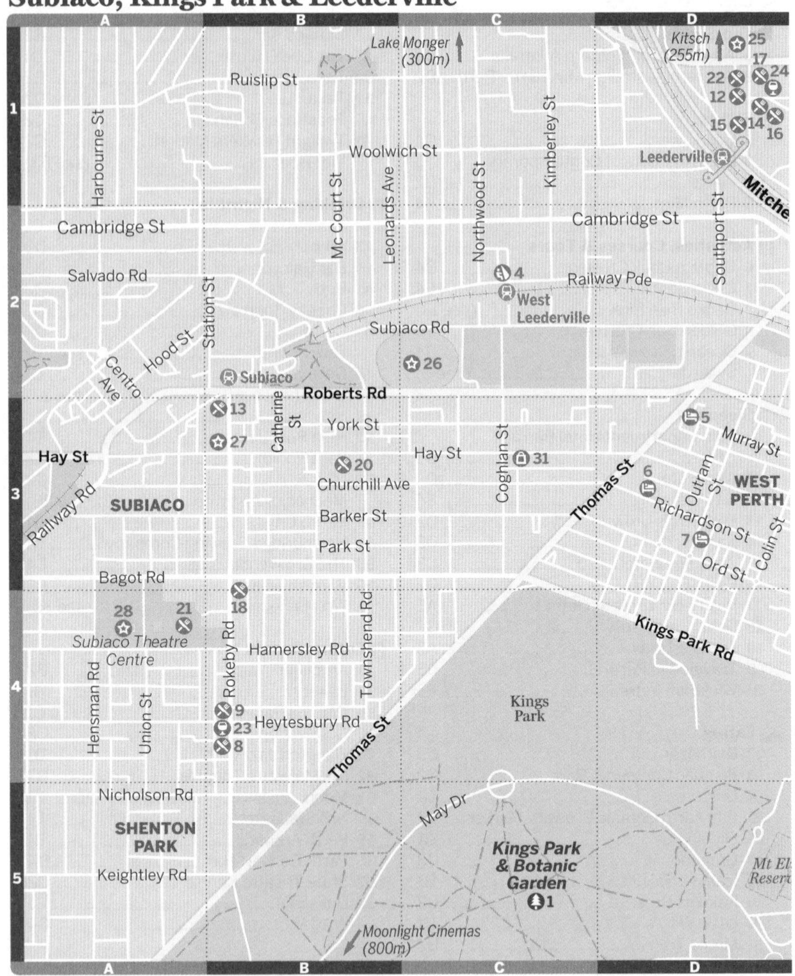

Activities

Whale Watching

The whale-watching season runs from mid-September to early December, when 30,000 whales take the 'Humpback Highway' up the coast. Tour operators offer either a refund or a repeat trip in the unlikely event that whales aren't spotted. Tour boats are fitted with underwater hydrophones, so you can to listen to the whales singing.

Mills Charters WHALE WATCHING
(08-9246 5334; www.millscharters.com.au; adult/child $80/65; 9am daily, 1.30pm Sat & Sun mid-Sep–Nov) Informative three- to four-hour trips departing from Hillarys Boat Harbour.

Oceanic Cruises WHALE WATCHING
(Map p54; 08-9325 1191; www.oceaniccruises.com.au; adult/child $77/34) Departs Perth's Barrack St Jetty or Fremantle's B Shed.

Cycling

Cycling is an excellent way to explore Perth. Kings Park has some good bike tracks and there are cycling routes along the Swan River, running all the way to Fremantle, and along the coast. Bikes can be taken free of charge on ferries at any time and on trains

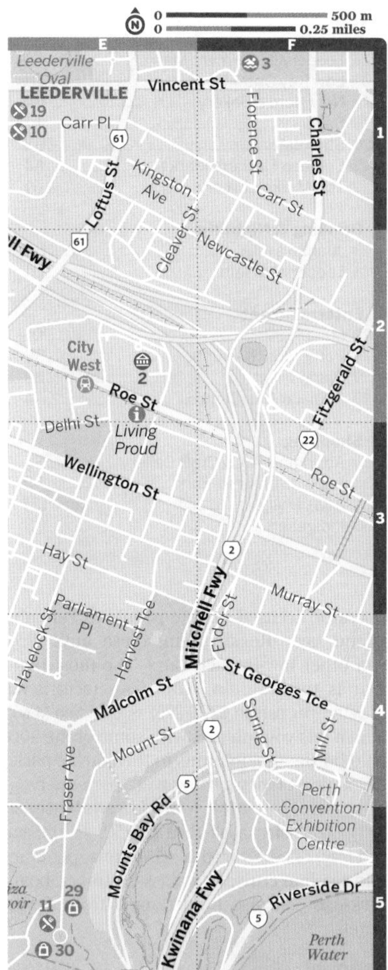

outside of weekday peak hours (7am to 9am and 4pm to 6.30pm) – with a bit of planning you can pedal as far as you like in one direction and return via public transport. Bikes can't be taken on buses at any time, except some regional coaches (for a small charge). For route maps, see www.transport.wa.gov.au/cycling/ or call into a bike shop.

About Bike Hire BICYCLE RENTAL
(Map p50; ☎08-9221 2665; www.aboutbikehire.com.au; 1-7 Riverside Dr, Causeway Car Park; per hour/day/week from $10/36/80; ⏰9am-5pm) Also hires kayaks (per hour/four hours $16/45).

Cycle Centre BICYCLE RENTAL
(Map p54; ☎08-9325 1176; www.cyclecentre.com.au; 326 Hay St; per day/week $25/65; ⏰9am-5.30pm Mon-Fri, 9am-4pm Sat, 1-4pm Sun) See the website for recommended rides.

Gecko Bike Hire BICYCLE RENTAL
(Map p54; www.geckobikehire.com.au; inside Emperor's Crown hostel, 85 Stirling St; per 4hr/day $22/33) Four locations around Perth, and further south in Bunbury and Busselton. See the website for route maps.

Other Activities

Surf Sail Australia WINDSURFING, KITESURFING
(Map p56; ☎1800 686 089; www.surfsailaustralia.com.au; 260 Railway Pde, Trial; ⏰10am-5pm Mon-Sat) When the afternoon sea breeze blusters in, windsurfers take to the Swan River, Leighton and beaches north of Perth. This is where you can hire or buy your gear.

Australasian Diving Academy DIVING
(Map p50; ☎08-9389 5018; www.ausdiving.com.au; 142 Stirling Hwy) Hires diving gear (full set per day/week $75/200) and offers diving courses (four-day open-water $495). There are a variety of sites in the vicinity, including several around Rottnest Island, and four wrecks.

Funcats SAILING
(Map p50; ☎0408 926 003; www.funcats.com.au; Coode St Jetty; per hour $40; ⏰10am-6pm Oct-Apr) These easy-to-sail catamarans are for hire on the South Perth foreshore. Each boat holds up to three people.

Surfschool SURFING
(Map p50; ☎08-9447 5637; www.surfschool.com; Scarborough Beach; adult/child $60/55; ⏰Oct-May) Two-hour lessons at Scarborough Beach (at the end of Manning St), including boards and wetsuits. Bookings essential.

Beatty Park Leisure Centre SWIMMING
(Map p56; ☎08-9273 6080; www.beattypark.com.au; 220 Vincent St; swimming adult/child $6/4.50; ⏰5.30am-9pm Mon-Fri, 6.30am-6pm Sat & Sun) This complex has indoor and outdoor pools, water slides and a gym. Turn left at the top of William St and continue on Vincent St to just past Charles St.

WA Skydiving Academy ADVENTURE SPORTS
(☎1300 137 855; www.waskydiving.com.au) Tandem jumps from 6000/8000/10,000/12,000ft from $260/300/340/380. Dropzone options include Perth, Mandurah and Pinjarra.

Subiaco, Kings Park & Leederville

Top Sights
1 Kings Park & Botanic Garden C5

Sights
2 Scitech E2

Activities, Courses & Tours
3 Beatty Park Leisure Centre F1
4 Surf Sail Australia C2

Sleeping
5 Murray Hotel D3
6 Richardson D3
7 The Outram D3

Eating
8 Boucla B4
9 Chez Jean-Claude Patisserie B4
10 Duende E1
11 Fraser's E5
12 Green's & Co D1
13 Jus Burgers B3
14 Jus Burgers D1
15 Kailis Bros D1
16 Leederville Farmers Market D1
17 Low Key Chow House D1
18 New Norcia Bakery B4
19 Sayers E1
20 Stimulatte B3
21 Subiaco Farmers Market A4
22 The Market Juicery D1

Drinking & Nightlife
23 Juanita's B4
24 Leederville Hotel D1

Entertainment
25 Luna D1
26 Patersons Stadium C2
27 Regal Theatre B3
28 Subiaco Arts Centre A4

Shopping
29 Aboriginal Art & Craft Gallery E5
30 Aspects of Kings Park E5
Atlas Divine .... (see 12)
31 Indigenart C3

Tours

Indigenous Tours WA CULTURAL TOUR
(www.indigenouswa.com) See Perth through the eyes of the local Wadjuk people. Options include the **Indigenous Heritage Tour** (0405 630 606; adult/child $50/15; 1.30pm & 3.30pm Mon-Fri) – a 90-minute guided walk around Kings Park – and an Indigenous-themed stroll (p81) around Fremantle. Tours can be booked online or through the visitor information centre; booking ahead is essential.

City Sightseeing Perth Tour BUS TOUR
(08-9203 8882; www.citysightseeingperth.com; adult/child from $30/12) Hop-on, hop-off double-decker bus tour, with loop routes taking in the central city, Kings Park and the Burswood Entertainment Complex. Tickets are valid for up to two days.

Two Feet & A Heartbeat WALKING TOUR
(1800 459 388; www.twofeet.com.au; per person $40-50) Daytime walking tours of Perth, and a popular after-dark 'Small Bar Tour'. Note 'Tight Arse Tuesdays' are just $20 for the Perth tour.

Rockingham Wild Encounters WILDLIFE TOURS
(08-9591 1333; www.rockinghamwildencounters.com.au; cnr Arcadia Dr & Penguin Rd) The only operator licensed to take people to Penguin Island near Rockingham, these guys also run other low-impact tours. The most popular is the **dolphin swim tour** (departs Val St Jetty; per person $205-225; 8am Sep-May), which lets you interact with some of the 200 wild bottlenose dolphins in the marine park. If you don't fancy getting wet, there are two-hour **dolphin-watch tours** (departs Mersey St Jetty, Shoalwater; adult/child $85/50; 10.45am Sep-May). There's also a 45-minute penguin and sea-lion cruise in a glass-bottomed boat. Pick-ups can also be arranged from Perth hotels.

Swan Jet BOAT TOUR
(Map p54; 1300 554 026; www.catalinaadventures.com.au; Barrack St Jetty; adult/child $55/45) Exciting jet boat blasts on the Swan River.

Captain Cook Cruises CRUISE
(Map p54; 08-9325 3341; www.captaincookcruises.com.au; adult/child from $38/21) Cruises to the Swan Valley or Fremantle, with an array of add-ons such as meals, wine tastings and tram rides.

Golden Sun Cruises CRUISE
(Map p54; 08-9325 9916; www.goldensuncruises.com.au; tours from $22) Well-priced cruises and a good option to get to Fremantle.

Beer Nuts BREWERY
(☎08-9295 0605; www.beernuts.com.au; per person from $60; ⏲Wed-Sun) Visits Swan Valley microbreweries and a rum distillery.

Out & About WINE TASTING
(☎08-9377 3376; www.outandabouttours.com.au; per person from $85) Wine-focused tours of the Swan Valley and historic Guildford. Some include river cruises, breweries, cheese and chocolate stops. Day trips also to Margaret River.

Swan Valley Tours FOOD, WINE TASTING
(☎03-9274 1199; www.svtours.com.au; per person from $65) Food- and wine-driven tours that cruise up to and/or drive through the Swan Valley.

Rottnest Air Taxi SCENIC FLIGHTS
(☎0411 264 547; www.rottnest.de) Thirty-minute joy flights over the city, Kings Park and Fremantle (per person $67 to $115), leaving from Jandakot airport.

Festivals & Events

Perth Cup HORSE RACING
(www.perthracing.org.au; ⏲1 Jan) New Year's Day sees Perth's biggest day at the races, with the party people heading to 'Tentland' for DJs and daiquiris.

Australia Day Skyworks FIREWORKS
(www.perth.wa.gov.au; ⏲26 Jan) Around 250,000 people come down to the riverside for a whole day of family entertainment, culminating in a 30-minute fireworks display at 8pm.

Perth International Arts Festival ARTS
(www.perthfestival.com.au; ⏲mid-Feb–early Mar) Artists such as Laurie Anderson, Dead Can Dance and Philip Glass perform alongside top local talent. Held over 25 days, it spans theatre, classical music, jazz, visual arts, dance, film and literature. Worth scheduling a trip around, especially for nocturnal types.

Kings Park Festival CULTURAL
(www.kingsparkfestival.com.au; ⏲Sep) Held throughout September to coincide with the wildflower displays, it includes live music every Sunday, guided walks and talks.

Perth Royal Show AGRICULTURE
(www.perthroyalshow.com.au; Claremont Showground; ⏲late Sep-early Oct) A week of fun-fair rides, spun sugar and showbags full of plastic junk. Oh, and farm animals.

Listen Out MUSIC
(www.listen-out.com.au; cnr Adelaide Tce & Riverside Dr, Ozone Reserve; ⏲late Sep) A one-day festival of international and local purveyors of danceable beats.

Awesome International Festival for Bright Young Things ARTS
(www.awesomearts.com; Perth Cultural Centre; ⏲school holidays Oct) This contemporary-arts festival held over 13-days celebrates young creativity with exhibitions, film, theatre, dance and wacky instruments. It strikes a balance between international performers and participation.

HOW TO MAXIMISE YOUR PERTH TRAVEL BUDGET

Everything you've heard is true. Perth is expensive, and central city accommodation is in especially high demand. Follow these tips to make the most of your dollars when visiting the city.

- Book accommodation as far ahead as possible.
- Accommodation can be significantly cheaper from Friday to Sunday.
- Consider a self-contained apartment with full cooking facilities.
- Perth B&Bs are usually good value.
- Consider Fremantle, especially for B&B accommodation, as a base while visiting Perth.
- Use Perth and Fremantle's free-of-charge Central Area Transit (CAT) bus services.
- Look out for lunch deals at central city pubs and cafes.
- Cheaper ethnic restaurants dot the streets around Northbridge, and there are good-value lunchtime food halls in central city shopping centres.
- Visit markets and other specialist stores for self-catering supplies.
- Free Perth attractions include Kings Park, the Art Gallery of Western Australia, the Perth Institute of Contemporary Arts and the Western Australian Museum.

Highgate & Mt Lawley

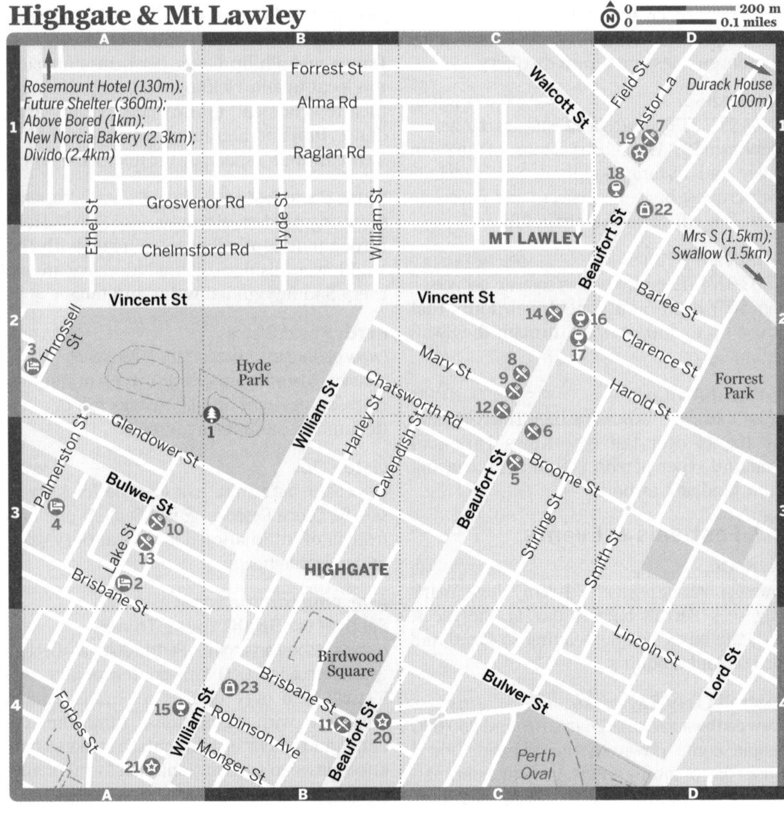

Highgate & Mt Lawley

Sights

1 Hyde Park B2

Sleeping

2 Hotel Northbridge A3
3 Pension of Perth A2
4 Witch's Hat A3

Eating

5 Ace Pizza C3
6 Beaufort St Merchant C3
7 Cantina 663 .... D1
8 El Público C2
9 Mary Street Bakery C2
Must Winebar .... (see 8)
10 Sayers Sister A3
11 Source Foods B4
12 St Michael 6003 .... C2
13 Tarts A3
14 Veggie Mama C2

Drinking & Nightlife

15 399 .... A4
16 Clarence's C2
17 Five Bar C2
18 Flying Scotsman D1
Must Winebar .... (see 8)
Velvet Lounge .... (see 18)

Entertainment

19 Astor D1
20 Lazy Susan's Comedy Den B4
21 Perth Steam Works A4

Shopping

22 Planet D1
23 William Topp B4

Sleeping

Perth is very spread out, so choose your location carefully. Northbridge is backpacker/boozer central, and can be noisy. The CBD and Northbridge are close to public transport, making hopping out to inner-city suburbs such as Leederville and Mt Lawley straightforward.

If you care most for the beach, consider staying there, as public transport to this part of town can be time-consuming.

Fuelled by the mining boom, Perth is an expensive town for accommodation. Book as early as you can.

City Centre

Kangaroo Inn HOSTEL $
(Map p54; ☎08-9325 3508; www.kangarooinn.com.au; 123 Murray St; dm $45-50, s/d $109/119;) Centrally located and near excellent cheap Asian food options, Kangaroo Inn is a very well-run recently opened addition to Perth's array of backpackers hostels. Private rooms and dorms are clean and modern, shared bathrooms are spotless, and there's a great rooftop chill-out area that's perfect for meeting other travellers.

Perth City YHA HOSTEL $
(Map p54; ☎08-9287 3333; www.yha.com.au; 300 Wellington St; dm $37-40, r with/without bathroom $125/100;) Occupying an impressive 1940s art-deco building by the train tracks, the centrally located YHA has a slight boarding-school feel in the corridors, but the rooms are clean and there are good facilities including a gym and a bar. Like many Perth hostels, it's popular with FIFO (fly-in, fly-out) mine workers, so the traditional YHA travellers' vibe has been diminished.

Riverview 42 Mt St Hotel APARTMENT $$
(Map p54; ☎08-9321 8963; www.riverviewperth.com.au; 42 Mount St; apt from $140;) There's a lot of brash new money up here on Mount St, but character-filled Riverview stands out as the best personality on the block. Its refurbished 1960s bachelor pads sit neatly atop a modern foyer and a relaxed cafe. Rooms are sunny and simple; the front ones have river views, while the back ones are quieter.

Pensione Hotel BOUTIQUE HOTEL $$
(Map p54; ☎08-9325 2133; www.pensione.com.au; 70 Pier St; d from $189;) Formerly the budget-oriented Aarons, this central-city 98-room property now features a shiny boutique sheen as the Pensione Hotel. The standard rooms definitely veer to cosy and (very) compact, but classy decor and a good location are two definite pluses in an expensive city.

City Waters MOTEL $$
(Map p54; ☎08-9325 1566; www.citywaters.com.au; 118 Terrace Rd; s/d $130/150;) Apricot-hued City Waters is one of a dying breed of old-fashioned Perth waterfront motels. Rooms are small and simple and face onto the car park, but they're clean and airy and the waterfront location is top-notch. Top-floor rooms are best; river views exist but are difficult to secure.

Travelodge Perth HOTEL $$
(Map p54; ☎08-9238 1888; www.travelodge.com.au; 417 Hay St; r from $189;) No surprises here, just unassuming well-kept rooms, some with views. Occasional online deals are good value in an expensive city.

Terrace Hotel BOUTIQUE HOTEL $$$
(Map p54; ☎08-9214 4444; www.terracehotelperth.com.au; 237 St Georges Tce; d from $432;) Opened in late 2012, the Terrace Hotel fills a heritage-listed terrace house in Perth's historic West End. There are just 15 deluxe rooms and suites, all with a clubby and luxurious ambience. Modern accoutrements include huge flat-screen TVs, Apple TV and iPads, and king-size four-poster beds with Egyptian-cotton linen.

Fraser Suites APARTMENT $$$
(Map p50; ☎08-9261 0000; http://perth.frasershospitality.com/en; 10 Adelaide Tce; apt $220-300;) At the quieter, eastern end of Perth's busy main drag, Fraser Suites offers elegant and modern apartments that are a good option for families or longer-stay visitors needing kitchen facilities. If you're here for the cricket, the hallowed turf of the Western Australian Cricket Association (WACA) stadium is a short stroll away. Try and secure a room with views of the Swan River.

Adina Apartment Hotel Barrack Plaza APARTMENT $$$
(Map p54; ☎08-9267 0000; www.tfehotels.com/brands/adina-apartment-hotels; 138 Barrack St; apt from $289;) The Adina's meticulously decorated apartment-sized hotel rooms are minimalist yet welcoming. All one-bedrooms have balconies, and rooms on Barrack St tend to have more natural light.

Northbridge

Most of Perth's hostels are in Northbridge, and it's possible to walk around and inspect rooms before putting your money down. Note that many hostels have long-term residents working in Perth, and this can alter the ambience for short-term visitors and travellers.

Witch's Hat HOSTEL **$**
(Map p60; ☎08-9228 4228; www.witchs-hat.com; 148 Palmerston St; dm/tw/d $36/88/99; ❄@📶) Witch's Hat is like something out of a fairy tale. The 1897 building itself could be mistaken for a gingerbread house, and the witch's hat (an Edwardian turret) stands proudly out the front, beckoning the curious to step inside. Dorms are light and uncommonly spacious, and there's a red-brick barbecue area out the back.

Emperor's Crown HOSTEL **$**
(Map p54; ☎08-9227 1400; www.emperorscrown.com.au; 85 Stirling St; dm $30-34, r with/without bathroom from $109/99; ❄@📶) One of Perth's best hostels has a great position (close to the Northbridge scene without being in the thick of it), friendly staff and high housekeeping standards. Granted, it's a bit pricier than most, but it's worth it.

One World Backpackers HOSTEL **$**
(Map p50; ☎08-9228 8206; www.oneworldbackpackers.com.au; 162 Aberdeen St; dm $31-33, d $82; @) Polished floorboards beam brightly in all the rooms of this nicely restored old house, and the dorms are big and sunny. The kitchen is large and functional, with everything provided, and there's a spacious lounge to relax in and plan your travels.

★ **Alex Hotel** BOUTIQUE HOTEL **$$**
(Map p54; ☎08-6430 4000; www.alexhotel.com.au; 50 James St; d from $190) The new Alex Hotel is more stylish evidence of the reinvention of Northbridge as a happening neighbourhood. Classy and compact rooms are decked out in neutral colours, stacked with fine linen and electronic gear, and the roof terrace has great city views. Relaxed shared spaces include a cafe and bar, and the Alex streetfront restaurant channels a retro European bistro.

Pension of Perth B&B **$$**
(Map p60; ☎08-9228 9049; www.pensionperth.com.au; 3 Throssell St; s/d from $150/165; ❄@📶) Pension of Perth's French belle-époque style lays luxury on thick: chaise lounges, rich floral rugs, heavy brocade curtains, open fireplaces and gold-framed mirrors. Two doubles with bay windows (and small bathrooms) look out onto the park, and there are two rooms with spa baths. Location wise, it's just across the road from gorgeous Hyde Park.

Hotel Northbridge HOTEL **$$**
(Map p60; ☎08-9328 5254; www.hotelnorthbridge.com.au; 210 Lake St; r from $175; ❄@) Hotel Northbridge isn't the hippest kid in town, but there's a spa bath in every room, and it's in a quieter part of a sometimes noisy neighbourhood. The classic pub rooms in the budget wing ($65) face onto a broad verandah but share toilets.

East Perth

Wickham Retreat HOSTEL **$**
(Map p54; ☎08-9325 6398; www.wickhamretreat.com; 25-27 Wickham St; dm $34-38, d $80; @📶) Located in a residential neighbourhood east of the city centre, Wickham Retreat has a quieter vibe than other hostels around town. Most of the guests are international travellers, drawn by the colourful rooms and dorms, and a funky astro-turf garden. Free food – including rice, fresh bread and vegies – stretches travel budgets eroded by Perth's high prices.

Sebel East Perth APARTMENT **$$$**
(Map p54; ☎08-9223 2500; www.accorhotels.com.au; 60 Royal St; apt from $270; ❄📶) Modern and chic apartments with self-contained kitchenettes and a classy hotel vibe. Adjacent Claisebrook Cove Promenade has a few nights' worth of restaurants, cafes and bars.

Highgate & Mt Lawley

★ **Above Bored** B&B **$$**
(Map p50; ☎08-9444 5455; www.abovebored.com.au; 14 Norham St; d $190-200; ❄📶) In a quiet residential neighbourhood, this 1927 Federation house is owned by a friendly TV scriptwriter. The two themed rooms in the main house have eclectic decor, and in the garden there's a cosy self-contained cottage with a kitchenette. In an expensive town for accommodation, Above Bored is great value. Northbridge and Mt Lawley are a short drive away.

★**Durack House** B&B $$
(Map p50; ☎08-9370 4305; www.durackhouse.com.au; 7 Almondbury Rd; r $195-215;) It's hard to avoid words such as 'delightful' when describing this cottage, set on a peaceful suburban street behind a rose-adorned white picket fence. The three rooms have plenty of old-world charm, paired with thoroughly modern bathrooms. It's only 250m from Mt Lawley station; turn left onto Railway Pde and then take the first right onto Almondbury Rd.

Subiaco & Kings Park

Murray Hotel HOTEL $$
(Map p56; ☎08-9321 7441; www.themurrayhotel.com; 718 Murray St; d $149-199;) Handily located near Kings Park, the Murray is an older hotel that's recently had a 21st-century makeover. Decor is sharp and modern, and although the hotel's 1970s provenance is not completely concealed, it's still good value in an expensive city. The pool is a cooling addition in a sultry WA summer, and Perth's free CAT bus service stops outside.

Richardson HOTEL $$$
(Map p56; ☎08-9217 8888; www.therichardson.com.au; 32 Richardson St; r from $530;) Ship-shaped and shipshape, the Richardson offers luxurious, thoughtfully designed rooms – some with sliding doors to divide them into larger suites. The whole complex has a breezy, summery feel, with pale marble tiles, creamy walls and interesting art. There's an in-house spa centre if you require additional pampering.

The Outram HOTEL $$$
(Map p56; ☎08-9322 4888; www.wyndhamap.com; 32 Outram St; r $320-380;) Discreet and understated, the Outram is stylish, with compact open-plan rooms, a bathroom with a walk-through shower, king-size beds and flat-screen TVs.

Beaches

Ocean Beach Backpackers HOSTEL $
(Map p50; ☎08-9384 5111; www.oceanbeachbackpackers.com.au; 1 Eric St, Cottesloe; dm/s/d $29/75/84; @) Offering (some) ocean views, this big, bright hostel in the heart of Cottesloe is just a short skip from the sand. Rooms are basic, but all have private bathrooms, and you'll probably just be here to sleep given the great location. Hire a bike to get around locally, or take advantage of the hostel's free bodyboards and surfboards.

Western Beach Lodge HOSTEL $
(Map p50; ☎08-9245 1624; www.westernbeach.com; 6 Westborough St, Scarborough; dm $33-36, d with shared bathroom $75; @) A real surfer hang-out, this sociable, homely hostel has surfboards and boogie boards available, and a good, no-frills feel.

Trigg Retreat B&B $$
(☎08-9447 6726; www.triggretreat.com; 59 Kitchener St, Trigg Beach; r $180-200; @) Quietly classy, this three-room B&B offers attractive and supremely comfortable queen bedrooms in a modern house a short drive from Trigg Beach. Each has fridge, TV, DVD player and tea- and coffee-making facilities. A full cooked breakfast is included in the rates.

Sunmoon Boutique Resort HOTEL $$
(Map p50; ☎08-9245 8000; www.sunmoon.com.au; 200 West Coast Hwy, Scarborough; r from $175;) Separated from Scarborough Beach by a busy road and a petrol station, this Balinese-themed complex has wooden pathways leading to shady palm gardens and fish ponds. Batik furnishings adorn large rooms with terracotta-tiled floors.

Other Areas

Discovery Holiday Parks – Perth CAMPGROUND $
(☎08-9453 6877; www.discoveryholidayparks.com.au; 186 Hale Rd, Forrestfield; powered sites for 2 people $42-50, units $159-179; @) This well-kept holiday park, 15km out of the city, has a wide range of cabins and smart-looking units, many with deck, TV and DVD player.

Peninsula APARTMENT $$
(Map p50; ☎08-9368 6688; www.thepeninsula.net; 53 South Perth Esplanade, South Perth; apt from $219; @) While only the front few apartments have full-on views, the Peninsula's waterfront location lends itself to lazy ferry rides and sunset strolls along the river. It's a sprawling, older-style complex, but it's kept in good nick. The apartments all have kitchenettes and there's a communal laundry room.

Eating

Where many of Australia's other state capitals might have a handful of top restaurants charging over $40 a main, in Perth those prices can be the norm for any establishment that considers itself above average. It's still possible to eat cheaply, especially in the Little Asia section of William St, Northbridge. Inner-city shopping centres all have food courts that are good for a cheap lunch.

Many restaurants are BYO, meaning you can bring your own wine; check first. Cafes are good places to go for a midrange meal.

The happening neighbourhoods for cafes and restaurants are Northbridge, Leederville and Mt Lawley, and the city centre has new options in the **Brookfield Place precinct** (www.brookfieldplace.com.au) on St George's Tce.

City Centre

Twilight Hawkers Market STREET FOOD **$**
(Map p54; www.twilighthawkersmarket.com; Forrest Chase; snacks & mains $10; ⏲4.30-9pm Fri mid-Oct–mid-Apr) Ethnic food stalls bring the flavours and aromas of the world to central Perth on Friday nights in spring and summer. Look forward to combining your Turkish *gözleme* (savoury crepe) or Colombian empanadas (deep-fried pastries) with regular live music from local Perth bands.

Toastface Grillah CAFE **$**
(Map p54; www.toastfacegrillah.com; Grand Lane; sandwiches $7-9; ⏲7am-4pm Mon-Fri, 9am-4pm Sat) Vibrant street art, excellent coffee and a sneaky laneway location combine with interesting toasted sandwiches such as the 'Pear Grillz' with blue cheese, pear and lime chutney. All this and a not-so-subtle Wu-Tang Clan reference too.

Mama Tran VIETNAMESE **$**
(Map p54; www.mamatran.com.au; 36-40 Milligan St; snacks & mains $8-14; ⏲7.30am-4pm Mon-Fri, 5.30-9pm Thu & Fri) Now you don't have to truck across to Northbridge for a hearty bowl of *pho* (Vietnamese noodle soup). The hip Mama Tran also serves excellent coffee, fresh rice-paper rolls and Asian salads. Grab a spot on one of the big shared tables and order up a storm including plump *banh mi ga* (Vietnamese chicken baguettes).

Secret Garden CAFE **$**
(Map p54; www.secretgardencafe.com.au; Murray Mews; mains $10-19; ⏲7am-3pm Mon-Fri; 📶) Tucked away down a boho laneway off Murray St, Secret Garden has good coffee, enticing counter food and all-day breakfasts for hangovers. Free wi-fi is the perfect partner to a robust espresso.

Taka JAPANESE **$**
(www.takaskitchen.iinet.net.au; mains $7-12; ⏲11am-9pm Mon-Sat) This straightforward Japanese eatery whips out standards such as teriyaki, udon and sushi. Great for a quick bite if you're out drinking. There are branches on **Barrack St** (Map p54; 150-152 Barrack St) and **Shafto Lane** (Map p54; Shops 5 & 6 Shafto Lane).

Greenhouse TAPAS **$$**
(Map p54; ☎08-9481 8333; www.greenhouseperth.com; 100 St Georges Tce; breakfast $10-20, shared plates $12-32; ⏲7am-late Mon-Fri, from 9am Sun) Ground-breaking design – straw bales, plywood, corrugated iron and exterior walls covered with 5000 pot plants – combines with excellent food at this tapas-style eatery. Middle Eastern and Asian influences inform a sustainably sourced menu including lamb tagine with kalamata olives and harissa, or prawns with coriander and Vietnamese-style *nuoc cham* sauce. At night, Greenhouse morphs into a good bar.

Stables Bar BISTRO **$$**
(Map p54; www.thestablesbar.com.au; 888 Hay St; tapas $12-16, mains $25; ⏲11am-late Mon-Sat) Concealed down a heritage arcade, Stables Bar manages to be both an energetic and bustling bar, and a worthwhile destination for interesting food. On weekend nights, craft beers, cocktails and a rowdier bar persona definitely take over, but at quieter times it is worth popping in for well-priced tapas and mains including crab linguine and lamb with baba ganoush and dukkah.

★**Restaurant Amusé** MODERN AUSTRALIAN **$$$**
(Map p54; ☎08-9325 4900; www.restaurantamuse.com.au; 64 Bronte St; degustation without/with wine pairing $130/210; ⏲6.30pm-late Tue-Sat) The critics have certainly been amused by this degustation-only establishment, regularly rated as one of Australia's finest. Ongoing accolades include being dubbed WA's number one eatery by *Gourmet Traveller* magazine every year since 2010. Book well ahead and come prepared for a culinary adventure. Look forward to a stellar WA-focused wine list, too.

Balthazar MODERN AUSTRALIAN **$$$**
(Map p54; ☎08-9421 1206; www.balthazar.com.au; 6 The Esplanade; small plates $16-24, mains $45-47; ⏲noon-late Mon-Fri, 6pm-late Sat) Low-lit, discreet and sophisticated, with a hipster soundtrack and charming staff, Balthazar's informal cool vibe is matched by exquisite

food and a famously excellent wine list. The menu here is refreshingly original, combining European and Asian flavours with not-at-all-reckless abandon.

Print Hall ASIAN, MODERN AUSTRALIAN $$$
(Map p54; www.printhall.com.au; 125 St Georges Tce; shared plates $14-36, mains $25-36; ⊙11.30am-midnight Mon-Fri, 4pm-midnight Sat) This sprawling complex in the Brookfield Place precinct includes the Apple Daily, featuring Southeast Asian–style street food, and the expansive Print Hall Dining Room, with an oyster bar and grilled WA meat and seafood. Don't miss having a drink and Spanish tapas in the rooftop Bob's Bar, named after Australia's larrikin former prime minister, Bob Hawke.

Other hip bars and restaurants dot nearby basements and laneways.

Northbridge

Little Willy's CAFE $
(Map p54; https://www.facebook.com/LittleWillys; 267 William St; mains $8-16; ⊙6am-6pm Mon-Fri, 8am-4pm Sat & Sun) It's tiny and it's on William St, and it's a go-to spot to grab a sidewalk table and tuck into robust treats such as the city's best breakfast burrito and Bircher museli. It's also a preferred coffee haunt for the hip Northbridge indie set. BYO skinny jeans.

Tak Chee House MALAYSIAN $
(Map p54; 1/364 William St; mains $11-17; ⊙11am-3pm & 5-9pm Tue-Sun) With Malaysian students crammed in for a taste of home, Tak Chee is our pick for one of the best Asian cheapies along William St. If you don't have a taste for satay, Hainan chicken or *char kway teo*, Thai, Vietnamese, Lao and Chinese flavours are all just footsteps away. Cash only; BYO wine or beer.

Viet Hoa VIETNAMESE $
(Map p54; www.viethoa.com.au; 349 William St; mains $10-23; ⊙10am-10pm) Don't be fooled by the bare-bones ambience of this corner Vietnamese restaurant – or you'll miss out on the fresh rice-paper rolls and top-notch *pho*. Greenery creeping up the beams gives the place an offbeat feel.

Source Foods CAFE $
(Map p60; www.sourcefoods.com.au; 289 Beaufort St; mains $10-19; ⊙7am-3pm Mon-Fri, from 8.30am Sat-Sun; 📶) An unassuming corner cafe committed to sustainable practices, Source Food's excellent breakfast options include a massive spinach and feta scramble. We're big fans of the tandoori chicken burger for lunch.

SELF-CATERING

Below we've listed the pick of the self-catering crop.

Boatshed Market (www.boatshedmarket.com.au; 40 Jarrad St, Cottesloe; ⊙6.30am-8pm) Upmarket shed stacked with fresh produce, meat, fish, delicatessen goods, pastries and bread.

Chez Jean-Claude Patisserie (Map p56; www.chezjeanclaudepatisserie.com.au; 333 Rokeby Rd, Subiaco; ⊙6am-6pm Mon-Fri) Line up with the locals for brioche and baguettes.

City Farm Organic Growers Market (Map p54; www.perthcityfarm.org.au; 1 City Farm Pl, East Perth; ⊙market 8am-4pm Tue-Fri, 8am-noon Sat, cafe 7am-3pm Mon-Fri, 7am-noon Sat) Local organic producers sell eggs, fruit, vegetables and bread, and there's also an excellent cafe.

Kailis Bros (Map p56; www.kailisbrosleederville.com.au; 101 Oxford St, Leederville; ⊙shop 8am-6pm, cafe 7am-late) Big, fresh seafood supplier with cafe attached.

Kakulas Bros (Map p54; www.kakulasbros.com.au; 183 William St, Northbridge; ⊙8am-5pm Mon-Sat, 11am-4pm Sun) Provisions store overflowing with sacks and vats of legumes, nuts and olives, plus a deli counter that's well stocked with cheese. There's another branch, Kakulas Sister (p83), down in Fremantle.

Subiaco Farmers Market (Map p56; www.subifarmersmarket.com.au; 271 Bagot Rd, Subiaco Primary School; ⊙8am-noon Sat) and **Leederville Farmers Market** (Map p56; www.leedervillefarmers.com.au; Newcastle St, car park; ⊙8am-noon Sun) Street eats, organic produce and family entertainment on Saturday (Subiaco) and Sunday (Leederville) mornings.

Flipside BURGERS $
(Map p54; www.flipsideburgerbar.com.au; 222 William St; burgers $11.50-15.50; 11.30am-9.30pm Tue-Sun) Gourmet burgers with the option of taking away to the bar upstairs, Mechanics Institute (p70).

★**Brika** GREEK $$
(Map p54; www.brika.com.au; 3/177 Stirling St; meze & mains $9-27; noon-late Wed-Sun) Presenting a stylish spin on traditional Greek cuisine, Brika is our favourite new Perth restaurant. The whitewashed interior is enlivened by colourful traditional fabrics, and menu highlights include creamy zucchini fritters, slow-cooked lamb, and chargrilled swordfish skewers. Definitely leave room for dessert of *ravani* (semolina cake), and consider a $12 lunchtime souvlaki if time or money is tight.

★**Pleased to Meet You** BISTRO, BAR $$
(Map p54; www.pleasedtomeetyou.com.au; 38 Roe St; shared plates $9-20; 5pm-late Mon-Thu, noon-late Fri-Sun) Ticking all the hipster culinary boxes with its dedication to Asian and South American street food, Pleased to Meet You presents bold flavours in a menu that's perfect for sharing over a few cocktails, WA wines or craft beers. Grab a spot at the shared tables and tuck into flavour hits such as coconut ceviche, duck tacos and grilled garlic oysters.

Izakaya Sakura JAPANESE $$
(Map p54; 08-9328 2525; www.izakayasakura.com.au; 2/182 James St; shared plates $10-15, mains $13-18) Small plates made for sharing feature at this stylish retreat from the occasional rough and tumble of Northbridge. The sushi and sashimi are superfresh, and other stand-out dishes include delicate tempura prawns and *takoyaki* (deep-fried octopus snacks). Come with a thirst for sake or cold beer, and work through the sensibly-priced menu. Bookings are recommended for Friday and Saturday nights.

Bivouac Canteen & Bar CAFE $$
(Map p54; www.bivouac.com.au; 198 William St; shared plates $10-28, pizzas $23-25; noon-late Tue-Sat) Mediterranean-style cuisine partners with a good wine list, and gourmet pizzas go well with boutique beers and artisan ciders. The coffee is excellent, and Bivouac's utilitarian decor is softened with a rotating roster of work from local artists.

Tarts CAFE $$
(Map p60; www.tartscafe.com.au; 212 Lake St; brunch $11-25, dinner $24-34; 7am-5pm Sat-Tue, 7am-11pm Wed-Fri) Massive tarts piled with berries, apples or lime curd; rich scrambled eggs tumbling off thickly sliced sourdough; mini custard tarts stacked with glazed strawberries. Packed like a picnic hamper on weekends, and a worthy bistro-style dinner option from Wednesday to Friday.

Sayers Sister CAFE $$
(Map p60; www.sayerssister.com.au; 236 Lake St; mains $12-27, tapas $8-15; 7am-4pm Sun-Thu, to 10pm Fri & Sat) Top-notch breakfasts and lunches – including feta scrambled eggs with green tea and vodka-smoked salmon – and a convenient Northbridge location. On Friday and Saturday nights shared tapas goes very well with a concise, but thoughtful, wine list.

Highgate, Mt Lawley & Maylands

Veggie Mama VEGETARIAN $
(Map p60; www.veggiemama.com.au; cnr Beaufort & Vincent Sts; mains $10-20; 8am-7pm Mon & Tue, 8am-9pm Wed-Fri, 9am-5pm Sat & Sun;) Loads of vegan and gluten-free options shine at this cute corner cafe where flavour is definitely not compromised. The menu includes delicious salads, smoothies, vegie curries and burgers; weekend breakfasts are very popular.

El Público MEXICAN $$
(Map p60; 0418 187 708; www.elpublico.com.au; 511 Beaufort St; snacks & shared plates $9-18; 5pm-midnight Mon-Fri, from 4pm Sat & Sun) Look forward to interesting and authentic spins on Mexican street food, all served as small plates that are perfect for sharing. Menu stand-outs include cuttlefish soft-shell tacos and salmon ceviche, and peanut butter *dulce de leche* (caramelised sugar and milk) praline for dessert. Bring along a few friends and groove to the occasional DJs.

Cantina 663 MEDITERRANEAN $$
(Map p60; 08-9370 4883; www.cantina663.com; 663 Beaufort St; mains $15-33; 7.30am-late Mon-Sat, to 3pm Sun) It's a mini culinary World Cup, featuring Spain, Portugal and Italy, at this cool but casual cantina with tables spilling into the arcade. Service can be a bit too cool for school, but it's worth waiting for dishes such as truffle risotto with chestnuts

and artichoke, or seared cuttlefish with pickled carrot, cucumber, radish and white wine.

Mrs S CAFE $$

(Map p50; www.mrsscafe.com.au; 178 Whatley Cres; mains $11-21; ⏲7am-5pm Tue-Fri, 8am-4pm Sat & Sun) Mrs S has a quirky retro ambience, the perfect backdrop for excellent home-style baking or a lazy brunch. Menus – presented in Little Golden children's books – feature loads of innovative variations on traditional dishes. Weekends are *wildly* popular, so try to visit on a weekday.

Mary Street Bakery CAFE $$

(Map p60; 507 Beaufort St; mains $12-21; ⏲7am-4pm) Crunchy and warm wood-fired baked goods, artisan bread and interesting cafe fare combine with what are quite probably Perth's best chocolate-filled doughnuts at this recent addition to the competitive dining scene in Mt Lawley. Spacious and sunny, it's a good way to start the day before exploring the area's retail scene. At lunchtime, a concise wine and beer selection also features.

Ace Pizza PIZZA $$

(Map p60; www.acepizza.com.au; 448 Beaufort St; snacks $8-16, mains & pizza $18-26; ⏲5.30pm-late) Cosy banquette seating fills this dark and dramatic retreat serving Perth's best thin-crust pizza. The menu stretches to other Italian-inspired wood-fired goodies, but most punters are here for the crispy, garlicky and smokey combinations of runny cheese, fresh herbs, and prosciutto or seafood. A concise selection of bar snacks makes it good for a relaxed beer or wine, too.

Beaufort Street Merchant CAFE $$

(Map p60; ☎08-9328 6299; www.beaufortmerchant.com; 488 Beaufort St; breakfast $16-20, lunch & dinner $24-37; ⏲7am-late) This Mt Lawley institution with a distinct Mediterranean influence is good for a leisurely brekky over newspapers and a couple of coffees. Go for the baked Spanish egg and bean cassoulet or stonking Big Breakfast, and work out what to order when you come back for dinner. How about the chilli-tinged *arrabiatta* (tomato and chilli) mussels or the fragrant lemon thyme gnocchi?

St Michael 6003 MODERN AUSTRALIAN $$$

(Map p60; ☎08-9328 1177; www.facebook.com/stmichael6003; 483 Beaufort St; 3/7 small plates per person $49/89; ⏲5-10pm Tue-Sat, noon-3pm Fri) Formerly the high-end eatery Jackson's, this new incarnation is slightly more casual, but still classy and elegant. Like many other eateries in Perth, the emphasis here is on smaller shared plates, but there's some serious culinary wizardry in the kitchen. Menu highlights include WA marron (freshwater lobster), scallops, quail and trout. Sign up for the seven-course menu for a leisurely treat.

Must Winebar FRENCH $$$

(Map p60; ☎08-9328 8255; www.must.com.au; 519 Beaufort St; bar snacks $9-24, mains $39-46; ⏲noon-midnight) One of Perth's best wine bars, Must is also one of the city's best restaurants. The Gallic vibe is hip, slick and a little bit cheeky, and the menu marries classic French bistro flavours with the best local produce. Oysters, bar snacks and charcuterie plates are more informal, but equally tasty, distractions.

Mt Hawthorn

New Norcia Bakery BAKERY, CAFE $

(Map p50; www.newnorciabaker.com.au; 163 Scarborough Beach Rd; mains $11-17; ⏲7am-6pm) Perth's best bread, delicious pastries and a bright cafe as well, this place gets crammed on the weekends. There's another more central **branch** (Map p56; Bagot Rd, The Cloisters; ⏲7.30am-6pm) in Subiaco for takeaway baked goodies.

Divido ITALIAN $$$

(Map p50; ☎08-9443 7373; www.divido.com.au; 170 Scarborough Beach Rd; mains $38-40, 5-course degustation $89; ⏲6pm-late Mon-Sat) Italian but not rigidly so (the chef's of Croatian extraction, so delicious Dalmatian-style doughnuts make it onto the dessert menu), this romantic restaurant serves handmade pasta dishes and expertly grilled mains. The five-course degustation menu is highly recommended for a night of culinary adventure.

Leederville

The Market Juicery CAFE $

(Map p56; www.facebook.com/Themarketjuicery; Shop 2, 139-141 Oxford St; salads $10-12, juices & smoothies $7-9; ⏲7am-3pm Mon-Sat) Superfood smoothies, cold-pressed juices and zingy salads all feature at this good-value lunch stop amid the funky retailers of Leederville. Wraps and bagels are also good. You'll the find The Market Juicery down an arcade behind Tom's Cafe.

Green's & Co CAFE $

(Map p56; 123 Oxford St; cakes $5-8; ⏲8am-midnight) Dive into great coffee and a 'how-do-I-choose?' selection of cakes, and see if your favourite band is featured on the posters adorning the walls.

Jus Burgers BURGERS $

(Map p56; www.jusburgers.com.au; 743 Newcastle St; burgers $12-16; ⏲11.30am-10pm) Carbon-neutral gourmet burgers. There's another branch in **Subiaco** (Map p56; 1 Rokeby Rd).

★ **Duende** TAPAS $$

(Map p56; ☎08-9228 0123; www.duende.com.au; 662 Newcastle St; tapas & mains $15-32; ⏲7.30am-late) Sleek Duende occupies a corner site amid the comings and goings of Leederville. Stellar modern-accented tapas are served, so make a meal of it or call in for a late-night glass of dessert wine and *churros*. We're partial to starting the day with an espresso and Duende's ham and Manchego cheese croquettes.

Sayers CAFE $$

(Map p56; www.sayersfood.com.au; 224 Carr Pl; mains $12-28; ⏲7am-3pm) This classy cafe has a counter groaning under the weight of an alluring cake selection. The breakfast menu includes smoked salmon with scrambled eggs and asparagus, while lunch highlights include a chermoula-spiced chicken salad with quinoa, pistachio and a lemon yoghurt dressing. Welcome to one of Perth's best cafes.

Low Key Chow House ASIAN $$

(Map p56; www.keepitlowkey.com.au; 140 Oxford St; mains $24-30; ⏲noon-3pm Fri-Sun, 5.30pm-10.30pm Wed-Sun) Noisy and bustling – just like the Southeast Asian street food eateries it references – eating at Low Key Chow House is a fun experience best shared with a group. Sup on cold Singha beer or punchy Asian cocktails, and order up a storm from a menu featuring the best of Malaysia, Vietnam, Thailand, Cambodia and Laos.

Kitsch ASIAN $$

(Map p50; www.kitschbar.com.au; 229 Oxford St; shared plates $11-25; ⏲5.30pm-midnight Tue-Sat) Southeast Asian–style street food, Thai beers and an eclectic, slightly overgrown garden make Kitsch a great spot for a few laid-back hours of tasty grazing. Expect to stay (and eat) longer than you planned.

Subiaco, Kings Park & Nedlands

Boucla CAFE $

(Map p56; www.boucla.com; 349 Rokeby Rd; mains $11-24; ⏲7am-5pm Mon-Fri, 7am-3.30pm Sat) A locals' secret, this Greek- and Levantine-infused haven is pleasingly isolated from the thick of the Rokeby Rd action. Baklava and cakes tempt you from the corner, and huge tarts filled with blue-vein cheese and roast vegetables spill off plates. The salads are great too.

Stimulatte CAFE $

(Map p56; www.stimulatte.com.au; 361 Hay St; brunch $11-18; ⏲6.30am-3pm Mon-Fri, 7.30am-1pm Sat) Make the short stroll from central Subiaco to this cool neighbourhood cafe. Big-format photos of New York adorn the walls, providing a cosmopolitan backdrop for interesting brunches and serious coffee. Try the Middle Eastern–influenced *shakshouka*, baked eggs in a spicy tomato sauce topped with hummus and dukkah.

Fraser's MODERN AUSTRALIAN $$$

(Map p56; ☎08-9481 7100; www.frasersrestaurant.com.au; Fraser Ave; mains $32-58; ⏲noon-late) Atop Kings Park, overlooking the city and the glittering Swan River, Fraser's is in a wonderful location. Thankfully, the food is also excellent, making it a popular spot for business lunches and romantic dinners on the terrace on balmy summer nights.

Beaches

Il Lido ITALIAN $$

(Map p50; www.illido.com.au; 88 Marine Pde, Cottesloe; mains $20-42; ⏲8am-late) Il Lido's alfresco area is popular with Cottesloe locals and their dogs, but we prefer the sunny interior of this self-styled 'Italian canteen'. Breakfast and coffee attract the early-bird swimmers, and throughout the day antipasto plates, pasta and risottos, alongside a good beer and wine list, continue the culinary buzz. Maybe linger for cocktails and an Indian Ocean sunset.

Cott & Co Fish Bar SEAFOOD $$

(Map p50; www.cottandco.com.au; 104 Marine Pde, Cottesloe Beach Hotel; bar snacks & oysters $9-14, mains $23-35; ⏲11am-late) The bistro at the Cottesloe Beach Hotel has been transformed into a sleek seafood restaurant and wine bar. Settle in with a few local oysters, a glass of Margaret River wine, and ease into the relaxing reverie of an Indian Ocean sunset. Out the back, the pub's formerly rowdy garden bar now channels a whitewashed Cape Cod vibe as The Beach Club.

Drinking & Nightlife

A local law change a few years ago has produced a salvo of quirky small bars that are distinctly Melbourne-ish in their hipness. They're sprouting up all over the place, including in the formerly deserted-after-dark city centre. Northbridge is also a happy hunting ground for more idiosyncratic drinking establishments. Many also offer interesting and tasty food.

One of the by-products of the mining boom has been the rise of the Cashed-Up Bogan (CUB) – young men with plenty of cash to splash on muscle cars, beer and drugs. A spate of fights and glassings in bars has caused many venues, particularly around Northbridge, to step up security. Most pubs now have lockouts, so you'll need to be in before midnight in order to gain entry. You may need to present photo ID to obtain entry and it would pay to keep your wits about you in pubs and on the streets after dark.

City Centre

Greenhouse COCKTAIL BAR
(Map p54; www.greenhouseperth.com; 100 St Georges Tce; ⏲7am-midnight Mon-Fri, from 9am Sat) In a city so in love with the great outdoors, a rooftop bar in the city centre makes perfect sense. Hip, eco-conscious Greenhouse mixes up a storm amid the greenery with great cocktails and an interesting beer and wine list. Good food is also available.

Lalla Rookh WINE BAR
(Map p54; www.lallarookh.com.au; Lower Ground Floor, 77 St Georges Tce; pizza $16-26, shared plates $14-21, 6 plates for $58; ⏲11.30am-midnight Mon-Fri, from 5pm Sat) Escape downstairs from the CBD to this cosy bar specialising in wine, craft beer and Italian food. Cocktails also come with a whisper of the Mediterranean, and the all-day menu encourages relaxed grazing over shared dishes. Our favourite combo is the chilli and king prawn pizza partnered with a zesty Feral Hop Hog Pale Ale from the nearby Swan Valley.

Bar Halcyon COCKTAIL BAR
(Map p54; www.bardehalcyon.com.au; Wolfe Lane; ⏲11.30am-late Tue-Fri, 4pm-late Sat) Concealed in the funky laneway that is Wolfe Lane, Bar Halcyon channels a Spanish vibe with sangria, tapas and *pinxtos* (savoury bar snacks), and a decent selection of cocktails and beer. DJs kick in most weekend nights, but it's also a top spot for a daytime coffee.

Helvetica BAR
(Map p54; www.helveticabar.com.au; rear 101 St Georges Tce; ⏲3pm-midnight Tue-Thu, noon-1am Fri, 6pm-1am Sat) Clever artsy types tap their toes to delicious alternative pop in this bar named after a typeface and specialising in whisky and cocktails. The concealed entry is off Howard St: look for the chandelier in the laneway.

Cheeky Sparrow BAR
(Map p54; www.cheekysparrow.com.au; 1/317 Murray St; ⏲6.30am-midnight Mon-Fri, from 4pm Sat) Cheeky Sparrow's multilevel labyrinth of leather banquettes and bentwood chairs is great for everything from brunch and coffee through to pizza and cheese and charcuterie plates. If you're feeling peckish later at night, pop in for robust bar snacks including chorizo and lime, and chilli cheese sliders. Cocktail fans certainly won't be disappointed. Access is via Wolfe Lane.

Hula Bula Bar COCKTAIL BAR
(Map p54; www.hulabulabar.com; 12 Victoria Ave; ⏲4pm-midnight Wed-Fri, 6pm-1am Sat, 4-10pm Sun) You'll feel like you're on *Gilligan's Island* in this tiny Polynesian-themed bar, decked out in bamboo, palm leaves and tikis. A cool but relaxed crowd jams in here on weekends to sip ostentatious cocktails out of ceramic monkey's heads.

Varnish on King WHISKY BAR
(Map p54; www.varnishonking.com; 75 King St; ⏲11.30am-midnight Mon-Fri, 4pm-midnight Sat) With interesting shopping and new cafes and bars, lower King St is emerging as a Perth hot spot. Amid the hipster barber shops and single-origin coffee, our favourite new opening is a brick-lined homage to American whisky. More than 40 types are available, and a decent beer and wine list is partnered by grown-up party food such as moreish fried chicken wings.

Wolf Lane COCKTAIL BAR
(Map p54; www.wolflane.com.au; Wolfe Lane; ⏲4pm-midnight Fri & Sat) Exposed bricks, classic retro furniture and high ceilings create a pretty decent WA approximation of a New York loft. A serious approach to cocktails and wine combines with an eclectic beer

selection, and bar snacks include share plates of Turkish bread and chorizo.

The Grosvenor PUB
(Map p54; www.thegrosvenorperth.com.au; cnr Hay & Hill Sts; ⌚11am-midnight) This classic corner pub – complete with wrought-iron balconies and one of Perth's best garden bars – draws a crowd of loyal locals, nearby desk jockeys and thirsty students. Decent wood-fired pizza too.

Ambar CLUB
(Map p54; www.boomtick.com.au/ambar; 104 Murray St; ⌚10pm-5am Fri & Sat) Perth's premier club for breakbeat, drum and bass, and visiting international DJs.

Northbridge

Northbridge is the rough-edged hub of Perth's nightlife, with pubs and clubs around William and James Sts. Recent openings have lifted the tone of the area.

Mechanics Institute BAR
(Map p54; www.mechanicsinstitutebar.com.au; 222 William St; ⌚noon-midnight Tue-Sat, to 10pm Sun) Negotiate the laneway entrance around the corner on James St to discover one of Perth's most down-to-earth small bars. Share one of the big tables on the deck or nab a stool by the bar. Craft beers are on tap, and you can even order in a gourmet burger from Flipside (p66) downstairs.

LOT 20 BAR
(Map p54; www.lot20.co; 198-206 William St, entrance on James St; ⌚10am-midnight Mon-Sat, to 10pm Sun) LOT 20 is more evidence of the ongoing transformation of rough and ready Northbridge into the home of more intimate and sophisticated small bars. The brick-lined courtyard is perfect on a warm WA evening, and on cooler nights the cosy interior is best experienced with a few bar snacks – try the Asian-style 'Son in Law Eggs' – and wine or craft beer.

Ezra Pound BAR
(Map p54; www.epbar.com.au; 189 William St; ⌚1pm-midnight Tue-Sat, to 10pm Sun) Down a much-graffitied lane leading off William St, Ezra Pound is favoured by Northbridge's bohemian set. It's the kind of place where you can settle into a red velvet chair and sip a Tom Collins out of a jam jar. Earnest conversations about Kerouac and Kafka are strictly optional.

399 BAR
(Map p60; www.399bar.com; 399 William St; ⌚4pm-midnight Mon-Sat, to 10pm Sun) This friendly neighbourhood bar has booths along one side and a long bar down the other, making it easy to interact with the engaging bar staff. Cocktails are artfully crafted, and there's a serious approach to beer and wine. Nearby are lots of good, cheap Asian restaurants.

Northbridge Brewing Company MICROBREWERY
(Map p54; www.northbridgebrewingco.com.au; 44 Lake St; ⌚8am-10pm Sun-Tue, to midnight Wed-Sat) The four beers brewed here are decent enough, but the real attraction is the occasional guest beers on tap from around Australia. The outdoor bar adjoining the grassy expanse of Northbridge Plaza is relaxed and easygoing, and various big screens dotted around the multilevel industrial space make it a good spot to watch live sport. Go the Dockers!

Bird BAR
(Map p54; www.williamstreetbird.com; 181 William St; ⌚noon-midnight Mon-Sat, to 10pm Sun) Cool indie bar with local bands, performers and DJs. Upstairs there's a brick-lined deck with city views.

Air CLUB
(Map p54; www.airclub.com.au; 139 James St; ⌚from 9pm Fri & Sat) Nonstop house, techno and trance.

Geisha CLUB
(Map p54; www.geishabar.com.au; 135a James St; ⌚11pm-6am Fri & Sat) A small and pumping, DJ-driven, gay-friendly club.

Metro City CLUB
(Map p54; www.metroconcertclub.com; 146 Roe St) Thumping superclub (capacity 2000), which doubles as a concert venue.

Highgate, Mt Lawley & Maylands

Five Bar CRAFT BEER
(Map p60; www.fivebar.com.au; 560 Beaufort St, Mt Lawley; ⌚noon-midnight Mon-Sat, to 10pm Sun) International and Australian craft beers – including seasonal and one-off brews from WA's best – make Mt Lawley's Five Bar worth seeking out by the discerning drinker. Wine lovers are also well catered for, and the menu leans towards classy comfort food.

GAY & LESBIAN PERTH

Perth is home to all of Western Australia's gay and lesbian venues. Before you get excited, let's clarify matters: it has precisely two bars and one men's sauna. Many other bars, especially around Highgate and Mt Lawley, are somewhat gay friendly, but it's hardly what you'd call a bustling scene.

For a head's up on what's on, pick up the free monthly newspaper *Out In Perth* (www.outinperth.com). **Pride WA** (www.pridewa.com.au) runs PrideFest, a 10-day festival from mid-November culminating in the Pride Parade.

Court (Map p54; www.thecourt.com.au; 50 Beaufort St; ⌚noon-midnight Sun-Thu, to 2am Fri & Sat) A large, rambling complex consisting of an old corner pub and a big, partly covered courtyard with a clubby atmosphere. Wednesday is drag night, with kings and queens holding court in front of a young crowd.

Connections (Map p54; www.connectionsnightclub.com; 81 James St, Northbridge; ⌚8pm-late Wed-Sat) DJs, drag shows and the occasional bit of lesbian mud wrestling.

Perth Steam Works (Map p60; www.perthsteamworks.com.au; 369 William St; admission $25; ⌚noon-1am Sun-Thu, to 2am Fri & Sat) Gay men's sauna. Entry on Forbes St.

Clarence's COCKTAIL BAR

(Map p60; www.clarences.com.au; 506 Beaufort St, Mt Lawley; ⌚4pm-late Mon-Fri, noon-late Sat, noon-10pm Sun) Clarence's energetic collage of small-bar buzz and intimate bistro dining is a dependable spot for good times along Mt Lawley's Beaufort St after-dark strip. Menu highlights include crab tacos, and sweetcorn and saffron arancini.

Must Winebar WINE BAR

(Map p60; www.must.com.au; 519 Beaufort St, Mt Lawley; ⌚noon-midnight) With cool French house music pulsing through the air and the perfect glass of wine in your hand (40 offerings by the glass, 500 on the list), Must is hard to beat. Upstairs is an exclusive, bookings-only Champagne bar.

Swallow WINE BAR

(Map p50; www.swallowbar.com.au; 198 Whatley Cres, Maylands; snacks $10-18; ⌚5pm-late Wed-Sat, 3-9pm Sun) Channeling an art-deco ambience with funky lampshades and vintage French advertising, Swallow is the kind of place you'd love as your local. Wine and cocktails are exemplary, and the drinks list includes Spanish wheat beers and French ciders. Check the website for live music from Thursday to Sunday.

Flying Scotsman PUB

(Map p60; www.facebook.com/scottoscottoscotto; 639 Beaufort St, Mt Lawley; ⌚11am-midnight) Old-style pub that attracts the Beaufort St indie crowd. A good spot for a drink before a gig up the road at the Astor (p72).

Velvet Lounge BAR

(Map p60; www.facebook.com/thevelvetlounge perth; 639 Beaufort St, Mt Lawley) Out the back of the Flying Scotsman is this small, red-velvet-clad lounge with ska, punk and indie beats.

Leederville

Leederville Hotel PUB

(Map p56; www.leedervillehotel.com; 742 Newcastle St; ⌚11am-late) Cool decor and good food ensure nights are huge at The Garden, the Leederville's decent stab at a 21st-century gastropub.

Subiaco & Kings Park

Juanita's BAR, CAFE

(Map p56; www.juanitas.com.au; 341 Rokeby Rd; ⌚9am-11pm Mon-Fri, 10am-1am Sat, noon-1am Sun) Welcome to Perth's most eclectic small (and we do mean small) bar. Tapas, shared platters and a concise selection of beer and wine partner with rescued 1960s furniture, walls trimmed with bric-a-brac, and a few outside tables. It's all thoroughly local, very charming, and a refreshing antidote to the flash, renovated pubs elsewhere in Subiaco.

Beaches

Elba BAR

(Map p50; www.elbacottesloe.com.au; 29 Napoleon St, Cottesloe; ⌚3pm-late Mon-Thu, noon-late Fri-Sun) In the swanky residential part of Cottesloe, not the chilled-out beach strip, Elba has taken its street name as inspiration and produced a slick Napoleonic bar complete with a gilt-framed portrait of the little man. Come dressed for cocktails, although perhaps in flat shoes out of deference. Small plates (obviously) complete the picture for a worthwhile evening assignation.

☆ Entertainment

Live Music

Ellington Jazz Club JAZZ

(Map p54; www.ellingtonjazz.com.au; 191 Beaufort St; 6.30pm-1am Mon-Thu, to 3am Fri & Sat, 5pm-midnight Sun) FREE There's live jazz nightly in this handsome, intimate venue. Standing-only admission is $10, or you can book a table (per person $15 to $20) for tapas and pizza.

Perth Arena LIVE MUSIC

(Map p54; www.pertharena.com.au; 700 Wellington St) Used for big concerts by major international acts such as Kanye West and The Rolling Stones. It's also used by the Perth Wildcats NBL basketball franchise.

Bakery LIVE MUSIC

(Map p54; www.nowbaking.com.au; 233 James St; 7pm-late) Run by Artrage, Perth's contemporary arts festival body, the Bakery draws an arty crowd. Popular indie gigs are held almost every weekend.

Amplifier LIVE MUSIC

(Map p54; www.amplifiercapitol.com.au; rear 383 Murray St) The good old Amplifier is one of the best places for live (mainly indie) bands. Part of the same complex is Capitol, used mainly for DJ gigs.

Moon LIVE MUSIC

(Map p54; www.themoon.com.au; 323 William St; 6pm-late Mon & Tue, 11am-late Wed-Sun) Low-key, late-night cafe with singer-songwriters on Wednesday nights, jazz on Thursdays, and poetry slams on Saturday afternoons from 2pm.

Universal LIVE MUSIC

(Map p54; www.universalbar.com.au; 221 William St; 3pm-late Wed-Sun) The unpretentious Universal is one of Perth's oldest bars and much-loved by soul, R&B and blues enthusiasts.

Rosemount Hotel LIVE MUSIC

(Map p50; www.rosemounthotel.com.au; cnr Angove & Fitzgerald Sts; noon-late) Local and international bands play regularly in this spacious art-deco pub with a laid-back beer garden.

Charles Hotel LIVE MUSIC

(Map p50; www.charleshotel.com.au; 509 Charles St) Hosts lots of live music, including the Legendary Perth Blues Club on Tuesday.

Astor CONCERT VENUE

(Map p60; www.liveattheastor.com.au; 659 Beaufort St) The beautiful art-deco Astor still screens the odd film but is mainly used for concerts these days.

Cabaret & Comedy

Devilles Pad CABARET

(Map p54; www.devillespad.com; 3 Aberdeen St; 6pm-midnight Thu, to 2am Fri & Sat) The devil goes to Vegas disguised as a 1950s lounge lizard in this extremely kooky venue. Punters are encouraged to dress to match the camp interiors (complete with erupting volcano). Burlesque dancers, live bands and assorted sideshow freaks provide the entertainment, and good food is available. Thursday is rock 'n' roll karaoke night, so bring along your Elvis A-game.

Lazy Susan's Comedy Den COMEDY

(Map p60; www.lazysusans.com.au; Brisbane Hotel, 292 Beaufort St; 8.30pm Tue, Fri & Sat) Shapiro Tuesday offers a mix of first-timers, seasoned amateurs and pros trying out new shtick (for a very reasonable $5). Friday is for more grown-up stand-ups, including some interstaters. Saturday is the Big Hoohaa – a team-based comedy wrassle. The Den is at the Brisbane Hotel.

Theatre & Classical Music

Check the *West Australian* (www.thewest.com.au) newspaper for what's on. Book through www.ticketek.com.au or www.ticketmaster.com.au.

His Majesty's Theatre THEATRE

(Map p54; www.hismajestystheatre.com.au; 825 Hay St) The majestic home to the **West Australian Ballet** (www.waballet.com.au) and **West Australian Opera** (www.waopera.asn.au), as well as lots of theatre, comedy and cabaret.

Perth Concert Hall CONCERT VENUE

(Map p54; www.perthconcerthall.com.au; 5 St Georges Tce) Home to the **Western Australian Symphony Orchestra** (WASO; www.waso.com.au).

State Theatre Centre THEATRE
(Map p54; www.statetheatrecentrewa.com.au; 174 William St) This complex includes the 575-seat Heath Ledger Theatre and the 234-seat Studio Underground. It's home to the Black Swan State Theatre Company and Perth Theatre Company.

Subiaco Arts Centre THEATRE
(Map p56; www.subiacoartscentre.com.au; 180 Hamersley Rd) Indoor and outdoor theatres used for drama and concerts; home to young people's theatre **Barking Gecko** (www.barkinggecko.com.au).

Regal Theatre THEATRE
(Map p56; www.regaltheatre.com.au; 474 Hay St, Subiaco) Popular musicals and stage shows.

Cinema

Somerville Auditorium CINEMA
(Map p50; www.perthfestival.com.au; 35 Stirling Hwy; ⌚Dec-Mar) A quintessential Perth experience, the Perth Festival's film program is held here on the University of WA's beautiful grounds surrounded by pines. Picnicking before the film is a must.

Luna CINEMA
(Map p56; www.lunapalace.com.au; 155 Oxford St) Art-house cinema in Leederville with Monday double features and a bar. Cheap tickets on Wednesdays.

Cinema Paradiso CINEMA
(Map p54; www.lunapalace.com.au; 164 James St) Art-house cinema in Northbridge. Cheap tickets on Tuesdays.

Moonlight Cinema CINEMA
(Map p50; www.moonlight.com.au; Synergy Parklands, Kings Park; ⌚Dec-Easter) Bring a picnic and blanket and enjoy a romantic moonlit movie; summer only.

Camelot Outdoor Cinema CINEMA
(Map p50; www.lunapalace.com.au; 16 Lochee St, Memorial Hall; ⌚Dec-Easter) Seated open-air cinema in Mosman Park.

Sport

In WA 'football' means Aussie Rules, and during the Australian Football League (AFL) season it's hard to get locals to talk about anything but the two local teams – the **West Coast Eagles** (www.westcoasteagles.com.au) and the **Fremantle Dockers** (www.fremantlefc.com.au).

Patersons Stadium STADIUM
(Subiaco Oval; Map p56; ☎08-9381 2187; www.patersonsstadium.com.au; 250 Roberts Rd) The home of Aussie Rules and big concerts.

WACA STADIUM
(Western Australian Cricket Association; Map p54; ☎08-9265 7222; www.waca.com.au; Nelson Cres) Main venue for interstate and international cricket.

NIB Stadium STADIUM
(Perth Oval; Map p54; www.nibstadium.com.au; Lord St) Home to **Perth Glory** (www.perthglory.com.au) soccer (football) and **Western Force** (www.westernforce.com.au) rugby.

HBF Stadium STADIUM
(Map p50; www.hbfstadium.com.au; Stephenson Ave, Mt Claremont) Home to **West Coast Fever** (www.westcoastfever.com.au) netball.

Shopping

City Centre

Murray St and Hay St Malls are the city's shopping heartland, while Leederville and Mt Lawley feature more eclectic shops. If you're after vintage or retro style head to Northbridge. Lower King St near Wellington St in the CBD is developing as a hub for independent retail stores and designers.

Pigeonhole CLOTHING, ACCESSORIES
(Map p54; www.pigeonhole.com; 9 Shafto Lane; ⌚10am-6pm Mon-Thu & Sat, to 9pm Fri) Hip local and international clothing, and stylish retro accessories and gifts.

78 Records MUSIC
(Map p54; www.78records.com.au; upstairs 255 Murray St Mall; ⌚9am-5pm Mon-Sat, from 11am Sun) Independent record shop. Also good for vinyl and tickets to rock and indie gigs.

Northbridge, Highgate & Mt Lawley

William Topp DESIGN
(Map p60; www.williamtopp.com; 452 William St; ⌚11am-6pm Tue-Fri, to 5pm Sat, to 4pm Sun) Cool designer knick-knacks.

Planet BOOKS, MUSIC
(Map p60; www.planetvideo.com.au; 636-638 Beaufort St; ⌚10am-late) Books, CDs and obscure DVDs.

Future Shelter HOMEWARES
(Map p50; www.futureshelter.com; 56 Angove St, North Perth; ⏲10am-5pm Mon-Sat) Quirky clothing, gifts and homewares designed and manufactured locally. Surrounding Angove St is an emerging hip North Perth neighbourhood.

Leederville

Leederville's Oxford St is the place for boutiques, eclectic music and bookshops.

Atlas Divine CLOTHING
(Map p56; 121 Oxford St; ⏲9am-9pm) Hip women's and men's clobber: jeans, quirky tees, dresses etc.

Subiaco & Kings Park

Rokeby Rd and Hay St boast fashion, art and classy gifts.

Indigenart ARTS
(Map p56; www.mossensongalleries.com.au; 115 Hay St; ⏲11am-4pm Wed-Sat) Indigenous art from around Australia, but with a focus on WA artists. Works include weavings, paintings on canvas, bark and paper, and sculpture.

Aboriginal Art & Craft Gallery ARTS
(Map p56; www.aboriginalgallery.com.au; Fraser Ave; ⏲10.30am-4.30pm Mon-Fri, 11am-4pm Sat & Sun) Work from around WA; more populist than high-end or collectable.

Aspects of Kings Park ARTS, SOUVENIRS
(Map p56; www.aspectsofkingspark.com.au; Fraser Ave; ⏲9am-5pm) Australian art, craft and books.

Other Areas

æ'lkemi CLOTHING
(Map p50; www.aelkemi.com; Times Square Centre, 337 Stirling Hwy; ⏲10am-5.30pm Mon-Sat) Top WA designer's signature store, showcasing feminine frocks and distinctive prints. Adjacent Claremont Quarter is an extensive mall.

Orientation

The city of Perth lies along a wide sweep of the Swan River. The river borders the city centre to the south and east, and links Perth to its neighbouring port city, Fremantle. Follow the river north from the city and you'll reach prosperous nooks such as Claisebrook Cove, lined with ostentatious houses, cafes and public sculpture.

Train tracks divide the city centre from the Northbridge entertainment enclave, immediately to the north. Here's where you'll find Perth's cultural institutions, most of its hostels and the lively Little Asia restaurant strip.

Continue northeast along Beaufort St and you'll reach the sophisticated suburbs of Highgate and Mt Lawley. Heading west there's Mt Hawthorn and hip Leederville. To the west of the central city rises Kings Park, with well-heeled Subiaco beyond it. Go further west and you'll hit the beaches.

Information

EMERGENCY

Police Station (☎13 14 44; www.police.wa.gov.au; 2 Fitzgerald St)

Sexual Assault Resource Centre (☎08-9340 1828, freecall 1800 199 888; www.kemh.health.wa.gov.au/services/sarc; ⏲24hr) Twenty-four-hour emergency service.

INTERNET ACCESS

Perth City offers free wi-fi access in Murray St Mall between William St and Barrack St.

State Library of WA (www.slwa.wa.gov.au; Perth Cultural Centre, 25 Francis St; ⏲9am-8pm Mon-Thu, 10am-5.30pm Fri-Sun; @ 📶) Free wi-fi and internet access.

MEDIA

Drum Media (www.facebook.com/drumperth) Music, film and culture listings.

Go West (www.gowesternaustralia.com.au) Backpacker magazine with information on seasonal work opportunities.

Urban Walkabout (www.urbanwalkabout.com) Eating, drinking and shopping highlights in key inner-Perth neighbourhoods and Fremantle.

West Australian (www.thewest.com.au) Local newspaper with entertainment and cinema listings.

X-Press Magazine (www.xpressmag.com.au) A good online source of live-music information. Also available as an app.

MEDICAL SERVICES

Lifecare Dental (☎08-9221 2777; www.dentistsinperth.com.au; 419 Wellington St; ⏲8am-8pm) In Forrest Chase.

Royal Perth Hospital (☎08-9224 2244; www.rph.wa.gov.au; Victoria Sq) In central Perth.

Travel Medicine Centre (☎08-9321 7888; www.travelmed.com.au; 5 Mill St; ⏲8am-5pm Mon-Fri) Travel-specific advice and vaccinations.

MONEY

ATMs are plentiful, there are currency-exchange facilities at the airport and major banks in the CBD.

POST

Main Post Office (GPO; Map p54; ☎13 13 18; 3 Forrest Pl; ⊙8.30am-5pm Mon-Fri, 9am-12.30pm Sat) Central location near the bus and train station.

TOURIST INFORMATION

i-City Information Kiosk (Map p54; Murray St Mall; ⊙9.30am-4.30pm Mon-Thu & Sat, to 8pm Fri, 11am-3.30pm Sun) Volunteers answer questions and run walking tours.

WA Visitor Centre (Map p54; ☎1800 812 808, 08-9483 1111; www.bestofwa.com.au; 55 William St; ⊙9am-5.30pm Mon-Fri, 9.30am-4.30pm Sat, 11am-4.30pm Sun) Excellent resource for information across WA.

WEBSITES

www.heatseeker.com.au Gig guide and ticketing.

www.perthnow.com.au Perth and WA news and restaurant reviews.

www.scoop.com.au Entertainment and dining information.

www.showticketing.com.au Gig guide and ticketing.

www.whatson.com.au Events and travel information.

Getting There & Away

AIR

For details on flights to Perth from international, interstate and Western Australian destinations, see the Transport chapter (p257).

BUS

Integrity Coach Lines (Map p54; ☎08-9274 7464; www.integritycoachlines.com.au; Wellington St Bus Station) Runs services between Perth and Port Hedland via Mt Magnet, Cue, Meekatharra and Newman. Also has a service from Perth to Geraldton on Indian Ocean Dr via Lancelin, Jurien Bay and Cervantes.

South West Coach Lines (☎08-9261 7600; www.transdevsw.com.au) Focuses on the southwestern corner of WA, running services from the Esplanade Busport (some starting at the domestic airport) to most towns in the region, including: Dunsborough (four hours, daily) via Mandurah, Bunbury and Busselton; Augusta (five hours, daily) via Bunbury, Busselton, Cowaramup and Margaret River; Manjimup (five hours, daily except weekends) via Mandurah, Bunbury, Balingup and Bridgetown.

Transwa (☎1300 662 205; www.transwa.wa.gov.au) Operates services from the bus terminal at East Perth train station to/from many destinations around the state. These include the following:

- SW1 to Augusta ($51, six hours, 12 per week) via Mandurah, Bunbury, Busselton and Dunsborough.
- SW2 to Pemberton ($53, 5½ hours, thrice weekly) via Bunbury, Balingup and Bridgetown.
- GS1 to Albany ($61, six hours, daily) via Mt Barker.
- GE2 to Esperance ($91, 10 hours, thrice weekly) via Mundaring, York and Hyden.
- N1 to Geraldton ($64, six hours, daily) and on to Northampton and Kalbarri.

TRAIN

Transwa runs the following services:

Australind (twice daily) Perth to Pinjarra ($17, 1¼ hours) and Bunbury ($31, 2½ hours).

MerredinLink (daily) East Perth to Toodyay ($17, 1¼ hours) and Northam ($20, 1½ hours).

Prospector (daily) East Perth to Kalgoorlie–Boulder ($86, seven hours).

Getting Around

TO/FROM THE AIRPORT

The domestic and international terminals of Perth's airport are 10km and 13km east of Perth respectively, near Guildford. Taxi fares to the city are around $40 from the domestic and international terminals, and about $60 to Fremantle.

Connect (☎1300 666 806; www.perthairportconnect.com.au) runs shuttles to and from central accommodation and transport options in the city centre (one way/return $15/30, every 50 minutes). Bookings are recommended for groups.

Transperth buses 36, 37 and 40 travel to the domestic airport from St Georges Tce (stop 10121), near William St ($4.40, 40 minutes, every 10 to 30 minutes, hourly after 7pm). A free transfer bus links the domestic and international terminals.

CAR & MOTORCYCLE

Driving in the city takes a bit of practice as some streets are one way and many aren't signed. There are plenty of car-parking buildings in the city centre but no free parks. For unmetered street parking you'll need to look well away from the main commercial strips and check the signs carefully.

A fun way to gad about the city is on a moped. **Scootamoré** (☎08-9380 6580; www.scootamore.com.au; 356a Rokeby Rd, Subiaco; day/3 days/week/month $45/111/200/400) hires 50cc scooters with helmets (compulsory) and insurance included (for those over 21, $500 excess).

PUBLIC TRANSPORT

Transperth (☎13 62 13; www.transperth.wa.gov.au) operates Perth's public buses, trains and ferries. There are Transperth information offices at Perth station (Wellington St), Wellington St bus station, Perth underground station (off Murray St) and the Esplanade Busport (Mounts Bay Rd). It has a good online journey planner.

Fares & Passes

From the city centre, the following fares apply for all public transport:

Free Transit Zone (FTZ) Covers the central commercial area, bounded (roughly) by Fraser Ave, Kings Park Rd, Thomas St, Newcastle St, Parry St, Lord St and the river (including the City West and Claisebrook train stations, to the west and east respectively).

Zone 1 Includes the city centre and the inner suburbs ($2.90).

Zone 2 Fremantle, Guildford and the beaches as far north as Sorrento ($4.40).

Zone 3 Hillarys Boat Harbour (AQWA), the Swan Valley and Kalamunda ($5.30).

Zone 5 Rockingham ($7.80).

Zone 7 Mandurah ($10.30).

DayRider Unlimited travel after 9am weekdays and all day on the weekend in any zone ($12.10).

FamilyRider Lets two adults and up to five children travel for a total of $12.10 on weekends, after 6pm weekdays and after 9am on weekdays during school holidays.

If you're in Perth for a while, consider buying a SmartRider card, covering bus, train and ferry travel. It's $10 to purchase, then you add value to your card. The technology deducts the fare as you go, as long as you tap in and tap out (touch your card to the electronic reader) every time you travel, including within the FTZ. The SmartRider works out 15% cheaper than buying single tickets and automatically caps itself at the DayRider rate if you're avoiding the morning rush hour.

Bus

As well as regular buses the FTZ is well covered during the day by the three free Central Area Transit (CAT) services. The Yellow and Red CATs operate east–west routes, Yellow sticking mainly to Wellington St, and Red looping roughly east on Murray St and west on Hay St. The Blue Cat does a figure eight through Northbridge and the south end of the city; this is the only one to run late – until 1am on Friday and Saturday nights only. Pick up a copy of the free timetable (widely available on buses and elsewhere) for the exact routes and stops. They run every five to eight minutes during weekdays and every 15 minutes on weekends. Digital displays at the stops advise when the next bus is due.

The metropolitan area is serviced by a wide network of Transperth buses. Pick up timetables from any of the Transperth information centres or use the online journey planner.

Ferry

The only ferry runs every 20 to 30 minutes between Barrack St Jetty and Mends St Jetty in South Perth – use it to get to the zoo or for a bargain from-the-river glimpse of the Perth skyline.

Train

Transperth operates five train lines from around 5.20am to midnight weekdays and until about 2am Saturday and Sunday. Your rail ticket can also be used on Transperth buses and ferries within the ticket's zone. You're free to take your bike on the train during nonpeak times. The lines and useful stops include the following:

Armadale Thornlie Line Perth, Burswood.

Fremantle Line Perth, City West, West Leederville, Subiaco, Shenton Park, Swanbourne, Cottesloe, North Fremantle, Fremantle.

Joondalup Line Esplanade, Perth Underground, Leederville.

Mandurah Line Perth Underground, Esplanade, Rockingham, Mandurah.

Midland Line Perth, East Perth, Mt Lawley, Guildford, Midland.

TAXI

Perth has a decent system of metered taxis, though the distances make frequent use costly and on busy nights you may have trouble flagging one down off the street. The two main companies are **Swan Taxis** (☎13 13 30; www.swantaxis.com.au) and **Black & White** (☎13 10 08; www.bwtaxi.com.au); both have wheelchair-accessible cabs.

FREMANTLE

POP 28,100

Creative, relaxed, open-minded: Fremantle's spirit is entirely distinct from Perth's. Perhaps it has something to do with the port and the city's working-class roots. Or the hippies, who first set up home here a few decades ago and can still be seen casually bobbling down the street on old bicycles. Or perhaps it's just that a timely 20th-century economic slump meant that the city retained an almost complete set of formerly grand Victorian and Edwardian buildings, creating a heritage precinct that's unique among Australia's cities today.

Whatever the reason, today's clean and green Freo makes a cosy home for performers, professionals, artists and more than a few eccentrics. There's a lot to enjoy here – fantastic museums, edgy galleries, pubs thrumming with live music and a thriving coffee culture. On weekend nights the city's residents vacate the main drag, leaving it to kids from the suburbs, who move in to party hard and loud.

History

This was an important area for the Wadjuk Noongar people, as it was a hub of trading paths. Some of these routes exist to this day in the form of modern roads. Before the harbour was altered, the mouth of the river was nearly covered by a sandbar and it was only a short swim from north to south. The confluence of the river and ocean, where Fremantle now stands, was known as Manjaree (sometimes translated as 'gathering place'). The Fremantle coast was called Booyeembara, while inland was Wallyalup, 'place of the eagle'.

Manjaree was mainly occupied in summer when the Wadjuk would base themselves here to fish. In winter they would head further inland, avoiding seasonal flooding.

Fremantle's European history began when the ship HMS *Challenger* landed in 1829. The ship's captain, Charles Fremantle, took possession of the whole of the west coast 'in the name of King George IV'. Like Perth, the settlement made little progress until convict labour was used. Convicts constructed most of the town's earliest buildings; some of them, such as the Round House, Fremantle Prison and Fremantle Arts Centre, are now among the oldest in WA.

As a port, Fremantle wasn't up to much until engineer CY O'Connor created an artificial harbour in the 1890s, destroying the Wadjuks' river crossing in the process. This caused such disruption to their traditional patterns of life that it's said that a curse was placed on O'Connor; some took his later suicide at Fremantle as evidence of its effectiveness.

The port blossomed during the gold rush and many of its distinctive buildings date from this period. Economic stagnation in the 1960s and 1970s spared the streetscape from the worst ravages of modernisation. It wasn't until 1987, when Fremantle hosted the America's Cup, that it transformed itself from a sleepy port town into today's vibrant, artsy city.

The cup was lost that year, but the legacy of a redeveloped waterfront remains. In 1995 the Fremantle Dockers played their first game, quickly developing one of the most fanatical fan bases in the Australian Football League (AFL). Their popularity was boosted by semifinals berths in 2010 and 2012, and a losing cameo in the final in 2013. We reckon it's only a matter of time before they go all the way.

Sights

★Fremantle Prison HISTORIC BUILDING
(08-9336 9200; www.fremantleprison.com.au; 1 The Terrace; single day tour adult/child $20/11, combined day tours $28/19, Torchlight Tour $26/16, Tunnels Tour adult/child over 12yr $60/40; 9am-5.30pm) With its foreboding 5m-high walls, the old convict-era prison still dominates Fremantle. Daytime tour options include the Doing Time Tour taking in the kitchens, men's cells and solitary-confinement cells. The Great Escapes Tour recounts famous inmates and takes in the women's prison. Book ahead for the Torchlight Tour focusing on macabre aspects of the prison's history, and the 2½-hour Tunnels Tour which includes an underground boat ride and subterranean tunnels built by prisoners.

Entry to the gatehouse, including the Prison Gallery, gift shop and Convict Cafe is free. In 2010 its cultural status was recognised as part of the Australian Convict Sites entry on the Unesco World Heritage List.

The first convicts were made to build their own prison, constructing it from beautiful pale limestone dug out of the hill on which it was built. From 1855 to 1991, 350,000 people were incarcerated here, although the highest numbers held at any one time were 1200

FREMANTLE FOR CHILDREN

You can let the littlies off the leash at **Esplanade Reserve**, watch buskers at the **market**, make sand castles at **Bathers Beach** or have a proper splash about at **South** or **Port Beaches**. Older kids might appreciate the creepier aspects of the prison and the innards of the submarine at the **Maritime Museum**, where they can also poke about on actual boats. **Adventure World** is nearby for funfair rides. Finish up with fish and chips at **Fishing Boat Harbour**.

Fremantle

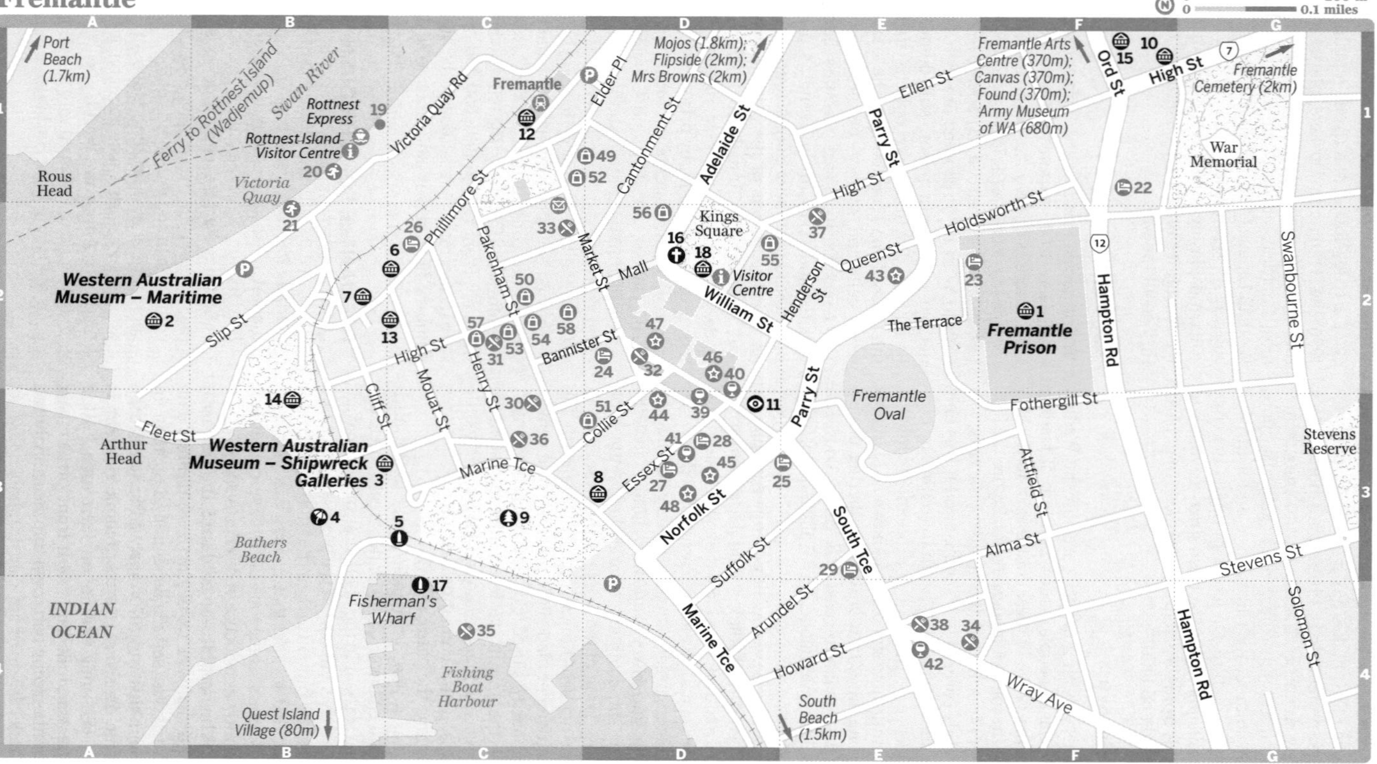
Port Beach (1.7km)
Ferry to Rottnest Island (Wadjemup)
Swan River
Rottnest Express
Rottnest Island Visitor Centre
Rous Head
Victoria Quay
Victoria Quay Rd
Fremantle
Elder Pl
Mojos (1.8km); Flipside (2km); Mrs Browns (2km)
Cantonment St
Adelaide St
Parry St
Ellen St
Fremantle Arts Centre (370m); Canvas (370m); Found (370m); Army Museum of WA (680m)
Ord St
High St
Fremantle Cemetery (2km)
War Memorial
Phillimore St
Western Australian Museum – Maritime
Slip St
Pakenham St
Market St
Mall
Kings Square
Visitor Centre
William St
Henderson St
QueenSt
Holdsworth St
The Terrace
Fremantle Prison
Hampton Rd
Swanbourne St
High St
Mouat St
Henry St
Bannister St
Cliff St
Collie St
Fremantle Oval
Fothergill St
Fleet St
Arthur Head
Western Australian Museum – Shipwreck Galleries
Marine Tce
Essex St
Norfolk St
South Tce
Attfield St
Stevens Reserve
Bathers Beach
Alma St
Stevens St
Suffolk St
Arundel St
Fisherman's Wharf
INDIAN OCEAN
Marine Tce
Howard St
Wray Ave
Solomon St
Fishing Boat Harbour
Quest Island Village (80m)
South Beach (1.5km)
200 m
0.1 miles

Fremantle

Top Sights
1 Fremantle Prison F2
2 Western Australian Museum – Maritime A2
3 Western Australian Museum – Shipwreck Galleries B3

Sights
4 Bathers Beach B3
5 Bon Scott Statue C3
6 Chamber of Commerce Building C2
7 Customs House B2
8 Esplanade Hotel D3
9 Esplanade Reserve C3
10 Fremantle Grammar School F1
11 Fremantle Markets D3
12 Fremantle Train Station C1
John Curtin Statue .... (see 18)
13 Old German Consulate C2
Pietro Porcelli Statue .... (see 16)
14 Round House B3
15 Samson House F1
16 St John's Anglican Church D2
17 To the Fishermen C4
18 Town Hall D2

Activities, Courses & Tours
19 Captain Cook Cruises B1
Fremantle Tram Tours .... (see 18)
20 Oceanic Cruises B1
21 STS Leeuwin II B2

Sleeping
22 Fothergills of Fremantle F1
23 Fremantle Prison YHA Hostel E2
24 Hougoumont Hotel D2
25 Norfolk Hotel E3
26 Old Firestation Backpackers C2
27 Pirates D3
28 Port Mill B&B D3
29 Terrace Central B&B Hotel E3

Eating
30 Bread in Common C3
31 Cafe 55 .... C2
32 Gino's D2
33 Kakulas Sister C2
34 Lenny the Ox E4
35 Little Creatures C4
36 Moore & Moore C3
37 Raw Kitchen E2
38 Wild Poppy E4

Drinking & Nightlife
Little Creatures .... (see 35)
39 Monk D3
Norfolk Hotel .... (see 25)
40 Sail & Anchor D2
41 Whisper D3
42 Who's Your Mumma E4

Entertainment
43 Fly by Night Musicians Club E2
44 Hoyts D3
45 Luna on SX D3
46 Metropolis Fremantle D2
47 Newport Hotel D2
48 X-Wray Cafe D3

Shopping
49 Aboriginart D1
50 Bodkin's Bootery C2
51 Chart & Map Shop D3
52 Didgeridoo Breath C1
Japingka .... (see 31)
53 Jarrahcorp C2
54 Love in Tokyo C2
55 MANY6160 .... D2
56 Mills Records D2
57 New Edition C2
58 Record Finder C2

men and 58 women. Of those, 43 men and one woman were executed on site, the last of which was serial killer Eric Edgar Cooke in 1964.

★ Western Australian Museum – Maritime MUSEUM

(www.museum.wa.gov.au; Victoria Quay; adult/child museum $10/3, submarine $10/3, museum & submarine $16/5; ⏲9.30am-5pm) Housed in an intriguing sail-shaped building on the harbour, just west of the city centre, the Maritime Museum is a fascinating exploration of WA's relationship with the ocean. Well-presented displays range from yacht racing to Aboriginal fish traps and the sandalwood trade. If you're not claustrophobic, take an hour-long tour of the submarine HMAS *Ovens*. The vessel was part of the Australian Navy's fleet from 1969 to 1997. Tours leave every half-hour from 10am to 3.30pm.

Various boats are on display in the museum including *Australia* II, the famous winged-keel yacht that won the America's Cup yachting race in 1983 (ending 132 years of American domination of the competition). Other boats include an Aboriginal bark canoe; an Indonesian outrigger canoe, introduced to the Kimberley and used by Indigenous people; and a pearl lugger used in Broome. Even a classic 1970s panel van (complete with fur lining) makes the cut – because of its status as the surfer's vehicle of choice.

★Western Australian Museum – Shipwreck Galleries MUSEUM
(www.museum.wa.gov.au; Cliff St; admission by donation; ⏲9.30am-5pm) Located within an 1852 commissariat store, the Shipwreck Galleries are considered the finest display of maritime archaeology in the southern hemisphere. The highlight is the **Batavia Gallery**, where a section of the hull of Dutch merchant ship *Batavia*, wrecked in 1629, is displayed. Nearby is a large stone gate, intended as an entrance to Batavia Castle, which was being carried when it sank.

Other items of interest include the inscribed pewter plate left on Cape Inscription by Willem de Vlamingh in 1697, positioned next to a replica of the plate left by Dirk Hartog in 1616 during the first confirmed European landing in WA.

Round House HISTORIC BUILDING
(☎08-9336 6897; www.fremantleroundhouse.com.au; Captains Lane; admission by donation; ⏲10.30am-3.30pm) Built from 1830 to 1831, this 12-sided stone prison is WA's oldest surviving building. It was the site of the colony's first hangings, and was later used for holding Aboriginal people before they were taken to Rottnest Island. On the hilltop outside is the Signal Station, where at 1pm daily a time ball and cannon blast were used to alert seamen to the correct time. The ceremony is re-enacted daily; book ahead if you want to fire the cannon.

To the Indigenous Noongar people, it's a sacred site because of the number of their people killed while incarcerated here. Freedom fighter Yagan was held here briefly in 1832. Beneath is an impressive 1837 Whalers' Tunnel carved through sandstone and used for accessing Bathers Beach, where whales were landed and processed.

Fremantle Arts Centre GALLERY
(Map p50; www.fac.org.au; 1 Finnerty St; ⏲10am-5pm) FREE An impressive neo-Gothic building surrounded by lovely elm-shaded gardens, the Fremantle Arts Centre was constructed by convict labourers as a lunatic asylum in the 1860s. Saved from demolition in the 1960s, it houses interesting exhibitions and the excellent Canvas (p83) cafe. During summer there are concerts, courses and workshops.

Fremantle Markets MARKET
(www.fremantlemarkets.com.au; cnr South Tce & Henderson St; ⏲8am-8pm Fri, 8am-6pm Sat & Sun) FREE Originally opened in 1897, these colourful markets were reopened in 1975 and today draw slow-moving crowds, combing over souvenirs such as plastic boomerangs and swan-shaped magnets. The fresh-produce section is a good place to stock up on snacks.

Army Museum of WA MUSEUM
(Map p50; www.armymuseumwa.com.au; Burt St; adult/child $10/7; ⏲11am-4pm Wed-Sun) Situated within the imposing Artillery Barracks, this little museum pulls out the big guns, literally. Howitzers and tanks line up outside, while inside you'll find cabinets full of uniforms and medals.

Gold-Rush Buildings

Fremantle boomed during the WA gold rush in the late 19th century, and many wonderful buildings remain that were constructed during, or shortly before, this period. High St, particularly around the bottom end, has some excellent examples including several old hotels.

Chamber of Commerce Building HISTORIC BUILDING
(16 Phillimore St) Continuing its original use since 1873.

St John's Anglican Church CHURCH
(Kings Sq) Built in 1882.

Fremantle Grammar School HISTORIC BUILDING
(200 High St) Built as an Anglican public school in 1885.

Town Hall HISTORIC BUILDING
(Kings Sq) Opened on Queen Victoria's jubilee in 1887.

Samson House HISTORIC BUILDING
(cnr Ellen & Ord Sts) A well-preserved 1888 colonial home owned by the National Trust.

Esplanade Hotel HISTORIC BUILDING
(Marine Tce) Attractive colonnaded hotel, built in 1896.

Old German Consulate HISTORIC BUILDING
(5 Mouat St) Built 1903; now a B&B.

Fremantle Train Station HISTORIC BUILDING
(Phillimore St) Built from Donnybrook sandstone in 1907; we're not sure why the swans are white rather than black.

Customs House HISTORIC BUILDING
(cnr Cliff & Phillimore Sts) Built in 1908 in Georgian style.

Public Sculptures

Enlivening Fremantle's streets are numerous bronze sculptures, many by local artist Greg James (www.gregjamessculpture.com).

In Fishing Boat Harbour is **To the Fishermen** (Fishing Boat Harbour), a cluster of bronze figures, unloading and carrying their catch up from the wharf. There's a lively statue of former member for Fremantle and wartime Labor prime minister **John Curtin** (1885–1945) in Kings Sq, outside the Town Hall. Nearby is a Greg James sculpture of fellow sculptor **Pietro Porcelli** (1872–1943), in the act of making a bust.

Bon Scott Statue STATUE

The most popular of Fremantle's public sculptures is Greg James' statue of Bon Scott (1946–80), strutting on a Marshall amplifier in Fishing Boat Harbour. The AC/DC singer moved to Fremantle with his family in 1956 and his ashes are interred in **Fremantle Cemetery** (Map p50; Carrington St). Enter the cemetery at the entrance near the corner of High and Carrington Sts. Bon's plaque is on the left around 15m along the path.

Beaches & Parks

Green spaces around Fremantle include **Esplanade Reserve** (Marine Tce), shaded by Norfolk Island pines and dividing the city from Fishing Boat Harbour. During summer, nearby **Bathers Beach** hosts a Saturday night market with music and food from 5pm to 9pm. A new waterfront restaurant also opened here in late 2014. **South Beach** is sheltered, swimmable, only 1.5km from the city centre and on the free CAT bus route. The next major beach is **Coogee Beach**, 6km further south.

Activities

Fremantle Trails WALKING

(www.visitfremantle.com.au) Pick up trailcards from the visitor centre for 11 self-guided walking tours: Art and Culture, Convict, CY O'Connor (a pioneering civil engineer), Discovery (a Fremantle once-over), Fishing Boat Harbour, Hotels and Breweries, Maritime Heritage, Manjaree Heritage (Indigenous), Retail & Fashion, Waterfront and Writers.

Oceanic Cruises WHALE WATCHING

(☎08-9325 1191; www.oceaniccruises.com.au; adult/child $69/29; ⊙mid-Sep–early Dec) Departs B Shed, Victoria Quay, at 10.15am for a two-hour tour. Days of operation vary by month, so check the website.

STS Leeuwin II SAILING

(☎08-9430 4105; www.sailleeuwin.com; Berth B; adult/child $99/69; ⊙Nov–mid-Apr) Take a three-hour trip on a 55m, three-masted tall ship; see the website for details of morning, afternoon or twilight sails. Sailings are from Friday to Sunday.

Tours

Fremantle Tram Tours CITY

(☎08-9433 6674; www.fremantletrams.com.au; ghostly tour adult/child $80/60, lunch & tram adult/child $89/54, triple tour adult/child $80/30, tram & prison adult/child $45/14) Looking like a heritage tram, this bus departs from the Town Hall on an all-day hop-on, hop-off circuit around the city (adult/child $26/5). The Ghostly Tour runs from 6.45pm to 10.30pm Friday and visits the prison, Round House and Fremantle Arts Centre (former asylum) by torchlight. Combos include Lunch & Tram (tram plus a lunch cruise on river), Triple Tour (tram, river cruise and Perth sightseeing bus), and Tram & Prison (incorporating the tram and Fremantle prison).

Captain Cook Cruises CRUISE

(Map p54; ☎08-9325 3341; www.captaincookcruises.com.au; C Shed; adult/child $28/16) Cruises between Fremantle and Perth (adult/child $28/16) departing Fremantle at 11.05am, 12.45pm and 3.30pm (the last is one-way only). A three-hour lunch cruise departs at 12.45pm (adult/child $69/46).

Fremantle Indigenous Heritage Tours WALKING TOUR

(☎0405 630 606; www.indigenouswa.com; adult/child $50/15; ⊙1.30pm Sat) Highly regarded tour covering the history of Fremantle and the Nyoongar and Wadjuk people. Book through the Fremantle visitors centre.

Two Feet & A Heartbeat WALKING TOUR

(☎1800 459 388; www.twofeet.com.au; per person $20-40; ⊙10am daily) Operated by a younger, energetic crew, tours focus on Fremantle's often rambunctious history. 'Tight Arse Tuesdays' are good value.

Festivals & Events

Laneway MUSIC

(www.fremantle.lanewayfestival.com; ⊙early Feb) WA's skinny-jean and floppy-fringe hipsters party to the planet's up-and-coming indie acts. The über-cool festival takes place around Fremantle's West End and Esplanade Reserve.

West Coast Blues 'n' Roots Festival MUSIC
(www.westcoastbluesnroots.com.au; late Mar–mid-Apr) Interpreting its remit widely, recent festivals have featured Steve Earle, Grace Jones, Elvis Costello and My Morning Jacket.

Blessing of the Fleet RELIGIOUS
(www.fremantleseafoodfestival.com.au; Esplanade Reserve, Fishing Boat Harbour; late Oct) An October tradition since 1948, brought to Fremantle by immigrants from Molfetta, Italy. It includes the procession of the Molfettese *Our Lady of Martyrs* statue (carried by men) and the Sicilian *Madonna di Capo d'Orlando* (carried by women), from St Patrick's Basilica (47 Adelaide St) to Fishing Boat Harbour, where the blessing takes place. An associated seafood festival also takes place nearby.

Fremantle Festival CULTURAL
(www.fremantle.wa.gov.au/festivals; late Oct-early Nov) In spring the city's streets and concert venues come alive with performances in Australia's longest-running festival.

Sleeping

Fremantle Prison YHA Hostel HOSTEL $
(08-9433 4305; www.yha.com.au/hostels/wa/perth-surrounds/fremantle-prison-yha/; 6a The Terrace, 6160; dm from $36-40, private room $156;) Newly opened in early 2015, Fremantle's iconic prison has a hostel wing with a mix of dorm-style accommodation and private rooms. Slightly more upmarket options include a private bathroom.

Pirates HOSTEL $
(08-9335 6635; www.piratesbackpackers.com.au; 11 Essex St; dm $31-33, r $80;) Attracting a diverse international crew, this sun- and fun-filled hostel in the thick of the Freo action is a top spot to socialise. Rooms are small and reasonably basic, but the bathrooms are fresh and clean. The kitchen area is well equipped, there's a shady courtyard, and eye-catching marine murals remind you that an ocean swim is minutes away.

Old Firestation Backpackers HOSTEL $
(08-9430 5454; www.old-firestation.net; 18 Phillimore St; dm $28-32, d $75-80;) There's entertainment aplenty in this converted fire station: free internet, foosball, movies and a sunny courtyard. Dorms have natural light and afternoon sea breezes, and there's a female-only section. The hippy vibe culminates in late-night guitar-led singalongs around the campfire; bring earplugs if you value sleep.

Woodman Point Holiday Park CAMPGROUND $
(08-9434 1433; www.aspenparks.com.au; 132 Cockburn Rd; sites for 2 people $47-49, d $120-215;) A particularly pleasant spot, 10km south of Fremantle. It's usually quiet, and its location makes it feel more summer beach holiday than outer-Freo staging post.

★ **Hougoumont Hotel** BOUTIQUE HOTEL $$
(08-6160 6800; www.hougoumonthotel.com.au; 15 Bannister St; d $200-255) Standard 'cabin' rooms are definitely compact, but very stylish and efficiently designed, and you can't beat the central location of this recently opened boutique hotel. Top-end toiletries, a hip, breezy ambience, and complimentary late-afternoon wine and snacks for guests reinforce the Hougoumont's refreshingly different approach to accommodation. Service from the multinational team is relaxed but professional.

Fothergills of Fremantle B&B $$
(08-9335 6784; www.fothergills.net.au; 18-22 Ord St; r $195-245;) Naked bronze women sprout from the front garden, while a life-size floral cow shelters on the verandah of these neighbouring mansions on the hill. Inside, the decor is in keeping with their venerable age (built in 1892), aside from the contemporary art scattered about – including some wonderful Aboriginal pieces. Breakfast is served in a sunny conservatory.

Terrace Central B&B Hotel B&B $$
(08-9335 6600; www.terracecentral.com.au; 79-85 South Tce; d $180-220;) Terrace Central may be a character-filled B&B at heart, but its larger size gives it the feel of a boutique hotel. The main section is created from an 1888 bakery and an adjoined row of terrace houses, and there are modern one- and two-bedroom apartments out the back. You'll find ample off-street parking.

Port Mill B&B B&B $$
(08-9433 3832; www.portmillbb.com.au; 3/17 Essex St; r $199-299;) One of the most luxurious B&Bs in town, Port Mill is clearly the love child of Paris and Freo. Crafted from local limestone (it was built in 1862 as a mill), inside it's all modern Parisian style, with gleaming taps, contemporary French furniture and wrought-iron balconies. French doors open out to the sun-filled decks, where you can tinkle the china on your breakfast platter.

Norfolk Hotel HOTEL $$
(08-9335 5405; www.norfolkhotel.com.au; 47 South Tce; s/d without bathroom $90/120, d with

bathroom $150;) While eucalypts and elms stand quietly in the sun-streaked beer garden, the old limestone Norfolk harbours a secret upstairs: its rooms. Far above your standard pub digs, they've all been tastefully decorated in muted tones and crisp white linen, and there's a communal sitting room. It can be noisy on weekends, but the bar closes at midnight.

Number Six APARTMENT **$$**
(08-9299 7107; www.numbersix.com.au; studios/1-bedroom apt from $105/160;) Self-contained, stylish studios, apartments and houses available for overnight to long-term stays in great locations around Freo.

Quest Harbour Village APARTMENT **$$$**
(Map p50; 08-9430 3888; www.questharbourvillage.com.au; Mews Rd, Challenger Harbour; apt from $280;) At the end of a wharf, this attractive, two-storey, sandstone and brick block of one- to three-bedroom apartments makes the most of its nautical setting; one-bedroom units have views over the car park to the Fishing Boat Harbour, while the others directly front the marina. Downstairs the rooms are light and simple, and the kitchens are fully equipped.

Eating

Although it doesn't have Perth's variety of fine-dining places, eating and drinking your way around town are two of the great pleasures of Freo. People-watching from outdoor tables on South Tce is a legitimate lifestyle choice. The Fremantle Markets are a good place to stock up on fruit and picnic items.

City Centre

Cafe 55 ASIAN **$**
(www.cafe55.com.au; 55 High St; mains $8-13; 7.30am-3pm Mon-Fri) Asian food with a Freo feel, this bright cafe's fragrant soups – *pho, bun bo Hue* (spicy beef noodle soup) and Malaysian laksa – are all fantastic. Plus there are Turkish toasted sandwiches and healthy, well-priced Asian-influenced salads ($8).

Kakulas Sister DELI **$**
(www.kakulassister.com.au; 29-31 Market St; 9am-5.30pm Mon-Sat, 11.30am-5pm Sun) This provedore – packed with nuts, quince paste and Italian rocket seeds – is a cook's dream, and an excellent spot to stock up on energy-filled snacks. If you've been to Kakulas Bros (p65) in Northbridge, you'll know the deal.

★ **Bread in Common** BISTRO, BAKERY **$$**
(www.breadincommon.com.au; 43 Pakenham St; shared platters $12-14, mains $21-26; 10am-10pm Mon-Fri, 9am-10pm Sat & Sun) Be initially lured by the comforting aroma of the in-house bakery, before staying on for cheese and charcuterie platters, or larger dishes such as chargrilled chicken with corn, ginger and coriander. There's an equal focus on comfort food and culinary flair, while big shared tables and a laid-back warehouse ambience encourage conversation over WA wines and Aussie craft beers and ciders.

Raw Kitchen VEGETARIAN **$$**
(www.therawkitchen.com.au; 181a High St; mains $18-24; 11am-4pm Mon-Thu, 11am-9pm Fri-Sun) Vegan, organic and sustainable, and therefore *very* Freo. Reset your chakra and boost your energy levels with the super-healthy but still very tasty food in this funky, brick-lined warehouse. A lot (but not all) of the menu showcases raw ingredients, but there's no trade off for taste. Gluten-free beer and sustainably-produced wine mean you don't have to be *too* virtuous.

Canvas CAFE **$$**
(Map p50; www.canvasatfremantleartscentre.com; Fremantle Arts Centre, Finnerty St; mains $12-25; 8am-3pm Mon-Fri, 8am-4pm Sat & Sun;) Freo's best cafe is in the shaded courtyard of the Fremantle Arts Centre with a menu channelling Middle Eastern, Spanish and North African influences. Breakfast highlights include baked-egg dishes – try the Israeli-style Red Shakshuka – and lunch presents everything from jerk chicken wraps to bouillabaisse and Tasmanian salmon. The concise drinks list includes craft beer, ciders and wine.

Moore & Moore CAFE **$$**
(www.mooreandmoorecafe.com; 46 Henry St; mains $11-20; 7am-4pm;) An urban-chic cafe that spills into the adjoining art gallery and overflows into a flagstoned courtyard. With great coffee, good cooked breakfasts, pastries, wraps and free wi-fi, it's a great place to linger. Look forward to the company of a few Freo hipsters, and the international crew of students studying at Fremantle's University of Notre Dame.

Gino's CAFE **$$**
(www.ginoscafe.com.au; 1 South Tce; mains $17-31; 6am-late;) Old-school Gino's is Freo's most famous cafe, and while it's become a tourist attraction in its own right, the locals

still treat it as their second living room, only with better coffee. You'll need to order and pay, then collect your own coffee.

Fishing Boat Harbour

Little Creatures PUB FOOD $$
(www.littlecreatures.com.au; 40 Mews Rd; pizzas $19-24, shared plates $8-24; 10am-midnight Mon-Fri, from 9am Sat & Sun;) Little Creatures is classic Freo: harbour views, fantastic brews (made on the premises) and excellent food. In a cavernous converted boatshed overlooking the harbour, it can get chaotic at times, but a signature Pale Ale with a wood-fired pizza will be worth the wait. More substantial shared plates include kangaroo with tomato chutney and grilled prawn skewers. No bookings.

North Fremantle

Flipside BURGERS $
(Map p50; www.flipsideburgers.com.au; 239 Queen Victoria St, North Fremantle; burgers $11.50-15.50; 5.30-9pm Tue-Thu, noon-2.30pm Thu, noon-9pm Fri-Sun) Gourmet burgers with the option of dining in next door at Mrs Browns.

South Fremantle

Public & Co BISTRO, TAPAS $$
(www.publicandco.com.au; 25 Duoro St; shared plates $15-24, mains & pizza $15-28; 6-10pm Wed-Fri, 8am-4pm & 6-10pm Sat, 8am-3pm Sun) Around 2.5km from central Fremantle, Public & Co is worth the journey for a relaxed meal in this spacious and airy corner bungalow. Shared plates – most with a Med or Asian spin – wood-fired pizza and top-notch burgers all reinforce a laid-back, WA-style approach to living. It also has one of the best craft beer selections in Perth.

Wild Poppy CAFE $$
(2 Wray Ave; breakfast $10-18, lunch $16-22; 7am-4pm;) Lace doilies, kitschy furniture and a stupendous collection of retro portaits and landscapes make this hip cafe in South Freo worth seeking out. Soup and salad specials team with good coffee, beer and cider, and the chilli eggs are a great way to start the day. For lunch ask if the prawn laksa is available.

Lenny the Ox CAFE $$
(www.facebook.com/LennytheOX; 20 Wray Ave; mains $15-22; 6.30am-5pm) A serious approach to coffee from bearded hipster baristas combines with real culinary nous at this airy cafe. Locals crowd in for excellent home-style baking and the first caffeine hit of the day, before returning for quirky spins on cafe classics. The baked beans served with black pudding, labneh and a fried egg will definitely set you up for the day.

Drinking & Nightlife

Most of Fremantle's big pubs are lined up along South Tce and there are some character-filled old taverns on High St. Freo's pubs have long been incubators for local musos, including world-famous-in-Australia acts such as Tame Impala, San Cisco and John Butler. A couple of interesting smaller bars also lurk in North and South Fremantle, and it's a good destination for fans of craft beer.

Little Creatures BREWERY
(www.littlecreatures.com.au; 40 Mews Rd, Fishing Boat Harbour; 10am-midnight Mon-Fri, from 9am Sat & Sun) Try the Little Creatures Pale Ale and Pilsner, and other beers and ciders under the White Rabbit and Pipsqueak labels. Keep an eye out also for one-off Shift Brewers' Stash beers. Creatures NextDoor is an adjacent lounge bar with regular live entertainment and DJs. Live jazz kicks off at 4.30pm on Sundays, and there's live comedy ($30) on Saturday nights from 8pm.

Who's Your Mumma BAR
(www.facebook.com/whosyourmummabar; cnr Wray Ave & South Tce; 4pm-midnight Mon-Sat, noon-10pm Sun) Industrial-chic lightbulbs and polished-concrete floors are softened by recycled timber at the laid-back Who's Your Mumma. An eclectic crew of South Freo locals crowd in for excellent cocktails, WA craft beer and moreish bar snacks including fluffy pork buns. Taco Thursdays are definitely good value with a Mexican accent.

Sail & Anchor PUB, CRAFT BEER
(www.sailandanchor.com.au; 64 South Tce; 11am-midnight Mon-Sat, to 10pm Sun) Welcome to the best destination for the travelling beer geek in Western Australia. Built in 1854, this Fremantle landmark has been impressively restored to recall much of its former glory. Downstairs is big and beer focused, with 27 taps delivering an ever-changing range of local and international craft beers. Occasional live music and decent bar food complete the picture.

Mrs Browns BAR
(Map p50; www.mrsbrownbar.com.au; 241 Queen Victoria St, North Fremantle; ⌚4.30pm-midnight Tue-Thu, noon-midnight Fri-Sun) Exposed bricks and a copper bar combine with retro and antique furniture to create North Fremantle's most atmospheric bar. The music could include all those cult bands you thought were *your* personal secret, and an eclectic menu of beer, wine and tapas targets the more discerning, slightly older bar hound. And you can order in burgers from Flipside next door.

Norfolk Hotel PUB
(www.norfolkhotel.com.au; 47 South Tce; ⌚11am-midnight Mon-Sat, to 10pm Sun) Slow down to Freo pace at this 1887 pub. Interesting guest beers create havoc for the indecisive drinker, and the pub food and pizzas are very good. We love the heritage limestone courtyard, especially when sunlight peeks through the elms and eucalypts. Downstairs, the Odd Fellow channels a bohemian small-bar vibe, and hosts regular live gigs from Tuesday to Saturday.

Monk CRAFT BEER
(www.themonk.com.au; 33 South Tce; ⌚11.30am-late Mon-Fri, 8.30am-late Sat & Sun) Park yourself on the spacious front terrace or in the chic interior, partly fashioned from recycled railway sleepers, and enjoy the Monk's own brews (kolsch, mild, wheat, porter, rauch, pale ale). The bar snacks and pizzas are also good, and guest beers and regular seasonal brews always draw a knowledgeable crowd of local craft-beer nerds.

Whisper WINE BAR
(www.whisperwinebar.com.au; 1/15 Essex St; ⌚noon-late Wed-Sun) In a lovely heritage building, this classy French-themed wine bar also does shared plates of charcuterie and cheese.

Entertainment

Fly by Night Musicians Club LIVE MUSIC
(www.flybynight.org; Parry St) Variety is the key at Fly by Night, a not-for-profit club that's been run by musos for musos for years. All kinds perform here, and many local bands made a start here. It's opposite the car park below the old Fremantle Prison.

X-Wray Cafe LIVE MUSIC
(www.facebook.com/xwray.fremantle; 3-13 Essex St; ⌚7am-midnight Mon-Sat, to 10pm Sun) There's something on every night (live jazz, rock, open piano) at this hipster hang-out, comprising a smallish indoor area and a large canvas-covered terrace. Light meals are available, kicking off with breakfasts.

Mojo's LIVE MUSIC
(Map p50; www.mojosbar.com.au; 237 Queen Victoria St, North Fremantle; ⌚7pm-late) Local and national bands (mainly Aussie rock and indie) and DJs play at this small place, and there's a sociable beer garden out the back. First Friday of the month is reggae night; every Monday is open-mic night.

Metropolis Fremantle LIVE MUSIC
(www.metropolisfremantle.com.au; 58 South Tce) A great space to watch a gig, it turns into a nightclub on the weekends. International and popular Australian bands and DJs perform here.

Newport Hotel LIVE MUSIC
(www.thenewport.com; 2 South Tce; ⌚noon-midnight Mon-Sat, to 10pm Sun) Local bands and DJs gig from Friday to Sunday. The Tiki Beat Bar is worth a kitsch cocktail or two.

Luna on SX CINEMA
(www.lunapalace.com.au; Essex St) Art-house cinema between Essex and Norfolk Sts. Cheaper Wednesday tickets.

Hoyts CINEMA
(www.hoyts.com.au; Collie St) Blockbuster heaven with cheaper tickets on Tuesdays.

Shopping

The bottom end of High St features interesting and quirky shopping. Fashion stores run along Market St, towards the train station. Queen Victoria St in North Fremantle is the place to go for antiques. Don't forget Fremantle Markets (p80) for clothes and souvenirs.

Japingka ARTS
(www.japingka.com.au; 47 High St; ⌚10am-5.30pm Mon-Fri, noon-5pm Sat & Sun) Specialising in Aboriginal fine art from WA and beyond. Purchases come complete with extensive notes about the works and the artists that painted them.

Aboriginart ARTS
(www.aboriginart.com.au; 6 Elder Pl; ⌚10am-4pm Wed-Mon) Contemporary and collectable art ethically sourced from Indigenous artists living in Australia's Central and Western desert areas.

Didgeridoo Breath ARTS & CRAFTS
(www.diggeridoobreath.com; 6 Market St; ⌚10.30am-5pm) The planet's biggest selection of didgeridoos, Indigenous Australian books and CDs, and how-to-play lessons ranging from one hour to four weeks. You'll probably hear the shop before you see it.

New Edition BOOKS
(www.newedition.com.au; cnr High & Henry Sts; ⌚9am-6pm) Recently relocated to a sunny corner location, and still a bookworm's dream with comfy armchairs for browsing.

MANY6160 ARTS & CRAFTS
(www.many6160.com; 2 Newman Ct; ⌚10am-5pm Fri-Sun) A boho mash-up of local artists' studios and pop-up galleries and shops fills the spacious ground floor of the former Myer department store.

Jarrahcorp FURNITURE
(www.jarrahcorp.com.au; cnr High & Pakenham Sts; ⌚11am-4pm Mon-Sat, noon-4pm Sun) Traditional and contemporary furniture and gifts crafted from jarrah and marri timber salvaged from old buildings or ancient logs.

Found ARTS & CRAFTS
(Map p50; www.fac.org.au; Fremantle Arts Centre, 1 Finnerty St; ⌚10am-5pm) The Fremantle Arts Centre shop stocks an inspiring range of WA art and craft.

Love in Tokyo CLOTHING
(www.loveintokyo.com.au; 61-63 High St; ⌚10am-5pm Mon-Sat, noon-4pm Sun) Local designer turning out gorgeously fashioned fabrics for women.

Record Finder MUSIC
(87 High St; ⌚10am-5pm) A treasure trove of old vinyl, including rarities and collectables.

Bodkin's Bootery SHOES
(www.bodkinsbootery.com; 72 High St; ⌚9am-5pm Mon-Sat, noon-5pm Sun) Handcrafted men's and women's boots and hats. Aussie as.

Chart & Map Shop MAPS
(www.chartandmapshop.com.au; 14 Collie St; ⌚10am-5pm) Maps and travel guides.

Mills Records MUSIC
(www.mills.com.au; 22 Adelaide St; ⌚9am-5.30pm Mon-Sat, noon-5pm Sun) Music, including some rarities, and concert tickets. Check out the 'Local's Board' for recordings by Freo and WA acts.

Information

See www.fremantlestory.com.au for visitor information. Online www.lovefreo.com is a good source of information on local openings and events.

For free wi-fi, try Moore & Moore (p83), or the FREbytes hot spot in the vicinity of the Town Hall and library.

Fremantle City Library (☎08-9432 9766; www.frelibrary.wordpress.com; Kings Sq, Town Hall; ⌚9.30am-5.30pm Mon, Fri & Sat, to 8pm Tue-Thu; @ 📶) Free wi-fi and internet terminals.

Visitor Centre (☎08-9431 7878; www.visitfremantle.com.au; Kings Sq, Town Hall; ⌚9am-5pm Mon-Fri, 9am-4pm Sat, 10am-4pm Sun) Bookings for accommodation, tours and hire cars.

Getting There & Away

Fremantle sits within Zone 2 of the Perth public-transport system (Transperth) and is only 30 minutes away by train. There are numerous buses between Perth's city centre and Fremantle, including routes 103, 106, 107, 111 and 158.

Another very pleasant way to get here from Perth is by taking the 1¼-hour river cruise run by Captain Cook Cruises (p81).

Getting Around

There are numerous one-way streets and parking meters in Freo. It's easy enough to travel by foot or on the free CAT bus service, which takes in all the major sights on a continuous loop every 10 minutes from 7.30am to 6.30pm on weekdays, until 9pm on Friday and 10am to 6.30pm on the weekend.

Bicycles (Fremantle Visitor Centre, Kings Sq; ⌚9.30am-4.30pm Mon-Fri, to 3.30pm Sat, 10.30am-3.30pm Sun) can be rented for free at the visitor centre, an ideal way to get around Freo's storied streets. A refundable bond of $200 applies.

Around Perth

Best Places to Eat

- RiverBank Estate (p101)
- Hotel Rottnest (p93)
- Rustico (p94)
- Jezebelle (p100)
- Lobster Shack (p110)

Best Places to Stay

- Cervantes Lodge & Pinnacles Beach Backpackers (p109)
- Amble Inn (p109)
- Rottnest Island Authority Cottages (p92)
- Lancelin Lodge YHA (p107)
- Centrebreak Beach Stay (p110)

Why Go?

Although Western Australia (WA) is huge, you don't have to travel too far from Perth to treat yourself to a taste of what the state has to offer. A day trip could see you frolicking with wild dolphins, snorkelling with sea lions, scooping up brilliant-blue crabs or spotting bilbies in the bush. Active types can find themselves canoeing, rafting, surfing, windsurfing, sandboarding, diving, skydiving and ballooning. Those who prefer pursuits less likely to ruffle one's hair can linger at vineyards or craft breweries, settle down for a culinary feast, or explore historic towns classified by the National Trust. To the north is the spectacular landscape of the Pinnacles Desert.

When to Go

Mandurah

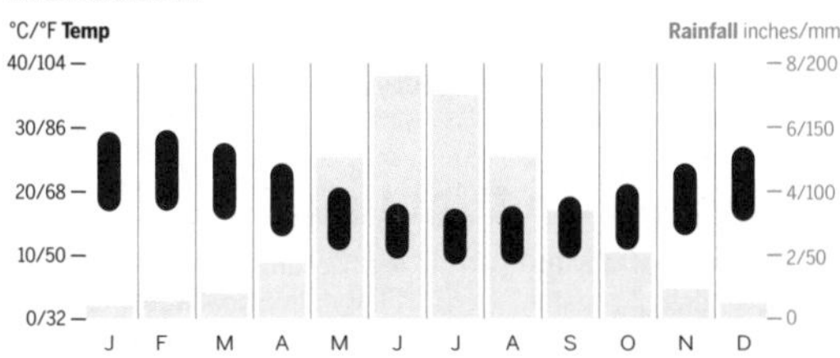

Mar Good beach weather and a fine time to spot thrombolites in Lake Clifton.

Jun Food and wine excellence at the Avon Valley Gourmet Food & Wine Festival.

Aug Wildflowers start to bloom; brave paddlers take on the Avon River Descent.

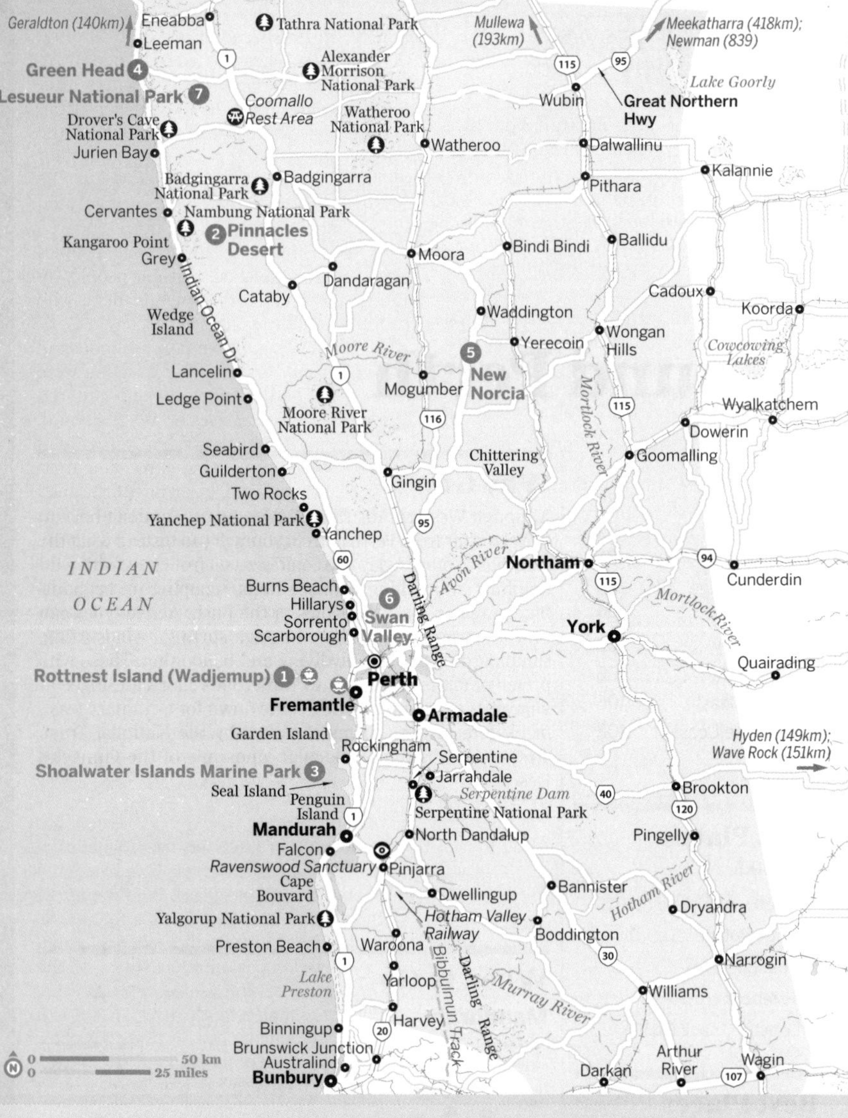

Around Perth Highlights

1. Cycling your way to a private slice of coastal paradise on **Rottnest Island** (Wadjemup; p89), then spending the afternoon swimming, sunning and snorkelling.
2. Enjoying a sublime sunset over the other-worldly **Pinnacles Desert** (p108).
3. Getting chipper with Flipper in **Shoalwater Islands Marine Park** (p94) off Rockingham.
4. Splashing about with sea lions at **Green Head** (p110).
5. Exploring the intriguing monastery town of **New Norcia** (p105).
6. Getting your foodie fix at the vineyards, breweries and artisan producers of the **Swan Valley** (p101).
7. Immersing yourself in the wonderful wildflowers of the **Lesueur National Park** (p108).

ROTTNEST ISLAND (WADJEMUP)

POP 475

'Rotto' has long been the family holiday playground of choice for Perth locals. Although it's only about 19km offshore from Fremantle, this car-free, off-the-grid slice of paradise, ringed by secluded beaches and bays, feels a million miles away.

Cycling around the 11km-long, 4.5km-wide island is a real pleasure, and it's easy to discover your own sandy beach. You're bound to spot quokkas, the island's only native land mammals. Also relatively common are New Zealand fur seals off magical West End, dolphins, and – in season – whales. King skinks are also common sunning themselves on the roads.

Snorkelling, fishing, surfing and diving are also all excellent on the island. There's not a lot to do here that's not outdoors, so postpone your day trip if the weather is bad. It can be quite unpleasant when the wind really kicks up.

Rotto is also the site of annual school leavers' and end-of-uni-exams parties, a time when the island is overrun by kids 'getting blotto on Rotto'. Depending on your age, it's either going to be the best time you've ever had or the worst – check the calendar before proceeding.

In early September, the annual **Rottofest** (www.rottofest.com.au) immerses the island in three days of music, film and comedy.

There is a fee per adult/child/family of $17/6/39.50 to visit the island. This fee is included in ferry costs.

History

The island was originally called Wadjemup (place across the water), but Wadjuk oral history recalls that it was joined to the mainland before being cut off by rising waters. Modern scientists date that occurrence to before 6500 years ago, making these memories some of the world's oldest. Archaeological finds suggest that the island was inhabited 30,000 years ago, but not after it was separated from the mainland.

Dutch explorer Willem de Vlamingh claimed discovery of the island in 1696 and named it Rotte-nest ('rat's nest', in Dutch) because of the king-sized 'rats' (which were actually quokkas) he saw there.

From 1838 it was used as a prison for Aboriginal men and boys from all around the state. At least 3670 people were incarcerated here, in harsh conditions, with around 370 dying (at least five were hanged). Although there were no new prisoners after 1903 (by which time holiday-makers from the mainland had already discovered the island), some existing prisoners served their sentences there until 1931. Even before the prison was built, Wadjemup was considered a 'place of the spirits', and it's been rendered even more sacred to Indigenous peoples because of the hundreds of their people, including prominent resistance leaders, who died there. Many avoid it to this day.

During WWI, approximately a thousand men of German or Austrian extraction were incarcerated here, their wives and children left to fend for themselves on the mainland. Ironically most of the 'Austrians' were actually Croats who objected to Austro-Hungarian rule of their homeland. Internment resumed during WWII, although at that time it was mainly WA's Italian population who were imprisoned.

There's an ongoing push to return the island to its original name. One suggested compromise is to adopt a dual name, Wadjemup/Rottnest.

Sights

Most of Rottnest's historic buildings, built mainly by Aboriginal prisoners, are grouped around Thomson Bay, where the ferry lands.

Quod HISTORIC SITE

(Kitson St) Built in 1864, this octagonal building with a central courtyard was once the Aboriginal prison block but is now part of the Rottnest Lodge hotel. During its time as a prison several men would share a 3m-by-1.7m cell, with no sanitation (most of the deaths here were due to disease). The only part of the complex that can be visited is a small whitewashed **chapel**. A weekly Sunday service is held at 9.30am.

Adjacent to the Quod is a wooded area where hundreds of Aboriginal prisoners are buried in **unmarked graves**. Until relatively recently, this area was used as a camping ground, but it's now fenced off with signs asking visitors to show respect to what is considered a sacred site. Plans are under way to convert the area into a memorial, in consultation with Aboriginal elders.

Rottnest Museum MUSEUM

(Kitson St; admission by gold-coin donation; ⏲ 11am-3.30pm) Housed in the old hay-store building, this little museum tells the island's natural

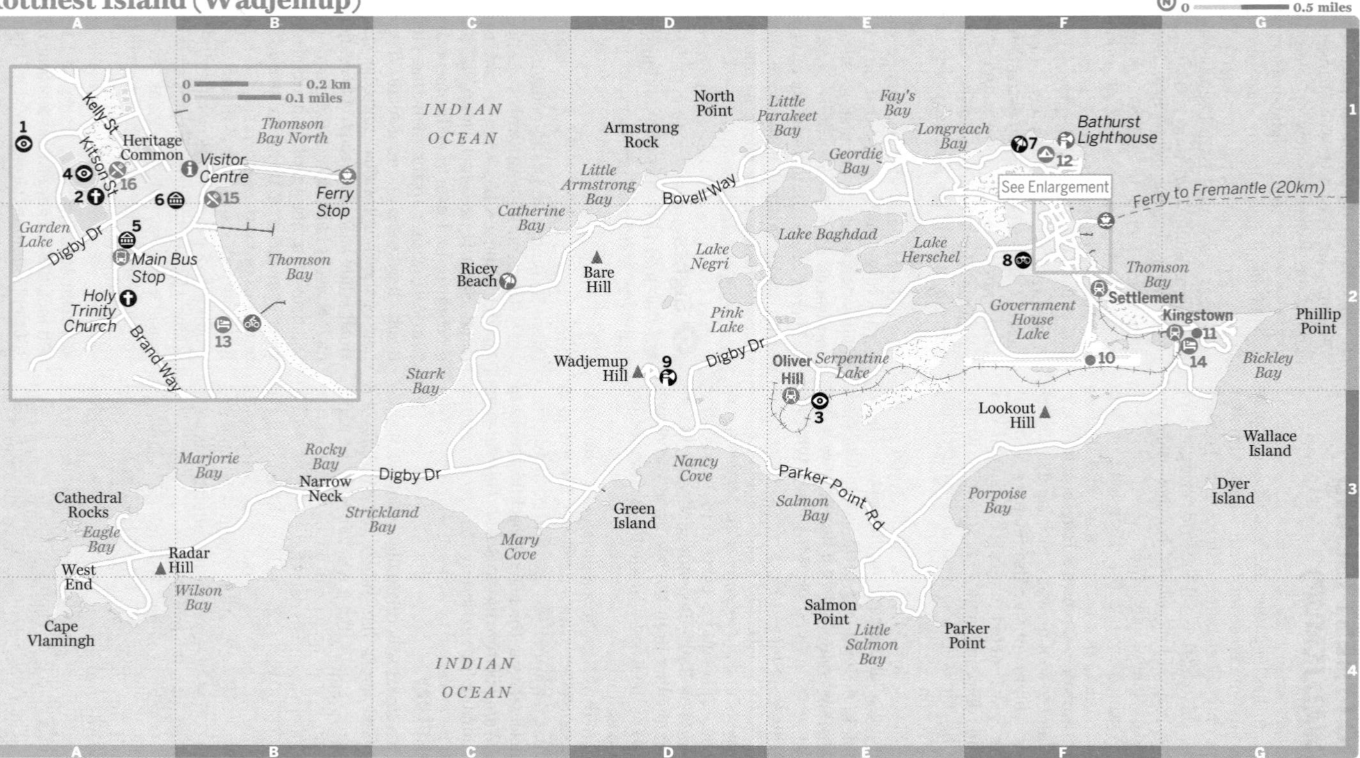
Rottnest Island (Wadjemup)
0 1 km
0 0.5 miles
INDIAN OCEAN
Armstrong Rock
North Point
Little Parakeet Bay
Fay's Bay
Longreach Bay
Bathurst Lighthouse
7
12
See Enlargement
Ferry to Fremantle (20km)
Little Armstrong Bay
Geordie Bay
Bovell Way
Catherine Bay
Lake Baghdad
Lake Herschel
8
Lake Negri
Thomson Bay
Settlement
Kingstown
11
14
Phillip Point
Ricey Beach
Bare Hill
Pink Lake
Government House Lake
Wadjemup Hill
9
Digby Dr
Oliver Hill
Serpentine Lake
10
Bickley Bay
Stark Bay
3
Lookout Hill
Wallace Island
Dyer Island
Marjorie Bay
Rocky Bay
Narrow Neck
Digby Dr
Nancy Cove
Parker Point Rd
Cathedral Rocks
Green Island
Salmon Bay
Porpoise Bay
Strickland Bay
Eagle Bay
Mary Cove
West End
Radar Hill
Wilson Bay
Cape Vlamingh
Salmon Point
Little Salmon Bay
Parker Point
INDIAN OCEAN
0 0.2 km
0 0.1 miles
1
Kelly St
Thomson Bay North
Heritage Common
Visitor Centre
4
Kitson St
16
Ferry Stop
2
6
15
Garden Lake
5
Digby Dr
Main Bus Stop
Thomson Bay
Holy Trinity Church
13
Brand Way

Rottnest Island (Wadjemup)

Sights
1 Aboriginal Burial Ground A1
2 Historic Chapel.. A1
3 Oliver Hill Battery E3
4 Quod A1
5 Rottnest Museum A2
6 Salt Store A1
7 The Basin F1
8 Vlamingh's Lookout...............................F2
9 Wadjemup Lighthouse D2

Activities, Courses & Tours
10 Rottnest Air Taxi F2
Rottnest Voluntary Guides ....(see 6)
11 Segway Tours G2

Sleeping
12 Allison Tentland F1
13 Hotel Rottnest...B2
14 Kingstown Barracks Youth Hostel G2
Rottnest Lodge .... (see 4)

Eating
15 Aristos.. B1
16 General Store A1
Hotel Rottnest...............................(see 13)
Riva.. (see 4)

and human history, warts and all, including dark tales of shipwrecks and incarceration.

Salt Store HISTORIC BUILDING
(Colebatch Ave) FREE A photographic exhibition in this 19th-century building looks at a different chapter of local history: when the island's salt lakes provided all of WA's salt (between 1838 and 1950). It's also the meeting point for walking tours.

Vlamingh's Lookout LOOKOUT
Not far away from Thomson Bay (go up past the old European cemetery), this unsigned vantage point offers panoramic views of the island, including its salt lakes. It's on View Hill, off Digby Dr.

Activities

Most visitors come for Rottnest's beaches and aquatic activities. **The Basin** is the most popular beach for family-friendly swimming as it's protected by a ring of reefs. Other popular spots are **Longreach Bay** and **Geordie Bay**, though there are many smaller secluded beaches such as **Little Parakeet Bay**.

Snorkelling & Diving

Excellent visibility, temperate waters, coral reefs and shipwrecks make Rottnest a top spot for scuba diving and snorkelling. There are snorkel trails with underwater plaques at Little Salmon Bay and Parker Point. The Basin, Little Parakeet Bay, Longreach Bay and Geordie Bay are also good. Rottnest Island Bike Hire (p93) has masks, snorkels and fins available, as well as kayaks, surfboards, paddleboards and scooters. The only wreck that is accessible to snorkellers without a boat is at Thomson Bay.

The Australasian Diving Academy (p57) organises wreck diving trips.

Surfing

The best surf breaks are at Strickland, Salmon and Stark Bays, towards the western end of the island.

Birdwatching

Rottnest is ideal for twitchers because of the varied habitats: coast, lakes, swamps, heath, woodlands and settlements. Coastal birds include pelicans, gannets, cormorants, bar-tailed godwits, whimbrels, fairy terns, bridled terns, crested terns, oystercatchers and majestic ospreys. For more, grab a copy of *A Bird's Eye View of Rottnest Island* from the visitor centre.

Tours

Check times online or at the Salt Store, or call the visitor centre.

Rottnest Voluntary Guides WALKING TOUR
(☎08-9372 9757; www.rvga.asn.au) FREE Free, themed walks leave from the central Salt Store daily, with topics including History, Reefs, Wrecks and Daring Sailors, Vlamingh Lookout and Salt Lakes, and the Quokka Walk. They also run tours of Wadjemup Lighthouse (adult/child $9/4) and Oliver Hill Gun & Tunnels (adult/child $9/4); you'll need to make your own way there for the last two.

Oliver Hill Train & Tour TRAIN RIDES
(www.rottnestisland.com; adult/child $29/16.50) The **Oliver Hill battery** was built in the 1930s and played a major role in the defence of the WA coastline and Fremantle harbour. This trip takes you by train to Oliver Hill (departing from the train station at 1.30pm) and includes the Gun & Tunnels tour run by Rottnest Voluntary Guides.

QUOKKAS

These cute little docile bundles of fur have suffered a number of indignities over the years. First Willem de Vlamingh's crew mistook them for rats as big as cats. Then the British settlers misheard and mangled their name (the Noongar word was probably *quak-a* or *gwaga*). But worst of all, a cruel trend of 'quokka soccer' by sadistic louts in the 1990s saw many kicked to death before a $10,000 fine was imposed; occasional cases are still reported. On a more positive note, the phenomenon of 'quokka selfies' briefly illuminated the internet in 2015 with various Rottnest marsupials achieving minor global fame on Instagram. Google 'Rottnest quokka selfies' to see the best of #quokkaselfie.

These marsupials of the macropod family (relatives of kangaroos and wallabies) were once found throughout the southwest but are now confined to mainland forests and a population of 8000 to 10,000 on Rottnest Island. Don't be surprised if one approaches looking for a titbit. Just say no, as human food isn't good for them.

Island Explorer Tour BUS TOUR
(www.rottnestisland.com; adult/child $20/12; departs every 1¼hr 8.45am-3pm) Handy hop-on, hop-off coach service stopping at 18 locations around the island. Includes a commentary and is a great way to get your bearings when you first arrive.

Rottnest Adventure Tour CRUISE
(www.rottnestexpress.com.au; adult/child $55/27; mid-Sep–late Apr) Ninety-minute cruises around the coast with a special emphasis on spotting wildlife. Packages are also available from Perth (adult/child $152/78) and Fremantle (adult/child $132/68). Check the website for other options including the Discover Rottnest coach tour and the Eco-Express snorkelling tour. From mid-September to late November two-hour whale-watching tours (adult/child ex Perth $77/34) are on offer.

Charter 1 SAILING
(0428 604 794; www.charter1.com.au; mid-Sep–Apr) Briny excursions departing from Fremantle include full-day sails (adult/child $229/149) including kayaking and snorkelling; guided snorkelling eco-tours ($129); and two-hour twilight sails (adult/child $48/29) leaving from Thompson Bay on Rottnest Island. Bring your own (BYO) chilled beverages for the sunset cruise.

Rottnest Air Taxi SCENIC FLIGHTS
(0411 264 547, 1800 500 006; www.rottnest.de) Ten-minute flights over the island ($45).

Segway Tours SEGWAY
(1300 808 180; www.segwaytourswa.com; cnr Kingstown Rd & Hospital Lane, Kingstown Barracks; 1hr/90min $89/129; tours depart 9am, 11am, 12.30pm & 2pm) Choose from the 90-minute Fortress Adventure Tour or the one-hour Kingstown Explorer option.

Sleeping

Rotto is wildly popular in summer and during school holidays, when accommodation is booked out for months in advance. Prices can rise steeply at these times. Check websites for off-peak deals combining transport to the island, especially when incorporating a weekday visit.

Kingstown Barracks Youth Hostel HOSTEL $
(08-9432 9111; www.rottnestisland.com; dm/f $51/111) This hostel is located in old army barracks that still have a rather institutional feel, and few facilities. Check in at the visitor centre before you make the 1.8km walk, bike or bus trip to Kingston.

Allison Tentland CAMPGROUND $
(08-9432 9111; www.rottnestisland.com; Thomson Bay; sites $36) Camping on the island is restricted to this leafy camping ground with barbecues. Be vigilant about your belongings, especially your food – cheeky quokkas have been known to help themselves.

Rottnest Island Authority Cottages COTTAGES $$
(08-9432 9111; www.rottnestisland.com; cottages $114-256) There are more than 250 villas and cottages for rent around the island. Some have magnificent beachfront positions and are palatial; others are more like beach shacks. Prices rise by around $60 for Friday and Saturday nights, and they shoot up by up to $120 in peak season (late September to April). Check online for the labyrinthine pricing schedule.

Rottnest Lodge HOTEL $$
(08-9292 5161; www.rottnestlodge.com.au; Kitson St; r $210-320;) It's claimed there are

ghosts in this comfortable complex, which is based around the former Quod and boys' reformatory school. If that worries you, ask for a room in the new section, looking onto a salt lake. The lodge's Riva restaurant (p93) channels Italian flavours amid the island's vaguely Mediterranean ambience, especially noticable when the sun is shining.

Hotel Rottnest HOTEL **$$$**
(08-9292 5011; www.hotelrottnest.com.au; 1 Bedford Ave; r $270-320;) Based around the former summer-holiday pad for the state's governors (built in 1864) the former Quokka Arms has been completely transformed by a stylish renovation. The whiter-than-white rooms in an adjoining building are smart and modern, if a tad pricey. Some have beautiful sea views.

Eating & Drinking

Most visitors to Rotto self-cater. The **general store** (www.rottnestgeneralstore.com.au) is like a small supermarket (and also stocks liquor), but if you're staying a while, you're better to bring supplies with you. Another option is to preorder food from the general store, and they'll equip your accommodation with food and drinks before your arrival.

Hotel Rottnest PUB FOOD **$$**
(www.hotelrottnest.com.au; 1 Bedford Ave; mains $25-38, pizza $20-26; 11am-late) It's hard to imagine a more inviting place for a sunset pint of Little Creatures than the astroturf 'lawn' of this chic waterfront hotel. A big glass pavilion creates an open and inviting space, and bistro-style food and pizzas are reasonably priced given the location and ambience. Bands and DJs regularly boost the laid-back island mood during summer.

Riva SEAFOOD **$$**
(Rottnest Lodge, Kitson St; lunch $18-20, dinner $24-38; noon-late) Classy Italian restaurant with a strong focus on grills and seafood. Prawns and salmon both receive an elegant touch of the Med, and there are also wood-fired pizzas and interesting spins on chicken and lamb.

Aristos SEAFOOD **$$$**
(www.aristosrottnest.com.au; Colebatch Ave; breakfast $10-23, lunch & dinner mains $27-49; 8am-late) An upmarket, but pricey, option for seafood, steaks and salads, fish and chips, burgers, ice cream or excellent coffee. Push the boat (way) out with a seafood platter for two people ($134).

Information

At the Thomson Bay settlement, behind the main jetty, there's a shopping area with an ATM.

Ranger (08-9372 9788) For fishing and boating information.

Visitor Centre (08-9372 9732; www.rottnestisland.com; Thomson Bay; 7.30am-5pm Sat-Thu, 7.30am-7pm Fri, extended hours in summer) Handles check-ins for all of the island authority's accommodation. There's a bookings counter at the Fremantle office (Map p78; 08-9432 9300; www.rottnestisland.com; E Shed, Victoria Quay), near where the ferry departs.

Getting There & Away

AIR

Rottnest Air-Taxi (0411 264 547; www.rottnest.de) Flies from Jandakot airport in four-seater (one way/same-day return/extended return $260/360/460) or six-seater planes (one-way/same-day/extended return $380/480/580). Prices include up to three passengers in the four-seater and five passengers in the six-seater.

BOAT

Rottnest Express (1300 467 688; www.rottnestexpress.com.au) Fremantle (B Shed, Victoria Quay; adult/child $83.50/47); Northport (Map p50; 1 Emma Pl, Northport, Rous Head; adult/child $83.50/47); Perth (Map p54; Pier 2, Barrack St Jetty; adult/child $103.50/57) Prices listed are for return day trips and include the island admission fee. Ferry schedules are seasonal, though those listed here are roughly the minimum: Perth (1¾ hours, once daily), Fremantle (30 minutes, five times daily) and North Fremantle (30 minutes, three times daily). Packages, including bike hire, snorkelling equipment, meals, accommodation and tours, are all available. The Perth and Fremantle departure points are handy to train stations.

Rottnest Fast Ferries (08-9246 1039; www.rottnestfastferries.com.au; adult/child $85/48.50) Departs from Hillarys Boat Harbour (40 minutes; three times daily), around 40 minutes' drive north of Perth. See www.hillarysboatharbour.com.au for public transport details. An additional 6pm ferry departs on Friday nights over summer. Packages also available.

Getting Around

BIKE

Rottnest is just big enough (and with enough hills) to make a day's ride good exercise.

Bikes can be booked in advance online or on arrival through **Rottnest Island Bike Hire** (☎08-9292 5105; www.rottnestisland.com; cnr Bedford Ave & Welch Way; per hour $13, 1/2/3/4/5 days $32/45/56/67/79; ⏰8.30am-4pm, to 5.30pm summer). Photo ID must be shown.

The ferry companies also hire bikes as part of an island package, and have them waiting for visitors on arrival. The visitor centre also hires bikes.

BUS

A free shuttle runs between Thomson Bay, the main accommodation areas and the airport, departing roughly every 35 minutes, with the last bus at 8pm.

The Island Explorer (p92) is a handy hop-on, hop-off coach service stopping at 18 locations around the island. It includes a commentary and is a great way to get your bearings when you first arrive. Between Geordie Bay and Thomson Bay it's free.

ROCKINGHAM

POP 100,000

Just 46km south of Perth, Rockingham's main attractions are good beaches and the Shoalwater Islands Marine Park, where you can observe dolphins, sea lions and penguins in the wild.

Rockingham was founded in 1872 as a port, although this function was taken over by Fremantle in the 1890s. There's still a substantial industrial complex to the north, at Kwinana.

Most places of interest are stretched along Rockingham Beach.

Sights & Activities

Shoalwater Islands Marine Park NATURE RESERVE

(www.marineparks.wa.gov.au; ⏰closed for nesting Jun–mid-Sep) Just a few minutes' paddle, swim or boat ride away from the shore is strictly protected **Penguin Island**, home to penguins, silver gulls, boardwalks, swimming beaches and picnic tables. Apart from birdwatching (pied cormorants, pelicans, crested and bridled terns, oystercatchers), day visitors can also swim and snorkel.

The **Penguin Island ferry** (Mersey Point Jetty; adult/child $15/12.50; ⏰hourly 9am-3pm mid-Sep–May) is run by Rockingham Wild Encounters (p58). Tickets that combine the ferry with entry to the penguin feeding at the island's discovery centre (adult/child $23/18.50) are available.

At low tide it's possible to wade the few hundred metres to the island across the sandbar. However, take heed of warning signs, as people have drowned here after being washed off the bar during strong winds and high tides.

West Coast Dive Park DIVING

(www.westcoastdivepark.com.au; permits per day/week $25/50) Diving within the Shoalwater Islands Marine Park became even more interesting after the sinking of the *Saxon Ranger*, a supposedly jinxed 400-tonne fishing vessel. Permits to dive at this site are available from the visitor centre. Contact the Australasian Diving Academy (p57) about expeditions to this and the wrecks of three other boats, two planes and various reefs in the vicinity.

Tours

Capricorn Seakayaking KAYAKING

(☎0427 485 123; www.capricornseakayaking.com.au; incl pick up at Rockingham train station $169; ⏰late-Sep–late Apr) Runs full-day sea-kayaking tours around Penguin and Seal Islands. Also includes wildlife watching and snorkelling.

Eating

Pengo's Cafe CAFE $

(153 Arcadia Dr; snacks & mains $8-20; ⏰8am-4.30pm Sep-May, reduced hours in winter) Good coffee, gourmet burgers and fresh salads shine at this excellent cafe near the Rockingham Wild Encounters ticket office. There's a nice alfresco deck and lots of grass for the kids to run around on.

Rustico CAFE $$

(www.rusticotapas.com.au; 61 Rockingham Beach Rd; shared plates $14-25, pizzas $17; ⏰noon-late) This stylish cafe is renowned for its authentic Spanish-style tapas. Secure a seat on the expansive corner terrace with ocean views, and tuck into free-range pork belly or scallops with chorizo. Good pizzas and larger shared plates are also available.

Information

Visitor Centre (☎08-9592 3464; www.rockinghamvisitorcentre.com.au; 19 Kent St; ⏰9am-5pm; @) Accommodation listings if you want to stay overnight.

Getting There & Around

Rockingham sits within Zone 5 of the Perth public transport system, **Transperth** (☎13 62 13; www.transperth.wa.gov.au). Regular trains depart from Rockingham station, via the Mandurah line, to Perth Underground/Esplanade ($7.70, 34 minutes) and Mandurah ($5.20, 18 minutes).

Rockingham station is around 4km southeast of Rockingham Beach and around 6km east of Mersey Point, from where the Penguin Island ferries depart; catch bus 551 or 555 to the beach or stay on the 551 to Mersey Point.

HEADING SOUTH

The fastest and simplest route south from Central Perth is to jump on the Kwinana Fwy. Rather than visiting Rockingham and the Peel Region as separate day trips, you could turn them into a 220km loop: Perth–Rockingham–Mandurah–Pinjarra–Dwellingup–Jarrahdale–Perth. A good overnight stop is Mandurah.

PEEL REGION

Taking in swaths of jarrah forest, historic towns and the increasingly glitzy coastal resort of Mandurah, the Peel Region can easily be tackled as a day trip from Perth or as the first stopping point of a longer expedition down the South Western Hwy (Rte 1).

As you enter the Peel, you'll pass out of Wadjuk country and into that of their fellow Noongar neighbours, the Pinjarup (or Binjareb) people.

Mandurah

POP 80,000

Shrugging off its fusty retirement-haven image, Mandurah has made concerted efforts to reinvent itself as an upmarket beach resort, taking advantage of its new train link to Perth's public-transport network. And, although its linked set of redeveloped 'precincts' and 'quarters' may sound a little pretentious, the overall effect is actually pretty cool. You can wander along the waterfront from the Ocean Marina (boats, cafes and the Dolphin Quay indoor market), past the Venetian Canals (glitzy apartments linked by Venetian-ish sandstone bridges), through the Boardwalk and Cultural Precinct (more eateries, visitor centre, cinema, arts centre), to the Bridge Quarter (still more restaurants and bars).

The bridge spans the Mandurah Estuary, which sits between the ocean and the large body of water known as the Peel Inlet. It's one of the best places in the region for fishing, crabbing, prawning (March and April) and dolphin spotting.

Sights & Activities

Several beautiful beaches are within walking distance of the Mandurah waterfront. **Town Beach** is just across from the marina, at the southern end of Silver Sands – perhaps the best of the ocean beaches. There's a designated, boat-free swimming area on the far side of the estuary, just north of Mandurah Bridge. Here dolphins have been known to swim up to unwitting kids for a frolic. Facing the ocean, west of the mouth of the estuary, is family-friendly **Doddi's Beach**.

Mandurah Cruises CRUISE
(☎08-9581 1242; www.mandurahcruises.com.au; Boardwalk) Take a one-hour Dolphin & Scenic Canal Cruise (adult/child $28/14; departs on the hour from 10am to 4pm), a half-day Murray River Lunch Cruise (adult/child $79/49; September to May) and, through December, a one-hour Christmas Lights Canal Cruise (adult/child $30/15), that gawps at millionaires' mansions under the pretence of admiring their festive displays. Other cruise options incorporate catching and cooking Mandurah's famous blue manna crabs, and a heritage cruise highlighting the region's history.

Mandurah Boat & Bike Hire BOATING, CYCLING
(☎08-9535 5877; www.mandurahboatandbikehire.com.au; Boardwalk) Chase the fish on a four-seat dinghy or six-seat pontoon (per hour/day from $50/320). Also hires out bikes (per hour/day $10/33).

Sleeping

Mandurah Ocean Marina Chalets MOTEL **$$**
(☎08-9535 8173; www.marinachalets.com.au; 6 The Lido; studios & chalets $116-176; P ❄ ☜) The ambience is a bit like a British holiday camp, but the chalets and motel units are spotless and modern with fully equipped kitchens. There's a shared barbecue area and crab-cooking facility, and the canals and restaurants of Ocean Marina and Dolphin Quay are a short walk away.

Seashells Resort RESORT $$
(08-9550 3000; www.seashells.com.au; 16 Dolphin Dr; apt from $216;) Seashells' apartments are cool and spacious, there's a beach on its doorstep and a lovely infinity-lipped pool just metres away. Check into one of its luxury beachfront villas and you may not want to leave.

Eating & Drinking

Restaurants and cafes abound on the Boardwalk and Dolphin Quay.

Cafe Moka CAFE $$
(www.cafemoka.com.au; Dolphin Quay; breakfast $12-20, lunch $13-28; 8am-4pm) Mandurah's best brekky option is well positioned to soak up the morning sun on the edge of the marina.

M on the Point RESTAURANT $$
(www.mbarandrestaurant.com.au; 1 Marco Polo Dr; pizzas $19-21, mains $24-39; noon-late) The classy bars and restaurants beneath the Sebel are the perfect place for a Sunday sundowner. Either kick back with a cold one and a gourmet pizza, or try sophisticated food such as grilled barramundi with a prawn wonton and yellow curry in the restaurant.

Taste & Graze CAFE $$
(www.tasteandgraze.com.au; Shop 3/4, 16 Mandurah Tce; shared plates & mains $14-32; 8am-4pm Sun-Wed, 5pm-late Thu-Sat) Back in town in 'old' Mandurah, and perfectly located to catch the afternoon sun. Outdoor seating and a versatile Modern Australian menu covering breakfast, lunch and shared smaller plates make this a cosmopolitan slice of cafe cool.

Taku Japanese Kitchen JAPANESE $$
(Scott's Plaza, Shop 2, 52 Mandurah Tce; mains $10-19; 11.30am-2.30pm & 5-9pm Tue-Sun) Located out of Mandurah's tourist glitz, this friendly family-run operation across the road from Mandurah's town beach turns out excellent tempura, sashimi and sushi.

Brighton Hotel PUB
(www.brightonmandurah.com.au; 10-12 Mandurah Tce) Watch the sun set over the estuary with a glass of wine, and return after 8pm on the weekends to move to the DJs.

Information

Visitor Centre (08-9550 3999; www.visitmandurah.com; 75 Mandurah Tce; 9am-5pm;) On the estuary boardwalk.

Getting There & Away

Mandurah is 72km from central Perth; take the Kwinana Fwy and follow the signs.

TRAIN

Mandurah sits within the outermost zone (7) of the Perth public-transport system and is the terminus of Transperth's Mandurah line. There are direct trains from Mandurah to Perth Underground/Esplanade ($10.20, 50 minutes) and Rockingham ($7.70, 18 minutes).

BUS

Transwa (1300 662 205; www.transwa.wa.gov.au) coach routes include the following:

- SW1 (12 per week) to East Perth ($17, 1½ hours), Bunbury ($17, two hours), Busselton ($25, 2¾ hours), Margaret River ($34, four hours) and Augusta ($37, 4¾ hours)
- SW2 (thrice weekly) to Balingup ($28, three hours), Bridgetown ($32, 3½ hours) and Pemberton ($43, 4½ hours)
- GS3 (weekly) to Denmark ($66, 7¼ hours) and Albany ($72, eight hours)

South West Coach Lines (08-9261 7600; www.transdevsw.com.au) has services to/from Perth's Esplanade Busport ($22, 1¼ hours, twice daily), Bunbury ($22, 1¼ hours, twice daily), Busselton ($22, 2½ hours, daily), Dunsborough ($22, 3¼ hours, daily) and Bridgetown ($32, 3¼ hours, weekdays).

Yalgorup National Park

Fifty kilometres south of Mandurah is this beautiful 120-sq-km coastal park, consisting of 10 tranquil lakes and their surrounding woodlands and sand dunes. The park is recognised as a wetland of international significance for seasonally migrating water birds, with 130 species identified.

Amateur scientists can visit the distinctive **thrombolites** of Lake Clifton, which are descendants of the earliest living organisms on earth (they are the only life form known to have existed over 650 million years ago). These rocklike structures are most easily seen when the water is low, particularly during March and April. There's a viewing platform on Mt John Rd off Old Coast Rd; keep an eye out for long-neck tortoises below the boardwalk. A 5km **walking track** starts from here and loops around the lake.

The **Lake Pollard trail** (6km) begins about 8km down Preston Beach North Rd (not Preston Beach Rd, as marked on some maps). The pleasant Martins Tank Lake campground is just to the right of the trail's entrance. The trail takes in tuart, jarrah and bull banksia on its way to the lake, which is also known for its black swans (October to March).

The **Heathlands trail** (4.5km) to Lake Preston starts at the information bay on Preston Beach Rd (before the turn-off to Preston Beach North Rd) and explores the tuart woodland. Further along Preston Beach Rd is **Preston Beach**.

Dwellingup

POP 550

Dwellingup is a small, forest-shrouded township with character, 100km south of Perth. Its reputation as an activity hub has been enhanced by the hardy long-distance walkers and cyclists passing through on the Bibbulmun Track and the Munda Biddi Trail respectively.

Sights & Activities

Forest Heritage Centre NATURE RESERVE
(www.forestheritagecentre.com.au; 1 Acacia St; adult/child $5.50/2.20; 10am-3pm) Set within the jarrah forest, this interesting rammed-earth building takes the shape of three interlinked gum leaves. Inside are displays about the forest's flora and fauna, and a shop that sells beautiful pieces crafted by the resident woodwork artists. Short marked trails lead into the forest, including an 11m-high canopy walk.

Hotham Valley Railway HISTORIC TRAIN
(08-6278 1111; www.hothamvalleyrailway.com.au; Forest Train adult/child $24/12, Restaurant Train $79, Steam Ranger adult/child $34/17; Forest Train departs 10.30am & 2pm Sat & Sun, Restaurant Train departs 7.45pm Sat, Steam Ranger departs 10.30am & 2pm Sun May-Oct) On weekends (and Tuesdays and Thursdays during school holidays), the Dwellingup **Forest Train** chugs along 8km of forest track on a 90-minute return trip. Every Saturday night and some Fridays, the **Restaurant Train** follows the same route, serving up a five-course meal in a 1919 dining car. A third option is the **Steam Ranger**, travelling 14km via Western Australia's steepest rail incline to Isandra Siding.

Dwellingup Adventures ADVENTURE SPORTS
(08-9538 1127; www.dwellingupadventures.com.au; cnr Marrinup & Newton St; 1-person kayaks & 2-person canoes per 3hr $30; 8.30am-5pm) Don't miss the opportunity to get out on the beautiful Murray River. Hire camping gear, bikes, kayaks and canoes, or take an assisted, self-guided paddling (full day per one-person kayak $107) or cycling tour (full day per one/two/three people $107/140/198). White-water rafting tours (per person $150) are available from June to October.

Information

Visitor Centre (08-9538 1108; www.murraytourism.com.au; Marrinup St; 9am-3pm) Interesting displays about the 1961 bushfires that wiped out the town, destroying 75 houses but taking no lives.

Jarrahdale & Serpentine National Park

POP 956

Established in 1871, Jarrahdale is an old mill village reached by a leafy 6km drive east from the South Western Hwy. The **Old Post Office** (www.jarrahdale.com; guided walk $5; 10am-2pm Sat, 10am-4pm Sun), built in 1896, houses a small local museum. Guided walks run by volunteers from the heritage society depart from here.

Picturesque Millbrook Winery has a tranquil setting overlooking a small lake. Lunch bookings are recommended, especially on weekends.

Jarrahdale sits on the northern fringes of **Serpentine National Park** (www.parks.dpaw.wa.gov.au; per car $12; 8.30am-5pm), a forested area with walking tracks, picnic areas and a leisurely 15m slide of water known as the **Serpentine Falls** (Falls Rd, off South Western Hwy). If you're in no hurry, take a pleasant detour through the park from Jarrahdale, following Kingsbury Dr to the **Serpentine Dam** before curving back to the highway.

DRYANDRA TO HYDEN

A beautiful forest, rare marsupials, stunning ancient granite-rock formations, salt lakes, interesting back roads and the unique Wave Rock are the scattered highlights of this widespread farming region.

Hyden & Wave Rock

Large granite outcrops dot the Central and Southern Wheat Belts, and the most famous of these is the multicoloured cresting swell of **Wave Rock**, 350km from Perth. Formed some 60 million years ago by weathering and water erosion, Wave Rock is streaked with colours created by run-off from local mineral springs.

To get the most out of Wave Rock, obtain the *Walk Trails at Wave Rock and The Humps* brochure from the **visitor centre** (☎08-9880 5182; www.waverock.com.au; Wave Rock; ⏲9am-5pm). Park at Hippos Yawn (no fee) and follow the shady track back along the rock base to Wave Rock (1km).

Sleeping

Wave Rock Cabins & Caravan Park CABIN $
(☎08-9880 5022; www.waverock.com.au; unpowered/powered sites from $28/35, cabins from $140, cottages from $160;) Accommodation can fill up quickly, so phone ahead for a spot amid the gum trees at Wave Rock Cabins & Caravan Park.

Wave Rock Motel MOTEL $$
(☎08-9880 5052; www.waverock.com.au; 2 Lynch St, Hyden; s/d from $105/150;) In Hyden, 4km east of Wave Rock, the Wave Rock Motel has well-equipped rooms, a comfy lounge with fireplace, and an indoor bush bistro.

Getting There & Away

This area is best seen with your own vehicle, ideally on the way to somewhere else. If heading to/from the Nullarbor, take the 300km unsealed direct Hyden–Norseman road, which will save 100km or so. Look for the brochure *The Granite and Woodlands Discovery Trail* at the Norseman or Wave Rock visitor centres.

ROCK & ROLL

At 350km from Perth, Wave Rock is a rather long day trip, and some people are disappointed by what's really a one-trick gig. However, you can spice up this trip by hunting out other, lesser-known granite outcrops and curiosities. All you need is a map and a sense of adventure. (Hint: most of the granite outcrops end in 'Rock'.) To get you started, try Kokerbin Rock, Jilakin Rock, Dragon Rocks and Yorkrakine Rock. Visitor centres en route can supply maps.

Transwa (☎1300 662 205; www.transwa.wa.gov.au) runs a bus from Perth to Hyden ($51, five hours) and on to Esperance ($53, five hours) every Tuesday, returning on Thursday. **Western Travel Bug** (☎08-9486 4222; www.travelbug.com.au; tours $185) offers a very long one-day tour or, alternatively, you could see it as part of a six-day southwest loop with **Western Xposure** (☎08-9414 8423; www.westernxposure.com.au; tours $770).

DARLING RANGE

Commonly known as the Perth Hills, this forest-covered escarpment provides the city with a green backdrop and offers great spots for picnicking, barbecues, bushwalking and rubbing shoulders with wild kangaroos. Leafy suburbs nestle at its feet, along with a few dozen wineries.

Kalamunda

POP 59,700

Kalamunda is a well-heeled township on the crest of the Darling Range. The area began as a timber settlement, but it's since become a quieter residential haven close to the city (it's a 30-minute drive from Perth).

The main shopping area on Haynes St has good pubs and cafes. Nearby is **Stirk Cottage** (www.kalamundahistoricalsociety.com; Kalamunda Rd; ⏲2-4pm Sun) FREE, built of mud, saplings and shingle in 1881.

For walkers, Kalamunda is the northern terminus of the **Bibbulmun Track**, which starts near the shops and heads into the forest of **Kalamunda National Park**.

From Zig-Zag Dr, just north of Kalamunda off Lascelles Pde, there are fantastic views over Perth to the coast. The drive through the forested hills to Mundaring via Mundaring Weir Rd is also wonderful, but watch out for kangaroos.

Getting There & Away

From Perth, buses 283, 295, 296, 298 and 299 all head to Kalamunda ($5.20, 47 minutes).

Mundaring

POP 38,300

Located 35km east of Perth, Mundaring is a laid-back spot with a small artistic community. Bisected by the busy Great Eastern Hwy, the township itself isn't particularly interesting, but the **Mundaring Arts Centre** (www.mundaringartscentre.com.au; 7190 Great Eastern

WORTH A TRIP

DRYANDRA WOODLAND

With small populations of threatened numbats, woylies and tammar wallabies, this isolated remnant of eucalypt forest 164km southeast of Perth hints at what the wheat belt was like before large-scale land clearing and feral predators wreaked havoc on local ecosystems. With numerous walking trails, it makes a great getaway from Perth.

The excellent **Barna Mia Animal Sanctuary**, home to endangered bilbies, boodies, woylies and marla, conducts 90-minute after-dark torchlight tours, providing a rare opportunity to see these creatures up close. Book through **Parks & Wildlife** (08-9881 9222; www.parks.dpaw.wa.gov.au; 7 Wald St, Narrogin; adult/child/family $14/7.50/37.50; 8.30am-4pm) for post-sunset tours on Monday, Wednesday, Friday and Saturday, and book early for peak periods.

While you can hoist your tent at the **Congelin Camp Ground** (08-9881 9200; adult/child $7.50/2.20), Dryandra is one place you should splurge. The **Lions Dryandra Village** (08-9884 5231; www.dryandravillage.org.au; adult/child $30/15, 2-/4-person cabins $70/90, 8-12 person cabins $130) is a 1920s forestry camp offering self-contained, renovated woodcutters' cabins complete with fridge, stove, fireplace, en suite and nearby grazing wallabies. Narrogin, serviced by Transwa buses, is 22km southeast.

Hwy; 10am-5pm Tue-Fri, 11am-3pm Sat & Sun) exhibits and sells the work of local artists.

Sights & Activities

John Forrest National Park NATIONAL PARK

(www.parks.dpaw.wa.gov.au; admission per car $12) The 16-sq-km John Forrest National Park, west of Mundaring, was the state's first national park. Protected areas of jarrah and marri trees are scattered about granite outcrops, waterfalls and a pool.

Beelu National Park NATIONAL PARK

(www.parks.dpaw.wa.gov.au) Immediately south of Mundaring is Beelu National Park, part of a continuous swath of forest that includes Kalamunda National Park. The **Perth Hills National Parks Centre** (08-9295 2244; www.dpaw.wa.gov.au; Allens Rd, off Mundaring Weir Rd; 9am-4pm) hosts Nearer to Nature kids' programs with a flora and fauna spin. There's a good **campground** (adult/child $7.50/2.20), well positioned for the Bibbulmun Track, which passes nearby.

From November to April, kick back in a deck chair at the open-air **Kookaburra Cinema** (08-9295 6190; www.kookaburracinema.com.au; Allen Rd; adult/child $15/10), just across the road from the park centre.

Mundaring Weir DAM

South of Beelu National Park is Mundaring Weir, a dam built 100 years ago to supply water to the goldfields more than 500km to the east. The reservoir is a blissful spot, with walking trails and a well-positioned pub. Come dusk, the whole area swarms with kangaroos.

Lake Leschenaultia LAKE

(8.30am-dusk) East of Mundaring and north of the Great Eastern Hwy, near Chidlow, is freshwater Lake Leschenaultia, a picturesque former railway dam, complete with a swimming pontoon.

Sleeping

Mundaring Weir Hotel HOTEL $

(08-9295 1106; www.mundaringweirhotel.com.au; Weir Village Rd; r $115-140;) Overlooking the weir, this 1898 pub has bucket loads of ramshackle character. Rooms are simple but tidy, with DVD players and microwaves. The rooms also open onto an amphitheatre, which mainly functions as a beer garden but occasionally hosts concerts.

Information

Visitor Centre (08-9295 0202; www.mundaringtourism.com.au; 7225 Great Eastern Hwy; 9.30am-4pm Mon-Sat, 10.30am-2.30pm Sun) Good for accommodation bookings including B&Bs and lodges in the Perth Hills.

Getting There & Away

You can reach Mundaring from Perth on public transport in just over an hour, by taking a train to Midland and then bus 320 ($6.20). From town it's another 6km to Mundaring Weir.

SWAN VALLEY

Perthites love to swan around this semirural valley on the city's eastern fringe to partake in the finer things in life: booze, nosh

ARALUEN BOTANIC PARK

South of Kalamunda, just off Brookton Hwy, is **Araluen Botanic Park** (www.araluenbotanicpark.com.au; 362 Croyden Rd, Roleystone; adult/child $4/2; ⏲9am-6pm). Constructed in the 1920s by the Young Australia League (YAL) as a bush retreat, the park was neglected for years and became overgrown. The state government purchased it in 1990 and has since restored its elaborate garden terraces, waterfalls and ornamental pool. The spring tulip displays are wonderful.

and the great outdoors. Perhaps in tacit acknowledgement that its wines will never compete with the state's more prestigious regions (it doesn't really have the ideal climate), the Swan Valley compensates with plenty of galleries, breweries, provedores and restaurants.

Guildford

The gateway to the Swan Valley is the National Trust–classified town of Guildford, established in 1829 around the same time as Perth and Fremantle. A clutch of interesting old buildings, one housing the visitor centre, make it the logical starting place for day trippers. Guildford is only 12km from central Perth and is well served by suburban trains.

History

Guildford is built on the confluence of three rivers and was an important meeting and ceremonial place for the Wadjuk people. When the British arrived and travelled up the Swan, access to fresh water led them to establish one of their first settlements here. In 1833, four years after the colony's founding, resistance leader Yagan was shot and decapitated in the Swan Valley.

The fertile valley land was soon being used for farming. Vines were first planted in the 1830s at Houghton's, but it was after the arrival of Croatian settlers (from around 1916) that the farmland was increasingly transformed into wine production.

Sights

The centre of Guildford town is Stirling Sq, at the intersection of Swan and Meadow Sts. The cluster of buildings opposite the square includes the **Old Courthouse** (1866), which houses the visitor centre and has interesting historical displays. In the same grounds are the **gaol** (Old Courthouse; adult/child $4/free; ⏲9.30am-2pm Wed & Fri, 9am-12.30pm Sat) and **Taylor's Cottage** (1863; admission included with gaol entry). Various **heritage walks** start from here; get information from the visitor centre or download a trail card from its website. Two kilometres east is **Woodbridge House** (Ford St; adult/child $5/3; ⏲1-4pm Thu-Sun), an 1885 colonial mansion overlooking the river.

Eating

Jezebelle CAFE $$
(☎08-6278 3538; www.jezebelle.com.au; 127 James St; tapas & shared plates $16-34, breakfast $14-26; ⏲noon-late Wed-Fri, 7am-10pm Sat, 7am-6pm Sun) An exciting selection of WA, Spanish and Italian wines partner with interesting tapas and shared plates at Guildford's Jezebelle. Try the Manchego cheese and capsicum croquettes with sweetcorn relish, or chicken and rabbit paella. Leisurely weekend breakfasts are equally classy.

Rose & Crown PUB FOOD $$
(www.rosecrown.com.au; 105 Swan St; mains $25-38) WA's oldest still-operating pub (1841) has a wonderful leafy beer garden and lots of different spaces to explore inside. Have a beer in the cellar bar, where there's a convict-built well, and check out the sealed-off tunnel that used to connect the hotel with the river.

Information

Visitor Centre (☎08-9379 9400; www.swanvalley.com.au; Old Courthouse, cnr Swan & Meadow Sts; ⏲9am-4pm) Information and maps, plus an interesting display on local history.

Getting There & Away

Guildford falls within Zone 2 of Perth's public transport system, and it's only $4.40 to get here by bus or by train on the Midland Line from Perth, East Perth or Mt Lawley stations.

Elsewhere in the Swan Valley

The Swan Valley vibe is more low-key and relaxed than Margaret River. There are more than 40 vineyards, concentrated mainly along busy West Swan Rd (the road leading north from the Guildford visitor centre) and the Great Northern Hwy (running parallel to the east). Look for the free *Food & Wine Trail Guide* at the Guildford visitor centre.

Sights

Gomboc Gallery GALLERY
(www.gomboc-gallery.com.au; 50 James Rd, Middle Swan; ⏲10am-5pm Wed-Sun) FREE One of WA's best commercial galleries, surrounded by an intriguing sculpture park.

Whiteman Park PARK
(www.whitemanpark.com; enter from Lord St or Beechboro Rd, West Swan; ⏲8.30am-6pm) Located in Caversham in West Swan, at 26 sq km this is Perth's biggest park, with over 30km of walkways and bike paths, and numerous picnic and barbecue spots. There are also train and tram rides for the kids, plus the following attractions:

➡ **Caversham Wildlife Park**
(www.cavershamwildlife.com.au; adult/child $25/11; ⏲9am-5.30pm, last entry 4.30pm) Part of the Whiteman Park estate, this wildlife park features cassowaries, echidnas, kangaroos, koalas, potoroos, quokkas and native birds. Say g'day to Neil, the very laid-back southern hairy wombat, for us. There are also farm shows for the kids.

➡ **Revolutions**
(www.whitemanpark.com.au; entry by gold-coin donation; ⏲10am-4pm) Museum celebrating transport in WA with horse-drawn wagons, camels, trains, boats and planes.

➡ **Motor Museum of WA**
(www.motormuseumofwa.asn.au; adult/child $10/7; ⏲10am-4pm) Vintage cars and motorbikes in Whiteman Park.

Eating & Drinking

In this 'Valley of Taste' eating and drinking go hand in hand, and many wineries and breweries have restaurants attached.

Lamont's TAPAS $$
(www.lamonts.com.au; 85 Bisdee Rd, Millendon; tapas $14.50-23; ⏲10am-5pm Thu-Sun) Look forward to lazy tastings and heaving plates of tapas under an open sky. The wine's very good, much of it grown in its Margaret River vineyard.

★ **RiverBank Estate** MODERN AUSTRALIAN $$$
(☎08-9377 1805; www.riverbankestate.com.au; 126 Hamersley Rd, Caversham; mains $38-44; ⏲tastings 10am-5pm, restaurant 11.30am-2.30pm) Our pick of the Swan Valley's restaurants, RiverBank winery is a wonderful place to while away a few hours over excellent Modern Australian cuisine. It's a little more dressed up than most other places and it charges for tastings if you're not dining in the restaurant, but we're willing to let that go when the food's this good. There's live jazz on the first Saturday of the month.

Sandalford RESTAURANT $$$
(www.sandalford.com; 3210 West Swan Rd, Caversham; tours $16, mains $24-45; ⏲tastings 10am-5pm, tours noon, lunch noon-3pm) Sandalford has the nicest surrounds of any of the Swan Valley wineries, and plays host to weddings and major concerts.

★ **Feral Brewing Company** CRAFT BEER
(www.feralbrewing.com.au; 152 Haddrill Rd; ⏲11am-5pm Sun-Thu, 11am-late Fri & Sat) Here's your chance to try some of Australia's best craft beers. Head brewer Brendan Varis is regularly lauded, with his always interesting brews including the mighty Hop Hog Pale Ale. Feral's barrel-aged and sour brews are also excellent when paired with Feral's robust pub-grub menu.

★ **Homestead Brewery** CRAFT BEER
(www.mandoonestate.com.au/homestead/; 10 Harris Rd, Caversham; ⏲10am-5pm Mon-Thu, 10am-late Fri, from 7.30am Sat & Sun) Located in the grounds of the award-winning Mandoon Estate winery, Homestead is the Swan Valley's newest craft brewery and one of WA's best. Standout brews include Kaiser's Choice, a zingy Hefeweizen wheat beer. Visit on weekend afternoons for garden picnics and Mediterranean-style barbecues inspired by the owners' Croatian heritage.

Mash CRAFT BEER
(www.mashbrewing.com.au; 10250 West Swan Rd, Henley Brook; ⏲11am-5pm Mon & Tue, 11am-late Wed-Sun) A lively barlike atmosphere and a selection of homemade lager, ales, wheat beer and cider. Interesting seasonal brews are always worth trying. Its hoppy Copycat American IPA was judged Aussie's best beer in 2014.

Houghton WINERY
(www.houghton-wines.com.au; Dale Rd, Middle Swan; ⏲10am-5pm) The Swan's oldest and best-known winery is surrounded by pleasant grounds, including a jacaranda grove. There's a gallery in the cellar where bushranger Moondyne Joe was caught, and a small display of old wine-making equipment.

Getting There & Away

To get around the Swan Valley you'll need to drive or take a tour.

For Whiteman Park, catch a train on the Midland Line from Perth to Bassendean Station. Switch to a bus to Ellenbrook and get off at Lord St (bus stop 15529).

AVON VALLEY

The lush, green Avon Valley – with its atmospheric homesteads with big verandahs, rickety wooden wagons and moss-covered rocks – was 'discovered' by European settlers in early 1830 after food shortages forced Governor Stirling to dispatch Ensign Dale to search the Darling Range for arable land. What he found was the upper reaches of the Swan River, but he presumed it was a separate river – which is why its name changes from the Swan to the Avon in Walyunga National Park. The valley was very soon settled, just a year after Perth was founded, and many historic stone buildings still stand proudly in the towns and countryside in the area.

This country traditionally belongs to the Balardung, one of the Noongar peoples.

York

POP 2100

Unrelentingly quaint, York is the most atmospheric spot in the Avon Valley and is a wonderful place to while away a couple of hours on a Sunday, when it's at its liveliest. Avon Tce is lined with restored heritage buildings, and the entire town has been classified by the National Trust.

Only 97km from Perth, York is the oldest inland town in WA, first settled in 1831, just two years after the Swan River Colony. The settlers here saw similarities between the Avon Valley and their native Yorkshire, so Governor Stirling bestowed the name York.

Convicts were brought to the region in 1851 and contributed to the development of the district; the ticket-of-leave hiring depot was not closed until 1872, four years after the transportation of convicts to WA ceased. During the gold rush, York prospered as a commercial centre, servicing miners who were heading to Southern Cross, a goldfields town 273km to the east. Most of its buildings date from this time.

Sights & Activities

Avon Tce is lined with significant buildings such as the town hall, Castle Hotel, police station, Old Gaol and Courthouse, and Settlers House. **Holy Trinity Church** (Pool St), by the Avon River, was completed in 1854 and features stained-glass windows designed by WA artist Robert Juniper, as well as a rare pipe organ. The suspension bridge across the Avon was built in 1906.

Residency Museum MUSEUM
(www.yorksoc.org.au; Brook St; adult/child $4/2; 1-3pm Tue, Wed & Thu, 11am-3.30pm Sat & Sun) Built in 1858, this museum houses some intriguing historical exhibits and poignant old black-and-white photos of York.

Motor Museum MUSEUM
(www.yorkwa.com.au/Motor.Museum; 116 Avon Tce; adult/child $9/4; 9.30am-3pm) A must for vintage-car enthusiasts.

Skydive Express SKYDIVING
(08-9444 4199; www.skydive.com.au; 3453 Spencers Brook Rd; tandem jumps 10,000/14,000ft $339/399) The Avon Valley is WA's skydiving centre; the drop zone is about 3km from town.

Sleeping & Eating

Faversham House B&B **$$**
(08-9641 1366; www.favershamhouse.com.au; 24 Grey St; r $125-255;) If you've ever wished you were 'to the manor born', indulge your fantasies in this grand stone mansion (1840). The rooms in the main house are large, TV-free and strewn with antiques; some have four-post beds. All have smallish private bathrooms. The cheaper rooms are in the old servants' quarters (naturally).

Jules Cafe CAFE **$**
(121 Avon Tce; snacks & mains $10-18; 8am-4pm Mon-Sat) Putting a colourful spin on heritage York since 1990, Jules Cafe channels a Lebanese heritage for top-notch kebabs, falafel and Middle Eastern sweets. A funky new-age accent is introduced with organic, vegie and gluten-free options.

Information

Visitor Centre (08-9641 1301; www.avonvalleywa.com.au; Town Hall, 81 Avon Tce; 10am-4pm)

Darling Range, Swan Valley & Avon Valley

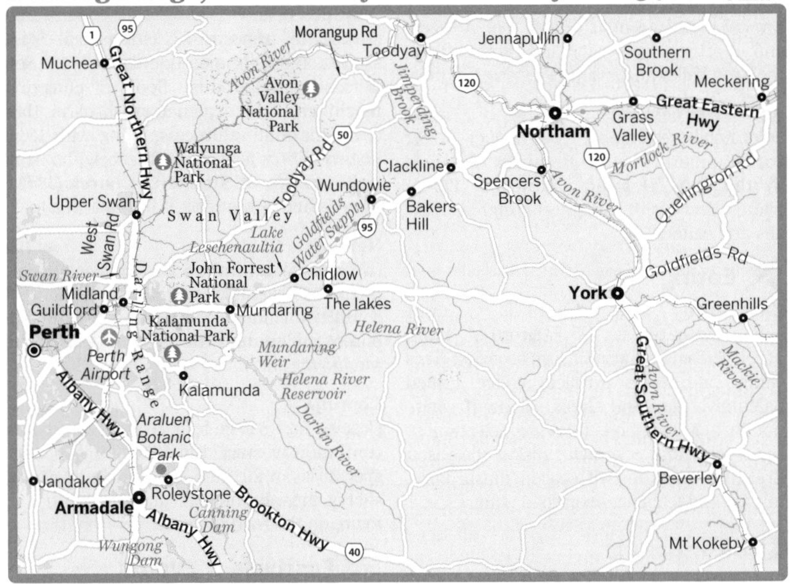

Getting There & Away

Transwa (☎1300 662 205; www.transwa.wa.gov.au) coach routes include the following:

- GE2 (three per week) to East Perth ($17, 1½ hours), Mundaring ($14, 47 minutes), Hyden ($40, 3¼ hours) and Esperance ($82, 8½ hours).
- GS2 to Northam ($8, 33 minutes, six per week), Mt Barker ($56, 5¼ hours, four per week) and Albany ($61, six hours, four per week).

Northam

POP 6000

This busy commercial centre is the major town of the Avon Valley. It's is a likeable place with some fine heritage buildings and pleasant cafes but little to justify a longer stay. The railway line from Perth once ended here and miners had to make the rest of the weary trek to the goldfields by road; it now continues all the way to Sydney.

In recent years, Northam has become the hub for various Avon Valley festivals.

Sights & Activities

Burlong Pool NATURAL POOL
This natural pool on the Avon River is a significant Noongar site, and is believed to be the summer home of the Wargal, the giant snakelike creature that created waterways and brought life to the land. It's customary to throw a handful of sand into the water out of respect. Follow the river southwest from the visitor centre for 3.5km along the river path called Dorntj Koorliny (Walking Together). Otherwise, take Fitzgerald Rd and continue to the end of Burlong Rd.

Morby Cottage HISTORIC BUILDING
(Katrine Rd; adult/child $2/1; 10.30am-4pm Sun) Built in 1836 as the home of John Morrell (founder of Northam), it now houses family heirlooms and early Northam memorabilia.

Old Railway Station Museum MUSEUM
(Fitzgerald St; adult/child $2/0.50; 10.30am-4pm Sun) Housed in a National Trust-registered building (1886) this museum showcases railway memorabilia.

Windward Adventures BALLOONING
(☎08-9621 2000; www.ballooning.net.au; weekday/weekend flights $300/350; Apr-Oct) Sunrise flights followed by a champagne breakfast.

Festivals & Events

Avon Valley Vintage Festival VINTAGE
(www.avonvalleywa.com.au; adult/child $12/free; first weekend of Mar) Three days of antiques and collectables, and vintage spins on fashion, cars and bicycles.

Avon Valley Gourmet Food & Wine Festival FOOD, WINE
(www.avonvalleywa.com.au; ⏲early Jun) A weekend of artisan food, wine and produce from the Avon Valley and around Western Australia.

Avon River Festival SPORTS
(www.avondescent.com.au; ⏲early Aug) Street parade, markets and fireworks followed by the Avon Descent, a gruelling 133km white-water event for power dinghies, kayaks and canoes.

Eating

Cafe Yasou CAFE $
(www.cafeyasou.com.au; 175 Fitzgerald St; mains $11-21; ⏲8am-4pm Mon-Fri, 8am-noon Sat) This sunny cafe serves excellent coffee, grilled haloumi cheese and Greek salads. If you're not in a Med mood, there's a selection of sandwiches and cakes. Our pick is the Yasou Breakfast, crammed with bacon, mushrooms, tomato and feta cheese on rosti potatoes.

Information

Visitor Centre (☎08-9622 2100; www.avonvalleywa.com.au; 2 Grey St; ⏲9am-4pm) Overlooking a picturesque portion of river with fountains and a compact island.

Getting There & Away

Transwa (☎1300 662 205; www.transwa.wa.gov.au) coach GS2 heads to East Perth ($20, 1½ hours, six per week), York ($8, 33 minutes, six per week), Mt Barker ($58, 5¾ hours, four per week) and Albany ($66, 6½ hours, four per week).

Northam is a stop on the AvonLink and Prospector lines, with trains to East Perth ($20, 1½ hours, 12 per week), Toodyay ($8, 20 minutes, 12 per week) and Kalgoorlie ($74, 5¼ hours, nine per week).

Toodyay

POP 1100

Historic Toodyay, only 85km northeast of Perth, is a popular weekend destination for browsing the bric-a-brac shops or having a beer on the verandah of an old pub. As you'd expect of a town classified by the National Trust, it has plenty of charming heritage buildings. Originally known by the name Newcastle, Toodyay (pronounced '2J'), came from the Aboriginal word *duidgee* (place of plenty); the name was adopted around 1910.

Sights & Activities

Connor's Mill MUSEUM
(Stirling Tce; admission $3; ⏲9am-4pm) Start at the top of this aged flour mill (1870) and descend through three floors of chugging machinery and explanatory displays that cover the milling process, along with local history. Entry is through the neighbouring visitor centre. **St Stephen's Church** (1862), directly across the road, is also worth a look.

Newcastle Gaol MUSEUM
(17 Clinton St; admission $3; ⏲10am-4pm) Built in the 1860s using convict labour, the gaol complex includes a courtroom, cells and stables. A gallery tells the story of bushranger Moondyne Joe.

Coorinja WINERY
(Toodyay Rd; ⏲10am-5pm Mon-Sat) Operating continuously since the 1870s, this winery specialises in fortified wines including port, sherry, muscat and Marsala. It's 6km out of town, on the road to Perth.

Festivals & Events

Moondyne Festival HERITAGE
(www.moondynefestival.com.au; ⏲1st Sun May) Costumed heritage hijinks in honour of Moondyne Joe (1826–1900), Western Australia's most infamous bushranger who had a knack for escaping from prison on multiple occasions.

Toodyay International Food Festival FOOD
(www.toodyayiff.wix.com/home; ⏲Aug) Held on the first weekend in August on the day before the Avon Descent.

Toodyay Agricultural Show AGRICULTURE
Early October.

Eating

Sozo Health Cafe CAFE $
(www.sozohealthcafe.com; 111c Stirling Tce; mains $9-20; ⏲10am-4pm Tue & Thu, 10am-8.30pm Wed, 9.30am-2pm Fri, 9.30am-8.30pm Sun) Juices, smoothies, healthy snacks and mains all feature at this laid-back cafe arrayed around a heritage courtyard. Look forward to a tasty menu packed with organic and gluten-free items. Wednesday night is 'Curry Night' and tapas take centre stage on Sunday evenings.

Cola Café & Museum CAFE $
(www.colacafe.com.au; 128 Stirling Tce; snacks $10-18; ⏲9am-4.30pm) Coca-Cola memorabilia runs amok here. Order a cola spider (Coke

with a scoop of ice cream) and a big burger and play 'name that song' with the retro tunes.

Information

Visitor Information Centre (☎08-9574 2435; www.toodyay.com; 7 Piesse St; ⊙9am-4pm) Tourist information and accommodation bookings.

Getting There & Away

Toodyay is a stop on the **Transwa** (☎1300 662 205; www.transwa.wa.gov.au), AvonLink and Prospector lines, with trains to East Perth ($17, 1¼ hours, seven per week), Northam ($8, 20 minutes, 12 per week) and Kalgoorlie ($78, 5½ hours, four per week).

Avon Valley National Park

Featuring granite outcrops, forests and wonderful fauna, **Avon Valley National Park** (www.parks.dpaw.wa.gov.au; per car $12; ⊙8am-4pm) is accessed from Toodyay and Morangup Rds. The Avon River flows through the centre of the park in winter and spring but is usually dry at other times.

The park is the northern limit of the jarrah forests, and jarrah and marri trees are mixed with wandoo woodland. Bird species include rainbow bee-eaters, honeyeaters, kingfishers and rufous treecreepers. In the understorey, honey possums and western pygmy possums hide among the dead leaves, and skinks and geckos scuttle about.

There are camp sites with basic facilities (eg pit toilets and barbecues).

NEW NORCIA

POP 70

The idyllic monastery settlement of New Norcia, 132km from Perth, consists of a cluster of ornate, Spanish-style buildings set incongruously in the Australian bush. Founded in 1846 by Spanish Benedictine monks as an Aboriginal mission, the working monastery today holds prayers and retreats, alongside a business producing boutique breads and gourmet goodies.

Sights

New Norcia Museum & Art Gallery MUSEUM, GALLERY
(☎08-9654 8056; www.newnorcia.wa.edu.au; Great Northern Hwy; combined museum & town tours adult/family $25/60; ⊙10am-4.30pm) New Norcia Museum & Art Gallery traces the history of the monastery and houses impressive art, including contemporary exhibitions and one of the country's largest collections of post-Renaissance religious art. The gift shop sells souvenirs, honeys, preserves and breads baked in the monks' wood-fired oven.

Abbey Church CHURCH
Inside the abbey church, try to spot the native wildlife in the sgraffito artworks that depict the Stations of the Cross. Look hard, as there's also an astronaut.

Tours

Town Tours TOUR
(www.newnorcia.wa.edu.au; adult/child $15/10; ⊙11am & 1.30pm) Guided two-hour town tours offer a look at the abbey church and the frescoed college chapels; purchase tickets from the museum.

Sleeping & Eating

New Norcia Hotel HOTEL $
(☎08-9654 8034; www.newnorcia.wa.edu.au; Great Northern Hwy; s/d without bathroom $75/95) New Norcia Hotel harks back to a more genteel time, with sweeping staircases, high ceilings, understated rooms (with shared bathrooms) and wide verandahs. An international menu ($15 to $36) is available at the bar or in the elegant dining room. Our pick is the ploughman's lunch served with New Norcia's own wood-fired sourdough bread.

Sit outside on the terrace and sample the delicious but deadly New Norcia Abbey Ale, a golden Belgian-style ale brewed especially for the abbey. Sunday is a good day to visit, either for a leisurely breakfast, or for popular wood-fired pizzas.

Monastery Guesthouse GUESTHOUSE $
(☎08-9654 8002; www.newnorcia.wa.edu.au; full board suggested donation $80) The abbey offers lodging in the Monastery Guesthouse within the walls of the southern cloister. Guests can join in prayers with the monks (and males can dine with them).

MOORA

POP 2574

Tall gums, wide streets, a pub with a wide verandah, a couple of galleries, a few B&Bs and a railway line (wheat trains only) define this agricultural service centre, all of which make it a good base to explore the surrounding area.

Transwa buses run to Perth ($31, three hours) and Geraldton ($48, four hours) along Rte 116.

Sights

The excellent **visitor centre** (08-9653 1053; www.moora.wa.gov.au; Moora Railway Station; 8.30am-4pm Mon-Fri; @) can supply a map of the local wildflowers and other sites including Jingemia Cave in **Watheroo National Park**. An interesting town walk takes in Moora's heritage buildings and murals.

Western Wildflower Farm GARDENS
(Midlands Rd; 9am-5pm Mon-Sat) FREE For hundreds of WA wildflowers, visit the Western Wildflower Farm, 19km north of Moora. Entrance is free, and morning and afternoon teas are served. The Wildflower Interpretative Education Centre at the farm is a great stop if you're heading out on a wildflower pilgrimage.

Sleeping & Eating

The visitor centre can arrange accommodation at well-maintained B&Bs – you'll need a car as most are slightly out of town.

Moora Caravan Park CARAVAN PARK $
(08-9651 0000; Dandaragan St; unpowered/powered sites $22/29, chalets $118-170) Moora Caravan Park offers basic, shady sites, and some comfortable modern chalets. Pay at the Gull service station.

Wheatbelt Gallery CAFE
(Padbury St; 9am-5pm Tue-Sat) The best coffee in town is at the Wheatbelt Gallery, opposite the visitor centre. It also doubles as a bar some evenings.

WONGAN HILLS

POP 1462

From the direction of New Norcia, take the back road via Yerecoin and you'll pass by the intriguing **Lake Ninan**, a huge saltpan. Wongan Hills, with its gently undulating country and myriad verticordias, makes a pleasant change from the flat wheat-belt towns, and there are plenty of trails for bushwalkers.

The **visitor centre** (08-9671 1973; www.wongantourism.com.au; The Station; 9am-5pm Mon-Sat, to 12.30pm Sun) has maps (and guides) for popular wildflower haunts such as **Mt Matilda** (8km return), 12km west of Wongan Hills, and **Christmas Rock** (behind the caravan park; 2km return). **Reynoldson Nature Reserve** (1km one way), 29km north of Wongan Hills, has spectacular verticordias, and you can drive to the top of **Mt O'Brien**, 11km west of Wongan Hills.

Transwa has services to Perth ($32, three hours), and Perenjori ($32, three hours) via Rte 115.

Sleeping & Eating

Wongan Hills Caravan Park CARAVAN PARK $
(08-9671 1009; www.wonganhillscaravanpark.com.au; Wongan Rd; unpowered/powered site $20/24, cabins & chalets $75-110) Wongan Hills Caravan Park has shady sites, a good kitchen and a few modern units.

Wongan Hills Hotel HOTEL $
(08-9671 1022; www.facebook.com/WonganHillsHotel; 5 Fenton Pl; hotel s/d $75/95, motel d $110, meals $20-32) Art-deco Wongan Hills Hotel offers classic hotel rooms, some opening onto the upstairs verandah, and modern motel rooms in a separate building. Meals are typical pub fare, including good pizzas.

SUNSET COAST

The coast road north of Perth leads to some popular spots for travellers. Within an hour's drive, Perth's outer suburbs give way to the bushland oasis of Yanchep National Park, with wonderful wildlife and walking trails.

The coastline ranges from tranquil bays at Guilderton, good for swimming and fishing, to windswept beaches at Lancelin, with excellent conditions for windsurfing and kitesurfing.

Yanchep

POP 2482

Yanchep and its close neighbour Two Rocks are effectively Perth's northernmost suburbs. The town was developed extensively during the 1980s by (now convicted fraudster) Alan Bond, and the legacy of this era includes a large marina and some dubious bits of sculpture (dolphins, a dragon and a giant Neptune).

To get to Yanchep by public transport, catch a train on the Joondalup line from Perth's Esplanade station to Clarkson, then catch bus 490.

Yanchep National Park NATIONAL PARK
(www.parks.dpaw.wa.gov.au; Wanneroo Rd; per car $12; visitor centre 9.15am-4.30pm) The woodlands and wetlands of Yanchep National Park are home to hundreds of species of fauna and flora, including koalas, kangaroos,

emus and cockatoos. The free *Wild About Walking* brochure outlines nine walking trails, from the 20-minute Dwerta Mia walk to the four-day Coastal Plain walk. Register with the park centre for longer walks.

The park features splendid caves, which can be viewed on 45-minute tours (adult/child $10/5; five per day). On weekends at 1pm and 2pm, local Noongar guides run excellent tours on Indigenous history, lifestyle and culture (adult/child $10/5), as well as didgeridoo and dance performances (adult/child $10/5).

Yanchep Inn MOTEL **$**
(08-9561 1001; www.yanchepinn.com.au; hotel r $80, old motel r $115, new motel r $170-210;) Within the national park, Yanchep Inn is more attractive from the outside than it is on the inside. The inn itself has basic rooms with shared facilities and a cafe downstairs. It's more comfortable in the newer of the two motel blocks, with lake views and rammed-earth walls, but perhaps a little overpriced. Prices jump up by $25 to $55 on weekends.

Guilderton

POP 150

Some 43km north of Yanchep, Guilderton is a popular and staggeringly beautiful family holiday spot. Children paddle safely near the mouth of the Moore River, while adults enjoy fishing and surfing on the ocean beach.

The name comes from the wreck of the *Vergulde Draeck,* part of the Dutch East India Company fleet, which ran aground nearby in 1656, reputedly carrying a treasure in guilders. Its original name was Gabbadah, meaning 'mouth of water', although many older Perthites still refer to it as Moore River.

The **Guilderton Caravan Park** (08-9577 1021; www.guildertoncaravanpark.com.au; 2 Dewar St; unpowered/powered sites $30/45, chalets $165) has self-contained chalets, but you'll need your own linen. There's also a cafe and general store, and a compact volunteer-run visitor centre (with erratic hours) next door.

Lancelin

POP 670

Afternoon offshore winds and shallows, protected by an outlying reef, make Lancelin perfect for windsurfing and kitesurfing, attracting action seekers from around the world. In January, wind-worshippers descend for the **Lancelin Ocean Classic** (www.lancelinoceanclassic.com.au) windsurfing race, starting at Ledge Point to the south.

The coral and limestone reef, no-fishing zone and dazzling white sands also make Lancelin a great snorkelling spot, while the mountainous soft, white dunes on the edge of town are good for sandboarding.

Activities

Makanikai Kiteboarding KITEBOARDING
(0406 807 309; www.makanikaikiteboarding.com; lessons from $200) Runs lessons in the fine art of kiteboarding and hires out gear; accommodation packages are also available.

Have a Chat General Store SANDBOARDING
(08-9655 1054; 104 Gingin Rd; 7am-6pm) Hires sandboards for $10 per two hours.

Sleeping & Eating

★**Lancelin Lodge YHA** HOSTEL **$**
(08-9655 2020; www.lancelinlodge.com.au; 10 Hopkins St; dm/d/f $30/85/105;) This laid-back hostel is well equipped and welcoming, with wide verandahs and lots of communal spaces to hang about in. The excellent facilities include a big kitchen, barbecue, wood-fire pizza oven, swimming pool, ping-pong table, volleyball court and free use of bikes and boogie boards.

Ledge Point Holiday Park CARAVAN PARK **$**
(1300 856 088; www.lphp.com.au; 742 Old Ledge Point Rd; 2-person sites $36-41, chalets & studios $120-230;) About 10 minutes' drive south of Lancelin, with excellent facilities and spotless accommodation ranging from caravan and camping sites to chalets and studios. Lots of family-friendly attractions include pedal carts and a jumping pillow. Ledge Point's beach – good for fishing and swimming – is around 500m away.

Lancelin Caravan Park CARAVAN PARK **$**
(08-9655 1056; Hopkins St; sites per person $14, on-site vans $70) Windsurfers love camping out at this neat park – not for the facilities and amenities, which are rudimentary, but for the beachfront location.

Windsurfer Beach Chalets APARTMENT **$$**
(08-9655 1454; www.lancelinaccommodation.com.au; 1 Hopkins St; d from $165) These self-contained two-bedroom chalets are near the windsurfing beach and are a good choice for groups of friends and families (each chalet sleeps up to six). They're functional and well equipped, and have a sun terrace

backing onto a grassy area. The operators can also arrange accommodation in Lancelin and nearby Ledge Point in a variety of self-contained holiday homes.

Endeavour Tavern PUB FOOD $$
(58 Gingin Rd; mains $18-38) A classic beachfront Aussie pub with a beer garden overlooking the ocean. The casual eatery serves decent seafood, pub-grub classics and wood-fired pizzas.

Getting There & Away

From Lancelin, **Integrity** (1800 226 339; www.integritycoachlines.com.au) buses leave from Lancelin Lodge YHA at 11.30pm on Tuesday and Thursday to Cervantes ($34, one hour), Jurien Bay ($34, 1¼ hours) and Geraldton ($50, four hours). Heading south, buses travel to Perth ($34, two hours), leaving Lancelin at 4.55am on Saturday and Monday mornings.

A new **Transwa** (1300 662 205; www.transwa.wa.gov.au) service is being trialled leaving East Perth at 2pm on Friday and Sunday and travelling to Geraldton via Lancelin ($22, 2¾ hours) and Cervantes.

TURQUOISE COAST

Stretching north of Lancelin to Port Denison, the relaxed Turquoise Coast is dotted with sleepy fishing villages, stunning beaches, extraordinary geological formations, rugged national parks and incredibly diverse flora. Offshore marine parks and island nature reserves provide a safe breeding habitat for Australian sea lions and other endangered species, while crayfishing brings in the dollars. Once somewhat isolated, the whole area has been brought within easy reach of Perth by the completion of the final section of Indian Ocean Dr between Lancelin and Cervantes.

Getting There & Away

Integrity runs three times a week along the coast between Perth and Geraldton and on to Exmouth and Broome.

Transwa has 2pm Friday and Sunday departures heading to Cervantes and Green Head from Perth. The Friday bus continues to Geraldton.

Cervantes & Pinnacles Desert

POP 480

Heading north from Lancelin on Indian Ocean Dr, you will pass the tiny fishing-shack villages of **Wedge Island** (http://wedgewa.com.au) and Grey, where access was previously 4WD-only along the beach. Pressure from developers and government mean the future of these communities is uncertain, and although there are no facilities for tourists, you are welcome to wander.

The laid-back crayfishing town of Cervantes, 198km north of Perth, makes a pleasant overnight stop for enjoying the Pinnacles Desert and a good base for exploring the flora of the Kwongan, the inland heathland of Lesueur National Park and Badgingarra National Park. There are also some lovely beaches on which to while away the time.

Grab a copy of the *Turquoise Coast Self Drive Map* from Cervantes' combined **post office and visitor centre** (08-9652 7700, 1800 610 660; www.visitpinnaclescountry.com.au; Cadiz St; 9am-5.30pm Mon-Fri, 9am-5pm Sat & Sun; @), which also supplies accommodation and tour information. The town's general store and liquor shop are also on this strip.

Sights & Activities

Just south of Cervantes, turn off for Lake Thetis where living stromatolites – the world's oldest organisms – inhabit the shoreline. Nearby Hansen Bay Lookout has excellent views across the coast. In town, walkways wend along the coastline and provide beach access.

★ **Nambung National Park** NATIONAL PARK
(per car $12) Situated 19km from Cervantes, Nambung is home to the spectacular **Pinnacles Desert**, a vast, alien-like plain studded with thousands of limestone pillars. Rising eerily from the desert floor, the pillars are remnants of compacted seashells that once covered the plain and, over millennia, subsequently eroded. A loop road runs through the formations, but it's more fun to wander on foot, especially at sunset, full moon or dawn, when the light is sublime and the crowds evaporate.

Nearby **Kangaroo Point** and **Hangover Bay** make nice picnic spots with barbecues and tables. The latter has the better swimming.

Lesueur National Park NATIONAL PARK
(per car $12) This botanical paradise, 50km north of Cervantes, contains a staggering 820 plant species, many of them rare and endemic, such as the pine banksia *(Banksia tricupsis)* and Mt Lesueur grevillea *(Gre-*

KWONGAN WILDFLOWERS

Take any road inland from the Turquoise Coast and you'll soon enter the Kwongan heathlands, where, depending on the season, the roadside verges burst with native wildflowers such as banksias, grevilleas, hakeas, calothamnus, kangaroo pasw and smokebush. While Lesueur National Park is an obvious choice for all things botanical, consider the following options.

Badgingarra National Park Three-and-a-half kilometres of walking trails, kangaroo paws, banksias, grass trees, verticordia and a rare mallee. The back road linking Badgingarra to Lesueur is particularly rich in flora. Obtain details from the Badgingarra Roadhouse. There's also a picnic area on Bibby Rd.

Alexander Morrison National Park Named after WA's first botanist. There are no trails, but you can drive through slowly on the Coorow Green Head Rd, which has loads of flora along its verge all the way from Lesueur. Expect to see dryandras, banksias, grevilleas, smokebush, leschenaultias and honey myrtles.

Tathra National Park Tathra has similar flora to Alexander Morrison National Park and the drive between the two is rich with banksias, kangaroo paws and grevilleas.

Coomallo Rest Area Orchids, feather flowers, black kangaroo paws, wandoo and river red gums can be found upstream and on the slopes of the small hill.

Brand Highway (Rte 1) The route's not exactly conducive to slow meandering, but the highway verges are surprisingly rich in wildflowers, especially either side of Eneabba.

If you're overwhelmed and frustrated by not being able to identify all these strange new plants, consider staying at **Western Flora Caravan Park** (☎08-9955 2030; wfloracp@activ8.net.au; Brand Hwy, North Eneabba; unpowered/powered sites $24/26, d $65, on-site vans $75, chalets $120), where the enthusiastic owners run free two-hour wildflower walks across their 65-hectare property every day at 4.30pm.

villea batrachioides). Late winter sees the heath erupt into a mass of colour, and the park is also home to the endangered Carnaby's cockatoo. An 18km circuit drive is dotted with lookouts and picnic areas. Flat-topped **Mt Lesueur** (4km return walk) has panoramic coastal views.

Tours

Many Perth-based companies offer day trips to the Pinnacles.

Pinnacle Helicopter Flights SCENIC FLIGHTS
(☎0428 880 066; www.pinnaclehelicopterflights.com.au; Pinnacles Discovery Centre, Nambung National Park; flights per person $95-190) Spectacular flights to see the beauty of the Pinnacles and the WA coastline from the air.

Turquoise Coast Enviro Tours SIGHTSEEING
(☎08-9652 7047; www.thepinnacles.com.au; 59 Seville St, Cervantes; full-day Kwongan tours $170) Cervantes local and ex-ranger Mike Newton runs a full-day Kwongan tour, including Lesueur National Park and the coast up to Leeman.

Sleeping

Prices surge during school holidays.

★**Cervantes Lodge & Pinnacles Beach Backpackers** HOSTEL $
(☎1800 245 232; www.cervanteslodge.com.au; 91 Seville St; dm $33, d with/without bathroom $130/90; @) In a great location behind the dunes, this relaxing hostel has a wide verandah, small and tidy dorms, a nice communal kitchen and a lounge area. Bright en-suite rooms, some with views, are next door in the lodge.

Pinnacles Holiday Park CARAVAN PARK $
(☎08-9652 7060; www.pinnaclesholidaypark.com.au; 35 Aragon St, Cervantes; unpowered & powered sites $25-49, cabins $90-105; wi-fi) Fantastic location right behind the dunes with plenty of shady, grassy sites and an on-site cafe.

Amble Inn B&B $$
(☎0429 652 401; 2150 Cadda Rd, Hill River; d from $170; air-con) High up on the heathland, about 25km east of Cervantes, this hidden gem of a B&B has beautiful thick stone walls, wide verandahs and superbly styled rooms. Watch the sunset over the coast from the nearby hill with a glass of your complimentary wine.

Cervantes Holiday Homes APARTMENT **$$**
(☎08-9652 7115; www.cervantesholidayhomes.com.au; cnr Malaga Ct & Valencia Rd, Cervantes; cottages from $140; ❄) These well-equipped, fully self-contained cottages are great value, especially for groups.

Pinnacles Edge Resort RESORT **$$**
(☎08-9652 7788; www.pinnaclesedgeresort.com.au; 7 Aragon St, Cervantes; d $150-220; ❄📶≋) Beautifully appointed luxury rooms, the more expensive ones with spas and balconies, are arranged around a central pool. There's an in-house restaurant and bar. The adjoining motel has cheaper, older-style doubles.

Eating

Seashells Cafe CAFE **$**
(☎08-9652 7060; 35 Aragon St, Cervantes; ⏲8am-4pm) With great coffee and the best view in town, the Seashell makes an excellent pit stop for breakfast or afternoon cake.

Lobster Shack SEAFOOD **$$**
(☎08-9652 7010; www.lobstershack.com.au; 11 Madrid St, Cervantes; ⏲shop 9am-5pm, lunch 11.30am-2.30pm, tours 12.30-2pm) Craving crayfish? They don't come much fresher than at this lobster factory–turned–lunch spot, where a delicious grilled cray, chips and salad will set you back $40. Lobster rolls are good value at $18. Tours (adult/child $15/7.50) and takeaway frozen seafood are also available.

Cervantes Country Club SEAFOOD **$$**
(☎08-9652 7123; Aragon St, Cervantes; mains & platters $25-49; ⏲6-9pm) The seafood platters at this humble sporting club (shorts and sandals are OK) are legendary, and include prawns, oysters, fish, calamari, crayfish (in season, extra $10), salad and mountains of chips.

Getting There & Away

Integrity (p108) runs three times a week to Perth ($44, three hours), Dongara ($34, two hours), Geraldton ($42, three hours) and Exmouth ($183, 14 hours). Transwa (p108) runs twice weekly to Perth ($34, three hours), Dongara ($22, two hours) and Geraldton ($40, three hours).

Jurien Bay

POP 1500

The largest town on the Turquoise Coast is likely to become quite a lot bigger after being selected as a regional 'Super Town'. Home to a hefty fishing fleet and lots of big houses, it's already rather spread out; however, there's a nice long swimming beach and great snorkelling and diving opportunities. Anglers have a choice of jetties and the lengthy foreshore walkway links several pleasant parks.

Accommodation in town caters mostly for Perth families. Holiday houses and apartments can be booked via local **real estate agents** (☎08-9652 2055; www.jurienbayholidays.com; Shop 1a, 34 Bashford St). Plan ahead for popular **Jurien Bay Tourist Park** (☎08-9652 1595; www.jurienbaytouristpark.com.au; Roberts St; sites $38, chalets $140-170), with its comfortable chalets right behind the beach. Next door, the **Jetty Cafe** (☎08-9652 1999; meals $10-17; ⏲7.30am-5pm) has a great position and good casual fare. For a beer or wine with lunch or dinner, try the eclectic international menu at the laid-back **Beach Bistro** (2/1 Roberts St; lunch $15-22, dinner $21-36; ⏲noon-9pm Wed-Mon).

To see the coastline from the air and land on the beach, see the team at **Skydive Jurien Bay** (☎1300 293 766, 08-9652 1320; www.skydivejurienbay.com; 65 Bashford St; 2440/3050/4270m jumps $300/350/450).

Green Head & Leeman

On the way to Green Head from Jurien Bay, stop at **Grigson Lookout** for a panoramic view of the coast and Kwongan. Tiny **Green Head** (population 280) has several beautiful bays; the horseshoe-shaped **Dynamite Bay** is the most spectacular and is sheltered for swimmers. There's good fishing, snorkelling, surfing and windsurfing here and at nearby **Leeman** (population 400).

Sea Lion Charters (☎0427 931 012; sealioncharters88@gmail.com; 24 Bryant St, Green Head; morning tours adult/child $150/75) offers a magical experience interacting in shallow water with playful sea lions who mimic your every move. It helps to be a good snorkeller.

Green Head has good sleeping and eating options, with the **Centrebreak Beach Stay** (☎08-9953 1896; www.centrebreakbeachstay.com.au; Lot 402, Ocean View Dr, Green Head; dm/d/f $35/150/190, meals $15-40; 📶) near Dynamite Bay also offering a licensed cafe. The shady **Green Head Caravan Park** (☎08-9953 1131; www.greenheadcaravanpark.com.au; 9 Green Head Rd, Green Head; unpowered/powered sites $20/28, on-site vans from $75) will suit most campers.

Heading north on Indian Ocean Dr, unmarked side-roads lead to lonely beaches and rocky cliffs begging to be explored.

Margaret River & the Southwest Coast

Best Places to Eat

- Laundry 43 (p117)
- Piari & Co (p118)
- Eagle Bay Brewing Co (p122)
- Vasse Felix (p123)
- Miki's Open Kitchen (p126)

Best Places to Stay

- Wildwood Valley Cottages (p122)
- Wharncliffe Mill Bush Retreat (p124)
- Acacia Chalets (p128)
- Burnside Organic Farm (p125)
- Foragers (p132)

Why Go?

The farmland, forests, rivers and coast of the lush, green southwestern corner of Western Australia (WA) contrast vividly with the stark, sunburnt terrain of much of the state. On land, world-class wineries and craft breweries beckon, and tall trees provide shade for walking trails and scenic drives. Offshore, bottlenose dolphins and whales frolic, and devoted surfers search for – and often find – their perfect break.

Unusually for WA, distances between the many attractions are short, and driving time is mercifully limited, making it a fantastic area to explore for a few days – you will get much more out of your stay here if you have your own wheels. Summer brings hordes of visitors, but in the wintry months from July to September the cosy pot-bellied stove rules and visitors are scarce, and while opening hours can be somewhat erratic, prices are much more reasonable.

When to Go

Margaret River

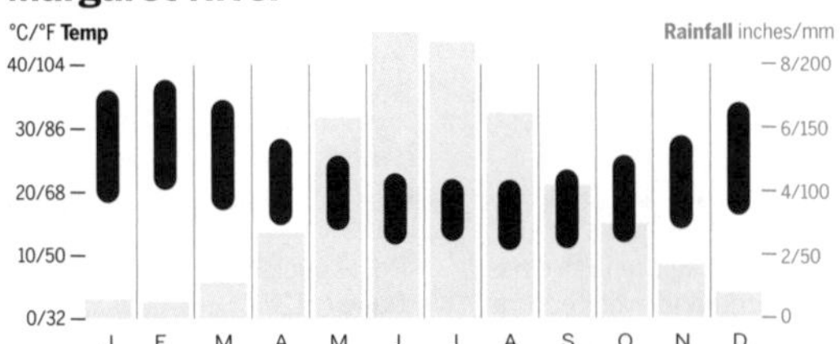

Jan Follow the party crowds from the Southbound festival to the beach.

Mar–Apr Catch the surf festival in Margaret River, and the Nannup Music Festival.

Aug Head to empty beaches, Margaret River wineries and Busselton's film festival.

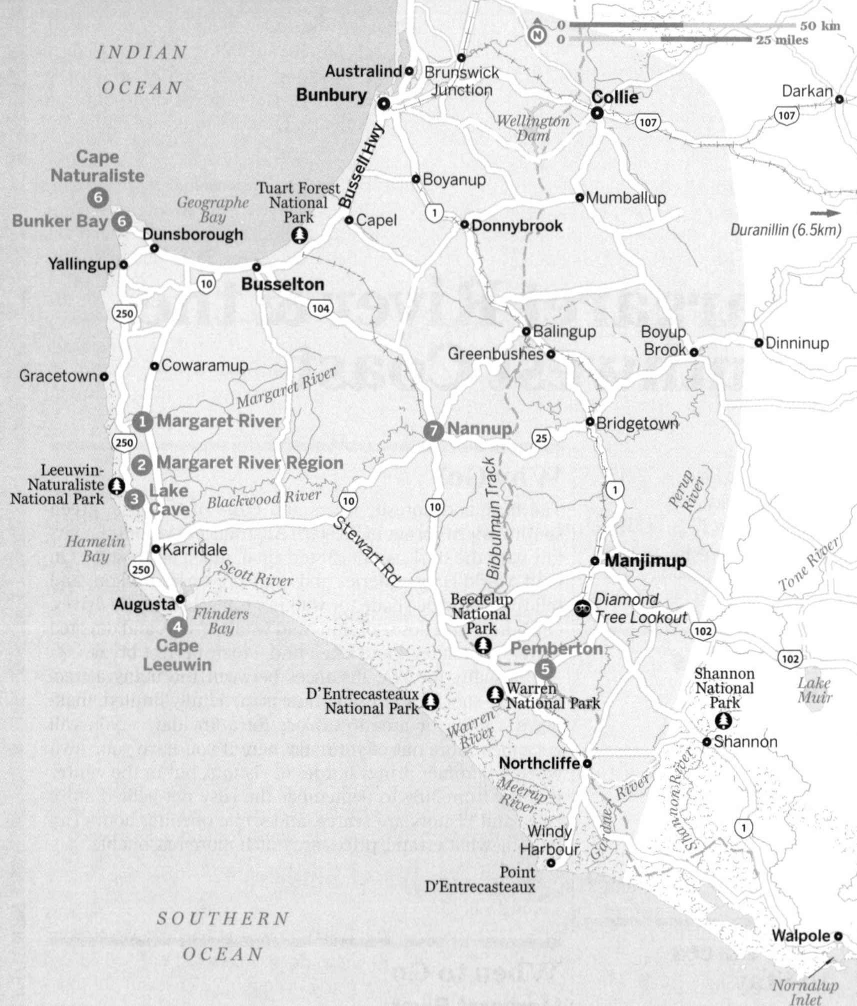

Margaret River & the Southwest Coast Highlights

1. Sampling the first-class wine, food and architecture of the vineyards of **Margaret River** (p119).
2. Getting active amid the dramatic seascapes and landscapes of the **Margaret River region** (p126).
3. Exploring the labyrinthine limestone caverns along Caves Rd, especially beautiful **Lake Cave** (p127).
4. Fronting up to the impressive coastline at Augusta's **Cape Leeuwin Lighthouse** (p128), at the confluence of the Indian and Southern Oceans.
5. Sinking into the dappled depths of the karri forests surrounding **Pemberton** (p131).
6. Revelling in the wild beauty of **Cape Naturaliste** (p118) and **Bunker Bay** (p118).
7. Canoeing from the forest to the sea along the Blackwood River, starting at **Nannup** (p129).

GEOGRAPHE BAY

Turquoise waters and 30km of excellent swimming beaches define this gorgeous bay. Positioned between the Indian Ocean and a sea of wine, the beachside towns of Busselton and Dunsborough attract hordes of holidaymakers. By WA standards, attractions are close together, making it perfect for leisurely touring. Accommodation prices can rise around 30% during summer and school holidays.

For 55,000 years the area from Geographe Bay to Augusta belonged to the Wardandi, one of the Noongar peoples. They lived a nomadic life linked to the seasons, heading to the coast in summer to fish, and journeying inland during the wet winter months.

The French connection to many of the current place names dates from an early-19th-century expedition by the ships *Le Géographe* and *Naturaliste*. Thomas Vasse, a crewman who was lost at sea, is remembered in the name of a village, river, inlet and Margaret River winery. According to local Wardandi, who found and fed him, he made it to shore but later died on the beach waiting for his ship to return.

Bunbury

POP 66,100

The southwest's only city is morphing from an industrial port into a seaside holiday destination. From Bunbury, the main route south branches to the Bussell Hwy (for Margaret River), and the South Western Hwy (to the southern forests and south coast). It's also the southernmost stop on the train network and a hub for regional buses.

The town centre has basically one main street (Victoria), and a few blocks to the west lies the beach. Immediately to the north, the redeveloped port features waterside restaurants.

The city lies at the western end of Leschenault Inlet. The area was named Port Leschenault after the botanist on Nicolas Baudin's ship *Le Géographe* in 1803, but British Governor James Stirling renamed it Bunbury after a lieutenant in charge of the original military outpost. The first British settlers arrived in 1838.

Sights

Bunbury Wildlife Park ZOO
(www.bunburywildlifepark.com.au; Prince Philip Dr; adult/child $9/5; 10am-5pm) Parrots, kangaroos, wallabies, possums, owls and emus all feature. Across the road, the **Big Swamp** wetlands has good walking tracks and stops for birdwatching. Head south on Ocean Dr, turn left at Hayward St and continue through the roundabout to Prince Philip Dr.

Bunbury Regional Art Galleries GALLERY
(www.brag.org.au; 64 Wittenoom St; 10am-4pm) FREE Housed in a restored pink convent (1897), this excellent gallery has a collection that includes works by Australian art luminaries Arthur Boyd and Sir Sidney Nolan.

St Mark's (Old Picton) Church CHURCH
(cnr Charterhouse Cl & Flynn St, East Bunbury) Built in 1842 using wattle and daub construction, this is WA's second-oldest church.

Activities

Mangrove Boardwalk WALKING
Mangrove Boardwalk (enter off Koombana Dr) meanders through the most southerly mangroves in WA, rich with more than 70 species of bird. Interpretive signs provide information about this 2500-year-old ecosystem.

Dekked Out Adventures KAYAKING
(08-9796 1000; www.dekkedout.com.au; 42 Elinor Bell Rd, Australind) Hires kayaks (single per half/full day $50/60) and sandboards (per half/full day $20/30).

Tuart Forest WALKING
This stretch of forest lined with tall trees runs along the southern end of Ocean Dr.

Sleeping

Wander Inn Backpackers HOSTEL $
(1800 039 032; www.bunburybackpackers.com.au; 16 Clifton St; incl breakfast dm $30-33, s/d $57/80;) Occupying a cheerful old blue-and-yellow house down a quiet side street between the beach and the main strip.

Dolphin Retreat YHA HOSTEL $
(08-9792 4690; www.dolphinretreatbunbury.com.au; 14 Wellington St; dm/s/d $32/57/82;) Around the corner from the beach, this small hostel is in a labyrinthine old house with hammocks and a barbecue on the back verandah.

Bunbury Glade Caravan Park CARAVAN PARK $
(08-9721 3800; www.glade.com.au; Timperley Rd; 2-person sites $25-38, cabins $70-105;) This spotless park is a five-minute drive from the centre of town on Blair St, the main road heading south.

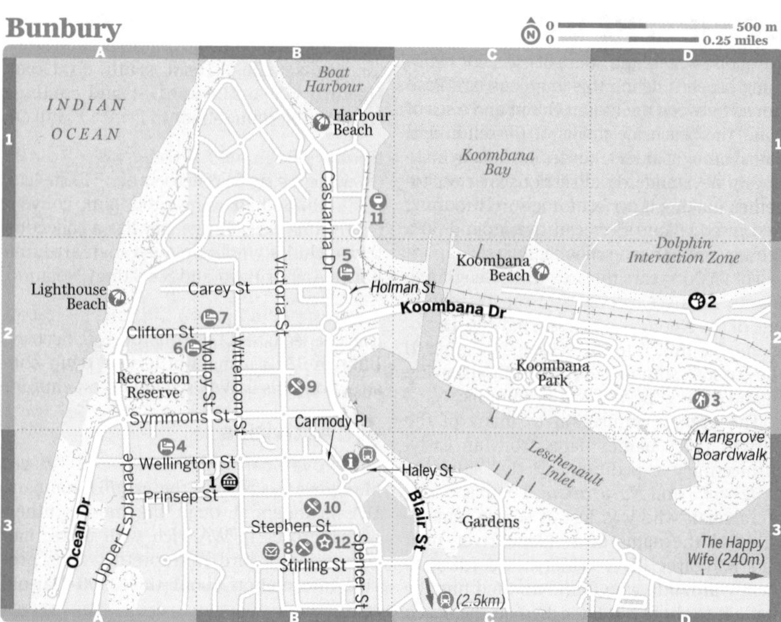

Bunbury

Sights

1 Bunbury Regional Art Galleries B3
2 Dolphin Discovery Centre D2

Activities, Courses & Tours

3 Mangrove Boardwalk D2

Sleeping

4 Dolphin Retreat YHA A3
5 Mantra B2
6 The Clifton A2
7 Wander Inn Backpackers B2

Eating

8 Café 140 .... B3
9 Kokoro B2
10 Mot's Cafe B3

Drinking & Nightlife

11 Mash B1

Entertainment

12 Prince of Wales B3

The Clifton MOTEL $$
(☎08-9721 4300; www.theclifton.com.au; 2 Molloy St; r $150-275;) For luxurious heritage accommodation, go for the top-of-the-range rooms in the Clifton's historic Grittleton Lodge (1885). Good-value motel rooms are also available.

Mantra APARTMENT $$$
(☎08-9721 0100; www.mantra.com.au; 1 Holman St; apt from $204;) The Mantra has sculpted a set of modern studios and apartments around four grain silos by the harbour. Deluxe rooms have spa baths and full kitchens.

Eating

Kokoro JAPANESE $
(30 Victoria St; mains $10-18; 11am-2.30pm & 6pm-late) Head to the cosy Kokoro and dine *izakaya* (Japanese bar)–style on Japanese tapas. Moreish highlights include creamy crab croquettes and tempura prawns, and the broader menu includes sushi and sashimi, as well as more robust teriyaki salmon and beef dishes. Lunch specials from $9.50 are good value.

Mot's Cafe MALAYSIAN $
(Shop 5, Central Arcade, 17 Prinsep St; snacks & mains $5-15; 10am-3pm Mon-Sat) Tasty Cocos Malay–style food from a friendly family orig-

inally from the Cocos Islands off the northwestern coast of Australia.

Happy Wife CAFE **$$**

(www.thehappywife.com.au; 98 Stirling St; mains $11-24; ⏲6.30am-3.30pm Mon-Fri, 7.30am-2.30pm Sat) Grab a spot in the garden of this Cape Cod–style cottage just a short drive from the centre of town. Excellent home-style baking and regular lunch specials make it worth seeking out. Try the Asian-style sticky pork salad with nashi pear, cabbage salad and toasted peanuts.

Café 140 CAFE **$$**

(www.cafe140.com.au; 140 Victoria St; mains $12-21; ⏲7.30am-4.30pm Mon-Fri, 8am-2pm Sat & Sun) Hip, onto-it staff make the funky Café 140 a top spot for a leisurely Bunbury breakfast. With one of WA's best salmon omelettes, good coffee, and lots of magazines and newspapers, you can kiss at least an hour of your travel schedule goodbye. Later in the day, gourmet burgers and grilled Turkish sandwiches are among the lunchtime stars.

Drinking & Entertainment

Mash CRAFT BEER

(www.mashbrewing.com.au; 2/11 Bonnefoi Blvd; ⏲11am-3pm Mon & Tue, to 9pm Wed-Sun) This waterfront microbrewery turns out seven regular beers, plus always interesting seasonal concoctions. Try the Copycat AIPA, champion brew at the Australian International Beer Awards in 2014. The food (mains $18 to $38) is decent pub grub, but service can be hit and miss.

Prince of Wales LIVE MUSIC

(41 Stephen St) Long-standing live-music venue.

Information

Visitor Centre (☎08-9792 7205; www.visitbunbury.com.au; Carmody Pl; ⏲9am-5pm Mon-Sat, 10am-2pm Sun) Located in the historic train station (1904).

Getting There & Around

BUS

Coaches stop at the **central bus station** (☎08-9722 7800; Carmody Pl), next to the visitor centre, or at the **train station** (Picton Rd, Woolaston).

Transwa (☎1300 662 205; www.transwa.wa.gov.au) routes include the following:

- SW1 (12 weekly) to East Perth ($31, 3¼ hours), Mandurah ($17, two hours), Busselton ($9.55, 43 minutes), Margaret River ($17, two hours) and Augusta ($25, 2½ hours).
- SW2 (three weekly) to Balingup ($14, 53 minutes), Bridgetown ($17, 1¼ hours) and Pemberton ($28, 2¼ hours).
- GS3 (daily) to Walpole ($45, 4½ hours), Denmark ($51, 5½ hours) and Albany ($58, six hours).

South West Coach Lines (☎08-9261 7600; www.transdevsw.com.au) Runs services to/from Perth's Esplanade Busport ($20.50, 2½ hours, three daily), Mandurah ($20.50, 1¼ hours, daily), Busselton ($11.50, 1¼ hours, four daily), Dunsborough ($18.50, 1¾ hours, daily) and Bridgetown ($18.50, 1¾ hours, daily).

TransBunbury (☎08-9791 1955; www.transdevsw.com.au/transbunbury/) Runs buses (30 minutes) between the central bus station and train station ($2.90; no Sunday service).

TRAIN

Bunbury is the terminus of the Transwa (p115) Australind train line, with two daily services to Perth ($31, 2½ hours) and Pinjarra ($17, 1¼ hours).

DOLPHIN DISCOVERY CENTRE

Around 60 bottlenose dolphins live in Bunbury's Koombana Bay year-round, their numbers increasing to around 260 in summer. The **Dolphin Discovery Centre** (☎08-9791 3088; www.dolphindiscovery.com.au; Koombana Beach; adult/child $10/5; ⏲9am-2pm Jun-Sep, 8am-4pm Oct-May) has a beachside zone where dolphins regularly come to interact with people in the shallows and you can wade in alongside them, under the supervision of trained volunteers. There are no guarantees of a close encounter, but they are more likely in the early mornings between November and April. Entry tickets are valid for three separate visits, a good option if you're in town for a few days.

To maximise your chances, there are **Eco Cruises** (1½hr cruise adult/child $49/35; ⏲11am daily Oct-May, 11am Sat & Sun Jun-Sep) and **Swim Encounter Cruises** (3hr cruises $149; ⏲7.30am mid-Oct–mid-Dec & Feb-Apr, 7.30am & 11.30am mid-Dec–Jan).

Volunteers must commit to at least six weeks' full-time involvement.

GEOGRAPHE WINE REGION

The **Geographe wine region** (www.geographewine.com.au) is the perfect primer for the glories of Margaret River. Geographe produces around 11% of the state's output from around 30 wineries, and the region's best-known brand is conveniently located halfway between Bunbury and Busselton. **Capel Vale** (www.capelvale.com.au; 118 Mallokup Rd, Capel) offers free tastings and Match restaurant overlooking the vines. It's located off the Bussell Hwy on the opposite side of the highway from Capel village.

Tuart Forest National Park

The tuart is a type of eucalypt that only grows on coastal limestone 200km either side of Perth, and this 20-sq-km strip squeezed between the Bussell Hwy and the Indian Ocean is the last pure tuart forest left. An alternative route to Busselton from Bunbury leads through the shade cast by these giants, some more than 33m tall.

Turn off the highway at Tuart Dr, 4km southwest of Capel. After 11km, turn right into Layman Rd for **Wonnerup House** (www.ntwa.com.au; 935 Layman Rd; adult/child $5/3; ⏲10am-4pm Thu-Mon), a National Trust homestead (1859). Continue past the seaside village of Wonnerup and follow the coast to Busselton.

Busselton

POP 15,400

Unpretentious and uncomplicated, Busselton is what passes for the big smoke in these parts. Surrounded by calm waters and white-sand beaches, its outlandishly long jetty is its most famous attraction. The family-friendly town has plenty of diversionary activities for lively kids, including sheltered beaches, water slides and animal farms. During school holidays, the population increases fourfold and accommodation prices soar.

Sights & Activities

Busselton Jetty JETTY
(☎08-9754 0900; www.busseltonjetty.com.au; adult/child $2.50/free, return train adult/child $11/6, Interpretive Centre admission free; ⏲Interpretive Centre 9am-5pm) Busselton's 1865 timber-piled jetty – the longest in the southern hemisphere (1841m) – reopened in 2011 following a $27-million refurbishment. A little **train** chugs along to the **Underwater Observatory** (adult/child incl train $29.50/14; ⏲9am-4.25pm), where tours take place 8m below the surface; bookings are essential. There's also an Interpretive Centre, an attractive building in the style of 1930s bathing sheds, about 50m along the jetty.

ArtGeo Cultural Complex GALLERY
(www.artgeo.com.au; 6 Queen St; ⏲10am-4pm) Grouped around the old courthouse (1856), this complex includes tea rooms, wood turners, an artist-in-residence and the Busselton Art Society's gallery, selling works by local artists.

Busselton Museum MUSEUM
(www.busseltonmuseum.org.au; Peel Tce; adult/child $8/3; ⏲10am-4pm Wed-Mon) Local history in an old butter factory.

Dive Shed DIVING
(☎08-9754 1615; www.diveshed.com.au; 21 Queen St) Runs regular dive charters along the jetty, to Four Mile Reef (a 40km limestone ledge about 6.5km off the coast) and to the scuttled navy vessel HMAS *Swan* (off Dunsborough).

Festivals & Events

Southbound MUSIC
(www.southboundfestival.com.au; ⏲early Jan) Start off the New Year with three days of alternative music and camping.

CinéfestOZ CINEMA
(www.cinefestoz.com; ⏲late Aug) Busselton briefly morphs into St-Tropez with this oddly glamorous festival of French and Australian cinema, including lots of Australian premieres and the odd Aussie starlet.

Sleeping

Accommodation sprawls along the beach for several kilometres either side of the town, so check the location if you don't have transport.

Beachlands Holiday Park CARAVAN PARK $
(☎1800 622 107; www.beachlands.net; 10 Earnshaw Rd, West Busselton; sites per 2 people $45, chalets from $142;) This excellent family-friendly park offers a wide range of accommodation amid shady trees, palms and flax bushes. Deluxe spa villas ($185) have corner spas, huge TVs, DVD players and full kitchens.

Observatory Guesthouse B&B $$
(☎08-9751 3336; www.observatoryguesthouse.com; 7 Brown St; d $145-155; ❄) A five-minute walk from the jetty, this friendly B&B has four bright, cheerful rooms. They're not overly big, but you can spread out on the communal sea-facing balcony and front courtyard.

Blue Bay Apartments APARTMENT $$
(☎08-9751 1796; www.bluebayapartments.com; 66 Adelaide St; apt from $140; ❄) Close to the beach, these good-value self-contained apartments are bright and cheery, each with private courtyard and barbecue.

Eating

★Laundry 43 CAFE $$
(www.laundry43.com.au; 43 Prince St; shared plates $14-29; ⏱9am-late Tue-Sat) Brick walls and a honey-coloured jarrah bar form the backdrop for Margaret River beers and wines, great cocktails, and classy shared plates and bigger dishes. Definitely get ready to linger longer than you planned. Wednesday nights offer live music from 7.30pm.

Goose CAFE $$
(www.thegoose.com.au; Geographe Bay Rd; breakfast $10-21, shared plates & mains $11-34; ⏱7am-late; 📶) Near the jetty, this stylish cafe has been reborn as a cool and classy bar and bistro. The drinks list bubbles away with WA craft beer and wine, and a versatile menu kicks off with eggy breakfasts, before graduating to shared plates including Vietnamese pulled-pork sliders, and larger dishes such as steamed mussels and seafood chowder.

Coco's Thai THAI $$
(55 Queen St; mains $16-22; ⏱5pm-late) A little place serving tasty Thai favourites and more adventurous dishes such as a delicious fish curry with apple. Loaded with fresh herbs, the prawn salad is also great. BYO.

Information

Visitor Centre (☎08-9752 5800; www.geographebay.com; end of Queen St, Busselton Foreshore; ⏱9am-5pm Mon-Fri, 9am-4.30pm Sat & Sun) Underneath the lighthouse near the pier.

Getting There & Around

Transwa (☎1300 662 205; www.transwa.wa.gov.au) Coach SW1 (12 weekly) stops on Peel Tce heading to/from East Perth ($37, 4¼ hours), Bunbury ($9.55, 43 minutes), Dunsborough ($8, 28 minutes), Margaret River ($14, 1½ hours) and Augusta ($17, 1¾ hours).

South West Coach Lines (☎08-9753 7700; www.transdevsw.com.au; 39 Albert St) Runs services to/from Perth's Esplanade Busport ($39, 3¾ hours, three daily), Bunbury ($11.50, one hour, three daily), Dunsborough ($11.50, 30 minutes, three daily) and Margaret River ($11.50, 50 minutes, three daily).

Dunsborough

POP 3400

Smaller and less sprawling than Busselton, Dunsborough is a relaxed, beach-worshipping town that goes bonkers towards the end of November when about 7000 'schoolies' descend. When it's not inundated with drunken, squealing teenagers, it's a thoroughly pleasant place to be. The beaches are better than Busselton's, but accommodation is more limited.

The name Dunsborough first appeared on maps in the 1830s, but to the Wardandi people it was always Quedjinup, meaning 'place of women'.

Activities

Cape Dive DIVING
(☎08-9756 8778; www.capedive.com; 222 Naturaliste Tce) There is excellent diving in Geographe Bay, especially since the decommissioned Navy destroyer HMAS *Swan* was purposely scuttled in 1997 for use as a dive wreck. Marine life has colonised the ship, which lies at a depth of 30m, 2.5km offshore.

Naturaliste Charters WHALE WATCHING
(☎08-9750 5500; www.whales-australia.com; adult/child $80/50; ⏱10am & 2pm Sep–mid-Dec) Two-hour whale-watching cruises from September to mid-December. From January to March the emphasis switches to an **Eco Wilderness Tour** showcasing beaches, limestone caves with Indigenous art, and wildlife including dolphins and New Zealand fur seals. Tours also run out of Augusta from mid-May to September.

Sleeping

There are many options for self-contained rentals in town depending on the season. The visitor centre has listings.

Dunsborough Beachouse YHA HOSTEL $
(☎08-9755 3107; www.dunsboroughbeachouse.com.au; 205 Geographe Bay Rd; dm $34-36, s/d $58/88; @📶) On the Quindalup beachfront,

this friendly hostel has lawns stretching languidly to the water's edge. It's an easy 2km cycle from the town centre.

Dunsborough Central Motel MOTEL $$
(☎08-9756 7711; www.dunsboroughmotel.com.au; 50 Dunn Bay Rd; r $130-175;) Centrally located in Dunsborough town, this well-run motel is good value, especially if you can snare an online midweek discount, which leaves more of your travel budget to enjoy the nearby wineries and breweries.

Eating & Drinking

Pourhouse BISTRO, PUB $$
(www.pourhouse.com.au; 26 Dunn Bay Rd; mains $19-31; ⏲4pm-late Mon-Sat, from 2pm Sun) Hip but not pretentious, with comfy couches, regular live bands, and an upstairs terrace for summer. The pizzas are excellent, and top-notch burgers come in a locally-baked sourdough bun. A considered approach to beer includes rotating taps from the best of WA's craft breweries and lots of bottled surprises.

Samudra CAFE $$
(www.samudra.com.au; 226 Naturaliste Tce; mains $14-23; ⏲7am-3pm Thu-Tue, to 10pm Wed) This funky garden cafe is one of WA's best vegetarian restaurants. Tasty wood-fired pizzas underpin a superhealthy menu of salads, wraps and smoothies, and there are plenty of shady places to sit and read or write. Samudra also offers relaxing and reinvigorating yoga classes, and surfing and spa retreats.

RED TAILS IN THE SUNSET

Between Cape Naturaliste and Cape Leeuwin is the most southerly breeding colony of the red-tailed tropicbird *(Phaethon rubricauda)* in Australia. From September to May, look for it soaring above Sugarloaf Rock, south of Cape Naturaliste. The viewpoint can be reached by a 3.5km boardwalk from the Cape Naturaliste lighthouse or by Sugarloaf Rd.

The tropicbird is distinguished by its two long, red tail streamers – almost twice its body length. Bring binoculars to watch this small colony soar, glide, dive and then swim with their disproportionately long tail feathers cocked up.

★**Piari & Co** BISTRO, BAR $$$
(☎08-9756 7977; www.piariandco.com.au; 5/54 Dunn Bay Rd; small plates $17-20, mains $35-38; ⏲10am-5pm Tue, 10am-11pm Wed-Fri, 5-11pm Sat) This relaxed and stylish bistro has a strong emphasis on local and seasonal produce. Small plates include Esperance scallops with crispy duck, and a subtle combination of citrus-cured salmon and mandarin gel. Mains such as pork belly and roast apple go well with a drinks list proudly showcasing Margaret River wines and craft beer. Bookings recommended.

Information

Visitor Centre (☎08-9752 5800; www.geographebay.com; 1/31 Dunn Bay Rd; ⏲9am-5pm Mon-Fri, 9.30am-4.30pm Sat & Sun) Information and bookings.

Getting There & Around

Transwa (☎1300 662 205; www.transwa.wa.gov.au) Coach SW1 (12 weekly) stops at the visitor centre, heading to/from East Perth ($40, 4½ hours), Bunbury ($14, 1¼ hours), Busselton ($8, 28 minutes), Margaret River ($9.55, 49 minutes) and Augusta ($17, 1¼ hours).
South West Coach Lines (☎08-9753 7700; www.transdevsw.com.au) Services to/from Perth's Esplanade Busport ($43.50, 4½ hours, daily), Bunbury ($18.50, 1¾ hours, daily) and Busselton ($11.50, 30 minutes, three daily).

Cape Naturaliste

Northwest of Dunsborough, Cape Naturaliste Rd leads to the excellent beaches of **Meelup**, **Eagle Bay** and **Bunker Bay**, and on to Cape Naturaliste. There are walks and lookouts along the way; pick up brochures from Dunsborough's visitor centre before heading out. Whales and hammerhead sharks like to hang out on the edge of Bunker Bay, where the continental shelf drops 75m. There's excellent snorkelling on the edge of the shelf at Shelley Cove.

Bunker Bay is home to **Bunkers Beach Cafe** (www.bunkersbeachcafe.com.au; Farm Break Lane; breakfast $14-25, lunch $16-34; ⏲8.30am-4pm), serving an adventurous menu only metres from the sand.

The **Cape Naturaliste lighthouse** (adult/child $14/7; ⏲tours every 30min 9.30am-4pm), built in 1903, can be visited on tours and there's also a free museum and a cafe. Above and Below (adult/child $30/15) packages are available, combining entry to Ngilgi Cave (p121).

MARGARET RIVER WINE REGION

With vineyard restaurants, artisan food producers, and some of Australia's most spectacular surf beaches and rugged coastline, the Margaret River wine region packs attractions aplenty into a compact area. Sleepy Yallingup conceals excellent beaches, restaurants and luxe accommodation, Margaret River township is the region's bustling foodie heart, and the best of the area's wineries are focussed around Cowaramup and Wilyabrup. Throughout the area, an excellent craft-beer scene bubbles away, and the road further south to the windswept Cape Leeuwin Lighthouse at Augusta is studded with spectacular underground caves.

Festivals & Events

Drug Aware Pro SPORTS
(www.aspworldtour.com; ⏲ Apr) Pro-surfing competition with concerts and fashion shows.

Margaret River Gourmet Escape FOOD & WINE
(www.gourmetescape.com.au; ⏲ late Nov) From Rick Stein and Heston Blumenthal to MasterChef's George Calombaris, the Gourmet Escape food and wine festival attracts the big names in global and Australian cuisine. Look forward to three days of food workshops, tastings, vineyard events and demonstrations. An inaugural added attraction in 2014 was a vineyard concert at Sandalford Estate featuring Kiwi music icon Neil Finn.

Tours

See local visitor centres for other options.

Bushtucker Tours GUIDED TOUR
(☎ 08-9757 9084; www.bushtuckertours.com; adult/child $95/40) The four-hour tour combines walking and canoeing up the Margaret River, and features aspects of Aboriginal culture along with uses for flora, and a bush-tucker lunch. Also runs a Winery & Brewery Tour (adult/child $95/40) around Margaret River.

Taste the South WINERY TOUR
(☎ 0438 210 373; www.tastethesouth.com.au; per person from $95) Wine and craft beer tours. Up to five breweries can be visited, and the special Hits with Kids tour combines children-friendly vineyards with activities including lamb feeding, sheep shearing and a chocolate factory.

CAPE TO CAPE TRACK

Stretching from Cape Naturaliste to Cape Leeuwin, the 135km **Cape to Cape Track** passes through the heath, forest and sand dunes of the **Leeuwin-Naturaliste National Park** (Caves Rd), all the while providing Indian Ocean views. Most walkers take about seven days to complete the track, staying in a combination of national-park camp sites and commercial caravan parks along the way, but you can walk it in five days or break up the route into day walks.

Harvest Tours WINERY TOUR
(☎ 0429 728 687; www.harvesttours.com.au; adult/child $155/55) Food and wine tour with an emphasis on organic, sustainable and ethical producers. Lunch is included at Cullen Wines (p124).

Wine for Dudes WINERY TOUR
(☎ 0427 774 994; www.winefordudes.com; tours $95) Includes a brewery, a chocolate factory, four wineries, a wine-blending experience and lunch.

Margaret River Tours WINERY TOUR
(☎ 0419 917 166; www.margaretrivertours.com) Runs winery tours (half-/full day $80/140) and can arrange charters.

Margies Big Day Out WINERY TOUR
(☎ 0416 180 493; www.margaretrivertourswa.com.au; tours $95) Three wineries, two breweries, cheese, chocolate and lunch.

Getting There & Away

Transwa (☎ 1300 662 205; www.transwa.wa.gov.au) Coach SW1 (12 weekly) from Perth to Augusta stops at Yallingup and Margaret River, with three coaches weekly continuing to Pemberton.

South West Coach Lines (☎ 08-9261 7600; www.transdevsw.com.au) Buses between Busselton and Augusta (12 weekly) stop at Cowaramup and Margaret River, linking with Perth on the weekends.

Yallingup & Around

POP 1070

Beachside Yallingup is a mecca for both surfers and wine aficionados. You're permitted to let a 'wow' escape when the surf-battered

Margaret River Wine Region

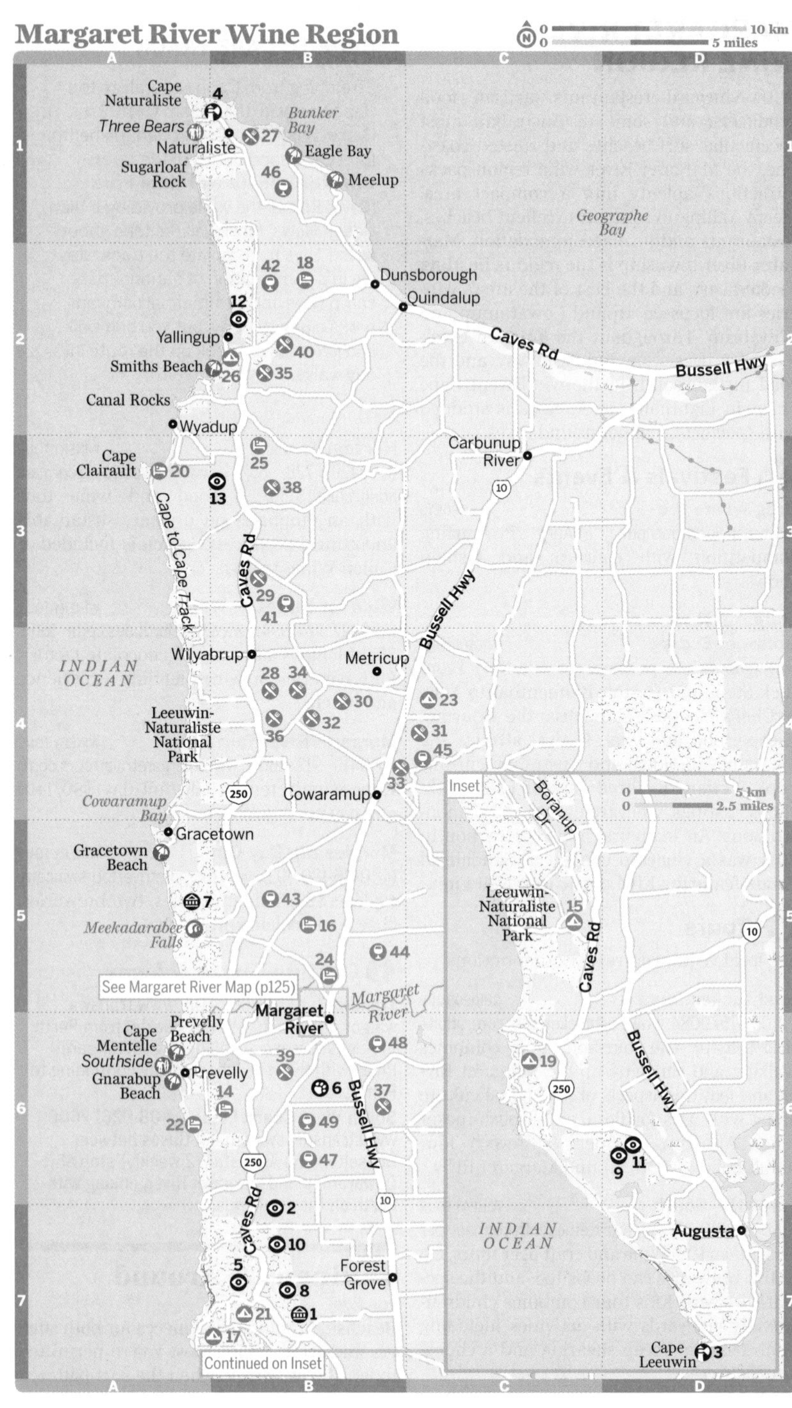

Margaret River Wine Region

Sights
1 Boranup Gallery B7
2 Calgardup Cave B7
3 Cape Leeuwin Lighthouse D7
4 Cape Naturaliste Lighthouse B1
5 CaveWorks & Lake Cave B7
6 Eagles Heritage B6
7 Ellensbrook Homestead A5
8 Giants Cave B7
9 Jewel Cave D6
10 Mammoth Cave B7
11 Moondyne Cave D6
12 Ngilgi Cave B2
13 Wardan Aboriginal Centre B3

Sleeping
14 Acacia Chalets B6
15 Boranup Campground C5
16 Burnside Organic Farm B5
Caves House .... (see 12)
17 Conto Campground B7
18 Empire Retreat B2
19 Hamelin Bay Holiday Park C6
20 Injidup Spa Retreat A3
Llewellin's .... (see 14)
Noble Grape Guesthouse .... (see 33)
21 Point Road Campground B7
22 Surfpoint A6
23 Taunton Farm Holiday Park C4
24 Wharncliffe Mill Bush Retreat B5
25 Wildwood Valley Cottages & Cooking School B3
26 Yallingup Beach Holiday Park B2

Eating
27 Bunkers Beach Cafe B1
28 Cullen Wines B4
29 Knee Deep in Margaret River B3
30 Margaret River Chocolate Company B4
31 Margaret River Dairy Company C4
32 Margaret River Nougat Company B4
33 Margaret Riviera B4
34 Providore B4
35 Studio Bistro B2
36 Vasse Felix B4
37 Watershed Premium Wines B6
38 Wills Domain B3
39 Xanadu B6
40 Yallingup Woodfired Bread B2

Drinking & Nightlife
Ashbrook .... (see 34)
41 Bootleg Brewery B3
42 Bush Shack Brewery B2
43 Cheeky Monkey Brewery B5
44 Colonial Brewing Co B5
45 Cowaramup Brewing Company C4
46 Eagle Bay Brewing Co B1
47 Leeuwin Estate B6
Margaret River Regional Wine Centre .... (see 33)
48 Stella Bella B6
Thompson Estate .... (see 34)
49 Voyager Estate B6

Information
National Park Information Centre .... (see 2)

coastline first comes into view. For romantic travellers, Yallingup means 'place of love' in the Wardandi Noongar tongue.

Beautiful walking trails follow the coast between here and Smiths Beach. Canal Rocks, a series of rocky outcrops forming a natural canal, are just past Smiths Beach.

Sights & Activities

Wardan Aboriginal Centre CULTURAL EXPERIENCE, GALLERY
(08-9756 6566; www.wardan.com.au; Injidup Springs Rd, Yallingup; experiences adult/child $20/10; 10am-4pm daily mid-Oct–mid-Mar, 10am-4pm Mon, Wed-Fri & Sun mid-Mar–mid-Jun & mid-Aug–mid-Oct, experiences Sun, Mon, Wed & Fri) Offers a window into the lives of the local Wardandi people. There's a gallery (free admission), an interpretive display on the six seasons that govern the Wardandi calendar (adult/child $8/3), and the opportunity to take part in various experiences including stone tool making, and boomerang and spear throwing. A guided bushwalk explores Wardandi spirituality and the uses of various plants for food, medicine and shelter.

Ngilgi Cave CAVE
(08-9755 2152; www.geographebay.com; Yallingup Caves Rd; adult/child $22/12; 9am-5pm) Between Dunsborough and Yallingup, this 500,000-year-old cave is associated in Wardandi spirituality with the victory of the good spirit Ngilgi over the evil spirit Wolgine. To the Wardandi people it became a kind of honeymoon location. A European man first stumbled upon it in 1899 while looking for his horse. Formations include the white **Mother of Pearl Shawl** and the equally beautiful **Arab's Tent** and **Oriental Shawl**. Tours depart every half-hour. Check online for other options.

More adventurous caving options include the two-hour Ancient Riverbed Tour (adult/child $60/39), the 45-minute Express Adventure Tour (adult/child $47/29), the

GETTING CRAFTY IN MARGARET RIVER

The Margaret River region's wine credentials are impeccable, but the area is also a destination for craft beer fans. Many breweries serve bar snacks and lunch.

Eagle Bay Brewing Co (www.eaglebaybrewing.com.au; Eagle Bay Rd, Dunsborough; ⌚11am-5pm) A lovely rural outlook, interesting beers and wines served in modern, spacious surroundings, and excellent food including crisp wood-fired pizzas ($20 to $24). Keep an eye out for Eagle Bay's Single Batch Specials.

Colonial Brewing Co (www.colonialbrewingco.com.au; Osmington Rd, Margaret River; ⌚11am-6pm) This modern microbrewery has great rural views and an excellent range of authentic beers including a witbier with coriander and mandarin, and a hop-fuelled India Pale Ale. Our favourite is the refreshing German-style Kölsch.

Bush Shack Brewery (www.bushshackbrewery.com.au; Hemsley Rd, Yallingup; ⌚10am-5pm) A small-scale brewery in a great bush setting. A healthy dose of innovation results in interesting brews such as chilli beer, lemon-infused lager and strawberry pale ale.

Cheeky Monkey Brewery (www.cheekymonkeybrewery.com.au; 4259 Caves Rd, Margaret River; ⌚10am-6pm) Set around a pretty lake, Cheeky Monkey has an expansive restaurant and lots of room for the kids to run around. Try the Hatseller Pilsner with bold New Zealand hops or the Belgian-style Hagenbeck Pale Ale. Decent food and apple and pear ciders means you'll make a day of it.

Bootleg Brewery (www.bootlegbrewery.com.au; off Yelverton Rd, Wilyabrup; ⌚11am-6pm) More rustic than some of the area's flashier breweries, but lots of fun with a pint in the sun – especially with live bands on Saturday. Try the award-winning Raging Bull Porter or the US West Coast–style Speakeasy IPA.

Cowaramup Brewing Company (www.cowaramupbrewing.com.au; North Treeton Rd, Cowaramup; ⌚11am-5pm) Modern microbrewery with an award-winning pilsner and a moreish English-style special pale ale. Four other beers and occasional seasonal brews also feature.

2½-hour Explorer Tour (adult/child $88/52), three-hour Crystal Crawl Tour (adults only, $110) and the four-hour Ultimate Ngilgi Adventure (adults only, $158). The Above & Below ticket (adult/child $30/15) includes entry to the Cape Naturaliste Lighthouse (p118).

Well-marked bushwalks start from here.

Yallingup Surf School SURFING
(☎08-9755 2755; www.yallingupsurfschool.com) Offers 90-minute lessons for beginners (one-hour lesson $50, three hours $125) and private coaching ($110).

Tours

Koomal Dreaming GUIDED TOUR
(☎0413 843 426; www.koomaldreaming.com.au; adult/child from $50/25) Yallingup local and Wardandi man Josh Whiteland runs tours showcasing Indigenous food, culture and music, usually also including bushwalking and exploration of the Ngilgi Cave.

Sleeping

Yallingup Beach Holiday Park CARAVAN PARK $
(☎08-9755 2164; www.yallingupbeach.com.au; Valley Rd; sites per 2 people $38, cabins $115-165; 📶) You'll fall asleep to the sound of the surf here, with the beach just across the road.

Caves House HOTEL $$
(Hotel Yallingup; ☎08-9750 1888; www.caveshousehotelyallingup.com.au; 18 Yallingup Beach Rd; d $150-210, ste $270-330; 📶) Sunday to Thursday rates at this restored heritage hotel are good value, and it's an atmospheric spot for a drink, with live gigs from 5pm on Friday and Sunday afternoons. Over summer, some of Australia's biggest touring bands sometimes drop by, and outdoor movies add to a laid-back holiday vibe.

★**Wildwood Valley Cottages & Cooking School** COTTAGE $$$
(☎08-9755 2120; www.wildwoodvalley.com.au; 1481 Wildwood Rd; cottages from $250; 📶) Lux-

ury cottages trimmed by native bush are arrayed across 50 hectares, and the property's main house also hosts the Mad About Food Cooking School with Sioban and Carlo Baldini. Sioban's CV includes cooking at Longrain and living in Tuscany, so the culinary emphasis is Thai or Italian. Cooking classes are $135 per person and usually run on a Wednesday.

Injidup Spa Retreat BOUTIQUE HOTEL **$$$**
(08-9750 1300; www.injidupsparetreat.com.au; Cape Clairault Rd; ste from $650;) The region's most stylish and luxurious accommodation, Injidup perches atop an isolated cliff south of Yallingup. A striking carved concrete and iron facade fronts the car park, while inside there are heated polished-concrete floors, 'eco' fires and absolute sea views. Each of the 10 suites has its own plunge pool. It's off Wyadup Rd.

Empire Retreat HOTEL **$$$**
(08-9755 2065; www.empireretreat.com; Caves Rd; ste $295-575;) Everything about the intimate Empire Retreat is stylish, from the Indonesian-inspired design to the attention to detail and service. The rooms are built around a former farmhouse, and a rustic but sophisticated ambience lingers. Check online for good packages combining accommodation and spa treatments.

Eating & Drinking

Yallingup Woodfired Bread BAKERY **$**
(189 Biddle Rd; 7am-6pm Mon-Sat) Look out for excellent sourdough, rye bread and fruit loaves at local shops and the Margaret River Farmers Market, or pick up some still-warm loaves at the bakery near Yallingup.

Wills Domain WINERY **$$$**
(www.willsdomain.com.au; cnr Brash & Abbey Farm Rds; mains $29-40, charcuterie platters $38; tastings 10am-5pm, lunch noon-3pm) Restaurant, gallery and wonderful hilltop views over vines. An innovative seven-course tasting menu (with/without wine match $139/99) is also available.

Studio Bistro MODERN AUSTRALIAN **$$$**
(08-9756 6164; www.thestudiobistro.com.au; 7 Marrinup Dr; small plates $15-20, mains $28-39, degustation menu with/without wine matches $135/95; 10am-5pm Thu-Mon, 6pm-late Fri & Sat) Studio Bistro's gallery focuses on Australian artists, while the garden restaurant showcases subtle dishes such as pan-fried fish with cauliflower cream, radicchio, peas and crab meat. Five-course degustation menus are offered on Friday and Saturday nights. Bookings recommended.

Cowaramup & Wilyabrup

POP 988

Cowaramup ('Cow Town' to some) is a couple of blocks of shops lining Bussell Hwy. Wilyabrup to the northwest is where the Margaret River wine industry began in the 1960s. This area has the highest concentration of wineries, and pioneers Cullen Wines and Vasse Felix are still leading the way.

Sleeping

Taunton Farm Holiday Park CARAVAN PARK **$**
(1800 248 777; www.tauntonfarm.com.au; Bussell Hwy, Cowaramup; sites $42, cottages $115-175;) There are plenty of farm animals for the kids to meet at one of Margaret River's best family-oriented campgrounds. For caravan and tenting buffs, the amenities blocks are spotless, and also scattered about are farm-style self-contained cottages.

Noble Grape Guesthouse B&B **$$**
(08-9755 5538; www.noblegrape.com.au; 29 Bussell Hwy, Cowaramup; s $140-160, d $145-190;) Noble Grape is more like an upmarket motel than a traditional B&B. Rooms offer a sense of privacy and each has a little garden courtyard.

Eating

Providore DELI **$**
(www.providore.com.au; 448 Tom Cullity Dr, Wilyabrup; 9am-5pm) Voted one of Australia's Top 100 Gourmet Experiences by *Australian Traveller* magazine – given its amazing range of artisan produce, including organic olive oil, tapenades and preserved fruits, we can only agree. Look forward to loads of free samples.

Margaret River Nougat Company CONFECTIONERY **$**
(www.margaretrivernougat.com.au; cnr Tom Cullity Dr & Miamup Rd; 10am-5pm) Visit the modern lakeside tasting room for award-winning French-style nougat. Our favourite is the salted caramel flavour.

Margaret Riviera DELI **$**
(www.margaretriviera.com.au; Bottrill St, Cowaramup; 10am-5pm) Gourmet food store stocking local produce including olive oils, preserves and cheeses.

BEST SURF SPOTS

- Margaret River Mouth
- Southside
- Three Bears
- Yallingup
- Injidup

Margaret River Chocolate Company CHOCOLATES $
(www.chocolatefactory.com.au; Harman's Mill Rd; 9am-5pm) Watch truffles being made and sample chocolate buttons.

Margaret River Dairy Company CHEESE $
(www.mrdc.com.au; Bussell Hwy; 9.30am-5pm) Cheese tastings north of Cowaramup.

★ **Vasse Felix** WINERY RESTAURANT $$$
(08-9756 5050; www.vassefelix.com.au; cnr Caves Rd & Harmans Rd S, Cowaramup; mains $32-39, 3-course menu $65, mains $32-39; cellar door 10am-5pm, restaurant 10am-3pm) Vasse Felix winery is considered by many to have the best fine-dining restaurant in the region, the big wooden dining room reminiscent of an extremely flash barn. The grounds are peppered with sculptures, while the gallery displaying works from the Holmes à Court collection is worth a trip in itself.

Knee Deep in Margaret River RESTAURANT $$$
(08-9755 6776; www.kneedeepwines.com.au; 61 Johnson Rd, Wilyabrup; mains $28-38, 3-/5-course degustation $70/90; cellar door 10am-5pm, lunch noon-3pm) Small and focused could be the motto here. Only a handful of mains are offered – crafted with locally sourced, seasonal produce – and the open-sided pavilion provides a pleasantly intimate vineyard setting.

Cullen Wines WINERY RESTAURANT $$$
(08-9755 5277; www.cullenwines.com.au; 4323 Caves Rd, Cowaramup; mains $25-38; 10am-4pm) Grapes were first planted here in 1966 and Cullen has an ongoing commitment to organic and biodynamic principles in both food and wine. Celebrating a relaxed ambience, Cullen's food is excellent, with many of the fruits and vegetables sourced from its own gardens.

Drinking

Margaret River Regional Wine Centre WINE
(www.mrwines.com; 9 Bussell Hwy, Cowaramup; 10am-7pm) A one-stop shop for Margaret River wine.

Ashbrook WINERY
(www.ashbrookwines.com.au; 448 Tom Cullity Dr, Wilyabrup; 10am-5pm) Ashbrook grows all of its grapes on site. Its award-winning rieslings are rightly lauded.

Thompson Estate WINERY
(www.thompsonestate.com; 299 Tom Cullity Dr, Wilyabrup; 11am-5pm Tue-Sun) A small-scale producer with an architectural award-winning tastings and barrel room.

Margaret River

POP 4500

Although tourists usually outnumber locals, Margaret River still feels like a country town. The advantage of basing yourself here is that after 5pm, once the wineries shut up shop, it's one of the few places with any vital signs. Plus it's close to the incredible surf of Margaret River Mouth and Southside, and the swimming beaches at Prevelly and Gracetown.

Margaret River spills over with tourists every weekend and gets very, *very* busy at Easter and Christmas (when you should book weeks, if not months, ahead). Accommodation prices tend to be cheaper midweek.

Sleeping

★ **Wharncliffe Mill Bush Retreat** ECO RETREAT $
(08-9758 8227; www.wharncliffemill.com.au; McQueen Rd, Bramley National Park; unpowered/powered sites $28/32, dm $25-30, safari tents & cabins $85-170;) Set amid shaded forests and around a former timber mill, Wharncliffe has accommodation ranging from simple shared dorms to safari tents and cosy wooden cabins. Solar power and sustainable environmental practices are encouraged, and there's plenty of excellent advice on local opportunities for bushwalking and mountain biking. Margaret River township is just 2km away, and mountain bikes can be hired (half-/full day $15/25).

Margaret River Lodge HOSTEL $
(08-9757 9532; www.margaretriverbackpackers.com.au; 220 Railway Tce; dm $30-32, r with/without bathroom $87/76;) About 1.5km southwest of the town centre, this clean, well-

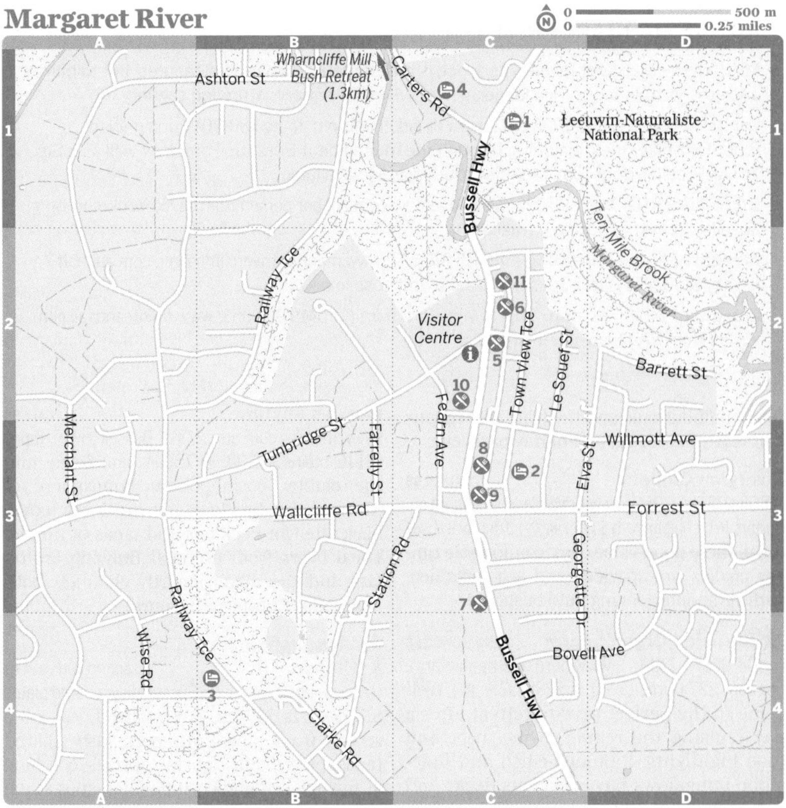

Margaret River

Sleeping
1 Edge of the Forest C1
2 Margaret River Backpackers YHA C3
3 Margaret River Lodge B4
4 Riverglen Chalets C1

Eating
5 Larder C2
6 Margaret River Bakery C2
7 Margaret River Farmers Market C3
8 Miki's Open Kitchen C3
9 Morries Anytime C3
10 Settler's Tavern C2
11 Swings Taphouse & Kitchen C2

Shopping
Tunbridge Gallery .... (see 5)

run hostel has a pool, volleyball court and football field. Dorms share a big communal kitchen, and a quieter area with private rooms has its own little kitchen and lounge.

Margaret River Backpackers YHA HOSTEL $
(☎08-9757 9572; www.margaretriverbackpackers.com.au; 66 Town View Tce; dm $36; ❄@📶) Located just a short walk from Margaret River township, this central option is popular with seasonal workers. Dorms are spartan, but there's a big deck out the back that's perfect for socialising.

Edge of the Forest MOTEL $$
(☎08-9757 2351; www.edgeoftheforest.com.au; 25 Bussell Hwy; r $160; ❄📶) Just a pleasant stroll from Margaret River township, the rooms here have all been recently renovated with new bathrooms and a chic Asian theme. Friendly owners have lots of local

ACTIVE MARGARET RIVER

Much of the Margaret River experience is based around sybaritic pleasures, but to balance the virtue-versus-vice ledger, get active in the region's stunning scenery.

Dirty Detours (08-9758 8312; www.dirtydetours.com; tours $80-90) Runs guided mountain-bike rides, including through the magnificent Boranup Forest, as well as a Sip 'n' Cycle cellar-door tour. Multiday tours are also available.

Edge Tours (0413 892 036; www.edgetours.com.au; per person from $175) Rock-climbing, abseiling, caving and sea kayaking.

Margaret River Climbing (0415 970 522; www.margaretriverclimbingco.com.au; half-/full day $130/250) Caving, rock climbing and abseiling.

Margaret River Kitesurfing & Windsurfing (0419 959 053; www.mrkiteandsail.com.au; 2hr from $75) Instruction and gear rental.

recommendations, and the leafy shared garden is perfect for an end-of-day barbecue.

Riverglen Chalets CHALETS $$
(08-9757 2101; www.riverglenchalets.com.au; Carters Rd; chalets from $175;) Just north of town, these good-value, very comfortable timber chalets are spacious and self-contained, with verandahs looking onto bushland.

★**Burnside Organic Farm** BUNGALOWS $$$
(08-9757 2139; www.burnsideorganicfarm.com.au; 287 Burnside Rd; d $280-325;) Welcome to the perfect private retreat after a day cruising the region's wine, beer and food highlights. Rammed-earth and limestone bungalows have spacious decks and designer kitchens, and the surrounding farm hosts a menagerie of animals and organic orchards. Guests can pick vegetables from the garden. Minimum two-night stay.

Eating & Drinking

Margaret River Bakery CAFE $
(89 Bussell Hwy; mains $10-18; 7am-4pm Mon-Sat) Elvis on the stereo, retro furniture and kitsch needlework art – the MRB has a rustic, playful interior. It's the perfect backdrop to the bakery's honest home-style baking, often with a vegie or gluten-free spin. Soak up the previous day's wine tasting with terrific burgers and pies.

Margaret River Farmers Market MARKET $
(www.margaretriverfarmersmarket.com.au; Lot 272 Bussell Hwy, Margaret River Education Campus; 8am-noon Sat) The region's organic and sustainable artisan producers come to town every Saturday. It's a top spot for breakfast. Check the website for your own foodie hit list.

Morries Anytime CAFE $$
(www.morries.com.au; 2/149 Bussell Hwy; tapas $11-16, mains $15-34; 7.30am-late) Settle into the clubby, cosmopolitan atmosphere of Morries' for breakfast or lunch, or come back later for cocktails and tapas or dinner. Local beers from Colonial Brewing are on tap, and the menu smartly channels both Asian and European flavours.

Swings Taphouse & Kitchen BISTRO, WINE BAR $$
(www.swings.com.au; 85 Bussell Hwy; shared plates $13-28, pizza $20-23; noon-late) Local wine served from taps, craft beer, tasty shared tapas plates and gourmet pizzas combine at this relaxed and cosmopolitan spot at the northern end of Margaret River township.

Settler's Tavern PUB FOOD $$
(www.settlerstavern.com; 114 Bussell Hwy; mains $16-36; 11am-midnight Mon-Sat, to 10pm Sun) There's live entertainment Thursday to Sunday at Settler's, so pop in for good pub grub and a beer, or choose a wine from the extensive list. Dinner options are limited in Margaret River, and Settler's is often wildly popular with locals and visitors. Try the mammoth Seafood Deluxe with a pint of the pub's own Great White Pale Ale.

Larder DELI $$
(www.thelarder.biz; 2/99 Bussell Hwy; 9.30am-6pm Mon-Sat, 10.30am-4pm Sun) Showcasing local Margaret River produce and gourmet foods, The Larder also sells takeaway meals ($15 to $17) – a good option for dinner – and comprehensive breakfast packs, picnic hampers and barbecue fixings ($50 to $95). Occasional cooking classes complete the tasty menu.

★Miki's Open Kitchen JAPANESE $$$
(☎08-9758 7673; www.facebook.com/mikisopenkitchen; 131 Bussell Hwy; small plates $12-16, large plates $28-37; ⏲6pm-late Tue-Sat) Secure a spot around the open kitchen and enjoy the irresistible theatre of the Miki's team creating innovative Japanese spins on the best of WA seafood and produce. Combine a Margaret River wine with the $55 multicourse tasting menu for the most diverse experience, and settle in to watch the laid-back Zen chefs work their tempura magic.

Shopping

Tunbridge Gallery ARTS
(www.tunbridgegallery.com.au; 101 Bussell Hwy; ⏲10am-5pm Mon-Sat, to 3pm Sun) Excellent Aboriginal art gallery featuring WA works.

Information

Visitor Centre (☎08-9780 5911; www.margaretriver.com; 100 Bussell Hwy; ⏲9am-5pm) Bookings and information, plus displays on local wineries.

Getting Around

Margaret River Beach Bus (☎08-9757 9532; www.margaretriverbackpackers.com.au) Minibus linking the township and the beaches around Prevelly ($10, three daily); summer only, bookings essential.

Around Margaret River

West of the Margaret River township, the coastline provides spectacular surfing and walks. Prevelly is the main settlement, with a few places to sleep and eat. Most of the sights are on Caves Rd or just off it.

Sights & Activities

CaveWorks & Lake Cave CAVE
(www.margaretriver.com; Conto Rd; single cave adult/child $22/10; ⏲9am-5pm, Lake Cave tours hourly 9.30am-3.30pm) The main ticket office for Lake, Mammoth and Jewel Caves (p128), CaveWorks also has excellent displays about caves, cave conservation and local fossil discoveries. There's also an authentic model cave and a 'cave crawl' experience. Behind the centre is Lake Cave, the prettiest of them all, where limestone formations are reflected in an underground stream. The vegetated entrance to this cave is spectacular and includes a karri tree with a girth of 7m.

Lake Cave is the deepest of all the caves open to the public. There are more than 300 steps down to the entrance (a 62m drop).

CaveWorks is 20km south of Margaret River, off Caves Rd. Single cave tickets include entry to CaveWorks. The Grand Tour Pass (adult/child $55/24), covering CaveWorks and all three caves, is valid for seven days, while the Ultimate Pass (adult/child $70/30) also includes Cape Leeuwin lighthouse.

Mammoth Cave CAVE
(www.margaretriver.com; Caves Rd; adult/child $22/10; ⏲9am-5pm) Mammoth Cave boasts a fossilised jawbone of *Zygomaturus trilobus,* a giant wombatlike creature, as well as other fossil remains and the impressive Mammoth Shawl formation. Visits are self-guided; an MP3 audio player is provided.

Calgardup & Giants Caves CAVES
(www.parks.dpaw.wa.gov.au) These two self-guided caves are managed by the Department of Environment and Conservation (DEC), which provides helmets and torches. **Calgardup Cave** (Caves Rd; adult/child $15/8; ⏲9am-4.15pm) has a seasonal underground lake and is an attractive illustration of the role of the caves in the ecosystem – a stream transports nutrients to the creatures living in the cave, while tree roots hang overhead. **Giants Cave** (Caves Rd; adult/child $15/8; ⏲9.30am-3.30pm school & public holidays only), further south, is deeper and longer and has some steep ladders and scrambles.

Ellensbrook Homestead HISTORIC BUILDING
(www.ntwa.com.au; Ellensbrook Rd; adult/child $4/2; ⏲10am-4pm Fri-Mon) Around 8km northwest of Margaret River, Ellensbrook (1857) was the first home of settlers Alfred and Ellen Bussell. The Wardandi people welcomed them, gave them Noongar names, and led them to this sheltered site. The basic ramshackle house is constructed of paperbark, driftwood, timber, lime, dung and hair. Between 1899 and 1917, Edith Bussell, who farmed the property alone for many years, established an Aboriginal mission. Children were taught to read and write, and two became beneficiaries of Edith's will.

A short walk leads to Meekadarabee ('bathing place of the moon'), a beautiful grotto set below trickling rapids and surrounded by lush bush, associated with a pair of star-crossed Indigenous lovers. The grounds are open even when the house isn't.

Boranup Gallery GALLERY
(www.boranupgallery.com; 7981 Caves Rd; ⌚10am-4pm) Local arts and crafts, 22km south of Margaret River, with a wide selection of jarrah furniture.

Boranup Drive SCENIC DRIVE
This 14km diversion runs along an unsealed road through Leeuwin-Naturaliste National Park's beautiful karri forest. Near the southern end there's a lookout offering sea views.

Eagles Heritage WILDLIFE RESERVE
(☎08-9757 2960; www.eaglesheritage.com.au; adult/child $17/10; ⌚10am-4.15pm Sat-Thu) Housing Australia's largest collection of raptors, this centre, 5km south of Margaret River, rehabilitates many birds of prey each year. There are free-flight displays at 11am and 1.30pm.

Sleeping

Surfpoint GUESTHOUSE $
(☎08-9757 1777; www.surfpoint.com.au; Reidle Dr, Gnarabup; s/d from $70/110; @ ᯤ ≋) This light and airy place offers the beach on a budget. The rooms are clean and well presented, and there's a very enticing little pool. Private rooms with en-suite facilities are good value.

National Park Campgrounds CAMPGROUND $
(www.parkstay.dpaw.wa.gov.au; sites per adult/child $7.50/2.20) The Department of Parks & Wildlife has three basic campgrounds within Leeuwin-Naturaliste National Park. **Conto Campground** (Conto Rd) has gas barbecues, toilets and running water; **Boranup Campground** (off Boranup Dr), under the tall trees off the southern end of Boranup Dr, can get damp in winter; **Point Road Campground** is only accessible by foot or 4WD from the northern end of Boranup Dr.

Llewellin's B&B $$
(☎08-9757 9516; www.llewellinsguesthouse.com.au; 64 Yates Rd; r $210-258; ᯤ) It may be a Welsh name, but the style's French provincial in the four upmarket yet homely guestrooms.

★ **Acacia Chalets** CHALET $$$
(☎08-9757 2718; www.acaciachalets.com.au; 113 Yates Rd; d $250-280; ❄) Private bushland – complete with marsupial locals – conceals three luxury chalets that are well located to explore the region's vineyards, caves and rugged nearby coastline. Limestone walls and honey-coloured jarrah floors are combined in some of the area's best self-contained accommodation. Spacious decks are equipped with gas barbecues.

Eating & Drinking

Watershed Premium Wines RESTAURANT $$$
(www.watershedwines.com.au; cnr Bussell Hwy & Darch Rd; cafe $16-29, restaurant $38-44; ⌚10am-5pm) Famous for its 'Awakening' cabernet sauvignon, and regularly rated as one of WA's best vineyard restaurants, dining options include an informal cafe and Watershed's classier restaurant with expansive views of a compact lake and trellised vines.

Xanadu RESTAURANT $$$
(☎08-9758 9531; www.xanaduwines.com; Boodjidup Rd; mains $32-39; ⌚10am-5pm, restaurant noon-3pm Thu-Mon) Escape into your own personal pleasure dome in the hip and chic restaurant filling Xanadu's vast space. The menu changes seasonally – we had terrific crispy skin snapper with anchovy mayonnaise. Definitely leave room for dessert.

Voyager Estate WINERY
(☎08-9757 6354; www.voyagerestate.com.au; Stevens Rd; ⌚10am-5pm, tours 11am Tue, Thu, Sat & Sun) The formal gardens and Cape Dutch–style buildings delight at Voyager Estate, the grandest of Margaret River's wineries. Tours of the estate are available ($25 to $75 including tastings and lunch).

Leeuwin Estate WINERY
(☎08-9759 0000; www.leeuwinestate.com.au; Stevens Rd; mains $31-39; ⌚10am-5pm daily, dinner Sat) An impressive estate with tall trees and lawns gently rolling down to the bush, Leeuwin Estate's Art Series chardonnay is one of the best in the country. Behind-the-scenes wine tours and tastings take place at 11am (adult/child $12.50/4). Big open-air concerts are regularly held here.

Stella Bella WINERY
(www.stellabella.com.au; 205 Rosabrook Rd; ⌚10am-5pm) No bells and whistles, just excellent wines with the prettiest labels in the region.

Information

National Park Information Centre (☎08-9757 7422; www.parks.dpaw.wa.gov.au; Calgardup Cave, Caves Rd; ⌚9am-4.15pm) National parks information.

Augusta & Around

POP 1700

Augusta is positioned at the mouth of the Blackwood River, 5km north of Cape Leeuwin, and quite separate from the main wine region. There are a few vineyards, but the vibe here is less epicurean, and more languid.

Sights & Activities

Operators running boat trips up the Blackwood River include **Absolutely Eco River Cruises** (☎08-9758 4003; cdragon@westnet.com.au; adult/child $30/15; ⊙Oct-May) and **Miss Flinders** (☎0409 377 809; adult/child $30/15; ⊙Oct-May).

Cape Leeuwin Lighthouse LIGHTHOUSE
(www.margaretriver.com; adult/child $8/5; ⊙9am-4.30pm) Wild and windy Cape Leeuwin, where the Indian and Southern Oceans meet, is the most southwesterly point in Australia. It takes its name from a Dutch ship that passed here in 1622. The lighthouse (1896), WA's tallest, offers magnificent views of the coastline. Tours leave every 40 minutes from 9am to 4.20pm (adult/child $20/13) – expect a short wait during the holiday season. The Ultimate Pass (adult/child $70/30) incorporates admission to the lighthouse with Jewel, Lake and Mammoth Caves.

Jewel Cave CAVE
(www.margaretriver.com; Caves Rd; adult/child $22/10; ⊙tours hourly 9.30am-3.30pm) The most spectacular of the region's caves, Jewel Cave has an impressive 5.9m straw stalactite, so far the longest seen in a tourist cave. Fossil remains of a Tasmanian tiger (thylacine), believed to be 3500 years old, were discovered here. It's located near the south end of Caves Rd, 8km northwest of Augusta.

The nearby **Moondyne Cave** (www.margaretriver.com; Caves Rd; Moondyne Experience $95; ⊙10am-2pm Tue & Fri Jun-Dec) can be visited on the Moondyne Experience, a subterranean adventure combining overalls, hard hats and torches. The tour concludes with lunch at Jewel Cave, and prior booking is essential. Children must be at least 12 years of age.

Augusta Historical Museum MUSEUM
(Blackwood Ave; adult/child $5/2; ⊙1-3pm) Interesting local exhibits.

Blackwood River Houseboats HOUSEBOATS
(☎08-9758 0181; www.blackwoodriverhouseboats.com.au; Westbay) Take care of your accommodation, river cruise and fishing trip all at once with a houseboat holiday. The houseboats are easy to drive and available for two-night/three-day hire (weekend $1000 to $1900) or for weekly hire ($2100 to $3800). A midweek rental will give you three nights for the weekend price.

Sleeping & Eating

Baywatch Manor YHA HOSTEL $
(☎08-9758 1290; www.baywatchmanor.com.au; 9 Heppingstone View, Augusta; dm $29, d with/without bathroom $93/73; @ 📶) Clean, modern rooms with creamy brick walls and antique furniture. There is a bay view from the deck and, in winter, a fire in the communal lounge. Some doubles have compact balconies.

Hamelin Bay Holiday Park CARAVAN PARK $
(☎08-9758 5540; www.hamelinbayholidaypark.com.au; Hamelin Bay West Rd; 2-person sites $28-45, cabins $90-220) Absolute beachfront, northwest of Augusta, this secluded place gets very busy during holiday times.

Best Western Georgiana Molloy MOTEL $$
(☎08-9758 1255; www.augustaaccommodation.com.au; 84 Blackwood Ave, Augusta; r $110-180) The decor's a little dated, but the spacious, self-contained units are stand-out value, each with a small garden area.

Deckchair Gourmet CAFE $
(Blackwood Ave, Augusta; mains $10-25; ⊙8am-3pm Mon-Sat, to noon Sun; 📶) Excellent coffee and good food. Try the bacon and egg wrap.

Information

Visitor Centre (☎08-9758 0166; www.margaretriver.com; cnr Blackwood Ave & Ellis St, Augusta; ⊙9am-5pm) Information and bookings.

SOUTHERN FORESTS

The tall forests of WA's southwest are simply magnificent, with towering gums (karri, jarrah, marri) sheltering cool undergrowth. Between the forests, small towns bear witness to the region's history of logging and mining. Many have redefined themselves as small-scale tourist centres where you can take walks, wine tours, canoe trips and trout- and marron-fishing expeditions.

Getting There & Away

Transwa (☎1300 662 205; www.transwa.wa.gov.au) coach routes include the following:

- SW1 (three weekly) to Nannup and Pemberton from East Perth, Bunbury, Busselton, Margaret River and Augusta.

- SW2 (three weekly) to Balingup, Bridgetown, Manjimup and Pemberton from East Perth, Mandurah and Bunbury.
- GS3 (daily) to Balingup, Bridgetown, Manjimup and Pemberton from Perth, Bunbury, Walpole, Denmark and Albany.

South West Coach Lines (☎08-9261 7600; www.transdevsw.com.au) runs services to the following locations:

- Nannup from Busselton (twice weekdays) and Bunbury (weekdays).
- Balingup, Bridgetown and Manjimup from Bunbury, Mandurah and Perth (daily).

Nannup

POP 500

Nannup's historic weatherboard buildings and cottage gardens have an idyllic bush setting on the Blackwood River. The Noongar-derived name means 'a place to stop and rest'; it's also a good base for bushwalkers and canoeists.

Sporadic but persistent stories of sightings of a striped wolflike animal, dubbed the Nannup tiger, have led to hopes that a Tasmanian tiger may have survived in the surrounding bush (the last known Tasmanian tiger, or thylacine, died in Hobart Zoo in 1936).

Activities

Blackwood River Canoeing CANOEING
(☎08-9756 1209; www.blackwoodrivercanoeing.com; hire per day from $25) Trips access the largely untouched jarrah forests framing southwest Australia's longest river, and multiday expeditions incorporate overnight camping. Blackwood River Canoeing provides equipment, basic instruction and transfers for canoeing paddles and longer expeditions. The best time to paddle is in late winter and early spring, when the water levels are up.

Festivals & Events

Nannup Music Festival MUSIC
(www.nannupmusicfestival.org) Held around early March, focusing on folk and world music.

Sleeping & Eating

Caravan Park CARAVAN PARK $
(☎08-9756 1211; www.nannupcaravanparks.com.au; sites $27-32) This riverside caravan park has overflow camping at two other nearby sites.

Holberry House B&B $$
(☎08-9756 1276; www.holberryhouse.com; 14 Grange Rd; r $140-190;) The decor might lean towards granny-chic, but this large house on the hill has charming hosts and comfortable rooms. It's surrounded by large gardens dotted with quirky sculptures (open to nonguests for $4).

Pickle & O CAFE $
(16 Warren Rd; snacks $7-12; ⏱10am-4pm) Good coffee, huge slabs of cheesecake, and smoked trout kebab wraps are all tasty reasons to stop in at this quirky combination of health food store and organic, sustainable cafe.

Nannup Bridge Cafe CAFE $$
(1 Warren Rd; breakfast & lunch $9-24, dinner $16-38; ⏱9am-2pm Tue-Sun, 6-8pm Wed-Sat) This riverfront cafe morphs into a bistro at night. Stand-out dishes include the pork belly and the sticky-date pudding.

Information

Visitor Centre (☎08-9756 1211; www.nannupwa.com; 4 Brockman St; ⏱9am-5pm Mon-Fri, 10am-3pm Sat, 10am-1pm Sun) Administers the neighbouring caravan park.

Bridgetown

POP 2400

Lovely Bridgetown is surrounded by karri forests and farmland, and spread around the Blackwood River. Weekends are busy, and the popular **Blues at Bridgetown Festival** (www.bluesatbridgetown.com.au) occurs annually on the second weekend of November.

Bridgetown's old buildings include **Bridgedale House** (Hampton St; admission by gold-coin donation; ⏱10am-2pm Sat & Sun), built of mud and clay by the area's first settler in 1862, and since restored by the National Trust.

Sleeping & Eating

Bridgetown Hotel HOTEL $$
(☎08-9761 1034; www.bridgetownhotel.com.au; 157 Hampton St; r $165-250, mains $17-29;) You don't expect quirky pizzas (pepperoni, lime and tequila; lamb and tzatziki) or large modern bedrooms with spa baths in an Australian country pub. This main street 1920s gem features both.

Bridgetown Riverside Chalets CHALET $$
(☎08-9761 1040; www.bridgetownchalets.com.au; 1338 Brockman Hwy; chalets from $140) On a rural riverside property, 5km up the road to Nannup, these four stand-alone wooden chalets

(complete with pot-bellied stoves and washing machines) sleep up to six in two bedrooms.

The Barking Cow CAFE $$
(88 Hampton St; breakfast $11-18, lunch $13-21; ⏲8am-2.30pm Mon-Sat) Colourful, cosy, and serving the best coffee in town, the Barking Cow is worth stopping at for daily vegetarian specials and world-famous-in-Bridgetown gourmet burgers.

Cidery CAFE $$
(www.thecidery.com.au; 43 Gifford Rd; mains $10-25; ⏲11am-4pm Sat-Thu, to 8pm Fri) Craft beer, cider and light lunches on outdoor tables by the river. On Friday nights from 5.30pm there's live music.

Information

Visitor Centre (☎08-9761 1740; www.bridgetown.com.au; 154 Hampton St; ⏲9am-5pm Mon-Fri, 10am-3pm Sat, 10am-1pm Sun; @) Includes apple-harvesting memorabilia.

Manjimup

POP 4300

Surrounded by spectacular forest, Manjimup is at the heart of WA's timber industry. For foodies it's known for something very different: truffles. During August especially, Manjimup's black Périgord truffles make their way onto top Australian menus.

Sights & Activities

Truffle & Wine Co FARM
(☎08-9777 2474; www.truffleandwine.com.au; Seven Day Rd, Manjimup; ⏲10am-4pm, lunch noon-3pm) To discover how the world's most expensive produce is harvested, follow your snout to the Truffle & Wine Co. Join a 2½-hour truffle hunt with the clever truffle-hunting Labradors on Saturday or Sunday from June to August (adult/child $60/30; book ahead). A three-course truffle-infused lunch ($65) is optional afterwards. Throughout the year there are plenty of truffle products to sample, and the attached provedore and cafe serves up cheese and charcuterie platters ($18 to $48), and coffee and cake.

Timber & Heritage Park PARK
(cnr Rose & Edward Sts; ⏲9am-5pm) Located in town this park has a little lake, free barbecues and logging paraphernalia, including a replica of One Tree Bridge.

One Tree Bridge & Glenoran Pool BRIDGE
(Graphite Rd) In a forest clearing 22km from town are the remains of One Tree Bridge. It was constructed from a single karri log carefully felled to span the width of the river but rendered unusable after the floods of 1966. Adjacent is gorgeous Glenoran Pool, a popular swimming hole.

Four Aces FOREST
(Graphite Rd) These four 300-plus-year-old karri trees sit in a straight line; stand directly in front and they disappear into one. There's a short loop walk through the surrounding karri glade, or a 1½-hour loop bushwalking trail from the Four Aces to One Tree Bridge.

Diamond Tree Lookout LOOKOUT
Nine kilometres south of Manjimup along the South Western Hwy is the Diamond Tree Lookout. Metal spikes allow you to climb this 52m karri, and there's a nature trail nearby.

Sleeping

Diamond Forest Cottages COTTAGES $$
(☎08-9772 3170; www.diamondforest.com.au; 29159 South Western Hwy; chalets $160-210; ❄) South of Manjimup, before the turn-off to Pemberton, is this collection of well-equipped wooden chalets with decks, scattered around a farm. Turkeys and sheep wander around, and there's a petting zoo and daily animal-feeding for the kids.

Information

Visitor Centre (☎08-9771 1831; www.manjimupwa.com; Giblett St; ⏲9am-5pm) Located in Manjim Park.

Pemberton

POP 760

Hidden deep in the karri forests, drowsy Pemberton produces excellent wine. If Margaret River is WA's Bordeaux, Pemberton is its Burgundy – producing excellent chardonnay and pinot noir, among other varietals. Wine tourism isn't as developed here, with some of the better names only offering tastings by appointment. Grab a free map listing cellar door opening hours from the visitor centre.

The national parks circling Pemberton are impressive. Aim to spend a day or two driving the Karri Forest Explorer tracks, walking the trails and picnicking in the green depths.

Activities

Salitage WINE TASTING

(☎08-9776 1195; www.salitage.com.au; Vasse Hwy; ⌚10am-4pm Fri-Tue) Salitage's pinot noir has been rated the state's best, while its chardonnay and sauvignon blanc are also very highly regarded. Hour-long vineyard tours leave at 11am; call ahead.

Pemberton Tramway TRAM RIDES

(☎08-9776 1322; www.pemtram.com.au; adult/child $24/12; ⌚10.45am & 2pm) Built between 1929 and 1933, the tram route travels through lush karri and marri forests to Warren River. A commentary is provided and it's a fun – if noisy – 1¾-hour return trip.

Mountford WINE TASTING

(www.mountfordwines.com.au; Bamess Rd; ⌚10am-4pm) The wines and ciders produced here are all certified organic, plus there's a gallery on site. It's located north of Pemberton and is easily incorporated into the Karri Forest Explorer circuit.

Pemberton Wine Centre WINE TASTING

(www.marima.com.au; 388 Old Vasse Rd; ⌚noon-4pm Mon-Fri) At the very heart of Warren National Park, this centre offers tastings of local wines and can compile a mixed case of your favourites.

Pemberton Pool SWIMMING

(Swimming Pool Rd) FREE Surrounded by karri trees, this natural pool is popular on a hot day – despite the warning sign (currents, venomous snakes). They breed them tough around here. Nearby is the trailhead for tracks making up the **Pemberton Mountain Bike Park** (www.pembertonvisitor.com.au/pages/pemberton-mountain-bike-park/). Trail maps can be downloaded from the website.

Tours

Pemberton Hiking & Canoeing HIKING, CANOEING

(☎08-9776 1559; www.hikingandcanoeing.com.au; half-/full day $50/100) Environmentally sound tours in Warren and D'Entrecasteaux National Parks and to the Yeagarup sand dunes. Specialist tours (wildflowers, frogs, rare fauna) are also available, as are night canoeing trips ($50) to spot nocturnal wildlife.

Pemberton Discovery Tours 4WD, MOUNTAIN BIKING

(☎08-9776 0484; www.pembertondiscoverytours.com.au; 12 Brockman St; adult/child $105/50) Half-day 4WD tours to the Yeagarup sand dunes and the Warren River mouth. Other tours focus on local vineyards, breweries and cideries, and the wild coastal scenery of D'Entrecasteaux National Park. Visit its central Pemberton location for local information and mountain-bike hire including details of nearby tracks and recommended rides.

Donnelly River Cruises BOAT TOUR

(☎08-9777 1018; www.donnellyrivercruises.com.au; adult/child $65/35) Cruises through 12km of D'Entrecasteaux National Park to the cliffs of the Southern Ocean.

Sleeping

Pemberton Backpackers YHA HOSTEL $

(☎08-9776 1105; www.yha.com.au; 7 Brockman St; dm/s/d $33/70/77; @ 📶) The main hostel is given over to seasonal workers, but you'll need to check-in here for a room in the separate cottage (8 Dean St) that's set aside for travellers. It's cute and cosy, but book ahead as it only has three rooms, one of which is a six-person dorm.

Best Western Pemberton Hotel HOTEL $

(☎08-9776 1017; www.pembertonhotel.bestwestern.com.au; 66 Brockman St; r from $115; 📶) Attached to a classic country pub, the comfortable accommodation occupies a striking new rammed-earth and cedar extension. The pub's friendly bistro is the best place for an evening meal in town.

Old Picture Theatre Holiday Apartments APARTMENT $$

(☎08-9776 1513; www.oldpicturetheatre.com.au; cnr Ellis & Guppy Sts; apt $160-210; ❄ 📶) The town's old cinema has been revamped into well-appointed, self-contained, spacious apartments with lots of jarrah detail and black-and-white movie photos. It offers good value for money and includes an on-site spa.

Pump Hill Farm Cottages COTTAGES $$

(☎08-9776 1379; www.pumphill.com.au; Pump Hill Rd; cottages $130-175) Families love this farm property, where kids are taken on a daily hay ride to feed the animals. Child-free folk will enjoy the ambience of the private, well-equipped cottages too.

★ **Foragers** COTTAGES $$$

(☎08-9776 1580; www.foragers.com.au; cnr Roberts & Northcliffe Rds; cottages $225-270; ❄)

Choose between very nice, simple karri cottages, or leap to the top of the ladder with the luxury eco-chalets. The latter are light and airy, with elegant, contemporary decor, eco-conscious wastewater systems and a solar-passive design. You're also right on hand to enjoy culinary treats at the adjacent Foragers Field Kitchen.

Marima Cottages COTTAGE **$$$**
(08-9776 1211; www.marima.com.au; 388 Old Vasse Rd; cottages $249-269) Right in the middle of Warren National Park, these four country-style rammed-earth-and-cedar cottages with pot-bellied stoves and lots of privacy are luxurious getaways. Look forward to marsupial company at dusk.

Eating & Drinking

Local specialities are trout and marron, a freshwater crayfish.

Holy Smoke CAFE, SELF-CATERING **$**
(www.holysmoke.com.au; Dickinson St; snacks $5-15; 10am-4pm Mon-Fri, from 9am Sat & Sun) Good coffee, tasty cakes and toasted sandwiches situated adjacent to the excellent Pemberton Fine Woodcraft Gallery. Especially good are the tasting platters of Holy Smoke's smoked meats, fish and pâtés.

Forest Fresh Marron SELF-CATERING **$**
(0428 887 720; www.forestfreshmarron.com.au; Pump Hill Rd; 10am-5pm Mon-Fri, 4.30-5.30pm Sat & Sun) Live, sustainably farmed marron for sale. Transport packs – to keep the wee beasties alive for up to 30 hours – and cooking pots are also available. It's 300m to the left of the caravan park.

Millhouse Cafe CAFE **$$**
(Brockman St; breakfast $10-21, lunch $10-16; 8am-4pm) Look forward to a few surprising South American spins on breakfast – try the Mexican corn tart with avocado – and good coffee at this cosy heritage cottage with wraparound verandahs. Marron and trout are on offer for lunch, and local art is often displayed on the walls.

Foragers Field Kitchen INTERNATIONAL **$$$**
(08-9776 1503; www.foragers.com.au; cnr Roberts & Northcliffe Rds; dinner $55-75) Join renowned chef Sophie Zalokar at one of her regular Friday or Saturday set dinners – options could include wood-fired Italian dishes or seasonal four-course menus – or sign up for one of her cooking classes (usually on a Wednesday night). Check the website's events calendar for dates. Booking at least 48 hours ahead is preferred.

Jarrah Jacks CRAFT BEER
(www.jarrahjacks.com.au; Lot 2 Kemp Rd; mains $20-26; 10am-5pm Thu-Tue) Vineyard views, six craft beers, and tasty food including marron salad, crispy squid, shared platters and robust burgers.

Information

Department of Parks & Wildlife (08-9776 1207; www.dpaw.wa.gov.au; Kennedy St; 8am-4.30pm) Information on local parks and bushwalks.

Visitor Centre (08-9776 1133; www.pembertonvisitor.com.au; Brockman St; 9am-4pm; @) Includes a pioneer museum and karri-forest discovery centre.

Karri Forest Explorer

Punctuated by glorious walks, magnificent trees and picnic areas, the Karri Forest Explorer tourist drive wends its way along 86km of scenic (partly unsealed) roads through three national parks (vehicle entry per park $12; four-week holiday pass $44).

Attractions include the **Gloucester Tree**, a fire-lookout tree laddered with a spiral metal stairway. If you're fit and fearless, climb 58m to the top.

The **Dave Evans Bicentennial Tree**, tallest of the 'climbing trees' at 68m, is in Warren National Park, 11km southwest of Pemberton. Its tree-house cage weighs 2 tonnes and can sway up to 1.5m in either direction in strong winds. The Bicentennial Tree one-way loop leads via **Maiden Bush** to the **Heartbreak Trail**, passing through 250-year-old karri stands. Nearby Drafty's Camp and Warren Campsite are great for overnighting (sites per adult/child $7.50/2.20).

The enchanting **Beedelup National Park**, 15km west of Pemberton on the Vasse Hwy (Rte 104) includes a scenic walk that crosses Beedelup Brook near **Beedelup Falls**. There are numerous bird species to be found in the tall trees. North of town, **Big Brook Arboretum** FREE features 'big' trees from all over the world.

Karri Forest Explorer

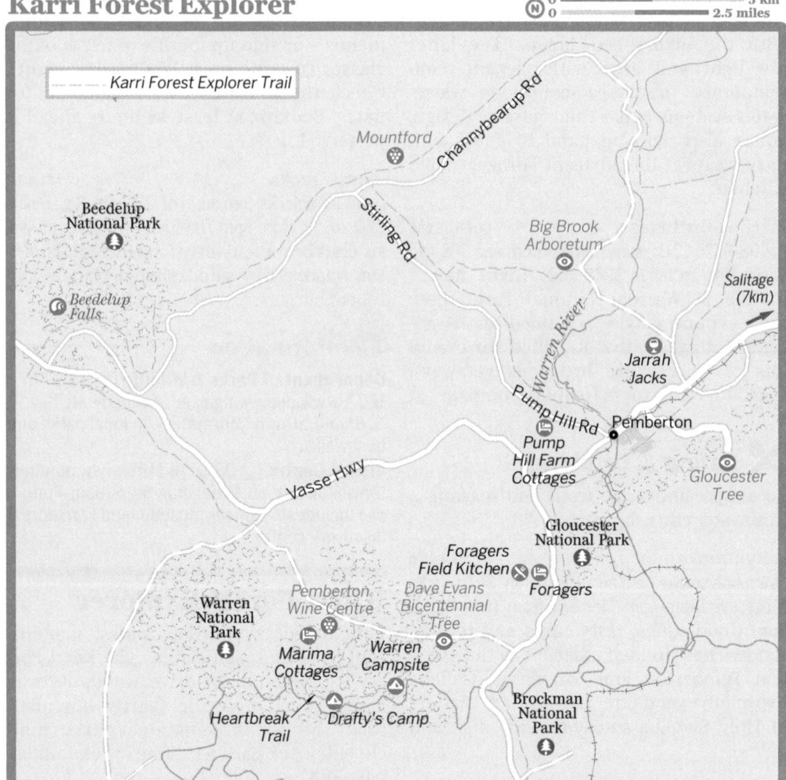

The track loops on and off the main roads, so you can drive short sections at a time. Grab a brochure from Pemberton's visitor centre.

Shannon National Park

The 535-sq-km **Shannon National Park** (entry per car/motorcycle $12/6) is on the South Western Hwy, 53km south of Manjimup. Until 1968 Shannon was the site of WA's biggest timber mill.

The 48km **Great Forest Trees Drive** is a one-way loop, split by the highway. Start at the park day-use area on the north of the highway. From here there's an easy 3.5km walk to the Shannon Dam and a steeper 5.5km loop to Mokare's Rock, with great views.

Further along, the 8km (return) Great Forest Trees Walk crosses the Shannon River. Off the southern part of the drive, boardwalks look over stands of giant karri at **Snake Gully** and **Big Tree Grove**.

In the park's southwest, a 6km (return) walking track links Boorara Tree with a lookout point over Lane Poole Falls.

There is a sizeable **campground** (www.parks.dpaw.wa.gov.au; sites per adult/child $10/6.60) with showers in the spot where the original timber-milling town used to be. A self-contained bunkhouse, **Shannon Lodge** (per night $66, bond $150), is available for groups of up to eight people; book this through Parks & Wildlife in Pemberton.

Southern WA

Includes ➡

Best Places to Eat

- York Street Cafe (p142)
- Mrs Jones (p139)
- Maleeya's Thai Cafe (p145)
- Pepper & Salt (p139)

Best Places to Stay

- Cape Howe Cottages (p139)
- Beach House at Bayside (p142)
- Esperance B&B by the Sea (p149)
- The Lily (p146)

Why Go?

Standing above the waves and cliffs of the rugged South Coast is an exhilarating experience. And on calm days, when the sea is aquamarine and white-sand beaches lie pristine and welcoming, it's an altogether different type of magnificent. Even busy summer holiday periods down here in the Great Southern are relaxed. It's just that bit too far from Perth for the holiday hordes.

Winter months bring pods of migrating whales, while the spectacular tingle trees of Walpole's Valley of the Giants are more super-sized evidence of nature's wonder.

For a change from the great outdoors, Albany – the state's earliest European settlement – has colonial and Anzac history, and Denmark has excellent wine, craft beer and good food.

From Esperance, strike out north to begin a compelling cross-country adventure across the Nullarbor Plain from Norseman, or continue on to the gold-mining past, present and future of rambunctious Kalgoorlie.

When to Go

Esperance

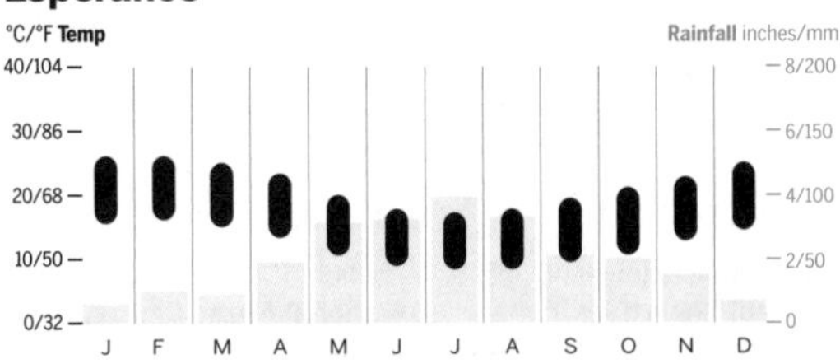

Jan The best beach weather – and it's not as hot or crowded as the west coast.

Sep Go wild for wild flowers and whales.

Dec Perfect weather for the Stirling Range and Porongurup National Parks.

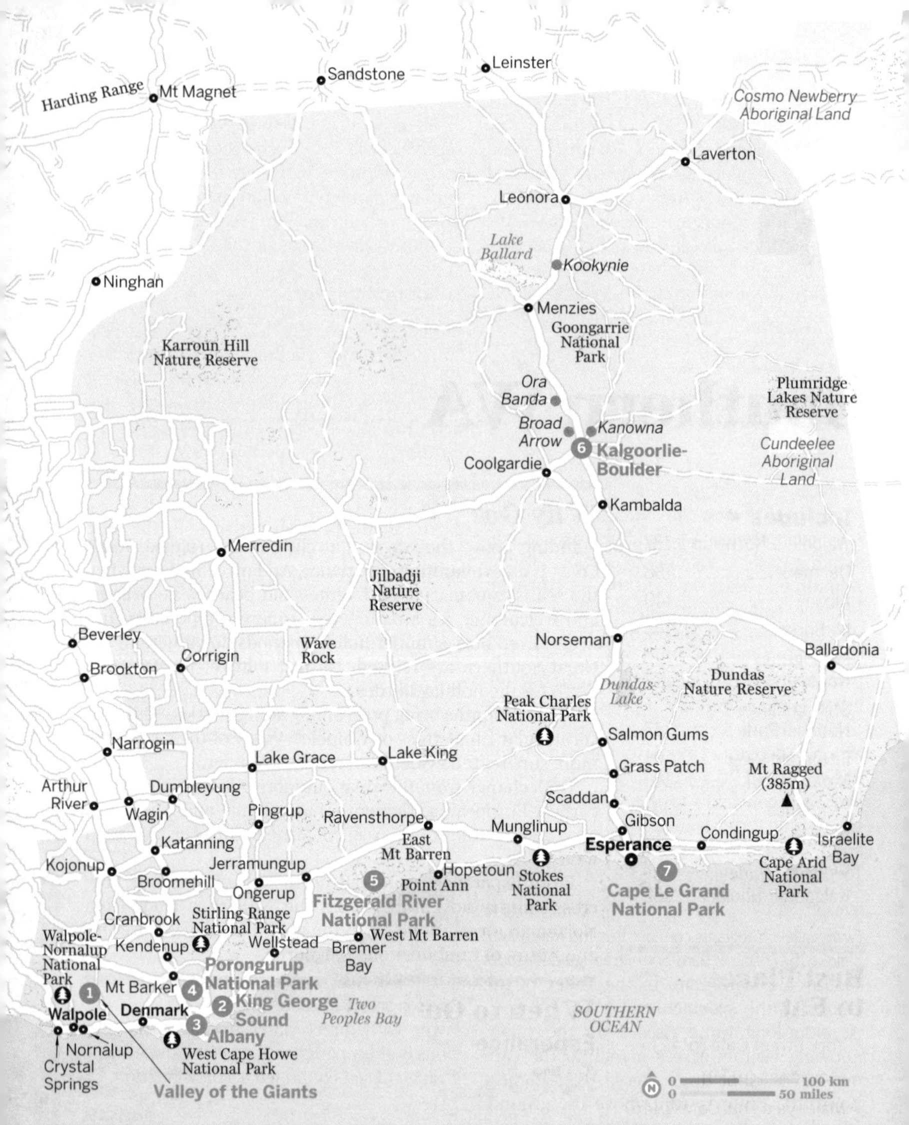

Harding Range
Mt Magnet
Sandstone
Leinster
Cosmo Newberry Aboriginal Land
Laverton
Leonora
Lake Ballard
Kookynie
Ninghan
Menzies
Goongarrie National Park
Karroun Hill Nature Reserve
Ora Banda
Plumridge Lakes Nature Reserve
Broad Arrow
Kanowna
6 Kalgoorlie-Boulder
Cundeelee Aboriginal Land
Coolgardie
Kambalda
Merredin
Jilbadji Nature Reserve
Beverley
Wave Rock
Norseman
Balladonia
Corrigin
Brookton
Dundas Lake
Dundas Nature Reserve
Peak Charles National Park
Salmon Gums
Narrogin
Lake Grace
Lake King
Grass Patch
Mt Ragged (385m)
Arthur River
Dumbleyung
Wagin
Pingrup
Scaddan
Ravensthorpe
Gibson
Munglinup
Condingup
Israelite Bay
Katanning
Esperance
East Mt Barren
Cape Arid National Park
Kojonup
Jerramungup
Hopetoun
Stokes National Park
7 Cape Le Grand National Park
Broomehill
Ongerup
5 Point Ann
Fitzgerald River National Park
Cranbrook
Stirling Range National Park
West Mt Barren
Walpole-Nornalup National Park
Kendenup
Wellstead
Bremer Bay
Porongurup National Park
Mt Barker
4
1
Walpole
Denmark
2 King George Sound
Two Peoples Bay
SOUTHERN OCEAN
3 Albany
Nornalup
Crystal Springs
West Cape Howe National Park
Valley of the Giants
0 100 km
0 50 miles

Southern WA Highlights

1 Walking among and above the giant tingle trees in the Valley of the Giants **Tree Top Walk** (p137).

2 Competing to see who can spot the most whales in Albany's **King George Sound** (p142).

3 Understanding the sacrifices made by brave soldiers 100 years ago at the **National Anzac Centre** (p141) in Albany.

4 Hiking among the tall trees and granite outcrops of **Porongurup National Park** (p144).

5 Wandering through wild flowers along the walking tracks of **Fitzgerald River National Park** (p146).

6 Feeling dwarfed in the depths of the spectacular Super Pit in **Kalgoorlie** (p152).

7 Swimming, surfing and soaking up the sun at the beaches of **Cape Le Grand National Park** (p150).

Walpole & Nornalup

The peaceful twin inlets of Walpole (pop 320) and Nornalup (pop 50) make good bases for exploring the heavily forested Walpole Wilderness Area – an immense wilderness incorporating a rugged coastline, several national parks, marine parks, nature reserves and forest conservation areas – covering a whopping 3630 sq km. Walpole is the bigger settlement, and it's here that the South Western Hwy (Rte 1) becomes the South Coast Hwy.

Sights & Activities

Walpole-Nornalup National Park NATURE RESERVE
(www.parks.dpaw.wa.gov.au) Giant trees include red, yellow and Rates tingle trees (all types of eucalypt, or gum, trees). Good walking tracks include a section of the Bibbulmun Track, which passes through Walpole to Coalmine Beach. Scenic drives include the Knoll Drive, 3km east of Walpole; the Valley of the Giants Road; and through pastoral country to Mt Frankland, 29km north of Walpole. Here you can climb to the summit for panoramic views or walk around the trail at its base. Opposite Knoll Drive, Hilltop Rd leads to a giant tingle tree; this road continues to the Circular Pool on the Frankland River, a popular canoeing spot. You can hire canoes from Nornalup Riverside Chalets.

Valley of the Giants NATURE RESERVE
(www.valleyofthegiants.com.au; Tree Top Walk adult/child $15/7.50; 9am-5pm, free guided tours 10.15am, 11.30am & 2pm) In the Valley of the Giants is the spectacular **Tree Top Walk.** A 600m-long ramp rises from the valley, allowing visitors access high into the canopy of the giant tingle trees. At its highest point, the ramp is 40m above the ground. It's on a gentle incline so it's easy to walk and is accessible by assisted wheelchair. At ground level, the Ancient Empire boardwalk (admission free) meanders through veteran red tingles, up to 16m in circumference and 46m high.

Conspicuous Cliffs LANDMARK
Midway between Nornalup and Peaceful Bay, Conspicuous Cliffs is a good spot for whale watching from July to November. There's a hilltop lookout and a steepish 800m walk to the beach.

Tours

WOW Wilderness Ecocruises CRUISE
(08-9840 1036; www.wowwilderness.com.au; adult/child $45/15) The magnificent landscape and its ecology are brought to life with anecdotes about Aboriginal settlement, salmon fishers and shipwrecked pirates. The 2½-hour cruise through the inlets and river systems leaves at 10am daily; book at the visitor centre.

Naturally Walpole Eco Tours ECOTOUR
(08-9840 1019; www.naturallywalpole.com.au) Half-day tours exploring the Walpole Wilderness (adult/child $95/55) and the Tree Top Walk (adult/child $105/60). Also customised winery and wild flower tours.

Sleeping

There are bush camping sites in the Walpole Wilderness Area, including at Crystal Springs and Fernhook Falls.

Walpole Lodge HOSTEL $
(08-9840 1244; www.walpolelodge.com.au; Pier St, Walpole; dm/s $27/45, d $65-90; @) This popular place is basic, open plan and informal, with great info boards and casual, cheery owners. En-suite rooms are excellent value.

Tingle All Over YHA HOSTEL $
(08-9840 1041; www.yha.com.au; 60 Nockolds St, Walpole; dm/s/d $31/54/74; @) Help yourself to lemons and chillies from the garden of this clean, basic option near the highway. Lots of advice on local walks is on offer.

Rest Point Holiday Village CARAVAN PARK $
(08-9840 1032; www.restpoint.com.au; Rest Point; 2-person sites $26, cabins $80-125) Set on wide lawns with direct water frontage, this spacious holiday park has shade for campers and a range of self-contained accommodation.

Riverside Retreat CHALETS $$
(08-9840 1255; www.riversideretreat.com.au; South Coast Hwy, Nornalup; chalets $150-210) On the banks of the beautiful Frankland River, these well-equipped chalets are great value, with pot-bellied stoves for cosy winter warmth, and tennis and canoeing as outdoor pursuits. Expect frequent visits from the local wildlife.

Nornalup Riverside Chalets CHALETS $$
(08-9840 1107; www.walpole.org.au/nornalupriversidechalets; Riverside Dr, Nornalup; chalets $110-180) Stay a night in sleepy Nornalup in

THE ROAD TO MANDALAY

About 13km west of Walpole, at Crystal Springs, is an 8km gravel road to **Mandalay Beach**, where the *Mandalay*, a Norwegian barque, was wrecked in 1911. The wreck eerily appears every 10 years or so after storms. See the photos at Walpole visitor centre. The beach is glorious, often deserted, and accessed by a boardwalk across sand dunes and cliffs. It's part of D'Entrecasteaux National Park.

these comfortable, colourful self-contained chalets, just a rod's throw from the fish in the Frankland River. The chalets are well spaced out, giving a feeling of privacy.

Eating

Thurlby Herb Farm CAFE **$$**
(www.thurlbyherb.com.au; 3 Gardiner Rd; mains $15-20; ⏲9am-5pm Mon-Fri) Thurlby offers light lunches and cakes accompanied by fresh-picked teas, as well as other herb-based products including soap and aromatherapy treatments. It's north of Walpole on the way to Mt Frankland National Park.

Top Deck Cafe CAFE **$$**
(25 Nockolds St, Walpole; mains $15-27; ⏲9am-2pm & 5.30-9pm) Tucked away in Walpole's main road, Top Deck kicks off with breakfast, and graduates to dinner options including spinach-and-feta pie and a daily curry special.

Information

The **Visitor Centre** (☎08-9840 1111; www.walpole.com.au; South Coast Hwy, Walpole; ⏲9am-5pm; @) is located in Pioneer Cottage.

Getting There & Away

Departing from the visitor centre, **Transwa** (☎1300 662 205; www.transwa.wa.gov.au) bus GS3 heads daily to/from Bunbury ($45, 4½ hours), Bridgetown ($26, 3¼ hours), Pemberton ($20, 1¾ hours), Denmark ($14, 42 minutes) and Albany ($22, 1½ hours).

Denmark

POP 2800

Denmark's beaches and coastline, river and sheltered inlet, forested backdrop and hinterland have attracted a varied, creative and environmentally aware community. Farmers, ferals, fishers and families all mingle during the town's four market days each year.

Denmark was established to supply timber to the early goldfields. Known by the Minang Noongar people as Koorabup (place of the black swan), there's evidence of early Aboriginal settlement in the 3000-year-old fish traps found in Wilson Inlet.

Sights & Activities

Denmark is located in the cool-climate Great Southern wine region and notable wineries include **Howard Park** (www.burchfamilywines.com.au; Scotsdale Rd; ⏲10am-4pm) and **Forest Hill** (www.foresthillwines.com.au; cnr South Coast Hwy & Myers Rd; ⏲10am-4pm). The latter features the excellent Pepper & Salt (p139) restaurant.

Surfing & Fishing

Surfers and anglers should head to ruggedly beautiful **Ocean Beach**. Accredited local instructor Mike Neunuebel gives **surfing lessons** (☎0401 349 8540; www.southcoastsurfinglessons.com.au; 2hr lessons incl equipment from $60).

Walking

To get your bearings, walk the **Mokare Heritage Trail** (a 3km circuit along the Denmark River), or the **Wilson Inlet Trail** (12km return, starting at the river mouth), which forms part of the longer **Nornalup Trail**. The **Mt Shadforth Lookout** has fine coastal views, and lush **Mt Shadforth Rd**, running from town to the South Coast Hwy west of town, makes a great scenic drive. A longer pastoral loop is via **Scotsdale Rd**. Attractions include alpaca farms, wineries, dairy farms, and arts and craft galleries.

Swimming

William Bay National Park, about 20km west of town, offers sheltered swimming in gorgeous **Greens Pool** and **Elephant Rocks**, and has good walking tracks. Swing by **Bartholomews Meadery** (www.honeywine.com.au; 2620 South Coast Hwy; ⏲9.30am-4.30pm) for a post-beach treat of mead (honey wine) or delicious home-made honey-rose-almond ice cream ($5).

Tours

Out of Sight! OUTDOORS
(☎08-9848 2814; www.outofsighttours.com; 5hr tour adult/child $150/75) 4WD nature trips exploring West Cape Howe National Park.

Denmark Wine Lovers Tour BUS TOUR
(☎0410 423 262; www.denmarkwinelovers.com.au) Full-day tours taking in Denmark wineries or heading further afield to Porongurup or Mt Barker.

Festivals & Events

Market Days MARKET
(www.denmarkarts.com.au) Four times a year (mid-December, early and late January and Easter) Denmark hosts riverside market days with craft stalls, music and food.

Festival of Voice MUSIC
(www.denmarkfestivalofvoice.com.au) Performances and workshops on the early June long weekend.

Sleeping

Blue Wren Travellers' Rest YHA HOSTEL $
(☎08-9848 3300; www.denmarkbluewren.com.au; 17 Price St; dm/d/f $28/80/120) Great info panels cover the walls and it's small enough (just 20 beds) to have a homey feel. Bikes can also be rented – $20 per day – and the friendly owner, Graham, is a whiz at bike repairs.

Denmark Rivermouth Caravan Park CARAVAN PARK $
(☎08-98481262; www.denmarkrivermouthcaravanpark.com.au; Inlet Dr; 2-person sites $30, cabins & chalets $135-210) Ideally located for nautical pursuits, this caravan park sits along Wilson Inlet beside the boat ramp. Some of the units are properly flash, although they are quite tightly arranged. There's also a kids playground and kayaks for hire.

31 on the Terrace BOUTIQUE HOTEL $$
(☎08-9848 1700; www.denmarkaccommodation.com.au; 31 Strickland St; r $115-155; ❄) Good-value, stylish en-suite rooms – some with balconies – fill this renovated corner pub in the centre of town. Compact apartments sleep up to five people.

★ **Cape Howe Cottages** COTTAGE $$$
(☎08-9845 1295; www.capehowe.com.au; 322 Tennessee Rd S; cottages $180-290; ❄) For a remote getaway, these five cottages in bushland southeast of Denmark really make the grade. They're all different, but the best is only 1.5km from dolphin-favoured Lowlands Beach and is properly plush – with a BBQ on the deck, a dishwasher in the kitchen and laundry facilities.

Celestine Retreat CHALETS $$$
(☎08-9848 3000; www.celestineretreat.com; 413 Mt Shadforth Rd; d $239-289; ❄) With just four spa chalets scattered over 13 hectares, there are stunning ocean and valley views at this luxury retreat. Romance is also on the agenda, with private spas, fluffy bathrobes and high-end bathroom goodies. Renovation aplenty was happening when we last dropped by.

Eating & Drinking

★ **Mrs Jones** CAFE $$
(☎0467 481 878; www.mrsjonescafe.com; 12 Mt Shadforth Rd; mains $9-18; ⌚7am-4pm) Denmark's best coffee is at this spacious spot. Settle in with locals and tourists for interesting cafe fare, often with an Asian or Mediterranean spin. The mixed platter ($42) with prawns, squid and salmon makes a great lunch for two.

★ **Pepper & Salt** MODERN AUSTRALIAN, ASIAN $$$
(☎08-9848 3053; www.pepperandsalt.com.au; 1564 South Coast Hwy, Forest Hill Vineyard; mains $38-42; ⌚noon-3pm Thu-Sun, from 6pm Fri) With his Fijian-Indian heritage, chef Silas Masih's knowledge of spices and herbs is wonderfully showcased in his fresh and vibrant food. Highlights include king prawns with chilli popcorn and lime mayonnaise, or the excellent tapas platter ($62), which effortlessly detours from Asia to the Middle East. Bookings essential.

Boston Brewery BREWERY
(www.willoughbypark.com.au; Willoughby Park Winery, South Coast Hwy; pizzas $17-18, mains $25-38; ⌚10am-7pm Mon-Thu, to 10pm Fri & Sat, to 9pm Sun) The industrial chic of the brewery gives way to an absolute edge-of-vineyard location, where wood-fired pizzas, meals and bar snacks go well with Boston's hoppy portfolio of four beers. The Willoughby Park Winery is also on site, and there's live music from 4pm to 8pm every second Saturday.

Information

The **Visitor Centre** (☎08-9848 2055; www.denmark.com.au; 73 South Coast Hwy; ⌚9am-5pm) has information, accommodation bookings, and a display on the local wine scene.

Getting There & Away

Transwa (☎1300 662 205; www.transwa.wa.gov.au) bus service GS3 heads daily to/from Bunbury ($51, 5½ hours), Bridgetown ($34, 4¾ hours), Pemberton ($28, 2¾ hours), Walpole ($14, 42 minutes) and Albany ($10, 42 minutes).

Albany

POP 25,200

Established shortly before Perth in 1826, the oldest European settlement in the state is now the bustling commercial centre of the southern region. Albany is a mixed bag comprising a stately and genteel decaying colonial quarter, a waterfront in the midst of sophisticated redevelopment and a hectic sprawl of malls and fast-food joints. Less ambivalent is its spectacular coastline, from Torndirrup National Park's surf-pummelled cliffs to Middleton Beach's white sands, and the calm waters of King George Sound.

The town is in an area that's seen the violence of weather and whaling. Whales are still a part of the Albany experience, but these days are hunted through a camera lens.

The **Bibbulmun Track** (www.bibbulmuntrack.org.au) ends (or starts) here, just outside the visitor centre.

History

The Minang Noongar people called this place Kinjarling (the place of rain) and be-

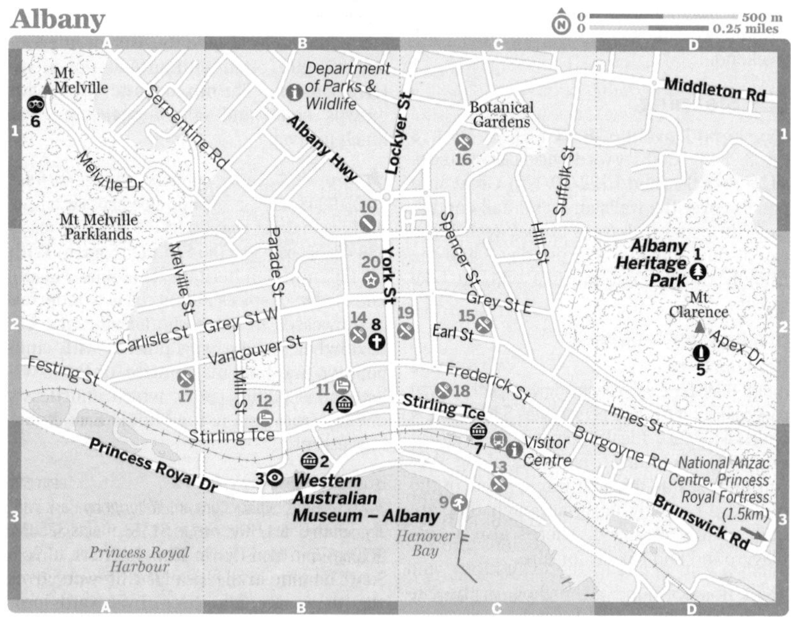

Albany

Top Sights
1 Albany Heritage Park D2
2 Western Australian Museum – Albany B3

Sights
3 Brig Amity B3
4 Courthouse B2
5 Desert Mounted Corps Memorial D2
6 Mt Melville Lookout Tower A1
7 Old Post Office C3
8 St John's Anglican Church B2

Activities, Courses & Tours
9 Albany Whale Tours C3
10 Southcoast Diving Supplies B1

Sleeping
11 1849 Backpackers B2
12 Albany Harbourside B2

Eating
13 Albany Boatshed Markets C3
14 Albany Farmers Market B2
15 Earl of Spencer C2
16 Lime 303 .... C1
17 Vancouver Cafe & Store A2
18 White Star Hotel C2
19 York Street Cafe C2

Entertainment
20 Town Hall B2

lieved that fighting Wargals (mystical giant serpents) created the fractured landscape.

Initial contacts with Europeans were friendly, with over 60 ships visiting between 1622 and 1826. The establishment of a British settlement was welcomed as it regulated the behaviour of sealers and whalers, who had been kidnapping, raping and murdering Minang people. Yet by the end of the 19th century, every shop in Albany refused entry to Aborigines, and control over every aspect of their lives (including the right to bring up their own children) had been lost.

For the British, Albany's raison d'être was its sheltered harbour, which made it a whaling port right up to 1978. During WWI it was the mustering point for transport ships for over 40,000 Australian and New Zealand Army Corps (Anzac) troops heading for Egypt and the Gallipoli campaign.

Sights

★ Albany Heritage Park PARK

Inaugurated in 2014, the Albany Heritage Park incorporates the National Anzac Centre, Princess Royal Fortress, Padre White Lookout, Desert Mounted Corps Memorial and the Ataturk Memorial.

➡ National Anzac Centre

(www.nationalanzaccentre.com.au; Forts Rd, Princess Royal Fortress; adult/child $24/12; ⏲9am-4pm) Opened for Albany's Anzac centenary commemorations in late 2014, this new museum remembers the men and women who left by convoy from Albany to fight in WWI. Excellent multimedia installations provide realism and depth to the exhibitions, and there is a profound melancholy in the museum's location overlooking the same body of water the troop ships left from.

Visitors are assigned one of 32 photographs remembering actual soldiers and nurses upon entry – including a German soldier and a Turkish soldier – and they can then follow their life story on interactive installations. The exact fate of each of the people in the 32 photographs is poignantly not revealed until the final stages of the museum.

➡ Princess Royal Fortress

(Forts Rd; included with entry to the National Anzac Centre; ⏲9am-5pm) As a strategic port, Albany was historically regarded as being vulnerable to attack. Built in 1893 on Mt Adelaide, this fort was initially constructed as a defence against potential attacks from the Russians and French, and the restored buildings, gun emplacements and views are very interesting.

➡ Mt Melville & Mt Clarence

There are fine views over the coast and inland from Mt Clarence and **Mt Melville**. On top of Mt Clarence is the **Desert Mounted Corps Memorial**, originally erected in Port Said, Egypt as a WWI memorial. It was irreparably damaged during the Suez crisis in 1956, and this copy was made from masonry salvaged from the original. Mt Clarence sits atop Albany Heritage Park.

★ Western Australian Museum – Albany MUSEUM

(www.museum.wa.gov.au; Residency Rd; admission by donation; ⏲10am-4.30pm) This branch of the state museum is split between two buildings. The newer Eclipse building has a kids' discovery section and a lighthouse exhibition. The restored 1850s home of the resident magistrate illuminates Minang Noongar history, local natural history and seafaring stories.

Brig Amity SHIP

(adult/child $5/2; ⏲10am-4.30pm) This full-scale replica of the brig that carried Albany's first British settlers from Sydney in 1826 was completed for the city's 150th anniversary. Around the brig is a heritage area worth exploring.

Great Southern Distillery DISTILLERY

(☎08-9842 5363; www.distillery.com.au; 252 Frenchman Bay Rd; tours $15; ⏲cellar door 10am-5pm, tours 1pm) Limeburners Single Malt whisky is the star at this waterfront distillery, but brandy, gin, absinthe and grappe also feature. Tours include tastings and there's a cafe offering tapas and snacks.

Historic Buildings

Near the foreshore is Albany's historic precinct. Take a stroll down Stirling Tce – noted for its Victorian shopfronts, **Courthouse** and **Old Post Office** – and up York St to **St John's Anglican Church** and Albany's **Town Hall** (www.albanytownhall.com.au; 217 York St). A guided walking-tour brochure is available from the visitor centre.

Beaches

East of the town centre, the beautiful Middleton and Emu Beaches face King George Sound and share one long stretch of family-friendly sand. In winter, you'll often see pods of mother whales and their calves here. Head around Emu Point to Oyster Harbour for swimming pontoons and even calmer waters.

A clifftop walking track hugs much of the waterfront between the town centre and Middleton Beach. Boardwalks continue along Emu Beach.

Activities

Whale Watching

After whaling ended in 1978, whales slowly began returning to the waters of Albany. Now southern right and humpback whales gather near the bays and coves of King George Sound from July to mid-October. You can sometimes spot them from the beach. Both **Albany Ocean Adventures** (08-9844 429 876; www.whales.com.au; adult/child $88/50; Jun-Oct) and **Albany Whale Tours** (08-9845 1068; www.albanywhaletours.com.au; Albany Waterfront Marina, cnr Princess Royal Dr & Toll Pl; adult/child $90/55; Jun-Oct) run whale-watching trips in season.

Diving

Albany's appeal as a top-class diving destination grew after the 2001 scuttling of the warship HMAS *Perth* to create an artificial reef for divers; visit www.hmasperth.com.au. **Southcoast Diving Supplies** (08-9841 7176; www.divealbany.com.au; 84b Serpentine Rd) can show you the underwater world.

Tours

Kalgan Queen BOAT TOUR
(08-9844 3166; www.albanyaustralia.com; Emu Point; adult/child $85/50; 9am Sep-Jun) Four-hour cruises up the Kalgan River in a glass-bottomed boat explain the history and wildlife of the area.

Sleeping

★**1849 Backpackers** HOSTEL $
(08-9842 1554; www.albanybackpackersaccommodation.com.au; 45 Peels Pl; dm $33, r $77; @) Flags from many nations provide a colourful international welcome at this well-run hostel. A huge, modern kitchen, sunny rooms and a laid-back ambience make this one of WA's best stays for budget travellers. Make sure you book in for the free barbecue on Sunday night.

Albany Discovery Inn GUESTHOUSE $
(08-9842 5535; www.discoveryinn.com.au; 9 Middleton Rd, Middleton Beach; s $65, d $90-100; @) Located close to the beach, Albany Discovery Inn features a cosy atmosphere with colourful rooms. Their cafe offers three-course evening meals for $20 and is also open for breakfast and lunch (mains $10 to $15). Outside dinner guests are welcome, but book ahead.

Emu Beach Holiday Park CARAVAN PARK $
(08-9844 1147; www.emubeach.com; 8 Medcalf Pde, Emu Point; sites $40, chalets $125-200;) Families love the Emu Beach area, and this friendly holiday park includes a BBQ area and a kids playground. Recently constructed motel units are spacious and modern.

Albany Harbourside APARTMENT $$
(08-9842 1769; www.albanyharbourside.com.au; 8 Festing St; d $159-219;) Albany Harbourside's portfolio includes spacious and spotless apartments on Festing St, and three other self-contained options arrayed around central Albany. Decor is modern and colourful, and some apartments have ocean views.

★**Beach House at Bayside** BOUTIQUE HOTEL $$$
(08-9844 8844; www.thebeachhouseatbayside.com.au; 33 Barry Ct, Collingwood Park; r $280-375;) Positioned right by the beach and the golf course in a quiet cul-de-sac, midway between Middleton Beach and Emu Point, this modern accommodation offers wonderful service. Rates include breakfast, afternoon tea, and evening port and chocolates.

Eating & Drinking

Albany Farmers Market FARMERS MARKET $
(www.albanyfarmermarket.com.au; Collie St; 8am-noon Sat) Weekly market with gourmet food and local artisan produce.

Albany Boatshed Markets MARKET $
(www.albanyboatshedmarkets.com; Princess Royal Dr, The Boatshed; 10am-1pm Sun) Local produce, arts and crafts, and wines from around the Great Southern area.

★**York Street Cafe** CAFE $$
(www.184york.com; 184 York St; breakfast & lunch $13-23, dinner $24-27; 7.30am-3pm Sun-Tue, 7.30am-late Wed-Sat;) The food is excellent at this cosmopolitan and versatile cafe on the main strip. Lunch includes Asian-style pork belly with spiced apple chutney on Turkish bread, while at dinner the attention turns to bistro items such as prosciutto-wrapped chicken on couscous. BYO wine.

Vancouver Cafe & Store CAFE $$
(☎08-9841 2475; 65 Vancouver St; mains $12-24, platters $32; ⏰8am-3.30pm) This heritage cafe features balcony views and delicious home baking. Toasted Turkish sandwiches combine with bigger dishes such as Moroccan lamb balls with pilaf and honey yoghurt, and good-value platters are a relaxed way to recharge over lunch.

White Star Hotel PUB FOOD $$
(72 Stirling Tce; mains $16-34; ⏰11am-late) With good beers on tap, excellent pub grub, a beer garden and lots of live music, this old pub gets a gold star. Sunday-night folk and blues gigs are a good opportunity to share a pint with Albany's laid-back locals.

Earl of Spencer PUB FOOD $$
(cnr Earl & Spencer Sts; mains $20-34; ⏰11.30am-late) Locals crowd in for the Earl's famous pie and pint deal or hearty lamb shanks. Live bands are regular visitors on weekends, often with a jaunty Irish brogue.

Lime 303 MODERN AUSTRALIAN $$$
(☎08-9845 7298; www.dogrockmotel.com.au; 303 Middleton Rd; mains $36-43; ⏰dinner 6pm-late, tapas 4.30-9pm) Pretty flash for regional WA, Lime 303 showcases local produce in dishes such as a creamy seafood moussaka with fish, scallops and prawns, and a confit duck and cabbage roll. More informal bar tapas are available from 4.30pm.

Information

Department of Parks & Wildlife (☎08-9842 4500; www.parks.dpaw.wa.gov.au; 120 Albany Hwy; ⏰8am-4.30pm Mon-Fri) For national park information.

Visitor Centre (☎08-9841 9290; www.amazingalbany.com; Proudlove Pde; ⏰9am-5pm) In the old train station.

Getting There & Away

Albany Airport (Albany Hwy) is 11km northwest of the city centre. **Skywest** (☎1300 660 088; www.skywest.com.au) has 18 flights a week to and from Perth (70 minutes).

Transwa (☎1300 662 205; www.transwa.wa.gov.au) services stop at the visitor centre. These include:

- GS1 to/from Perth ($61, six hours) and Mt Barker ($9.55, 39 minutes) daily.
- GS2 to/from Perth ($58, eight hours), Northam ($66, 6½ hours), York ($61, six hours) and Mt Barker ($9, 41 minutes) four times a week.
- GS3 to/from Bunbury ($58, six hours), Bridgetown ($45, 4¾ hours), Pemberton ($37, 3½ hours), Walpole ($22, 1½ hours) and Denmark ($9, 42 minutes) daily.

ALBANY TO ESPERANCE ALTERNATIVES

The rural 480km of South Coast Hwy (Rte 1) between Albany and Esperance is a relatively unpopulated stretch. Break up the first leg by taking the Albany Hwy (Rte 30) to Mt Barker, and then head east to Porongurup. Then travel north through the Stirling Ranges, and turn east again through Ongerup, and rejoin the highway at Jerramungup. This route adds 57km to the trip.

At Ongerup, the **Yongergnow Malleefowl Centre** (☎08-9828 2325; www.yongergnow.com.au; adult/child $8/4; ⏰10am-4pm Sat-Mon, Wed & Thu) is devoted to the conservation of a curious endangered bird that creates huge mounds to incubate its chicks.

Near Jerramungup is **Fitzgerald River National Park** – base yourself at Hopetoun or Bremer Bay. Note that Bremer Bay is best reached by taking the South Coast Hwy from Albany.

Getting Around

Loves (☎08-9841 1211) runs local bus services. The visitor centre has information on getting to Emu Point and Middleton Beach.

Around Albany

Discovery Bay MUSEUM
(☎08-9844 4021; www.discoverybay.com.au; Frenchman Bay Rd; adult/child $29/12; ⏰9am-5pm) When the Cheynes Beach Whaling Station ceased operations in November 1978, few could have guessed that the formerly gore-covered decks would eventually be covered in tourists discovering the area's bleakly fascinating story. An attached museum screens films about sharks and whales, and displays giant skeletons, harpoons, whaleboat models and scrimshaw (etchings on whalebone). Outside there's the rusting *Cheynes IV* whale chaser and station equipment to inspect. Free guided tours depart on the hour from 10am to 3pm. Part of the wider Discovery Bay complex is a new Australian wildlife park and botanic garden (adult/child $15/8) with plants endemic to the area. There are good ocean views from

the elevated sight, but the fledgeling gardens need a few years to develop more, and the animals – including koalas, pademelons and wallaroos – are cared for in fairly compact areas.

Torndirrup National Park NATIONAL PARK
(Frenchman Bay Rd) FREE Covering much of the peninsula enclosing the southern reaches of Princess Royal Harbour and King George Sound, this national park features windswept, ocean-bashed cliffs. **The Gap** is a natural cleft in the rock, channelling surf through walls of granite. Close by is the **Natural Bridge**. Further east, the **Blowholes** are spectacular. Rocky coves such as **Jimmy Newells Harbour** and **Salmon Holes** are popular with surfers. Better for swimmers are **Misery Beach** or **Frenchman Bay** on the peninsula's more sheltered side.

There's a challenging 10km-return bushwalk (five hours plus) over Isthmus Hill to Bald Heads.

Two Peoples Bay NATURE RESERVE
(Two Peoples Bay Rd) Around 20km east of Albany, Two Peoples Bay is a scenic 46-sq-km nature reserve with a good swimming beach.

Waychinicup National Park NATIONAL PARK
(Cheyne Beach Rd; park admission free, camp site adult/child $7.50/2.20) In a beautiful spot by the Waychinicup River, Gilbert's potoroos and scrub birds are often seen.

Mt Barker

POP 1770

Mt Barker (50km north of Albany) is the gateway to the Porongurup and Stirling Range National Parks. It's also the hub for the local wine industry. Pick up the *Mt Barker Wineries* map from the town's visitor centre and see www.mountbarkerwine.com.au.

Sights & Activities

Around 5km south of town, **Mt Barker** has excellent views. Southwest of Mt Barker, on the rolling grounds of the Egerton-Warburton estate, is the photogenic **St Werburgh's Chapel** (1872).

West Cape Howe Wines WINERY
(www.westcapehowewines.com.au; 14923 Muirs Hwy; ⏲cellar door 10am-5pm) In lovely grounds around 10km west of Mt Barker, West Cape Howe Wines are regular award winners for their riesling, merlot and cabernet sauvignon.

Plantagenet Wines WINE TASTING
(www.plantagenetwines.com; Albany Hwy; ⏲10am-4.30pm) Plantagenet Wines' cellar door is conveniently situated in the middle of town.

Mt Barker Police Station Museum MUSEUM
(Albany Hwy; adult/child $5/free; ⏲10am-3pm Sat & Sun) Mt Barker has been settled since the 1830s and the convict-built 1868 police station and gaol have been preserved as a museum.

Banksia Farm GARDENS
(☎08-9851 1770; www.banksiafarm.com.au; Pearce Rd; guided tours $20; ⏲tours 10am Mon-Fri mid Mar-mid Jun, daily mid Aug-mid Nov) See all 78 types and 24 subtypes of Australia's banksia plant at the Banksia Farm. There's also a cafe and B&B accommodation (singles/doubles from $95/150). From mid-August to mid-November 'Orchid Hunt' tours ($25) leave daily at 2pm.

Sleeping

Nomads Guest House GUESTHOUSE
(☎08-9851 2131; www.nomadsguesthousewa.com.au; 12 Morpeth St; s/d/yurts/chalets $70/90/100/110) A surprising sight is the authentic Mongolian yurt (felt tent) and gallery of Mongolian and Chinese art in the grounds of Nomads Guest House. The owners frequently rescue orphaned joeys (baby kangaroos), so don't be surprised to see a few temporary marsupial visitors in the main house.

Porongurup National Park

The 24-sq-km, 12km-long **Porongurup National Park** (entry per car $12) has 1100-million-year-old granite outcrops, panoramic views, beautiful scenery, large karri trees and some excellent bushwalks.

Bushwalks range from the 100m **Tree-in-the-Rock** stroll to the harder **Hayward and Nancy Peaks** (5.5km loop). The **Devil's Slide** (5km return) passes through karri forest to the stumpy vegetation of the granite zone. These walks start from the main day-use area (Bolganup Rd). **Castle Rock Trail to Balancing Rock** (3km return) starts further east, signposted off the Mt Barker–Porongurup Rd. The **Castle Rock Granite Skywalk Trail** (4.4km return, two hours) negotiates a steep and spectacular path up the rock. The final 200m ascent to the summit

Porongurup National Park

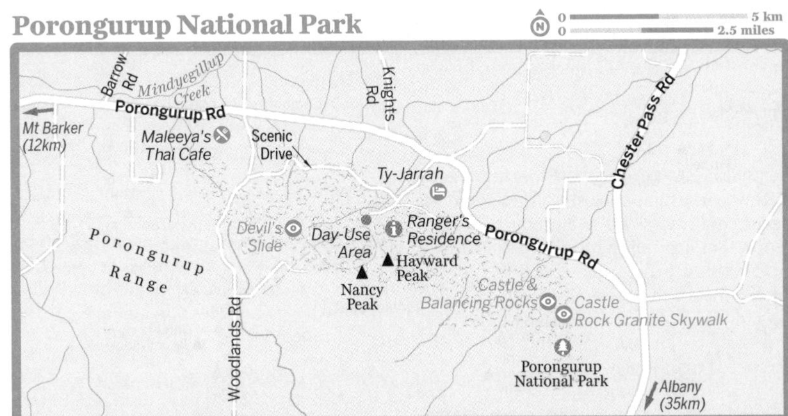

incorporates a steep rocky scramble and a vertical 7m ladder.

Porongurup is also part of the Great Southern wine region and there are 11 wineries in the vicinity. See www.porongurup.com.

Sleeping & Eating

There is no accommodation within the national park, but Ty-Jarrah is close by. Eating options are very limited.

Ty-Jarrah CHALET $$
(☎08-9853 1255; www.tyjarrah.com; 3 Bolganup Rd; ste/chalets $135/150) Located in a shady forest setting, these self-contained A-frame chalets are cosy and comfortable.

★ **Maleeya's Thai Cafe** THAI $$
(☎08-9853 1123; www.maleeya.com.au; 1376 Porongurup Rd; mains $25-33; ⊙11.30am-3pm & 6-9pm Fri-Sun) Foodies and chefs venture to Porongorup for some of WA's most authentic Thai food. Curries, soups and stir-fries all come punctuated with fresh herbs straight from Maleeya's garden, and other ingredients are organic and free range. Bookings recommended.

Stirling Range National Park

Rising abruptly from the surrounding flat and sandy plains, the Stirling Range's propensity to change colour through blues, reds and purples captivates photographers during the spectacular wild flower season from late August to early December. It's also recognised by the Noongar people as a place of special significance – a place where the spirits of the dead return. Every summit has an ancestral being associated with it, so it's appropriate to show proper respect when visiting.

This 1156-sq-km national park consists of a single chain of peaks pushed up by plate tectonics to form a range 10km wide and 65km long. Running most of its length are isolated summits, some knobbly and some perfect pyramids, towering above broad valleys covered in shrubs and heath. Bluff Knoll (Bular Mai), at 1095m, is the highest point in the southwest.

Park fees are charged at the start of Bluff Knoll Rd (entry per car/motorcycle $12/6).

Activities

The Stirlings are renowned for serious **bushwalking**. Keen walkers can choose from **Toolbrunup** (for views and a good climb; 1052m, 4km return) and **Bluff Knoll** (a well-graded tourist track; 1095m, 6km return). **Mt Hassell** (848m, 3km return) and **Talyuberlup** (783m, 2.6km return) are popular half-day walks.

Challenging walks cross the eastern sector include those from **Bluff Knoll to Ellen Peak** (three days), or the shorter traverse from **The Arrows to Ellen Peak** (two days).

Sleeping & Eating

Stock up on food in Mt Barker.

Stirling Range Retreat CARAVAN PARK $
(☎08-9827 9229; www.stirlingrange.com.au; 8639 Chester Pass Rd; unpowered/powered 2-person sites $32/34, cabins $55-95, units $145-185;

Stirling Range National Park

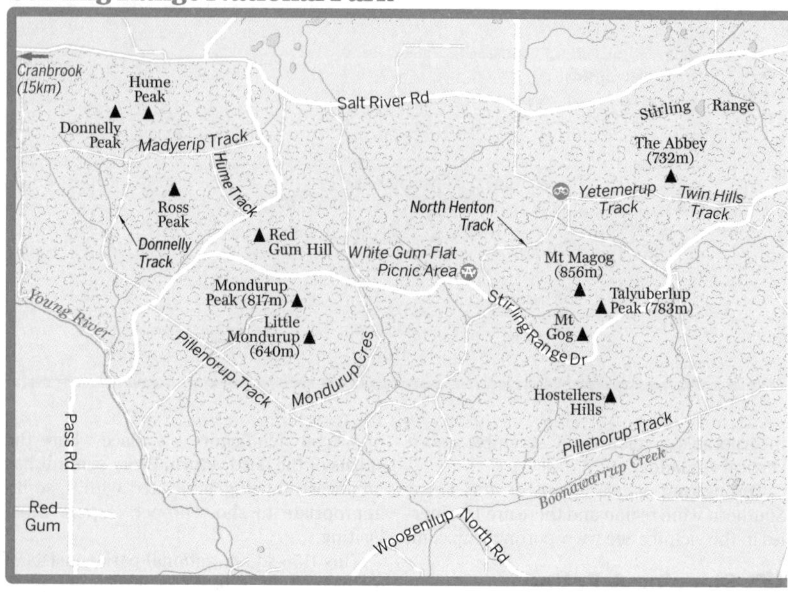

(❄@🏊) 🍃 On the park's northern boundary, this shaded area offers camp sites, cabins and vans, and self-contained, rammed-earth units. Wild flower and orchid bus tours and walkabouts (three hours, per person $49) are conducted from mid-August to the end of October. The swimming pool only opens from November to April.

Mount Trio Bush Camping & Caravan Park CARAVAN PARK **$**
(☎08-9827 9270; www.mttrio.com.au; Salt River Rd; unpowered/powered sites per person $13/15) Rustic bush campground on a farm property close to the walking tracks, north of the centre of the park. It has hot showers, a kitchen, free gas BBQs and a campfire pit. Guided walks from 90 minutes to one day are on offer.

★ **The Lily** COTTAGES **$$**
(☎08-9827 9205; www.thelily.com.au; Chester Pass Rd; cottages $149-179) These cottages 12km north of the park are grouped around a working windmill. Accommodation is self-contained, and meals are available for guests at the neighbouring restaurant. Call to enquire which nights the restaurant is open to the public and to arrange mill tours ($50, minimum of four people). There's also private accommodation in a restored 1944 Dakota aircraft.

Fitzgerald River National Park

Midway between Albany and Esperance, this gem of a park (entry per car/motorcycle $12/6) has been declared a Unesco Biosphere Reserve. Its 3300 sq km contain half of the orchid species in WA (more than 80, 70 of which occur nowhere else), 22 mammal species, 200 species of bird and 1700 species of plant (20% of WA's described flora species).

Walkers will discover beautiful coastline, sand plains, rugged coastal hills (known as 'the Barrens') and deep, wide river valleys. In season, you'll almost certainly see whales and their calves from the shore at **Point Ann**, where there's a lookout and a heritage walk that follows a short stretch of the 1164km **No 2 rabbit-proof fence**.

The three main 2WD entry points to the park are from the South Coast Hwy (Quiss Rd and Pabelup Dr), Hopetoun (Hamersley Dr) and Bremer Bay (along Swamp and Murray Rds). All roads are gravel, and likely to be impassable after rain, so check locally before you set out.

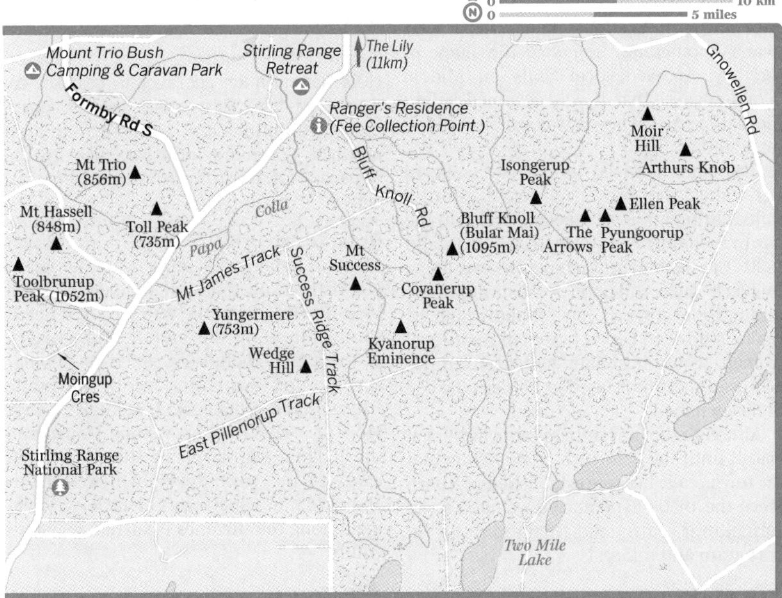

Bookending the park are the sleepy coastal settlements of **Bremer Bay** and **Hopetoun**, both with white sand and shimmering waters. To the east of Hopetoun is the scenic but often rough **Southern Ocean East Drive**, heading to beach camping sites at **Mason Bay** and **Starvation Bay**. If you're in a 2WD vehicle, don't head to Esperance this way.

Sleeping

Quaalup Homestead CAMPGROUND $
(08-9837 4124; www.whalesandwildflowers.com.au; Quaalup Rd; sites per person from $12, cabins $100-125) This 1858 homestead is secluded deep within the park's southern reaches. Electricity is solar generated, and forget about mobile-phone coverage. Accommodation includes a bush camp site with gas BBQs and cosy units and chalets. Quaalup Rd is reached from Pabelup Dr.

Parks & Wildlife Camp sites CAMPGROUND $
(www.parks.dpaw.wa.gov.au; sites per adult/child $10/2.20) Camp sites at St Mary Inlet (near Point Ann) and Four Mile Beach can be reached by 2WD. Others at Hamersley Inlet, Whale Bone Beach, Quoin Head and Fitzgerald Inlet are acccessible by 4WD or on foot.

Hopetoun Motel & Chalet Village MOTEL $$
(08-9838 3219; www.hopetounmotel.com.au; 458 Veal St, Hopetoun; r $140-200;) Rammed-earth complex with comfy beds and quality linen.

Information

Deck Treasures (www.decktreasures.com.au; Veal St, Hopetoun; 9am-12.30pm Nov-Apr;), in Hopetoun, has information on local wildlife and recommended driving routes.

Esperance

POP 9600

Framed by aquamarine waters and pristine white beaches, Esperance sits in solitary splendour on the Bay of Isles. But despite its isolation, families still travel from Perth or Kalgoorlie just to plug into the easygoing vibe and great beach life. For travellers taking the coastal route across the continent, it's the last sizeable town before the Nullarbor.

Picture-perfect beaches dot the even more remote national parks to the town's southeast, and the pristine environment of the 105 islands of the offshore Recherche Archipelago are home to fur seals, penguins and sea birds.

History

Esperance's Indigenous name, Kepa Kurl (water boomerang), refers to the shape of the bay. Archaeological finds on Middle Island suggest that it was occupied before the last Ice Age, when it was still part of the mainland.

Esperance received its current name in 1792 when the *Recherche* and *Espérance* sailed through the archipelago and into the bay to shelter from a storm. In the 1820s and 1830s the Recherche Archipelago was home to Black Jack Anderson – Australia's only pirate. From his base on Middle Island he raided ships and kept a harem of Aboriginal women, whose husbands he had killed. He was eventually murdered in his sleep by one of his own men.

Although the first settlers came in 1863, it wasn't until the gold rush of the 1890s that the town really became established as a port. Since the 1950s Esperance developed as an agricultural centre, and it continues to export grain and minerals.

Sights & Activities

Esperance Museum MUSEUM
(cnr James & Dempster Sts; adult/child $6/2; ⌚1.30-4.30pm) Glass cabinets are crammed with quirky collections of sea shells, frog ornaments, tennis rackets and bed pans. Bigger items include boats, a train carriage and the remains of the USA's spacecraft *Skylab*, which made its fiery re-entry at Balladonia, east of Esperance, in 1979.

Museum Village HISTORIC BUILDING
The museum consists of galleries and cafes occupying various restored heritage buildings; markets are held here every second Sunday morning. Aboriginal-run **Kepa Kurl Art Gallery** (www.kepakurl.com.au; cnr Dempster & Kemp Sts; ⌚10am-4pm Mon-Fri, market Sun) has reasonably priced works by local and Central Desert artists.

Lake Warden Wetland System WETLANDS
Esperance is surrounded by extensive wetlands, which include seven large lakes and over 90 smaller ones. The 7.2km-return **Kepwari Wetland Trail** (off Fisheries Rd) takes in **Lake Wheatfield** and **Woody Lake**, with boardwalks, interpretive displays and good birdwatching. **Lake Monjimup**, 14km to the northwest along the South Coast Hwy, is divided by Telegraph Rd into a conservation area (to the west) and a recreation area (to the east).

Cannery Arts Centre GALLERY
(1018 Norseman Rd; admission by gold-coin donation; ⌚1-4pm) Has artists studios, interesting exhibitions and a shop selling local artwork. For more local art, pick up the *Esperance Art Trail* brochure at the visitor centre.

Great Ocean Drive SCENIC DRIVE
Many of Esperance's most dramatic sights can be seen on this well-signposted 40km loop. Starting from the waterfront, it heads southwest along the breathtaking stretch of coast that includes a series of popular surfing and swimming spots, including **Blue Haven Beach** and **Twilight Cove**. Stop at rugged **Observatory Point** and the lookout on **Wireless Hill**. A turn-off leads to the **wind farm**, which supplies about 23% of Esperance's electricity. Walking among the turbines is surreal when it's windy.

Tours

Esperance Island Cruises BOAT TOUR
(☎08-9071 5757; www.woodyisland.com.au; 72 The Esplanade) Tours include Esperance Bay and Woody Island in a power catamaran (half/full day $120/185), getting close to fur seals, sea lions, Cape Barren geese and (with luck) dolphins. In January, there's a ferry to Woody Island (adult/child return $60/30).

Kepa Kurl Eco Cultural Discovery Tours CULTURAL TOUR
(☎08-9072 1688; www.kepakurl.com.au; Museum Village; adult/child $105/90, min 2 people) Explore the country from an Aboriginal perspective: visit rock art and waterholes, sample bush food and hear ancient stories.

Eco-Discovery Tours DRIVING TOUR
(☎0407 737 261; www.esperancetours.com.au) Runs 4WD tours along the sand to Cape Le Grand National Park (half/full day $105/195, minimum of two/four people) and two-hour circuits of Great Ocean Dr (adult/child $60/45).

Aussie Bight Expeditions 4WD TOUR
(☎0427 536 674; www.aussiebight.com; half/full day $90/160; ⌚Aug & Sep) Specialist wild flower tours from late August to September.

Esperance Diving & Fishing DIVING, FISHING
(☎08-9071 5111; www.esperancedivingandfishing.com.au; 72 The Esplanade) Takes you wreck diving on the *Sanko Harvest* (two-tank dive including all gear $260) or charter fishing throughout the archipelago.

Sleeping

Woody Island Eco-Stays CAMPGROUND $
(☎08-9071 5757; www.woodyisland.com.au; sites per person $25, on-site tents $41-61, huts $140-165; ⊙mid Dec-Jan, mid Apr-early May; ❄) It's not every day you get to stay in an A-class nature reserve. Choose between leafy camp sites (very close together) or canvas-sided bush huts, a few of which have a private deck and their own lighting. Power is mostly solar, and rainwater supplies the island – both are highly valued. Count on adding on a $60 return ferry transfer as well.

Blue Waters Lodge YHA HOSTEL $
(☎08-9071 1040; www.yha.com.au; 299 Goldfields Rd; dm/d/tr $28/74/95) On the beachfront about 1.5km from the town centre, this rambling place feels a little institutional, but management are friendly and it looks out over a tidy lawn to the water. Hire bikes to cycle the waterfront.

★ **Esperance B&B by the Sea** B&B $$
(☎08-9071 5640; www.esperancebb.com; 34 Stewart St; s/d $125/180; ❄) This great-value beachhouse has a private guest wing and the views from the deck overlooking Blue Haven Beach are breathtaking, especially at sunset. It's just a stroll from the ocean and a five-minute drive from central Esperance.

Clearwater Motel Apartments MOTEL $$
(☎08-9071 3587; www.clearwatermotel.com.au; 1a William St; s $110, d $140-195; ❄) The bright and spacious rooms and apartments here have balconies and are fully self-contained, and there's a well-equipped shared barbecue area. It's just a short walk from both the waterfront and town.

Driftwood Apartments APARTMENT $$
(☎0428 716 677; www.driftwoodapartments.com.au; 69 The Esplanade; apt $165-220; ❄) Each of these seven smart blue-and-yellow apartments, right across from the waterfront, has its own BBQ and outdoor table setting. The two-storey, two-bedroom units have decks and a bit more privacy.

Eating & Drinking

Taylor's Beach Bar & Cafe CAFE $$
(www.taylorsbeachbar.com.au; Taylor St Jetty; breakfast $13-24, lunch & dinner $20-30; ⊙10am-late Mon-Fri, 7am-late Sat & Sun; 📶) This sprawling cafe by the jetty serves cafe fare, burgers, seafood and salads. Locals hang out at the tables on the grass or read on the terrace. Focaccia sandwiches ($11 to $14) are good value if you're heading for the beach, and it's good for a glass of wine or chilled pint of Little Creatures beer. Ask about occasional live music.

Ocean Blues CAFE $$
(19 The Esplanade; mains $11-35; ⊙8am-8.30pm Tue-Sat, 8am-4pm Sun) Wander in sandy-footed and order a simple lunch (burgers, salads, sandwiches) from this unpretentious eatery. Dinners are more adventurous, representing good value for the price.

Pier Hotel PUB FOOD $$
(www.pierhotelesperance.net.au; 47 The Esplanade; mains $20-35; ⊙11.30am-late) Lots of beers on tap, wood-fired pizzas and good-value bistro meals conspire to make the local pub a firm favourite with both locals and visitors.

Coffee Cat CAFE
(⊙7am-2pm Mon-Fri) WA's hippest mobile coffee caravan also serves up yummy home-baked cakes and muffins. Grab an early-morning java to fuel you for a stroll along Esperance's flash new esplanade. Look for the caravan along the waterfront.

S'Juice JUICES
(juices & smoothies $7-9; ⊙9am-4pm Mon-Fri, to 3pm Sat & Sun) Colourful caravan with excellent juices and smoothies, and a few warming soups in cooler months. Usually located in the car park opposite the Pier Hotel.

Information

Parks & Wildlife (☎08-9083 2100; www.parks.dpaw.wa.gov.au; 92 Dempster St) National parks information.

Visitor Centre (☎08-9083 1555; www.visitesperance.com; cnr Kemp & Dempster Sts; ⊙9am-5pm Mon-Fri, to 2pm Sat, to noon Sun) In the museum village.

Getting There & Away

Esperance Airport (Coolgardie-Esperance Hwy) is 18km north of the town centre. **Virgin Australia** (☎1300 660 088; www.virginaustralia.com) has around three flights per day to and from Perth (1¾ hours). **Transwa** (☎1300 662 205; www.transwa.wa.gov.au) services stop at the visitor centre:

➡ GE1 to/from Perth ($91, 10¼ hours, thrice weekly)

➡ GE2 to/from Perth ($91, 10 hours), Mundaring ($90, 9¼ hours), York ($82, 8½ hours) and Hyden ($56, five hours) thrice weekly

➡ GE3 to/from Kalgoorlie ($58, five hours, thrice weekly), Coolgardie ($56, 4¾ hours, weekly) and Norseman ($31, 2¼ hours, thrice weekly)

Around Esperance

Cape Le Grand National Park NATIONAL PARK
(entry per car/motorcycle $12/6, sites adult/child $10/2.20) Starting 60km east of Esperance, Cape Le Grand National Park boasts spectacular coastal scenery, dazzling beaches and excellent walking tracks. There's good fishing, swimming and camping at **Lucky Bay** and **Le Grand Beach**, and day-use facilities at gorgeous **Hellfire Bay**. Make the effort to climb **Frenchman Peak** (a steep 3km return, allow two hours), as the views from the top and through the rocky 'eye', especially during the late afternoon, are superb. The 15km Le Grand Coastal Trail links the bay, or you can do shorter stretches between beaches.

Cape Arid National Park NATIONAL PARK
(entry per car/motorcycle $12/6, sites adult/child $10/2.20) On the Great Australian Bight and edging the Nullarbor Plain, rugged and isolated Cape Arid National Park has good bushwalking, great beaches and crazy squeaky sand. Whales (in season), seals and Cape Barren geese are seen regularly here. Most of the park is 4WD-accessible only, although the Thomas River Rd leading to the shire camp site suits all vehicles.

There's a challenging walk to the top of Tower Peak on Mt Ragged (3km return, three hours).

SOUTHERN OUTBACK

The southern outback is an iconic Australian experience. Almost-empty roads run relentlessly towards South Australia (SA) via the Nullarbor Plain, and up to the Northern Territory (NT). This was (and is) gold-rush country, with the city of Kalgoorlie-Boulder as its hub, while less-sustainable gold towns now lie sunstruck, isolated and deserted. Aboriginal people have lived for an age in this region, which early colonists found unforgiving until the allure of gold made it worthwhile to stay.

History

Gold was discovered at Southern Cross in 1888, inspiring one of the world's last great gold rushes. Around 50 towns quickly sprouted, but enthusiasm and greed often outweighed common sense, and typhoid, inadequate water, housing and food led to many fatalities in the mining camps.

The area's population dwindled along with the gold, and today Kalgoorlie-Boulder is the only real survivor. Explore other diminished towns and prodigious mining structures along the 965km Golden Quest Discovery Trail (www.goldenquesttrail.com).

Stretching 560km from the Perth foothills, the 1903 Golden Pipeline brought water to the goldfields. It was a lifeline for the towns it passed through and filled Kalgoorlie with the sense of a future, with or without gold. The present-day Great Eastern Hwy follows the pipeline's route, incorporating heritage pumping stations and information signs.

ℹ Getting There & Away

AIR

Qantas (☎13 13 13; www.qantas.com.au) Kalgoorlie to Perth and Adelaide.

NOT NULLAR-BORING AT ALL

'Crossing the Nullarbor' is an iconic Australian trip. It's absolutely about the journey as much as the destination, so relax and enjoy the big skies and forever horizons.

All roadhouses sell food and fuel and have accommodation ranging from often barren camp sites to basic budget rooms and motels. There's free roadside camping with toilets and tables about every 250km.

Ensure your vehicle is up to the distance and carry more drinking water than you think you'll need. Fuel prices are high and there's a distance between fuel stops of about 200km.

See www.nullarbornet.com.au for touring information.

Skippers Aviation (☎1300 729 924; www.skippers.com.au) Perth–Leonora–Laverton and Perth–Wiluna–Meekathara routes.

Virgin Australia (☎13 67 89; www.virgin-australia.com) Kalgoorlie to Perth, Melbourne, Sydney and Brisbane.

BUS

Transwa (☎1300 662 205; www.transwa.wa.gov.au) Kalgoorlie to Esperance ($58.20, five hours) via Coolgardie and Norseman.

Goldrush Tours (☎1800 620 440; www.goldrushtours.com.au) Weekly service from Kalgoorlie to Laverton ($82, 4½ hours) via Menzies and Leonora, departing Thursday and returning Friday.

TRAIN

Transwa runs the *Prospector* service from East Perth to Kalgoorlie ($86, seven hours, daily).

Norseman

POP 860

From the crossroads township of Norseman head south to Esperance, north to Kalgoorlie, westwards to Hyden and Wave Rock, or east across the Nullarbor. Note the 300km road from Hyden and Wave Rock to Norseman is unsealed, but is suitable for 2WD vehicles in dry conditions. Check at Norseman or Hyden before setting out.

Stretch your legs at the **Beacon Hill Mararoa Lookout**, where there's a walking trail, and stop at the **Historical Museum** (Battery Rd; adult/child $3/1; ⏲10am-1pm Mon-Sat). Pick up the **Dundas Coach Road Heritage Trail** brochure, for a 50km loop drive with interpretive panels.

Sleeping

Great Western Motel MOTEL $
(☎08-9039 1633; www.norsemangreatwesternmotel.com.au; Prinsep St; r $120; ❄≋) 'Budget' and 'lodge' rooms in an older block are perfectly adequate, but the rammed-earth 'motel' rooms are much nicer. There's a cafe-restaurant on site.

Gateway Caravan Park CARAVAN PARK $
(☎08-9039 1500; www.acclaimparks.com.au; 23 Prinsep St; sites $35-40, cabins $132-158; ❄) Decent cabins and a bushy atmosphere.

Information

Visitor Centre (☎08-9039 1071; www.norseman.info; 68 Roberts St; ⏲9am-5pm Mon-Fri, 9.30am-4pm Sat & Sun) Lots of Nullarbor information.

Eyre Highway (the Nullarbor)

The 2700km Eyre Hwy crosses the southern edge of the vast **Nullarbor Plain**, parallel with the **Trans-Australia Railway** to the north.

John Eyre was the first European to cross this unforgiving stretch of country in 1841. After the 1877 telegraph line was laid, miners trekked to the goldfields under blistering sun and through freezing winters. By 1941 a rough-and-ready road carried a handful of vehicles, and in 1969 the road was sealed to the SA border. In 1976, the last coastal stretch was surfaced, with the Nullarbor region ending at the cliffs of the Great Australian Bight.

From Norseman it's 725km to the SA border, and a further 480km to Ceduna. From Ceduna, it's still another 793km to Adelaide.

Norseman to Eucla

Around the 100km mark from Norseman is **Fraser Range Station** (☎08-9039 3210; www.fraserrangestation.com.au; unpowered/powered sites $22/30, budget s/tw/d/f $55/95/95/120, cottage r $155) with heritage buildings and a camping ground. Next is **Balladonia** (193km), where the **Balladonia Hotel Motel** (☎08-9039 3453; www.balladoniahotelmotel.com.au; unpowered/powered sites $19/28, dm $50, r from $130; ❄@≋) has a small museum including debris from *Skylab*'s 1979 return to earth nearby.

Balladonia to Cocklebiddy is around 210km. The first 160km to **Caiguna** includes Australia's longest stretch of straight road (145km), ending at Caiguna's **John Eyre Motel** (☎08-9039 3459; caigunarh@bigpond.com; unpowered/powered sites $20/25, d $85-120, tr/q $130/140; ❄).

Birds Australia's **Eyre Bird Observatory** (☎08-9039 3450; www.birdlife.org.au/visit-us/observatories/eyre; full board adult/child $90/45) is in the isolated 1897 former Eyre Telegraph Station, 50km south of Cocklebiddy. Book ahead for accommodation. Day visitors are welcome ($10 per vehicle), but the last 10km are soft sand and 4WD accessible only; 2WD travellers who want to stay can arrange pick-up with the wardens. There's no camping.

At **Madura**, 91km east of Cocklebiddy and near the Hampton Tablelands, the **Madura Pass Oasis Inn** (☎08-9039 3464; maduraoasis@

THE WORLD'S LONGEST GOLF COURSE

Stretching 1362km from Kalgoorlie, south to Norseman and across the desolate Nullarbor Plain to Ceduna, the **Nullarbor Links** (www.nullarborlinks.com; 18 holes $50) is a unique 18-hole, par-72 course.

Purchase your scorecard from the Kalgoorlie, Norseman or Ceduna visitor centres, and follow the directions along the route. Clubs are available for hire at each rocky and sandy hole ($5).

bigpond.com; unpowered/powered sites $15/25, r $105-125;) has a very welcome pool.

In **Mundrabilla**, 116km further east, the **Mundrabilla Motel Hotel** (08-9039 3465; mundrabilla@bigpond.com.au; unpowered/powered sites $20/25, r $80-110;) has cheaper fuel prices than roadhouses further west.

Just before the SA border is **Eucla**, surrounded by stunning sand dunes and pristine beaches. Visit the atmospheric ruins of the 1877 **telegraph station**, 5km south of town and gradually being engulfed by the dunes; the remains of the old jetty are a 15-minute walk beyond. The **Eucla Motor Hotel** (08-9039 3468; euclamotel@bigpond.com; unpowered/powered sites $10/20, r $45-110;) has good camping and spacious rooms.

Coolgardie

POP 800

In 1898 sleepy Coolgardie was the third-biggest town in WA, with a population of 15,000, six newspapers, two stock exchanges, more than 20 hotels and three breweries. It all took off just hours after Arthur Bayley rode into Southern Cross in 1892 and dumped 554oz of Coolgardie gold on the mining warden's counter. The only echoes that remain are stately historic buildings lining the uncharacteristically wide main road.

Sights & Activities

Goldfields Museum & Visitor Centre MUSEUM

(08-9026 6090; www.coolgardie.wa.gov.au; Bayley St, Warden's Court; adult/child $4/2; 8.30am-4.20pm Mon-Fri, 10am-3pm Sat & Sun) Goldfields memorabilia including information about former US president Herbert Hoover's days on the goldfields in Gwalia, as well as the fascinating story of Modesto Varischetti, the 'Entombed Miner'.

Warden Finnerty's Residence HISTORIC BUILDING

(www.nationaltrust.org.au; 2 McKenzie St; adult/child $4/2; 11am-4pm Thu-Tue) Built in 1895 for Coolgardie's first mining warden and magistrate.

Sleeping & Eating

Coolgardie Goldrush Motel MOTEL $

(08-9026 6080; www.coolgardiemotels.com.au; 49-53 Bayley St; r $125-150;) With bright linen, spotless bathrooms and flat-screen televisions, the Goldrush's compact but colourful rooms are very comfortable. The attached restaurant serves excellent homemade pies.

Kalgoorlie-Boulder

POP 28,300

With well-preserved historic buildings, Kalgoorlie-Boulder is an outback success story, and is still the centre for mining in this part of the state.

Historically, mine workers would come straight to town to spend up at Kalgoorlie's infamous brothels, or at pubs staffed by skimpies (scantily clad female bar staff). Today 'Kal' is definitely more family-friendly – mine workers must reside in town and cannot be transient 'fly-in, fly-out' labour.

It still feels a bit like the Wild West though, and the heritage pubs and skimpy bar staff are reminders of a more rambunctious past.

There are historical and modern mining sites to discover, and Kalgoorlie is a good base from which to explore the ghost towns in the surrounding area.

History

Long-time prospector Paddy Hannan set out from Coolgardie in search of another gold strike. He stumbled across the surface gold that sparked the 1893 gold rush, and inadvertently chose the site of Kalgoorlie for a township.

When surface sparkles subsided, the miners dug deeper, extracting the precious metal from the rocks by costly and complex processes. Kalgoorlie quickly prospered, and the town's magnificent public buildings, constructed at the end of the 19th century, are evidence of its fabulous wealth.

Despite its slow decline after WWI, Kal is still the largest producer of gold in Australia. What was a Golden Mile of small mining operators' head frames and corrugated-iron shacks is now the overwhelmingly huge Super Pit.

Sights & Activities

The city's main drag, Hannan St has retained many of its original gold rush–era buildings, including several grand hotels and the imposing town hall. Outside is a drinking fountain in the form of a statue of Paddy Hannan holding a water bag.

Super Pit LOOKOUT
(www.superpit.com.au; Outram St; ⏲7am-7pm) The view is staggering here, with building-sized trucks zig-zagging up and down the huge hole and looking like kids' toys. Take a fascinating tour with Kalgoorlie Tours & Charters.

Western Australian Museum – Kalgoorlie-Boulder MUSEUM
(www.museum.wa.gov.au; 17 Hannan St; suggested donation $5; ⏲10am-4.30pm) The impressive Ivanhoe-mine head frame marks this excellent museum's entrance; take the lift to look over the city. An underground vault displays giant nuggets and gold bars, and there's also a fantastic collection of trade-union banners.

School of Mines Mineral Museum MUSEUM
(cnr Egan & Cassidy Sts; ⏲9am-noon Mon-Fri, closed school holidays) FREE Geology displays including replicas of big nuggets discovered locally.

Royal Flying Doctor Service Visitor Centre TOUR
(☎08-9093 7595; www.flyingdoctor.net; Kalgoorlie-Boulder Airport; admission by donation; ⏲10am-3pm Mon-Fri, tours 10.15am year-round, additional tour 2pm May-Oct) See how the Flying Doctors look after the people of the outback.

Tours

Kalgoorlie Tours & Charters BUS TOUR
(☎08-9021 2211; www.kalgoorlietours.com.au; 250 Hannan St; adult/child $70/45; ⏲9.30am & 1.30pm Mon-Sat) Explore the Super Pit on 2½ hour tours. Shorter 90-minute tours (adult/child $45/25) run on demand during school holidays. All participants must wear long trousers and enclosed shoes.

Goldrush Tours BUS TOUR
(☎1800 620 440; www.goldrushtours.com.au; adult/child $150/75) Heritage jaunts around Kalgoorlie-Boulder and day tours to Lake Ballard's sculptures.

Questa Casa HISTORICAL TOUR
(☎08-9021 4897; www.questacasa.com; 133 Hay St; tours $25; ⏲tours 3pm) Still operational, this is the last of the gold rush–era brothels that once lined Hay St. Tours conducted at 3pm for curious visitors (18 and older only).

Festivals & Events

Kalgoorlie Market MARKET
(Hannan St, St Barbara's Sq) First Sunday of the month.

Boulder Market Day MARKET
(Burt St) Held at Loopline Reserve Railway Park on the third Sunday of the month.

Kalgoorlie-Boulder Racing Round RACING
(www.kbrc.com.au; ⏲Sep) Locals and a huge influx of visitors dress up to watch horses race. Accommodation can be difficult to secure.

Sleeping

Most accommodation targets the mining industry. Smarter places tend to be overpriced, and hostels and pubs are often full of long-stayers.

Kalgoorlie Backpackers HOSTEL $
(☎08-9091 1482; www.kalgoorliebackpackers.com.au; 166 Hay St; dm/s/d $33/60/85; ❄@≋) Partly located in a former brothel, this hostel is in a central location, and is a good place to find out about work opportunities.

Discovery Holiday Parks CARAVAN PARK $
(www.discoveryholidayparks.com.au; sites $21-51, r $60, units $119-179; ❄@≋) **Kalgoorlie** (☎08-9039 4800; 286 Burt St, Kalgoorlie); **Boulder** (☎08-9093 1266; 201 Lane St, Boulder) Sister complexes with sizeable and well-fitted-out A-frame chalets and cabins, grassy tent sites, playgrounds and pools.

Rydges Kalgoorlie HOTEL $$
(☎08-9080 0800; www.rydges.com; 21 Davidson St; r from $209; ❄@≋) Kalgoorlie's best accommodation is located in a residential area between Kalgoorlie and Boulder. In an oasis

of lush native bush, the rooms are spacious and very comfortable.

Railway Motel MOTEL $$
(☎08-9088 0000; www.railwaymotel.com.au; 51 Forrest St; r from $135; ❄🏊) Opposite the train station with bright, spruced-up rooms. Adjacent two-bedroom apartments are spacious and comfortable.

Langtrees BOUTIQUE HOTEL $$$
(☎08-9026 2181; www.langtreeshotel.com; 181 Hay St; d $300) Formerly a famous brothel, Langtrees has 10 themed rooms including an Afghan boudoir or the Holden-On room that's perfect for recovering petrolheads. Less ostentatious rooms are also available.

Eating

Relish CAFE $
(162 Hannan St; breakfast $8-16, lunch $10-14; ⌚6am-3pm Mon-Fri, 7am-2pm Sat & Sun) The best coffee in town along with interesting food such as lamb-and-feta frittata, vegetarian wraps and sweet-potato-and-chorizo tart. Check out local art in the adjacent whitewashed laneway.

Hoover's Cafe PUB FOOD $$
(www.palacehotelkalgoorlie.com/hoovers-cafe/; 137 Hannan St; mains $11-26; ⌚8am-5pm; 📶) At the Palace Hotel, this pub dining room serves good-value, tasty food. Upstairs is the flash **Balcony Bar & Restaurant** (mains $36-47; ⌚from 5pm) serving steak and seafood.

Lemongrass THAI $$
(5/84-90 Brockman St; mains $18-22; ⌚11.30am-2.30pm Mon-Sat, 4.30-9pm daily) A healthy, lighter option in a town better known for robust pub grub.

Paddy's Ale House PUB FOOD $$
(135 Hannan St, Exchange Hotel; mains $17-30; ⌚11am-late) Classic counter meals including steaks and bangers-and-mash and lots of live TV sport.

Drinking & Entertainment

The gold rush–era pubs of Hannan St are full of hard-drinking blokes and female bar staff clad in underwear, suspenders and high heels. Pick your pub carefully if you prefer your bar staff not in skimpy uniform.

Palace Hotel PUB
(www.palacehotelkalgoorlie.com.au; 137 Hannan St) Watch the street life from the relatively demure balcony bar or descend to the Gold Bar for live bands, DJs and skimpies.

Information

Department of Parks & Wildlife (☎08-9080 5555; www.parks.dpaw.wa.gov.au; 32 Brookman St; ⌚8am-5pm Mon-Fri) Information on the Goldfields Woodlands National Park.

Visitor Centre (☎08-9021 1966; www.kalgoorlietourism.com; Town Hall, cnr Hannan & Wilson Sts; ⌚8.30am-5pm Mon-Fri, 9am-2pm Sat & Sun) Accommodation bookings and information.

CANNING STOCK ROUTE & GUNBARREL HIGHWAY

Wiluna, 300km north of Leonora, is the start or finish point for two of Australia's most extreme 4WD adventures – the Canning Stock Route and the Gunbarrel Hwy. These rough, remote routes head through unforgiving wilderness for thousands of kilometres. They can only be safely traversed from April to September. Don't attempt them at all without checking with visitor centres and Parks & Wildlife offices first as they're completely weather-dependent. HEMA Maps' detailed *Great Desert Tracks – North West Sheet* is essential.

The **Canning Stock Route** (www.exploroz.com/TrekNotes/WDeserts/Canning_Stock_Route.aspx) runs 2006km northeast to Halls Creek, crossing the Great Sandy and Gibson Deserts, and is a route to be taken very seriously. If you're starting from Wiluna, pick up road and safety information from the **shire office** (☎08-9981 8000; www.wiluna.wa.gov.au; Scotia St). You'll need a permit to cross the Birrilburru native-title area.

Taking the old **Gunbarrel Highway** (www.exploroz.com/TrekNotes/WDeserts/Gunbarrel_Highway.aspx) from Wiluna to Warakurna near the NT border (where it joins the Outback Way) is a long, rough, heavily corrugated trip through sand dunes. Like the Canning, it's strongly recommended you drive this in a convoy with other vehicles, and you carry all supplies – including fuel and water – for the duration of your trip with you. Let the police posts at either end of both tracks know your movements.

North of Kalgoorlie-Boulder

Heading north from Kalgoorlie-Boulder, the Goldfields Hwy is surfaced to Wiluna (580km north), the starting point for the 4WD Canning Stock Route and Gunbarrel Hwy. Branching east, the road from Leonora is sealed to Laverton (367km northeast of Kalgoorlie), the starting point for the unsealed Great Central Rd (Outback Way).

Many gravel roads are fine for regular cars, but rain can quickly close them. All the (non-ghost) towns have pub accommodation, caravan parks with cabins, fuel stops and grocery stores.

Kanowna, Broad Arrow & Ora Banda

Easy day trips north from Kalgoorlie include the gold ghost towns of Kanowna (18km northeast), Broad Arrow (38km north) and Ora Banda (65km northwest). Little remains of Kanowna apart from the foundations of its 16 hotels (!), but its pioneer cemetery is interesting. Broad Arrow was featured in *The Nickel Queen* (1971), the first full-length feature film made in WA. At the beginning of the 20th century it had a population of 2400. Now there's just one pub, popular with Kal locals at weekends. The 1911 **Ora Banda Historical Inn** (☎08-9024 2444; www.orabanda.com.au; sites per 2 people $20-30, r $75-120) has a beer garden, simple accommodation and dusty camping.

Menzies & Lake Ballard

The once thriving but now tiny township of Menzies, 132km from Kalgoorlie, is best known as the turn-off for the stunning **Antony Gormley sculptures** on **Lake Ballard**, an eye-dazzling salt lake 51km northwest of town. Camp here for free. There are toilets and a barbecue area.

The **Menzies visitor centre** (☎08-9024 2702; www.menzies.wa.gov.au; Shenton St; ⏲9am-4.30pm Mon-Fri, 9am-1pm Sat & Sun; @📶) has information on visiting the sculptures and other local sites, and runs the neighbouring **caravan park** (☎08 9024 2702, after hours 0448 242 041; sites per 2 people $22-30). It also houses the **Spinifex Art Gallery**, exhibiting works from the Tjuntjuntjarra community, located 750km to the east.

> **ℹ PERMITS, PLEASE**
>
> The Canning Stock Route and Outback Way traverse various pockets of Aboriginal land and travellers must obtain a permit from the Department of Aboriginal Affairs (DAA; www.daa.wa.gov.au) to cross them. It's usually a quick online process, but if you're planning to stay and camp rather than merely pass through, additional approvals are required from the affected community; allow up to two weeks.

Kookynie

Midway between Menzies and Leonora, a good dirt road leads 25km to Kookynie, another interesting ghost town, where the **Kookynie Grand Hotel** (☎08-9031 3010; puseymin@bigpond.com; s/d $80/100) pulls pints and offers beds. Quiet **Niagara Dam**, 10km from Kookynie, has bush camping.

Leonora

North of Kookynie (237km from Kalgoorlie), Leonora is the area's service centre for mining exploration and farming. Old public buildings and pubs line the main street near the **visitor centre** (☎08-9037 7016; www.leonora.wa.gov.au; Tower St; ⏲9am-4pm Mon-Fri). Just 4km southwest of town, **Gwalia Historic Site** was occupied in 1896 and deserted in 1963, after the pit closed. With houses and household goods disintegrating intact, it's a strangely fascinating ghost town. The **museum** (www.gwalia.org.au; adult/child $10/5; ⏲9am-4pm) is full of wonderful curios, and there's a good audio tour ($2). **Hoover House** (☎08-9037 7122; www.gwalia.org.au; s $120-150, d $130-160; ❄), the 1898 mine manager's house, is named for Gwalia's first mine manager, Herbert Hoover, who later became the 31st president of the United States. It's beautifully restored, and you can stay overnight in one of the antique-strewn bedrooms.

Laverton

Laverton crouches on the edge of the Great Victoria Desert. The **visitor centre** (☎08-9031 1361; www.laverton.wa.gov.au; Augusta St; ⏲9.30am-4.30pm Mon-Fri, 9am-1pm Sat & Sun) is combined with the **Great Beyond – Explorers' Hall of Fame** (adult/child $10/5), which uses technology to tell pioneer stories. The not-for-profit **Laverton Outback Gallery** (www.laverton-outback-gallery.com.au; 4 Euro St; ⌚9am-5pm) is a great place to purchase paintings, necklaces, woomeras and boomerangs – 80% of the price goes straight to the Aboriginal artist.

Laverton marks the start of the Outback Way. Expect to overnight and/or stock up on supplies of fuel and water here, and *definitely* check at the visitor centre for current road conditions.

Outback Way (Great Central Road)

The unsealed **Outback Way** (www.outbackway.org.au) links Laverton with Winton in central Queensland, via the red centre of the Northern Territory. From Laverton it is a mere 1098km to Yulara, 1541km to Alice Springs and 2720km to Winton!

The road is sandy and corrugated in places, but it's wide and suitable for all vehicles. It can be closed for several days after rain. Fuel is available at roughly 300km intervals on the WA side.

Coming from Laverton, three WA roadhouses (www.ngaanyatjarraku.wa.gov.au) all provide food, fuel and limited mechanical services – **Tjukayirla** (☎08-9037 1108; tjukayirlaroadhouse@bigpond.com; unpowered/powered sites $20/30, s $75, units $120-160; ⌚9am-5pm Mon-Fri, 9am-2pm Sat & Sun) at 315km, **Warburton** (☎08-8956 7656) at 567km and **Warakurna** (☎08-8956 7344; warakurnaroadhouse@bigpond.com) at 798km. All offer camping (around $25 per person), budget rooms (around $70) and self-contained units (around $160). Book ahead as rooms are limited. The Tjukayirla roadhouse offers tours to caves with 5000-year-old rock art.

At Warburton visit the **Tjulyuru Cultural & Civic Centre** (☎08-8956 7966; www.tjulyuru.com; ⌚8.30am-4.30pm Mon-Fri) containing an extensive collection of Ngaanyatjarra Aboriginal paintings.

Warakurna, Warburton and Giles run on NT time, 1½ hours ahead of WA time.

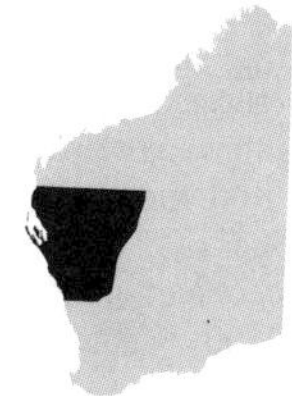

Monkey Mia & the Central West

Includes ➡

Best Places for Sunset

- Steep Point (p170)
- Fishermens Lookout (p159)
- Red Bluff (p165)
- Shark Bay Hotel (p170)
- Horrocks (p168)

Best Places to Stay

- Gnaraloo Station (p174)
- Ospreys Beach Chalet (p162)
- Dongara Breeze Inn (p159)
- Bentwood Olive Grove (p160)
- Hamelin Station (p168)

Why Go?

The pristine coastline and sheltered turquoise waters of Malgana country draw tourists and marine life from around the world. Aside from the dolphins of Monkey Mia, the submerged sea-grass meadows of World Heritage–listed Shark Bay host dugongs, rays, sharks and turtles. On land, rare marsupials take refuge in remote national parks, and limestone cliffs, red sand and salt lakes litter a stark interior.

Further south in the land of the Nhanda people, the gorges of Kalbarri invite adventurers to explore their depths, while wild flowers carpet the plains, and ospreys wheel away from battered Indian Ocean cliffs as humpback whales migrate slowly southwards.

Vegies are ripening in Carnarvon as anglers and board riders check the tides, and windsurfers are waiting for the 'Doctor' (strong afternoon sea breeze) to blow. In Geraldton, good cafes, weekend markets and an excellent museum combine with Indian Ocean views along the city's foreshore.

When to Go

Monkey Mia

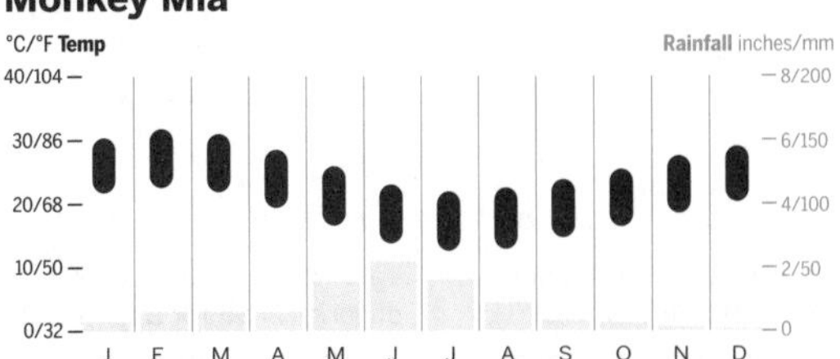

Jun–Aug The winter swells pump the breaks off Gnaraloo and Quobba.

Aug & Sep Kalbarri erupts in wild flowers.

Nov–Feb Windsurfers clutch their sails from Geraldton to Carnarvon.

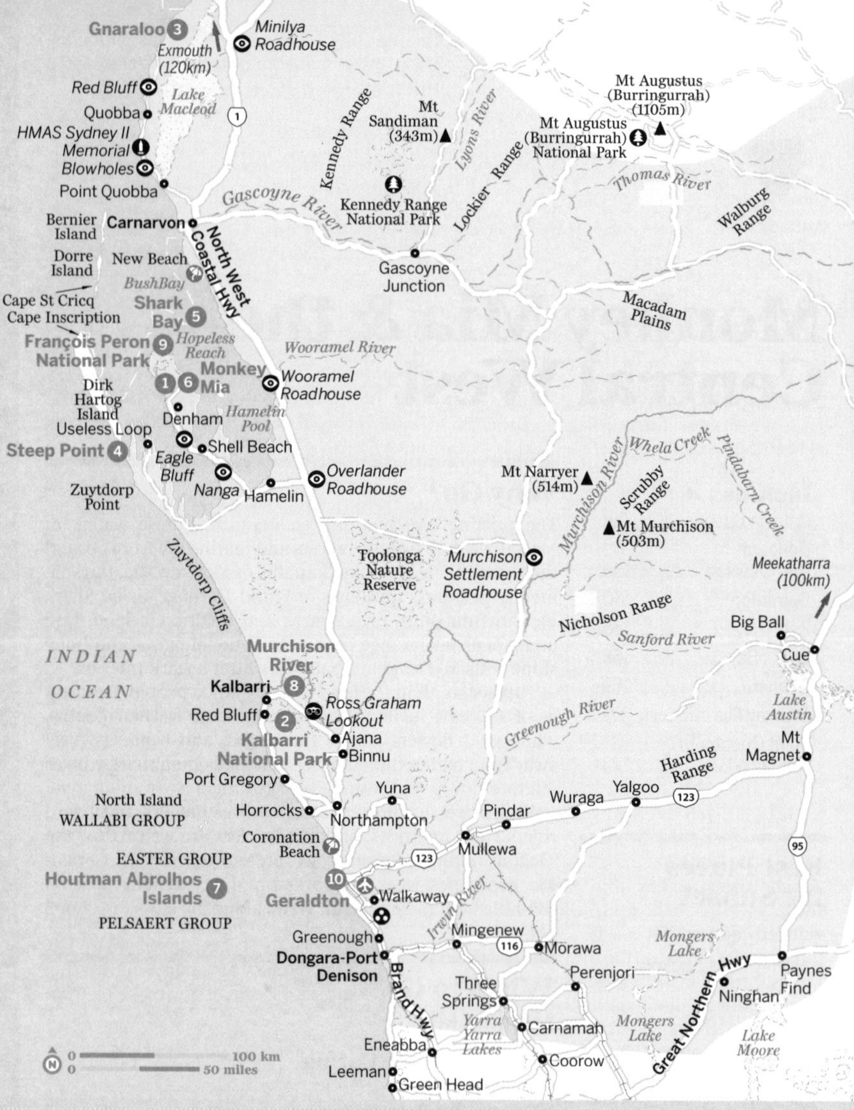

Monkey Mia & the Central West Highlights

1. Watching the dolphins feed at **Monkey Mia** (p171).
2. Canoeing at **Kalbarri National Park** (p165).
3. Surfing the Tombstones break at **Gnaraloo** (p174).
4. Driving out to the mainland's most westerly tip, **Steep Point** (p170).
5. Sailing out to look for dugongs in **Shark Bay** (p168).
6. Immersing yourself in Malgana culture on a **Wula Guda Nyinda** (p171) tour at Monkey Mia.
7. Diving on ancient shipwrecks at the **Houtman Abrolhos Islands** (p164).
8. Horse riding along the **Murchison River** (p165).
9. Spotting marine life from a coastal walk in the **François Peron National Park** (p171).
10. Soaking up some coffee and culture in **Geraldton's** (p160) museums, galleries and cafes.

Getting There & Around

AIR

Virgin Australia (13 67 89; www.virginaustralia.com) Perth to Geraldton.

Skippers (1300 729 924; www.skippers.com.au) Perth to Geraldton, Shark Bay and Carnarvon.

Qantas (13 13 13; www.qantas.com.au) Perth to Geraldton.

BUS

Integrity (1800 226 339; www.integritycoachlines.com.au) Sunday, Tuesday and Thursday evening departures from Perth to Broome stopping at Geraldton, Kalbarri and Carnarvon.

Transwa (1300 662 205; www.transwa.wa.gov.au) Buses between Perth and Kalbarri, Geraldton and Dongara along the Brand Hwy (Rte 1).

BATAVIA COAST

From tranquil Dongara-Port Denison to the remote, wind-scoured Zutydorp Cliffs stretches a dramatic coastline steeped in history, littered with shipwrecks and abounding in marine life. While the region proved the undoing of many early European sailors, today modern fleets make the most of a lucrative crayfish industry.

Dongara-Port Denison

POP 3100

Pretty little Dongara and Port Denison, twin seaside towns 359km from Perth, make an idyllic spot to break up a long drive. Surrounded by beautiful beaches, walking trails and historic buildings, the towns have a laid-back atmosphere. Port Denison has good beaches and accommodation, while Dongara's main street, shaded by century-old figs, offers the best eating.

Sights & Activities

The 12 itineraries in the free *Walk Dongara Denison* brochure include the **Irwin River Nature Trail**, where you might spot black swans, pelicans or cormorants. The **Heritage Trail** booklet ($2) details a 1.6km route linking buildings including 1860s **Russ Cottage** (Point Leander Dr), with a kitchen floor made from compacted anthills. The cells in the old police station hold the **Irwin District Museum** (08-9927 1404; admission $2.50; 10am-noon Mon-Sat), showcasing historical displays.

Denison Beach Marina brims with crayfish boats while sunsets are dazzling from nearby **Fishermens Lookout**.

Sleeping

Note that accommodation is more expensive during public and school holidays.

★**Dongara Breeze Inn** GUESTHOUSE $
(08-9927 1332; www.dongarabackpackers.com.au; 32 Waldeck St, Dongara; dm/s/d $30/80/85) The cheapest beds in town look onto a leafy garden at this popular lodging, which has stylish doubles with a chic Asian ambience, rustic dorms (in a vintage railway carriage) and free bike use for guests. The shared spaces arrayed around the garden are very appealing.

Dongara Tourist Park CARAVAN PARK $
(08-9927 1210; www.dongaratouristpark.com.au; 8 George St, Port Denison; unpowered/powered sites $26/37, 1-/2-bedroom cabins $110/150;) The best camping option has shaded, spacious sites behind South Beach. The two-bed cabins on the hill have great views, and there's a lush pergola for dining outdoors.

Dongara Old Mill Motel MOTEL $
(08-9927 1200; www.dongaraoldmillmotel.com.au; 58 Waldeck St, Dongara; s/d 105/110;) Good-value renovated rooms, friendly owners and a palm-trimmed swimming pool make this place worthy of an overnight stay. Good eating and drinking in central Dongara is a pleasant stroll away.

Port Denison Holiday Units APARTMENT $
(08-9927 1104; www.dongaraaccommodation.com.au; 14 Carnarvon St, Port Denison; d $125-135;) These spotless, spacious, self-catering units, some with views, are just a block from the beach.

Eating

Starfish Cafe CAFE $
(0448 344 215; White Tops Rd, Port Denison; mains $10-30; 8am-2pm Wed-Sun) Hidden away in the South Beach car park, this casual snack shack offers coffee, jaffles, winter soups and summer salads.

Priory Hotel PUB, BISTRO $$
(08-9927 1090; www.prioryhotel.com.au; 11 St Dominics Rd, Dongara; mains $15-42;) There's a touch of *Picnic at Hanging Rock* about this leafy former nunnery and ladies college with its period furniture, polished floorboards, black-and-white photos and wide

verandahs. Sundays bring roasts and woodfired pizza, several nights offer live music and steaks are available every evening.

Dongara Hotel Motel RESTAURANT $$
(☎08-9927 1023; www.dongaramotel.com.au; 12 Moreton Tce, Dongara; d $145, mains $22-42; ⏰7am-10pm; 📶) Locals love the Dongara's legendary servings of fresh seafood, steaks and 'Asian Corner' curries, *mie goreng* and *pad thai*. The motel rooms, popular with corporates, are surprisingly stylish.

Information

Telecentre (CRC; ☎08-9927 2111; 11 Moreton Tce, Dongara; internet $5 per hr; ⏰8.30am-4.30pm Mon-Fri; @) Internet access.

Visitor Centre (☎08-9927 1404; www.irwin.wa.gov.au; 9 Waldeck St, Dongara; ⏰9am-5pm Mon-Fri, to noon Sat) In Dongara's old post office.

Getting There & Around

Dongara-Port Denison is accessible via the Brand Hwy, Indian Ocean Dr or Midlands Rd (Rte 116).

Transwa buses run daily to Perth ($56, five hours) and Geraldton ($14, one hour). **Integrity** runs three times a week to Perth ($56, five hours) and Geraldton ($34, one hour), and to Exmouth ($172, 13 hours). Buses arrive and depart from the visitor centre.

For a taxi, call ☎08-9927 1555.

Geraldton

POP 39,000

Capital of the midwest, sun-drenched 'Gero' is surrounded by excellent beaches offering myriad aquatic opportunities – swimming, snorkelling, surfing and, in particular, wind- and kitesurfing. The largest town between Perth and Darwin has huge wheat-handling and fishing industries that make it independent of the fickle tourist dollar, and seasonal workers flood the town during crayfish season. Still a work in progress, Gero blends big-city sophistication with small-town friendliness, offering a strong arts culture, a blossoming foodie scene and some great local music.

Sights

★Western Australian Museum – Geraldton MUSEUM
(☎08-9921 5080; www.museum.wa.gov.au; 1 Museum Pl; admission by donation; ⏰9.30am-4pm) At one of the state's best museums, intelligent multimedia displays relate the area's natural, cultural and Indigenous history. The Shipwreck Gallery documents the tragic story of the *Batavia*, while video footage reveals the sunken HMAS *Sydney II*. Enquire about sailing open days held on the longboat moored behind the museum.

Cathedral of St Francis Xavier Church CHURCH
(☎08-9921 3221; www.geraldtondiocese.org.au; Cathedral Ave; ⏰tours 10am Mon & Fri, 4pm Wed) Arguably the finest example of the architectural achievements of the multi-skilled Monsignor John Hawes. The cathedral's striking features include imposing twin towers with arched openings, a central dome, Romanesque columns and boldly striped walls.

Geraldton Regional Art Gallery GALLERY
(☎08-9964 7170; www.artgallery.cgg.wa.gov.au; 24 Chapman Rd; ⏰10am-5pm Tue-Sun) FREE With an excellent permanent collection, including paintings by Norman Lindsay and Elizabeth Durack, this gallery also presents

GREENOUGH

Located 24km south of Geraldton, the rural area of historic Greenough makes a pleasant overnight stay. Sights such as the **Central Greenough Historical Settlement** (☎08-9926 1084; www.centralgreenough.com; Brand Hwy; adult/child $6/3, cafe meals $10-28; ⏰9am-4pm, from 10am Nov-Dec & Feb-Mar), with its handful of 19th-century buildings, and the **Pioneer Museum** (www.greenoughmuseum.com; Phillips Rd; adult/child $5/free; ⏰9.30am-3.30pm) detail early settler life and offer a chance to stretch the legs, although the area's main attractions are its excellent food and lodgings. Around 2km north of Central Greenough, look out for the quirky **Leaning Trees**, twisted into idiosyncratic shapes by incessant Indian Ocean gusts.

Bentwood Olive Grove (☎08-9926 1196; www.bentwood.com.au; Brand Hwy; d $130-160; ❄) has a long connection to gourmet food, though its focus is now on accommodation, with a beautiful stone cottage sleeping up to six. The Transwa daily service to Geraldton will drop you on the Brand Hwy entrance.

THE WILD FLOWER WAY

Inland east from Geraldton, Rte 123 leads to wheat silos, wild flowers and little one-pub towns that are a hive of activity between August and September as minibuses full of senior travellers zoom around hunting blossoms. Accommodation includes caravan parks, pubs and motels, and there are regular transport links with Transwa. In wild flower season, local visitor centres sometimes run minibuses to the best sites.

Morawa, Mingenew & Mullewa

The 'three Ms' form a triangle that buzzes during wild flower season but offers limited appeal to travellers outside this time. Morawa and Mullewa both have distinctive churches designed by Monsignor John Hawes.

Coalseam Conservation Park (www.parks.dpaw.wa.gov.au/park/coalseam; camping per person $7), 34km northeast of Mingenew on the Irwin River, has everlastings (paper daisies), a short loop walk, and ancient fossil shells embedded in the cliffs.

Mullewa is famous for its wreath flower, *Lechenaultia macrantha*. The town holds an annual wild flower show at the end of August. In season, the roads heading northeast to Yalgoo are normally carpeted in everlastings.

Perenjori

Perenjori, 360km from Perth, is a pretty town surrounded by abundant wildlife and, from July to November, stunning wild flowers. The **visitor centre** (☎08-9973 1105; www.perenjori.wa.gov.au; Fowler St; ⏲9am-4pm Mon-Fri Jul-Oct), also home to the **pioneer museum** (adult/child $2/0.50), has self-drive brochures including *The Way of the Wildflowers* and *Monsignor Hawes Heritage Trail*. They can provide access to the beautiful **St Joseph's Church**, designed by the prolific Hawes.

provocative contemporary work and regular touring exhibitions.

Old Geraldton Gaol Craft Centre HISTORIC BUILDING
(☎08-9921 1614; Bill Sewell Compiex, Chapman Rd; ⏲10am-3.30pm Mon-Sat) The crafts are secondary to the gloomy cells that housed prisoners from 1858 to 1986, and the historic documents that detail their grim circumstances.

HMAS Sydney II Memorial MONUMENT
(www.hmassydneymemorial.com.au; Mt Scott; ⏲tours 10.30am) FREE Commanding the hill overlooking Geraldton is this memorial commemorating the 1941 loss of the *Sydney* and its 645 men after a skirmish with the German raider *Kormoran*.

Activities

Most activities are water-based, but there is also an excellent network of bike paths, including the 10km-long coastal route from **Tarcoola Beach to Chapman River**. Grab the *Local Travelsmart Guide* from the visitor centre. Bikes can be hired from **Revolutions** (☎08-9964 1399; www.revolutions-geraldton.com.au; 2c Jensen St; bike hire per day $20; ⏲9am-5.30pm Mon-Fri, to noon Sat).

G-Spot Xtreme WINDSURFING
(☎08-9965 5577; www.gspotxtreme.com.au; 241a Lester Ave; hire per day windsurfers from $100, kayaks 2/4 hours from $30/45; ⏲10am-4pm Tue-Fri, 10am-1pm Sat) Hire or buy windsurfing and kiteboarding equipment and kayaks.

Batavia Coast Dive Academy DIVING
(☎08-9921 4229; www.facebook.com/bataviacoastdive; 118 Northwest Coastal Hwy; local dives with/without equipment $140/100; ⏲9am-5pm Mon-Fri, 8am-1pm Sat, 10am-noon Sun) Offers open-water courses (full PADI $630) and a range of diving trips, including chartered trips to the Houtman Abrolhos Islands (from $300 per person per day).

Midwest Surf School SURFING
(☎0419 988 756; http://surf2skool.com; lessons from $60, board hire $30) Courses for absolute beginners through to advanced at Geraldton's back beach.

KiteWest KITEBOARDING
(☎0449 021 7840449 021 784; www.kitewest.com.au; coaching per hr from $50) Kiteboarding courses, surfing lessons and paddleboarding tuition. Also 4WD camping tours and fishing, scenic and wild flower daytrips (per person from $95).

Geraldton

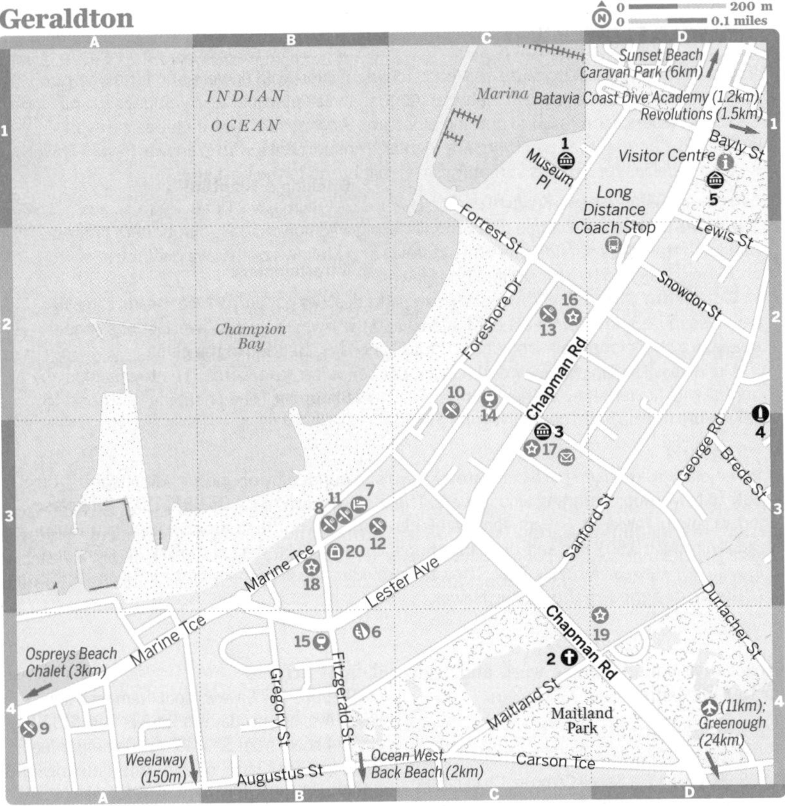

Sleeping

Expect price hikes for school and public holidays.

Foreshore Backpackers HOSTEL $
(☎ 08-9921 3275; www.foreshorebackpackers.com.au; 172 Marine Tce; dm/s/d $30/50/70; @) This rambling central hostel is full of hidden nooks, sunny balconies and world-weary travellers. It's very close to good bars and cafes, and a good place to find a job, lift or travel buddy.

Sunset Beach Holiday Park CARAVAN PARK $
(☎ 1800 353 389; www.sunsetbeachpark.com.au; Bosley St; powered sites $38, cabins $110-145) About 6km north of the CBD, Sunset Beach has roomy, shaded sites just a few steps from a lovely beach, and an ultramodern camp kitchen with the biggest plasma TV on the entire coast.

★ **Ospreys Beach Chalet** COTTAGE $$
(☎ 0447 647 994; enerhkalm@gmail.com; 40 Bosuns Cr, Point Moore; 2 persons from $155) Both ospreys and beach are nearby this sustainably restored cottage, which began life as a proof-of-concept project. Rainwater tanks and solar panels complement recycled materials in a restoration that doesn't skimp on comfort. There are plenty of outdoor areas and the rear native garden is a gem.

Ocean West APARTMENT $$
(☎ 08-9921 1047; www.oceanwest.com.au; 1 Hadda Way; 1-/3-bedroom apt from $133/213;) Don't let the '60s brick put you off; these fully self-contained units have all been tastefully renovated, making them one of the better deals in town. The wildly beautiful back beach is just across the road.

Weelaway B&B $$
(☎ 08-9965 5232; www.weelaway.com.au; 104 Gregory St; r $100-135, 2-bedroom cottages from

Geraldton

Top Sights
1 Western Australian Museum – Geraldton C1

Sights
2 Cathedral of St Francis Xavier Church C4
3 Geraldton Regional Art Gallery C3
4 HMAS Sydney II Memorial D3
5 Old Geraldton Gaol Craft Centre D1

Activities, Courses & Tours
6 G-Spot Xtreme B4

Sleeping
7 Foreshore Backpackers B3

Eating
8 Culinary HQ B3
9 Geraldton Fish Market A4
10 Go Health Lunch Bar C2
11 Jaffle Shack B3
12 Provincial B3
13 Saltdish C2

Drinking & Nightlife
14 Freemasons Hotel C2
15 Vibe B4

Entertainment
16 Breakers Bar C2
17 Camel Bar C3
18 Orana Cinemas B3
19 Queens Park Theatre D4

Shopping
20 Yamaji Art B3

$165;) Weelaway offers rooms in a heritage-listed house dating from 1862. There are formal lounge rooms, shady verandahs, and a well-stocked library, and it's all within walking distance of the centre of town.

Eating

Free barbecues and picnic tables dot the foreshore.

Jaffle Shack CAFE **$**
(www.facebook.com/TheJaffleShack; 188 Marine Tce; snacks $6-12; 7.30am-4pm Mon-Fri, to 3pm Sat, to 1pm Sun) The humble jaffle (toasted sandwich) is showcased at this rustic cafe. Fillings range from classic Aussie combos such as Vegemite and cheese, to butter chicken and raita, or Vietnamese-style pulled pork. Leave room for a Nutella one for dessert, and pop back later in the day for Gero's best ice-cream milkshakes. Damn fine coffee, too.

Geraldton Fish Market SEAFOOD **$**
(365 Marine Tce; 8.30am-5.30pm Mon-Fri, to noon Sat) Secure briny fresh fish and seafood for your next ad-hoc, al-fresco Aussie feast, or stock up on tasty treats including smoked fish and pickled octopus. Delicious ready-made seafood curries are good value at $14.95.

Go Health Lunch Bar CAFE **$**
(08-9965 5200; 122 Marine Tce; light meals around $11; 8.30am-3pm Mon-Sat;) Vegetarians can rejoice at the choice of fresh juices and smoothies, excellent espresso, healthy burritos, lentil burgers, focaccias and other light meals from this popular lunch bar in the middle of the mall.

Culinary HQ CAFE **$**
(08-9964 8308; www.culinaryhq.com.au; 202 Marine Tce; lunch $14.50; 7am-4pm Mon-Fri, 8am-1pm Sat) An eclectic gourmet menu changes weekly at this bustling providore and includes soups, baguettes and cooked meals that are also available for take-away – perfect for that hostel or campervan reheat.

★ **Saltdish** CAFE **$$**
(08-9964 6030; 35 Marine Tce; breakfast $8-20, lunch $16-32; 7.30am-4pm Mon-Fri;) The hippest cafe in town serves innovative, contemporary brekkies, light lunches and industrial-strength coffee, and screens films in its courtyard on summer evenings. Try the sweetcorn and coriander fritters. BYO wine or beer.

Provincial MODERN AUSTRALIAN **$$**
(08-9964 1887; www.theprovincial.com.au; 167 Marine Tce; tapas $8-20, pizza $14-20, mains $20-30; 4.30pm-late Tue-Sat) Stencil art adorns this atmospheric wine bar serving up tapas, wood-fired pizzas and more robust main courses. Try the zesty coconut prawn curry with a pint of zingy White Rabbit Belgian Pale Ale. Service can be slightly haphazard, but The Provincial has a coolly cosmopolitan vibe. Live music most Friday and Saturday nights.

OFF THE BEATEN TRACK

HOUTMAN ABROLHOS ISLANDS

Better known as 'the Abrolhos', this archipelago of 122 coral islands, 60km off the coast of Geraldton, is home to amazing wildlife including sea lions, green turtles, carpet pythons, over 90 seabird species and the Tammar wallaby. Much of the flora is rare, endemic and protected, and the surrounding reefs offer great diving thanks to the warm Leeuwin Current, which allows tropical species such as *Acropora* (staghorn) coral to flourish further south than normal.

These gnarly reefs have claimed many ships over the years, including the ill-fated *Batavia* (1629), and *Hadda* (1877), and you can dive on the wreck sites, as well as follow a number of self-guided dive trails (see the WA Fisheries *Abrolhos Islands Information Guide* for details). Because the general public can't stay overnight, divers (and surfers) normally need a multi-day boat charter. If you're content with a day trip where you can bushwalk, picnic, snorkel or fish, then flying in is your best bet.

Batavia Coast Dive Academy (p161) Can help get a boat together.

Shine Aviation Services (☎08-9923 3600; www.shineaviation.com.au; 90min/full-day tours $175/240) Full-day tours include a landing on the Abrolhos Islands and snorkelling.

Geraldton Air Charter (☎08-9923 3434; www.geraldtonaircharter.com.au; Brierly Terminal, Geraldton Airport; half-/full-day tours $240/550) Some trips include the Pinnacles to the south.

Drinking

Freemasons Hotel PUB

(☎08-9964 3457; www.thefreemasonshotel.wix.com/home#; cnr Marine Tce & Durlacher St; meals $18-33; 11am-late) The heritage-listed Freo has been serving beer to thirsty travellers since the 1800s. Nowadays it's a popular hang-out, with live music, DJs and open-mic and trivia nights complemented by a good range of bar meals.

Entertainment

Live-music and clubbing options include **Vibe** (☎08-9921 3700; 38-42 Fitzgerald St; from 11pm Thu-Sun), **Breakers** (☎08-9921 8924; www.facebook.com/breakersgeraldton; 41 Chapman Rd; from 9pm), **Camel Bar** (☎08-9965 5500; 20 Chapman Rd), the Provincial (p163) and the Freemasons Hotel. There is also a **cinema** (☎08-9965 0568; www.orana-cinemas.com.au; cnr Marine Tce & Fitzgerald St) and **theatre** (☎08-9956 6662; www.queensparktheatre.com.au; cnr Cathedral Ave & Maitland St).

Shopping

Yamaji Art ARTS

(☎0487 420 237, 08-9965 3440; www.yamajiart.com; 205 Marine Tce; varied, call first) A good opportunity to purchase Yamaji arts, bowls, didgeridoo and music. Opening hours can be flexible, so phone ahead.

Information

There's free wi-fi at the **library** (☎08-9956 6659; www.library.cgg.wa.gov.au; 37 Marine Tce; wi-fi 1st hr free; from 9am Tue-Sat, from 1pm Sun & Mon; @) and across central Geraldton.

Sun City Books & Internet Corner (☎08-9964 7258; 49 Marine Tce; 9am-5pm Mon-Fri, to 1pm Sat; @) Internet access and second-hand books.

Visitor Centre (☎08-9921 3999; www.geraldtontourist.com.au; Bill Sewell Complex, Chapman Rd; 9am-5pm Mon-Fri, 10am-4pm Sat & Sun) Accommodation, tours and transport bookings.

Getting There & Around

AIR

Virgin Australia and Qantas both fly daily between Perth and Geraldton. Skippers flies direct to/from Carnarvon a few times weekly. The airport is 12km from Marine Tce.

BUS

Integrity runs three bus services per week linking Geraldton to Perth ($63, six hours), Carnarvon ($115, six hours) and Exmouth ($156, 11 hours). Transwa has daily inland services to Perth ($68, six hours) and thrice weekly services to Kalbarri ($28, two hours). There's also a twice-weekly service to Meekatharra ($76, seven hours). All long-distance buses leave from the **old railway station**, where there is also a Transwa booking office.

TAXI

Call ☎131 008.

Kalbarri

POP 2000

Magnificent red-sandstone cliffs terminate at the Indian Ocean. The beautiful Murchison River snakes through tall, steep gorges before ending treacherously at Gantheaume Bay. Wild flowers line paths frequented by kangaroos, emus and thorny devils, while whales breach just offshore, and rare orchids struggle in the rocky ground. To the north, the towering line of the limestone Zuytdorp Cliffs remains aloof, pristine and remote.

Kalbarri is surrounded by stunning nature, and there's great surfing, swimming, fishing, bushwalking, horse riding and canoeing both in town and in Kalbarri National Park. While the vibe is mostly low key, school holidays see Kalbarri stretched to the limit.

Sights & Activities

Kalbarri has cycle paths along the foreshore, and you can ride out to **Blue Holes** for snorkelling, **Jakes Point** for surfing and fishing, and **Red Bluff Beach**, 5.5km away.

Lookouts along the coast are perfect for watching the sunset. Look for wild flowers along Siles Rd, River Rd and near the airport. The visitor centre publishes wild flower updates in season.

Ask at the visitor centre about other activities including quad biking, skydiving and fishing.

★ **Kalbarri National Park** NATIONAL PARK
(per car $12) With its magnificent river red gums and Tumblagooda sandstone, the rugged Kalbarri National Park contains almost 2000 sq km of wild bushland, stunning river gorges and savagely eroded coastal cliffs. There's abundant wildlife, including 200 species of birds, and spectacular wild flowers between July and November.

A string of lookouts dot the impressive coast south of town and the easy **Bigurda Trail** (8km one way) follows the cliff tops between **Natural Bridge** and **Eagle Gorge**; from July to November you may spot migrating whales. Closer to town are **Pot Alley**, **Rainbow Valley**, **Mushroom Rock** and **Red Bluff**, the latter accessible via a walking trail from Kalbarri (5.5km one way).

The river gorges are east of Kalbarri, 11km down Ajana Kalbarri Rd to the turn-off, and then 20km unsealed to a T-intersection. Turn left for lookouts over **The Loop** and the superb **Nature's Window** (1km return). Bring lots of water for the unshaded **Loop Trail** (8km return). Turning right at the T leads to **Z-Bend** with a breathtaking lookout (1.2km return) or you can continue steeply down to the gorge bottom (2.6km return). Head back to Ajana Kalbarri Rd and travel a further 24km before turning off to **Hawk's Head**, where there are great views and picnic tables, and **Ross Graham lookout**, where you can access the river. It's possible to **hike** 38km from Ross Graham to The Loop in a demanding four-day epic, but be warned: there are no marked trails and several river crossings.

Pelican Feeding WILDLIFE WATCHING
(08-9937 1104; 8.45am) FREE Kalbarri's most popular attraction takes place on the waterfront. Look for the compact wooden viewing area and wait for the hungry birds to rock up.

Kalbarri Boat Hire CANOEING
(08-99371245; www.kalbarriboathire.com; Grey St; kayak/canoe/surf cat/powerboat per hr $15/15/45/50) Also runs four-hour breakfast and lunch canoe trips down the Murchison (adult/child $70/50).

Kalbarri Abseil CANYONING
(08-9937 1618; www.abseilaustralia.com.au; half-day abseiling $80, full-day canyoning $135; abseiling year round, canyoning Apr-Nov) Abseil into the sheer gorges of Kalbarri National Park, then float along the bottom on inner tubes. Canyoning includes a fairly strenuous 12km hike.

Kalbarri Sandboarding SANDBOARDING
(08-9937 2377; www.sandboardingaustralia.com.au; adult/child $80/70) Muck around on sand dunes, then go for a snorkel on these fun half-day tours.

Kalbarri Adventure Tours CANOEING
(08-9937 1677; www.kalbarritours.com.au; adult/child from $75/55) Combine canoeing, bushwalking and swimming around the national park's Z-Bend/Loop area. Full- and half-day tours available.

Big River Ranch HORSE RIDING
(08-9937 1214; www.bigriverranch.net; off Ajana Kalbarri Rd.; 90min trail rides $85) Track through the beautiful Murchison River floodplain on horseback. All experience levels are catered for. Camping (per person $15) and rustic bunkhouse rooms (per person $25) available.

Kalbarri

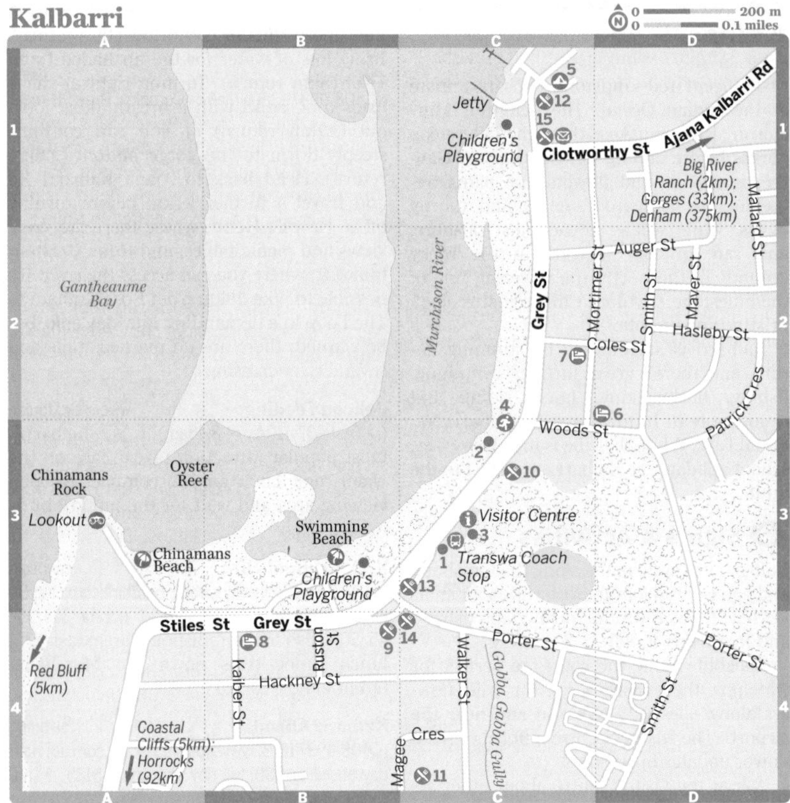

Kalbarri

Activities, Courses & Tours
1 Kalbarri Air Charter C3
2 Kalbarri Boat Hire C3
3 Kalbarri Wilderness Cruises C3
4 Pelican Feeding C3

Sleeping
5 Anchorage Caravan Park C1
6 Kalbarri Backpackers D2
7 Kalbarri Reef Villas C2
8 Pelican Shore Villas B4
Pelican's Nest .... (see 6)

Eating
9 Angies Cafe B4
10 Black Rock Cafe C3
11 Finlay's Fresh Fish BBQ C4
12 Gorges Café C1
13 Kalbarri Motor Hotel C3
14 Restaurant Upstairs C4
15 The Jetty Seafood Shack C1

Tours

The visitor centre can arrange all tour bookings.

Kalbarri Air Charter SCENIC FLIGHT
(☎08-9390 0999; www.kalbarriaircharter.com.au; 62 Grey St; flights $69-315) Offers 20-minute scenic flights over the coastal cliffs, and longer flights over gorges, the Zuytdorp Cliffs, Monkey Mia and the Abrolhos Islands. The River Gorges & Coastal Cliffs tour (45 minutes, $132) is a spectacular combo.

Kalbarri Wilderness Cruises CRUISE
(☎08-9937 1601; www.kalbarricruises.com; adult/child $46/25) Informative two-hour nature cruises along the Murchison.

Reefwalker Adventure Tours WHALE WATCHING
(☎0417 931 091; www.reefwalker.com.au; adult/child $85/55) Spot migrating humpbacks (from July to November). Also runs ocean fishing and sightseeing tours.

Sleeping

Try and avoid school holidays when prices sky rocket.

Kalbarri Backpackers HOSTEL $
(☎08-9937 1430; www.yha.com.au; cnr Woods & Mortimer Sts; dm/d $29/77, bike hire $20; @ ≋) This nice, shady hostel with a decent pool and barbecue is one block back from the beach. Bikes are available for hire.

Anchorage Caravan Park CARAVAN PARK $
(☎08-9937 1181; www.kalbarrianchorage.com.au; cnr Anchorage Lane & Grey St; powered sites $37, cabins with/without bathroom $100/80; ≋) The best option for campers, Anchorage has roomy, nicely shaded sites that overlook the river mouth.

Pelican Shore Villas APARTMENT $$
(☎08-9937 1708; www.pelicanshorevillas.com.au; cnr Grey & Kaiber Sts; villas $136-188; ❄ ≋) These modern and stylish town houses have the best view in town.

Pelican's Nest MOTEL $$
(☎08-9937 1598; www.pelicansnestkalbarri.com.au; 45-47 Mortimer St; d $120-180; ❄ @ ≋) In a quiet location a short walk from the beach, the Nest has a selection of neat motel-style rooms and good facilities.

Kalbarri Reef Villas APARTMENT $$
(☎08-9937 1165; www.reefvillas.com.au; cnr Coles & Mortimer Sts; units $141-195; ❄ ≋) One block behind the foreshore, these fully self-contained, two-storey, two-bedroom apartments face onto a palm-filled garden.

Eating & Drinking

There are supermarkets at the two shopping centres.

Angies Cafe CAFE $
(☎08-9937 1738; Shop 6, 46 Grey St; meals $8-22; ⏰7am-4pm) Great little cafe serving fresh, tasty meals with a good selection of salads.

The Jetty Seafood Shack FISH & CHIPS $
(opposite the Marina; meals $11-25, burgers $9-13; ⏰4.30-8.30pm Mon-Sat) Excellent fish and chips, gourmet burgers, and take-away salads (to make you feel at least slightly healthy). Pop across the road and dine at one of the outdoor picnic tables.

★ **Gorges Café** CAFE $$
(☎08-9937 1200; Marina Complex, Grey St; meals $8-25; ⏰7am-3pm Mon-Fri, to 2pm Sat & Sun) Just opposite the jetty with excellent breakfasts and lunches, and friendly service. Try the breakfast wrap or the lemon pepper squid. Look forward to the best coffee in town.

Black Rock Cafe CAFE $$
(80 Grey St; mains $15-40; ⏰7am-10pm Tue-Sun) Friendly service, versatile opening hours, very good seafood, and a contender for Kalbarri's best place to watch an Indian Ocean sunset.

Finlay's Fresh Fish BBQ SEAFOOD $$
(☎08-9937 1260; 24 Magee Cres; mains $15-40; ⏰5pm-late Tue-Sun) Simple barbecue seafood dinners at this Kalbarri institution come with piles of chips and lashings of mayonnaise-packed salads. Don't miss the walls packed with a few decades' strata of kitsch Australiana and Oz popular culture. BYO drinks.

Kalbarri Motor Hotel PUB $$
(☎08-9937 1400; 50 Grey St; pizzas $22, mains $22-37) The garden bar's our favourite spot for a sunset beer. Occasional live bands on Friday and Saturday nights.

Restaurant Upstairs MODERN AUSTRALIAN $$$
(☎08-9937 1033; 2 Porter St, upstairs; mains $25-44; ⏰6pm-late Wed-Mon) The specials board sometimes confuses culinary ambition with talent, but stick to the core menu of seafood and Asian-influenced mains, and you'll be satisfied at the classiest dining spot in town. Book ahead and ask for a spot on the verandah. Good service and a decent wine list seal the deal.

Information

There are ATMs at the shopping centres on Grey and Porter Sts.

Visitor Centre (☎1800 639 468; www.kalbarri.org.au; Grey St; ⏰9am-5pm Mon-Sat, 10am-2pm Sun) Book accommodation and tours. There's internet at the adjacent library.

Getting There & Around

Getting to/from Perth ($80, nine hours) and Geraldton ($28, two hours) by bus is easiest with **Transwa**, which departs from the visitor centre. Heading to/from points further north, the only option is with **Integrity**, which has three

WORTH A TRIP

HORROCKS & PORT GREGORY

The tiny seaside villages of Horrocks and Port Gregory, 92km and 68km south of Kalbarri, respectively, are as quiet as they come. Horrocks, the smaller and prettier of the two, has the dune-side **Horrocks Beach Caravan Park** (☎08-9934 3039; www.horrocksbeachcaravanpark.com.au; sites $24-33, cabins $75-100; 📶) and good-value **Beachside Cottages** (☎08-9934 3031; www.horrocksbeachsidecottages.com; 5 Glance St, Horrocks; d $85-95). Port Gregory, on the far side of the mysterious Pink Lakes, and with a fringing reef, is great for fishing and snorkelling. **Port Gregory Caravan Park** (☎08-9935 1052; www.portgregorycaravanpark.com.au; powered sites $32, cabins $100-125) is your best choice.

departures per week heading to Exmouth ($146, 10 hours) and on to Broome. To link with these services, catch a shuttle linking Kalbarri to/from the Ajana-Kalbarri turn-off. Shuttles should be pre-booked with Integrity or via Kalbarri Backpackers (p167).

Kalbarri Auto Centre (☎08-9937 1290) rents 4WDs and sedans from around $60 per day. Bikes are available from Kalbarri Backpackers and the **entertainment centre** (☎08-9937 1105; www.kalbarripirate.com; 15 Magee Cres; per half/full day $10/20; ⏰9am-5pm Fri-Mon & Wed).

For a taxi, call ☎0419 371 888.

SHARK BAY

The World Heritage–listed area of Shark Bay, stretching from Kalbarri to Carnarvon, consists of more than 1500km of spectacular coastline, containing turquoise lagoons, barren finger-like peninsulas, hidden bays, white-sand beaches, towering limestone cliffs and numerous islands. It's the westernmost part of the Australian mainland, and one of WA's most biologically rich habitats, with an array of plant and animal life found nowhere else on earth. Lush beds of sea-grass and sheltered bays nourish dugongs, sea turtles, humpback whales, dolphins, stingrays, sharks and other aquatic life. On land, Shark Bay's biodiversity has benefited from Project Eden, an ambitious ecosystem-regeneration program that has sought to eradicate feral animals and reintroduce endemic species. Shark Bay is also home to the amazing stromatolites of Hamelin Pool.

The Malgana, Nhanda and Inggarda peoples originally inhabited the area, and visitors can take Indigenous cultural tours to learn about Country. Shark Bay played host to early European explorers and many geographical names display this legacy. In 1616, Dutch explorer Dirk Hartog nailed a pewter dinner plate (now in Amsterdam's Rijksmuseum) to a post on the island (WA's largest) that now bears his name.

ℹ Getting There & Away

Shark Bay airport is located between Denham and Monkey Mia. **Skippers Aviation** flies to/from Perth six times weekly.

The closest **Integrity** approach for buses is the Overlander Roadhouse, 128km away on the North West Coastal Hwy. **Shark Bay Car Hire** (☎08-9948 3032, 0427 483 032; www.carhire.net.au/shuttle-service/; 65 Knight Tce, Denham; shuttle $70, car/4WD hire per day $95/185) runs a connecting shuttle (book at least 24 hours ahead).

Overlander Roadhouse to Denham

Twenty-nine kilometres along Shark Bay Rd from the Overlander Roadhouse is the turn-off for **Hamelin Pool**, a marine reserve with the world's best-known colony of **stromatolites**. These coral-like formations consist of cyanobacteria almost identical to organisms that existed 3.5 billion years ago, and through their use of photosynthesis, are considered largely responsible for creating our current atmosphere, paving the way for more complex life. There's an excellent boardwalk with information panels, best seen at low tide.

The nearby 1884 **Telegraph Office** (admission $5.50; ⏰check at shop) houses a museum containing possibly the only living stromatolites in captivity. The **Postmasters Residence** has a cafe and is the office for the tiny **Hamelin Pool Caravan Park** (☎08-9942 5905; www.hamelinpoolcaravanpark.com; Hamelin Pool; unpowered/powered sites $22/27, units $90; ❄).

Along the road you pass the turn-off for **Hamelin Station** (☎08-9948 5145; www.hamelinstationstay.com.au; sites per person $12, s/d/f $70/100/110, unit $150), which has lovely rooms in converted shearers' quarters, top-class amenities and somewhat arid camp sites. There's great bird life at the nearby waterhole.

As Shark Bay Rd swings north, you'll pass the turn-off for **Useless Loop** (a closed salt-mining town), **Edel Land** and **Steep Point**, the Australian mainland's most westerly tip.

The dusty former sheep station of **Nanga Bay Resort** (08-9948 3992; www.nangabayresort.com.au; Nanga Bay; unpowered/powered sites $25/30, dongas/motel r/huts/villas $50/165/180/250;) has a range of accommodation. Some accommodation options need a spruce-up, but there's a decent on-site restaurant and access to a sparkling, arcing beach.

Inside the vermin-proof fence, and 55km from the Hamelin turn-off, is the road to deserted **Shell Beach**, where tiny cockle shells, densely compacted over time, were once quarried as building material for places such as the Old Pearler Restaurant in Denham.

You'll pass turn-offs to bush camp sites before reaching **Eagle Bluff**, which has clifftop views overlooking an azure lagoon. You may spot turtles, sharks or manta rays.

Denham

POP 1500

Beautiful, laid-back Denham, with its aquamarine sea and palm-fringed beachfront, makes a great base for trips to the surrounding Shark Bay Marine Park, nearby François Peron and Dirk Hartog Island National Parks, and Monkey Mia, 26km away.

Australia's westernmost town originated as a pearling base, and the streets were once paved with pearl shell.

There's a pub, a supermarket, a bakery, cafes and take-aways on Knight Tce.

Sights & Activities

Shark Bay World Heritage Discovery Centre MUSEUM
(08-9948 1590; www.sharkbayvisit.com; 53 Knight Tce; adult/child $11/6; 9am-6pm) Informative and evocative displays of Shark Bay's ecosystems, marine and animal life, Indigenous culture, early explorers, settlers and shipwrecks.

Little Lagoon PICNIC SPOT
Little Lagoon, 4km from town, has picnic tables and barbecues. Don't be surprised if an emu wanders by.

Ocean Park AQUARIUM
(08-9948 1765; www.oceanpark.com.au; Shark Bay Rd; adult/child $20/15; 9am-4pm) On a spectacular headland just before town, this family-run aquaculture farm features an artificial lagoon where you can observe feeding sharks, turtles, stingrays and fish on a 60-minute guided tour. Also on offer are full-day 4WD tours to François Peron National Park ($180) and Steep Point ($350) with bushwalks and snorkelling. A new half-day tour focuses on South Peron ($75).

Tours

Shark Bay Scenic Flights SCENIC FLIGHT
(0417 919 059; www.sharkbayair.com.au) Flights include 15-minute Monkey Mia fly overs ($59) and a sensational 40-minute trip over Steep Point and the Zuytdorp Cliffs ($195).

Shark Bay Coaches & Tours BUS TOUR
(08-9948 1081; www.sharkbaycoaches.com.au; tours $150) Half-day bus tours and transfers to Monkey Mia from Denham (per person $12, minimum $60).

Sleeping

Expect school-holiday surcharges for accommodation.

Bay Lodge HOSTEL $
(08-9948 1278; www.baylodge.info; 113 Knight Tce; dm/d from $34/100; @) Every room at this YHA-associated hostel has its own en suite, kitchenette and TV/DVD. Ideally located across from the beach, it also has a great pool, a larger common kitchen, and a free shuttle bus to Monkey Mia for guests.

SEASIDE BUSH CAMPING

Shark Bay shire offers a choice of four coastal bush camp sites – **Goulet Bluff**, **Whalebone**, **Fowlers Camp** and **Eagle Bluff** – all 20km to 40km south of Denham in the area known as South Peron. To camp here, you must first obtain a permit ($10 per vehicle) from the Shark Bay visitor centre (p171). While this is easily arranged via phone (if yours has any reception), in practice it's better to scope the sites first, then get the permit. There are no facilities and a one-night limit applies to the whole area.

OFF THE BEATEN TRACK

WAY OUT WEST IN EDEL LAND

The Australian mainland's westernmost tip is **Steep Point**, just below **Dirk Hartog Island**. It's a wild, wind-scarred, barren clifftop with a beauty born of desolation and remoteness. The **Zuytdorp Cliffs** stretch away to the south, the limestone peppered with blowholes, while leeward, bays with white sandy beaches provide sheltered camp sites. The entire area is known as **Edel Land**, and is a proposed national park. Anglers catch game fish from the towering cliffs, but few tourists make the 140km rough drive down a dead-end road to reach the point.

Access is via Useless Loop Rd, and is controlled by the **Department of Parks & Wildlife** (www.parks.dpaw.wa.gov.au; entry permit per vehicle $12, sites per person $19). There is a ranger station at **Shelter Bay**, with camping nearby; at Steep Point (rocky and exposed); and at **False Entrance** to the south. Sites are limited and must be booked in advance. There is also accommodation at the **Dirk Hartog Island Eco Lodge** (08-9948 1211; www.dirkhartogisland.com; full board per person $290-350, min 2-night stay; Mar-Oct;). Rates include excellent gourmet seafood meals.

You'll need a high-clearance 4WD as the road deteriorates past the Useless Loop turn-off (approximately 100km from Shark Bay Rd). Tyres should be deflated to 20psi. Ensure you bring ample water and enough fuel to return to the Overlander Roadhouse (185km) or Denham (230km). During winter, a barge runs from Shelter Bay to Dirk Hartog Island (bookings essential). See www.sharkbay.org.au for details and downloadable permits. Hire-car companies will not insure for this road, though tours can be arranged from Denham. Steep Point is definitely more easily reached by boat, but that's not the Point, is it?

Beachfront units ($130) have great ocean views.

Denham Seaside Tourist Village CARAVAN PARK **$**
(08-9948 1242; www.sharkbayfun.com; Knight Tce; unpowered/powered sites $36/43, units $95-160;) This lovely, shady park on the water's edge is the best in town, though you will need to borrow the drill for your tent pegs. Cover up at night against the insects and ring first if arriving after 6pm.

Oceanside Village CABIN **$$**
(08-9948 3003; www.oceanside.com.au; 117 Knight Tce; cabins $160-200;) These neat self-catering cottages with sunny balconies are perfectly located directly opposite the beach.

Tradewinds APARTMENT **$$**
(1800 816 160; www.tradewindsdenham.com.au; Knight Tce; units $145-165;) Spacious, fully self-contained, modern units right across from the beach.

Eating & Drinking

★Ocean Restaurant CAFE **$$**
(www.oceanpark.com.au; Shark Bay Rd; mains $26-32; 9am-5pm;) The most refined lunch in Shark Bay also comes with the best view. Inside Ocean Park, overlooking turquoise waters, you can partner beer and wine with tapas, all-day brekkies and local seafood. The platter for two people ($42) is excellent value. Fully licensed.

Old Pearler Restaurant SEAFOOD **$$$**
(08-9948 1373; 71 Knight Tce; meals $30-53; from 5pm Mon-Sat) Built from shell bricks, this atmospheric nautical haven serves fantastic seafood. The exceptional platter features local snapper, whiting, cray, oysters, prawns and squid – all grilled, not fried. BYO drinks; bookings recommended.

Shark Bay Hotel PUB
(08-9948 1203; www.sharkbayhotelwa.com.au; 43 Knight Tce; dinner $22-38; 10am-late) Sunsets are dynamite from the front beer garden of Australia's most westerly pub.

Information

For information, interactive maps and downloadable permits., check out www.sharkbay.org.au.

There are ATMs at Heritage Resort and Shark Bay Hotel, and internet access at the **Community Resource Centre** (CRC; 08-9948 1787; 67 Knight Tce; @).

Department of Parks & Wildlife (08-9948 2226; www.parks.dpaw.wa.gov.au; 61-63 Knight Tce; 8am-5pm Mon-Fri) Park passes and information.

Shark Bay Visitor Centre (08-9948 1590; www.sharkbayvisit.com; 53 Knight Tce; 9am-6pm) Accommodation, tour bookings and bush-camping permits for South Peron.

François Peron National Park

François Peron National Park NATIONAL PARK
(per vehicle $12) Covering the whole peninsula north of Denham is an area of low scrub, salt lakes and red sandy dunes, home to the rare bilby, mallee fowl and woma python. There's a scattering of rough camp sites alongside brilliant white beaches, all accessible via 4WD (deflate tyres to 20psi). Don't miss the fantastic **Wanamalu Trail** (3km return), which follows the clifftop between Cape Peron and Skipjack Point. Spot marine life in the crystal waters below.

Note that 2WD vehicles can enter only as far as the old **Peron Homestead**, where there's a walk around the shearing sheds, and an artesian-bore hot tub. Tours to the park start at around $180 per person from Denham or Monkey Mia. Groups should consider hiring a 4WD from Denham for the same price.

Monkey Mia

Watching the wild dolphins turn up for a feed each morning in the shallow waters of **Monkey Mia** (adult/child/family $8.50/3.20/17), 26km northeast of Denham, is a highlight of every traveller's trip to the region. Watch the way they herd fish upside down, trying to trap them against the surface. The pier makes a good vantage point. The first feed is around 7.45am, but you'll see them arrive earlier. Stay around after the session, as the dolphins commonly come a second or third time.

Note that visitors are restricted to the edge of the water, and only a lucky three people per session are selected to wade in and help feed the dolphins.

Monkey Mia Visitors Centre (08-9948 1366; 8am-4pm) has information and tours.

You can volunteer to work full time with the dolphins for between four and 14 days – it's popular, so apply several months in advance and specify availability dates, though sometimes there are last-minute openings. Contact the **volunteer coordinator** (08-9948 1366; monkeymiavolunteers@westnet.com.au).

Tours

Wula Guda Nyinda Aboriginal Cultural Tours CULTURAL TOUR
(0429 708 847; www.wulaguda.com.au; 90min tours adult/child from $60/30) Learn 'how to let Country talk to you' on these excellent bushwalks led by local Aboriginal guide Darren 'Capes' Capewell. You'll pick up some local Malgana language and identify bush tucker and Indigenous medicine. The sunset 'Maru Maru Dreaming' tours (adult/child $60/30) are magical. There are also snorkelling and kayak tours (adult half/full day $140/185) and exciting 4WD adventures ($185).

Aristocat II CRUISES
(1800 030 427; www.monkey-mia.net; 1-/2½hr tours $50/86) Cruise in comfort on this large catamaran, and you might see dugongs, dolphins and loggerhead turtles. You'll also stop off at the Blue Lagoon Pearl Farm.

Wildsights ADVENTURE TOUR
(1800 241 481; www.monkeymiawildsights.com.au) On the small *Shotover* catamaran you're close to the action; 2½-hour wildlife cruises start from $89. There are also 1½-hour sunset cruises ($39) and full-day 4WD trips to François Peron National Park ($195); discounts are available for multiple trips.

Sleeping & Eating

Monkey Mia Dolphin Resort RESORT $$
(1800 653 611; www.monkeymia.com.au; tent sites per person $16, van sites from $44, dm/d $30/109, garden units $229, beachfront villas $329;) With a stunning location the only accommodation option in Monkey Mia caters to campers, backpackers, package and top-end tourists. The staff are friendly, and the backpacker 'shared en suites' are good value, but the top-end rooms are expensive. It can also get very crowded. The restaurant has sensational water views but meals are overpriced, while the backpacker bar has cheaper food and excitable backpackers.

Getting There & Away

There is no public transport to Monkey Mia from Denham. If you stay at Bay Lodge (p169) in Denham, you can use its shuttle but it only runs alternate days. Other options are hiring a car or bicycle, or using the shuttle from Shark Bay Coaches (p169).

GASCOYNE COAST

This wild, rugged, largely unpopulated coastline stretches from Shark Bay to Ningaloo, with excellent fishing and waves that attract surfers from around the world. Subtropical Carnarvon, the region's hub, is an important fruit- and vegetable-growing district, and farms are always looking for seasonal workers. The 760km Gascoyne River, WA's longest, is responsible for all that lushness, though it flows underground for most of the year. Inland, the distances are huge and the temperatures high; here you'll find the ancient eroded rocks of the Kennedy Range.

Carnarvon

POP 9000

On Yinggarda country at the mouth of the Gascoyne River, fertile Carnarvon, with its fruit and vegetable plantations and thriving fishing industry, makes a pleasant stopover between Denham and Exmouth. This friendly, vibrant town has quirky attractions, a range of decent accommodation, well-stocked supermarkets and great local produce. The tree-lined CBD exudes a tropical feel, and the palm-fringed waterfront is a relaxing place to amble. The long picking season from March to January ensures plenty of seasonal work.

The last weekend of October sees the town taken over by desert drivers and riders competing in the gruelling 511km **Gascoyne Dash** (Gassy Dash; www.gasdash.com).

Sights & Activities

Carnarvon's luxuriant plantations along North and South River Rds provide a large proportion of WA's fruit and veg; grab the *Gascoyne Food Trail* (www.gascoynefood.com.au) brochure from the visitor centre.

You can walk or ride 2.5km along the old tramway to the **Heritage Precinct** on Babbage Island (www.carnarvonheritage.com.au), once the city's port. **One Mile Jetty** (adult/child $5/free; 9am-4.30pm) provides great fishing and views; walk or take the quirky **Coffee Pot Train** (adult/child $10/5) to the end. The nearby **Lighthouse Keepers Cottage** (Heritage Precinct; 10am-1pm) FREE has been painstakingly restored; don't miss the view from the top of the creaky water tower in the **Railway Station Museum** (9am-5pm) FREE.

The palm-lined **walking path** along the side of the Fascine (the body of water at the end of Robinson St) is a pleasant place for a sunset wander.

OTC Dish LANDMARK

(Mahony Ave) Established jointly with NASA in 1966, the OTC Dish at the edge of town tracked the *Gemini* and *Apollo* space missions, as well as Halley's Comet before closing in 1987. The fascinating **Carnarvon Space and Technology Museum** (www.carnarvonmuseum.org.au; Mahony Ave; adult/child $7/5; 10am-2pm, shorter hrs outside tourist season) is nearby, expanded in late 2014 with an interactive mock-up of a *Saturn V* command module.

Gwoonwardu Mia GALLERY

(08-9941 1989; wwww.gahcc.com.au; 146 Robinson St; 10am-3pm Mon-Fri) Gwoonwardu Mia, built to depict a cyclone, represents the five local Aboriginal language groups and houses a cultural centre and art gallery. Highlights include the poignant oral testimonies from Aboriginal elders in the award-winning Burlganjya Wanggaya (Old People Talking) exhibition.

Bumbak's FARM TOUR

(08-9941 8006; 449 North River Rd; 1hr tours $8.80; shop 9am-4pm Mon-Fri, tours 10am Mon, Wed & Fri Apr-Oct) Bumbak's, a working banana and mango plantation, offers tours of the plantation and sells a variety of fresh and dried fruit, preserves and yummy homemade ice cream.

Sleeping

Most accommodation is spread out along the 5km feeder road from the highway. Try to arrive before 6pm.

Fish & Whistle HOSTEL $

(08-9941 1704; Beardaj@highway1.com.au; 35 Robinson St; s/d/tw $50/60/60, motel r $120;) Travellers love this big, breezy backpackers with its wide verandahs, bunk-free rooms and excellent kitchen. There are air-con motel rooms out the back and the **Port Hotel** serving decent beer downstairs. The owners can help guests find seasonal jobs and provide transport to orchards and farms.

Coral Coast Tourist Park CARAVAN PARK $

(08-9941 1438; www.coralcoasttouristpark.com.au; 108 Robinson St; powered sites $35-45, cabins & units $75-205;) This pleasant, shady park, with tropical pool and grassy sites, is

MONKEY MIA & THE CENTRAL WEST CARNARVON

the closest to the town centre. There's a variety of well-appointed cabins, a decent camp kitchen, and bicycles for hire.

Carnarvon Central Apartments APARTMENT **$**
(☎08-9941 1317; www.carnarvonholidays.com; 120 Robinson St; 2-bedroom apt $140; ❄) These neat, fully self-contained apartments are popular with business travellers.

Hospitality Inn MOTEL **$$**
(Best Western; ☎08-9941 1600; www.carnarvon.wa.hospitalityinns.com.au; 6 West St; d $159-179) The best of the motels in town. Rooms are clean and quiet and there's a nice on-site restaurant (meals $19 to $42).

Eating

A good option to enjoy the local seafood is to cook your own on the free barbecues along the Fascine and at Baxter Park. There's also good dining at Carnarvon's handful of pubs.

Self-caterers should check out the delicious produce at the **Gascoyne Arts, Crafts & Growers Market** (www.gascoynefood.com.au/growers-market; Civic Centre car park; ⏲8-11.30am Sat May-Oct). The market is proudly plastic-free, so BYO bag.

River Gums Cafe CAFE **$**
(Margaret Row, off Robinson St; burgers & salads $7-10; ⏲10am-3pm Wed-Sun May-Oct) Legendary choc-topped banana smoothies, top-notch burgers and home baking are served at this rustic garden cafe in the middle of a fruit plantation.

Morel's Orchard MARKET **$**
(☎08-9941 8368; 486 Robinson St; ⏲8.30am-5.30pm mid Apr-mid Oct) Local fresh fruit and vegetables, as well as natural fruit ice creams. Our favourite are the frozen chocolate-dipped strawberries.

The Crab Shack SEAFOOD **$$**
(☎08-9941 4078; Small Boat Harbour; ⏲9am-5pm Mon-Sat Mar-Dec) Fill your esky with freshly steamed crabs, prawns, mussels, shucked oysters and fish fillets. Tasty crab cakes and prawn burgers are also available.

Gwoonwardu Mia Community Café CAFE **$$**
(☎08-9941 3127; 146 Robinson St; snacks $12.50, juices & smoothies $7; ⏲8am-3pm Mon-Fri) Located in the Gwoonwardu Mia complex, this training centre for Indigenous youth serves tasty snacks – try the breakfast wrap with eggs and chorizo – and the best fruit juices in town.

Information

ATMs are on Robinson St.

The **Visitor Centre** (☎08-9941 1146; www.carnarvon.org.au; Civic Centre, 21 Robinson St; ⏲9am-5pm Mon-Fri, to noon Sat; @) has information, maps and produce.

Getting There & Around

Skippers flies daily to Perth and weekly to Geraldton.

Integrity runs three times a week to Exmouth ($92, four hours), Geraldton ($115, six hours) and Perth ($167, 12 hours). Buses depart from the visitor centre.

Bikes can be hired from Coral Coast Tourist Park (p172).

For a taxi, call ☎131 008.

Point Quobba to Gnaraloo Bay

While the North West Coastal Hwy heads inland, the coast north of Carnarvon is wild, windswept and desolate, a favourite haunt of surfers and fisherfolk. Not many make it this far, but those who do are rewarded by huge winter swells, high summer temperatures, relentless winds, amazing marine life, breath-taking scenery and some truly magical experiences.

Turn down Blowholes Rd, 12km after the Gascoyne bridge, then proceed 49km along the sealed road to the coast. The **blowholes** (waves spraying out of limestone chimneys during a big swell) are just left of the T-intersection. **Point Quobba**, 1km further south, has beach shacks, excellent fishing, some gritty **camp sites** (sites per person $11), and not much else.

Heading right from the T onto dirt, after 8km you'll come across a lonely little cairn staring out to sea, commemorating HMAS *Sydney II*. Two kilometres further is **Quobba Station** (☎08-9948 5098; www.quobba.com.au; unpowered/powered sites per person $13/15, cabins & cottages per person $35-60), with plenty of rustic accommodation, a small store and legendary fishing.

Still on Quobba, 60km north of the homestead, **Red Bluff** (☎08-9948 5001; www.quobba.com.au; unpowered sites per person $15, shacks per person $20, bungalows/safari retreats $180/$200) is a spectacular headland with a wicked surf break and excellent fishing, and is the southern boundary of Ningaloo Marine Park. Accommodation comes in all forms, from exposed camp sites and palm shelters, to exclusive upmarket tents with balconies and superb views. Red Bluff's first shark attack happened in 2012.

The jewel, however, is at the end of the road around 150km from Carnarvon: **Gnaraloo Station** (08-9942 5927; www.gnaraloo.com; unpowered sites per person $20-25, cabins d $120-180;) . Surfers from around the world come every winter to ride the notorious **Tombstones**, while summer brings turtle monitoring (08-9315 4809; www.gnaraloo.com/conservation/gnaraloo-turtle-conservation-program; Oct-Apr) and windsurfers trying to catch the strong afternoon sea breeze, the Carnarvon Doctor. There's excellent snorkelling close to shore and the coastline north from **Gnaraloo Bay** is eye-burningly pristine. You can stay in rough camp sites next to the beach at **3-Mile**, or there's a range of options up at the homestead, the nicest being stone cabins with uninterrupted ocean views – great for spotting migrating whales (June to November) and sea eagles. Gnaraloo is dedicated to sustainability and has implemented a number of visionary environmental programs. The station is always looking for willing workers. Just be aware this is a working station in the Australian outback, not a luxury resort.

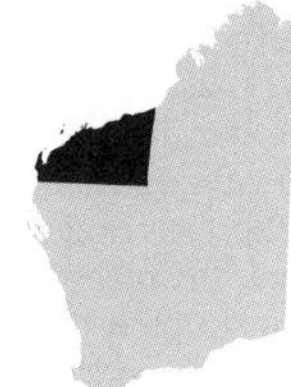

Coral Coast & the Pilbara

Includes ➡

Best Places to Eat

- Whalers Restaurant (p182)
- Karijini Eco Retreat (p192)
- Bills on the Ningaloo Reef (p179)
- The BBqFather (p183)
- Silver Star (p194)

Best Places to Swim

- Turquoise Bay (p186)
- Coral Bay (p178)
- Hamersley Gorge (p191)
- Fern Pool (p190)
- Deep Reach Pool (p190)

Why Go?

Lapping languidly on the edge of the Indian Ocean, the shallow, turquoise waters of the Coral Coast nurture a unique marine paradise. Lonely bays, deserted beaches and crystal-clear lagoons offer superb snorkelling and diving among myriad sea life, including humpback whales, manta rays and loggerhead turtles. World Heritage Ningaloo Reef is one of the very few places you can swim with the world's largest fish, the gentle whale shark. Development is low-key, towns few and far between, and seafood and sunsets legendary.

Inland, miners swarm like ants over the high, eroded ranges of the Pilbara, while ore trains snake down to a string of busy ports stretching from Dampier to Port Hedland. But hidden in the hills are two beautiful gems – Karijini and Millstream Chichester National Parks, home to spectacular gorges, remote peaks, deep tranquil pools and abundant wildlife.

When to Go

Exmouth

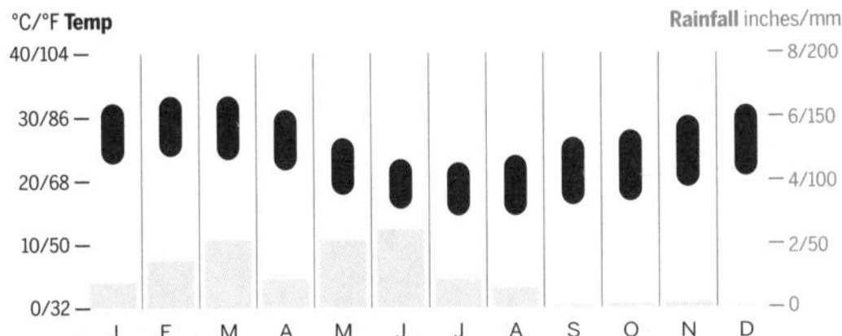

Apr–Jul Whale shark season – don't miss the swim of a lifetime.

Sep & Oct Karijini's gorges warm up and wild flowers blanket the ranges.

Nov–Mar Ningaloo is full of turtle love, eggs and hatchlings.

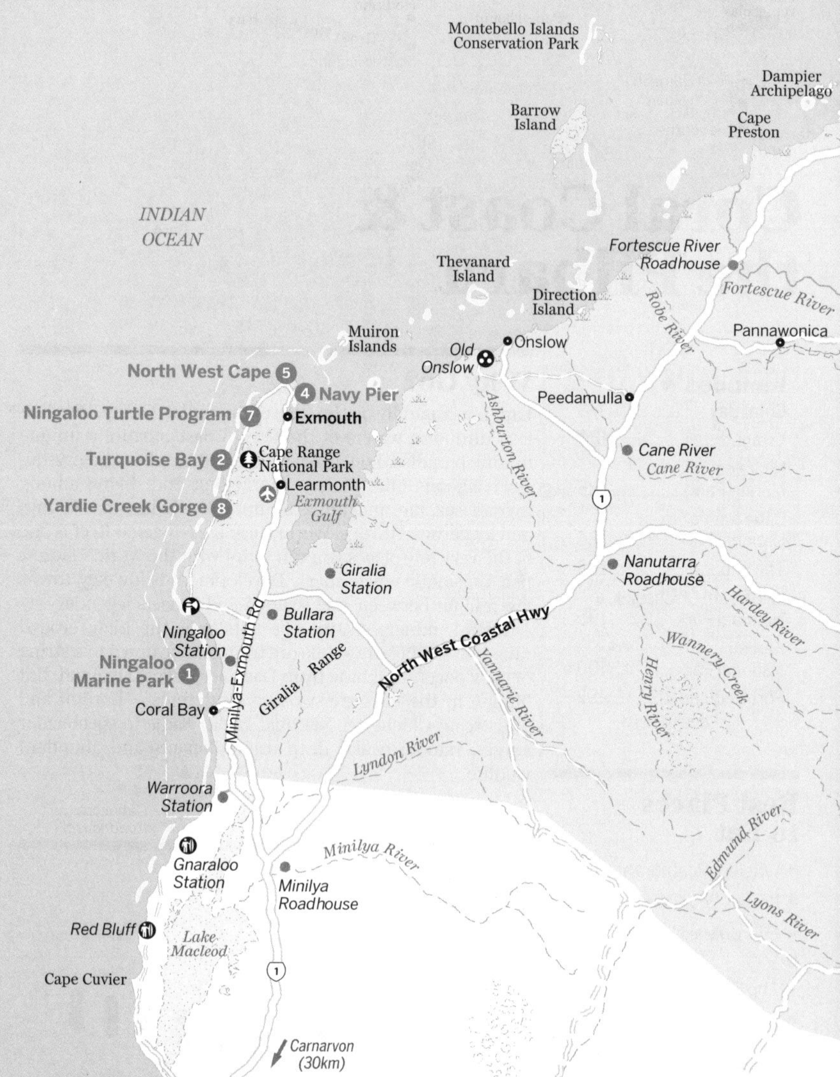

Coral Coast & the Pilbara Highlights

1 Swimming with 'gentle giant' whale sharks in **Ningaloo Marine Park** (p185).

2 Snorkelling over marine life at **Turquoise Bay** (p186) in Ningaloo Marine Park.

3 Descending into the 'centre of the earth' on an adventure tour through the gorges of **Karijini National Park** (p190).

4 Scuba diving off the **Navy Pier** (p185) at Point Murat, one of the world's finest shore dives.

5 Watching the annual humpback-whale migration from the lighthouse at **North West Cape** (p185).

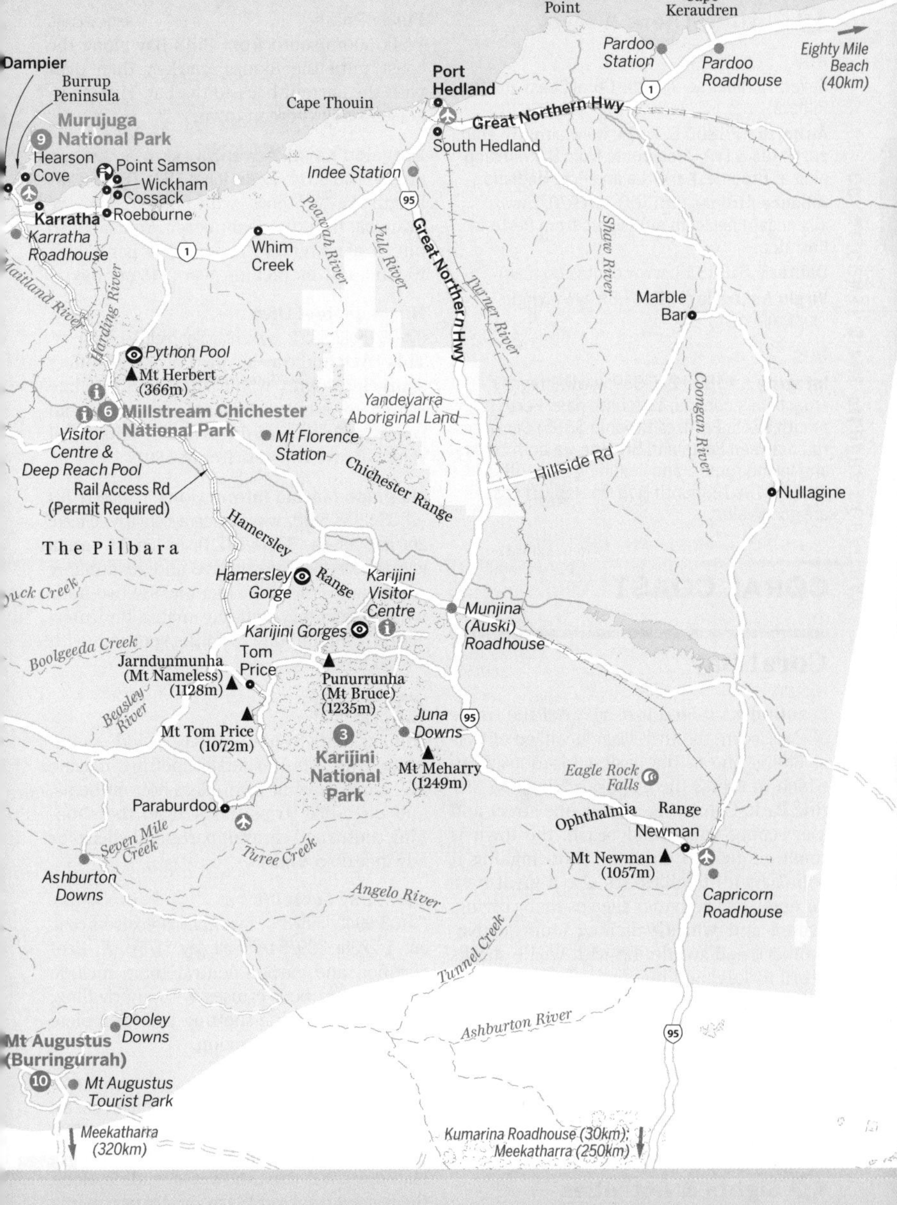

6 Cooling off in an idyllic waterhole at **Millstream Chichester National Park** (p190).

7 Tracking turtles on remote beaches with the **Ningaloo Turtle Program** (p182).

8 Spotting rare black-flanked rock wallabies on a cruise into stunning **Yardie Creek Gorge** (p187).

9 Being welcomed to Country on an **Indigenous cultural tour** (p188) to Murujuga National Park.

10 Scaling the country's biggest, most remote monolith, **Mt Augustus** (p189).

Getting There & Away

AIR

Several airlines service the Coral Coast and the Pilbara.

Airnorth (1800 627 474; www.airnorth.com.au; Tue & Fri) Circle route from Darwin stopping at Broome, Karratha and Port Hedland.

Alliance Airlines (1300 780 970; www.allianceairlines.com.au) Flights from Perth to Karratha.

Qantas (13 13 13; www.qantas.com.au)

Virgin Australia (13 67 89; www.virgin-australia.com)

BUS

Integrity (1800 226 339; www.integrity-coachlines.com.au; 12-month pass Perth to Exmouth $245, Perth to Broome $365) Services run between Perth and Broome via both coastal and inland routes, and including Exmouth and Karijini. The 12-month Hop On Hop Off passes are good value.

CORAL COAST

Coral Bay

POP 255

Beautifully situated just north of the tropic of Capricorn, the tiny seaside village of Coral Bay is one of the easiest locations from which to access the exquisite Ningaloo Marine Park. Consisting of only one street and a sweeping white-sand beach, the town is small enough to enjoy on foot, making it popular with families. It's also a great base for outer-reef activities such as scuba diving, fishing and whale watching (June to November), and swimming with whale sharks (April to July) and manta rays.

Development is strictly limited, so expect higher prices for food and accommodation. Exmouth, 152km away, has more options. There are ATMs at the shopping centre and the Peoples Park grocer, and internet access at some of the tour outlets and Fins Cafe. The town is chockers from April to October.

Sights & Activities

Fish feeding occurs on the beach at 3.30pm most days. Sunsets are sublime from the lookout above the beach car park.

Bill's Bay BEACH

(P) Keep to the southern end when snorkelling; the northern end (Skeleton Bay) is a breeding ground for reef sharks.

Purdy Point SNORKELLING

Walk 500m south from Bill's Bay along the coast until the 8km/h marker, then drift with the current back to the bay. Hire snorkel gear anywhere in town.

Ningaloo Kayak Adventures KAYAKING

(08-9948 5034; 2/3hr tours $50/70) Various length kayak tours with snorkelling are available from the main beach. You can also hire a glass-bottom canoe ($25 per hour), wetsuit and snorkelling gear ($15 per day).

Ningaloo Reef Dive DIVING

(08-9942 5824; www.ningalooreefdive.com) This PADI and eco-certified dive crew offers snorkelling with whale sharks ($390, late March to July) and manta rays ($140, all year), half-day reef dives ($180) and a full range of dive courses (from $450).

Ningaloo Marine Interactions SNORKELLING

(08-9948 5190; www.mantaraycoralbay.com.au; 2hr/half/full day $75/170/210; Jun-Oct, manta rays all year) Informative and sustainably run tours to the outer reef include two-hour whale watching, half-day manta-ray interaction and full-day wildlife spotting with snorkelling.

Tours

Popular tours from Coral Bay include swimming with whale sharks, spotting marine life, coral viewing from glass-bottom boats, and quad-bike trips. Book from the shopping centre and caravan parks and check for advance discounts.

Coral Bay Ecotours BOAT TOUR

(08-9942 5885; www.coralbayecotours.com.au; 1/2/3hr $39/54/75, all day $175) Eco-certified and carbon-neutral tours include glass-bottom boat cruises with snorkelling, and all-day wildlife-spotting trips complete with manta-ray interaction.

Coral Coast Tours DRIVING TOUR

(0427 180 568; www.coralcoasttours.com.au; half-day 4WD adult/child $135/78, full-day 4WD adult/child $185/124, snorkelling 2/3hr $55/75) Half-day 4WD trips showcase wildlife along the rugged tracks of Warroora Station, while full-day trips follow the coastal track to Yardie Creek and the Cape. There are also reef tours, and airport transfers ($88) continuing on to Exmouth ($110).

Coastal Adventure Tours ADVENTURE TOUR

(08-9948 5190; www.coralbaytours.com.au; 2/2.5hr quad bike $110/130, sailing from $75)

STATION STAYS

If you're sick of cramped caravan parks and want somewhere a little more relaxed and off the beaten track, consider a station stay. Scattered around the Coral Coast are a number of pastoral stations offering a range of rustic accommodation – be it an exquisite slice of empty coast, dusty home paddock, basic shearers' digs or fully self-contained, air-conditioned cottages. Don't expect top-notch facilities; most sites don't have any at all. Power and water are limited; the more self-sufficient you are, the more enjoyable the stay – remember, you're getting away from it all. You will find loads of wildlife, previously unseen stars, oodles of space, and some fair-dinkum outback.

Some stations offer wilderness camping away from the homestead (usually by the coast) and you'll need a 4WD and chemical toilet. These places tend to cater for fisher-types with boats and grey nomads who stay by the week.

Certain stations only offer accommodation during the peak season (April to October).

Giralia (08-9942 5937; www.giraliastation.com.au; Burkett Rd, 110km north of Coral Bay; camping per person $10, donga $70, cottage $160, homestead s/d $220/300;) Popular with fishermen and well set-up for travellers, there's a bush camping area with amenities, dongas, a family cottage and air-conditioned homestead rooms with breakfast and dinner included. The coast is 40 minutes away by 4WD. Meals and liquor available.

Bullara (08-9942 5938; www.bullara-station.com.au; Burkett Rd, 70km north of Coral Bay; camping $13, tw/d/cottage $110/140/200; Apr-Oct) Near the Minilya road junction and 2WD accessible, there's several rooms in the renovated shearers' quarters, a three-bedroom cottage and unpowered camping with amenities.

Warroora (08-9942 5920; www.warroora.com; Minilya Exmouth Rd, 47km north of Minilya; camping per day/week $10/50, r per person $30, cottages $150) Offers wilderness camp sites along the coast (some 2WD accessible) and cheap rooms in the shearers' quarters as well as a self-contained cottage and homestead. Chemical toilets for hire (per day $15).

Ningaloo Station (08-9942 5936; www.ningaloostation.com.au; Minilya Rd, 85km north of Coral Bay; sites per week $35, bond $100) Not to be confused with the marine park, the original station offers limited, totally self-sufficient bush sites on pristine coastline.

More a booking service than an individual operator, the combined quad bike and snorkelling trips get rave reviews. You can also book sailing excursions, glass-bottom boat tours and manta-ray interaction.

Sleeping & Eating

Avoid school holidays and book well ahead for peak season (April to October). Consider self-catering, as eating out is expensive.

Peoples Park Caravan Village CARAVAN PARK $
(08-9942 5933; www.peoplesparkcoralbay.com; sites unpowered/powered $41/47, 1-/2-bedroom cabins $250/270, hilltop villas $295;) This excellent park offers grassy, shaded sites and a variety of fully self-contained cabins. Friendly staff keep the modern amenities and spacious camp kitchen spotless, and it's the only place with freshwater showers. The hilltop villas have superb views, there are plenty of BBQs scattered around, and internet access is available at nearby Fins Cafe.

Ningaloo Club HOSTEL $
(08-9948 5100; www.ningalooclub.com; Robinson St; dm $28-32, d with/without bathroom $120/95;) Popular with the party crowd, this hostel is a great place to meet people, and boasts a central pool, a well-equipped kitchen and onsite bar. The rooms could be cleaner, and forget about sleeping before the bar closes. It also sells bus tickets (coach stop outside) and discounted tours.

★**Bills on the Ningaloo Reef** MODERN AUSTRALIAN $$
(08-9385 6655; Robinson St; lunch $16-24, dinner $18-28; 11am-late) This new gastropub immediately ups the ante for fine dining in a location where the other food offerings look decidedly tired. Try the fabulous fish curry, a selection of tapas or wash down the 'bucket of prawns' with a refreshing boutique ale.

Fins Cafe INTERNATIONAL $$
(08-9942 5900; Peoples Park; dinner mains $24-46; breakfast, lunch & dinner;) Casual,

outdoor BYO with ever-changing blackboard menu showcasing local seafood, curries and safe classics.

Getting There & Around

Coral Bay is 1144km north of Perth and 152km south of Exmouth. The closest airport (p183) is Learmonth, 118km to the north. Groups should consider hiring a car.

Integrity (☎1800 226 339; www.integrity coachlines.com.au; outside Ningaloo Club) Coaches run three times a week to Perth ($203, 16 hours) and Exmouth ($47, 90 minutes), and once a week to Karijini ($177, 12 hours).

Coral Coast Tours (☎0427 180 568; www.coralcoasttours.com.au; adult/child $88/44) Airport shuttle between Coral Bay and Learmonth

Exmouth

POP 2500

Once a WWII submarine base, Exmouth didn't flourish until the 1960s brought the Very Low Frequency (VLF) communications facility to North West Cape. Simultaneously, fishing (especially prawns) and resources exploration commenced, both still thriving today (gas flares are visible from Vlamingh Head at night).

With World Heritage protection of Ningaloo Reef, tourism provides the bulk of visitors, many coming to see the magnificent and enigmatic whale sharks (April to July). Peak season (April to October) sees this laid-back town stretched to epic proportions, but don't be put off, it's still the perfect base to explore nearby Ningaloo Marine and Cape Range National Parks. Alternatively, just relax, wash away the road dust and enjoy the local wildlife; emus wandering the footpaths, roos lounging in the shade, goannas ambling across the highway and corellas, galahs and ringnecks screeching and swooping through the trees.

Sights & Activities

Exmouth is flat, hot and sprawling, with most of the attractions located outside town and no public transport. Most activities are water based. Turtle volunteering (p182) is popular from November to January.

Snorkellers and divers head to Ningaloo Marine Park (p185) or the Muiron Islands (p187). Try to find the informative Parks & Wildlife (DPaW) book *Dive and Snorkel Sites in Western Australia*. Several dive shops in town offer PADI courses.

A set of cycle paths ring Exmouth and continue north to Harold E Holt Naval Base (HEH), where the road continues to Bundegi Beach; watch out for dingos! Ask around for bike hire.

Town Beach BEACH
(1km east of Murat Rd; P) An easy walk from town, this beach is popular with kiteboarders when an easterly is blowing.

Sewerage Works BIRDWATCHING
(Willersdorf Rd) Good water-bird viewing here and at the golf course next door.

Exmouth Cape Horses HORSE RIDING
(☎0400 886 576; www.exmouthcapehorses.com.au; 1hr ride $70) These short, beautiful beach rides along Exmouth Gulf are suitable for all skill levels and ages.

Tours & Courses

Swim with whale sharks, spot wildlife, dive, snorkel, kayak, surf and fish to your heart's content – the visitor centre (p183) has the full list of tours available. Some are seasonal.

Outside whale-shark season, marine tours focus on manta rays. You need to be a capable snorkeller. Be wary of snorkelling on what may essentially be a dive tour – the action may be too deep. It's normally 30% cheaper if you stay on the boat. Most ocean tours depart from **Tantabiddi** on the western cape and include free transfers from Exmouth. Check conditions carefully regarding 'no sighting' policies and cancellations.

Kings Ningaloo Reef Tours WILDLIFE TOUR
(☎08-9949 1764; www.kingsningalooreeftours.com.au; snorkeller/observer $385/285) Long-time player Kings gets rave reviews for its whale shark tours. It's renowned for staying out longer than everyone else, and has a 'next available tour' no-sighting policy.

Ningaloo Ecology Cruises BOAT TOUR
(☎1800 554 062; www.ningalootreasures.com.au; 1/2½hr $50/70) Has one-hour glass-bottom boat trips (April to October), and longer 2½-hour trips (all year) including snorkelling.

Birds Eye View SCENIC FLIGHTS
(☎0427 996 833; www.ningaloomicrolights.com.au; Exmouth Aerodrome; 30-/60-/90-min flight $199/299/399) Don't want to get your feet wet but still after adrenalin? Get some altitude on these incredible microlight flights over the Cape and (longer flights only) Ningaloo Reef.

Exmouth

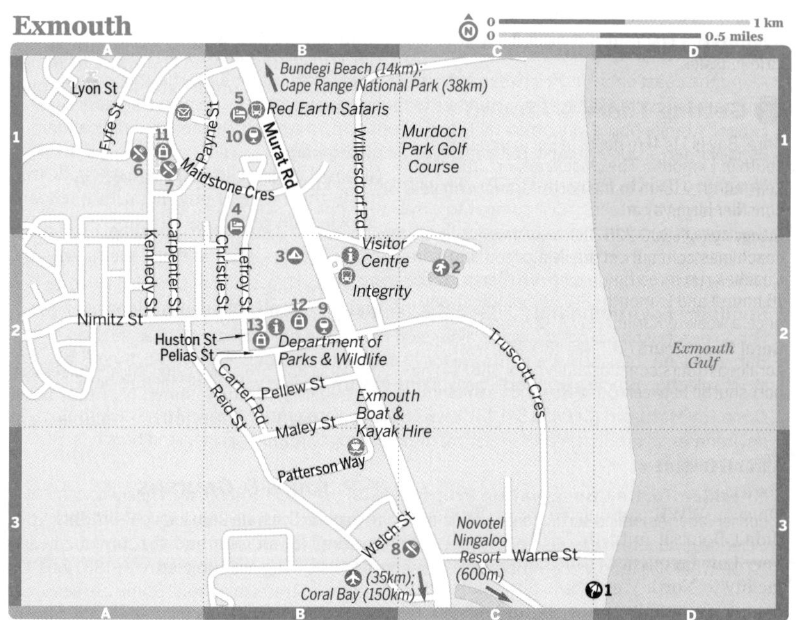

Exmouth

Sights
1 Town Beach ... D3

Activities, Courses & Tours
2 Sewerage Works ... C2

Sleeping
3 Exmouth Ningaloo Caravan & Holiday Resort ... B2
4 Ningaloo Lodge ... B1
5 Potshot Hotel Resort ... B1

Eating
6 5 Kennedy St ... A1
BBqFather ... (see 3)
7 See Salt ... A1
8 Whalers Restaurant ... C3

Drinking & Nightlife
9 Grace's Tavern ... B2
10 Potshot Hotel ... B1

Shopping
11 Exmouth Shopping Centre ... A1
12 Ningaloo Kite & Board ... B2
13 Reef Beef ... B2

Montebello Island Safaris CRUISE
(0419 091 670; www.montebello.com.au; Apr-Nov) Has a permanent houseboat moored at the Montebello Islands for maximum marine love on a six-night tour (per person $3000).

Capricorn Kayak Tours KAYAKING
(0427 485 123; www.capricornseakayaking.com.au; half-/1-/2-/5-day tour $99/179/665/1650) Capricorn offers single- and multi-day kayaking and snorkelling tours along the lagoons of Ningaloo Reef.

Ningaloo Whaleshark-N-Dive DIVING
(1800 224 060; www.ningaloowhalesharkndive.com.au) Offers daily dives to Lighthouse Bay ($185) and the Muiron Islands ($210) as well as longer live-aboard tours to the Muiron and Montebello Islands. Dive courses also available from intro ($255) to full PADI ($620).

Sleeping

Accommodation is limited so book ahead, especially for the peak season (April to October).

NINGA TURTLE TRACKERS

Along the coast each year between November and March, volunteer turtle-monitoring programs provide exciting opportunities for active involvement in local conservation. Expect strange hours, uncomfortable conditions and immense satisfaction. Applications usually open around August, but check individual programs.

Ningaloo Turtle Program (NTP; www.ningalooturtles.org.au; Exmouth; 5 weeks $1300; Nov-Mar) Volunteers must commit to a five-week period, spending most of that time at a remote base. Work from sunrise for five hours collecting data on turtle nesting, habitat and predation, then the rest of the day is free. Your fee covers all equipment, meals, accommodation, transport from Exmouth and insurance.

Pendoley Environmental (08-9330 6200; www.penv.com.au; Port Hedland; Nov-Jan) Pendoley's tagging program works alongside the oil and gas industry at sites such as Barrow Island. Typical placements are for 17 days with all expenses covered, there's a strict selection process and you'll be working mostly at night with minimal free time.

Care for Hedland (0439 941 431; www.careforhedland.org.au; Nov-Mar) Grass-roots environmental group runs volunteer monitoring programs on Port Hedland beaches from November.

Gnaraloo Turtle Conservation Program (GTCP; 08-9315 4809; www.gnaraloo.com/conservation/gnaraloo-turtle-conservation-program; Quobba Coast via Carnarvon; Oct-Apr) Science graduates (any discipline) prepared to commit for six months can apply to GTCP where all food, accommodation, transport and training are supplied.

Exmouth Ningaloo Caravan & Holiday Resort CARAVAN PARK $
(08-9949 2377; www.exmouthresort.com; Murat Rd; unpowered/powered sites $38/49, dm/d $39/80, chalets from $205; P ❄ 📶 🏊) Across from the visitor centre, this friendly, spacious park has grassy sites, self-contained chalets, four-bed dorms, an on-site restaurant and even a pet section. If you're camping, this is your best bet.

Potshot Hotel Resort RESORT $
(Excape Backpackers YHA; 08-9949 1200; www.potshotresort.com; Murat Rd; dm/d $30/72, motel d $145, studios $245, apt from $270; P ❄ @ 📶 🏊) A town within a town, this bustling resort has 10-bed dorms, standard motel rooms, luxury Osprey apartments, several bars and a disco. The backpacker rooms can be noisy, but the apartments are good value for a group.

Ningaloo Lodge GUESTHOUSE $$
(1800 880 949; www.ningaloolodge.com.au; Lefroy St; d $150; P ❄ 📶 🏊) These clean, tastefully appointed motel rooms are one of the better deals in town, with a modern communal kitchen, barbecue, shady pool and free wi-fi.

Eating & Drinking

Some popular haunts have relocated or been renamed. There is a supermarket, bakery and several take aways at Exmouth Shopping Centre (p183).

Grace's Tavern (08-9949 1000; Murat Rd; noon-11pm) and **Potshot Hotel** (08-9949 1200; Murat Rd; 10am-late) are your drinking options and both serve decent pub meals.

★ **Whalers Restaurant** SEAFOOD $$
(08-9949 2416; whalersrestaurant.com.au; 27 Murat Rd, inside Exmouth Escape; mains $29-40; 6pm-late) Recently relocated, this Exmouth institution is famous for its delicious Creole-influenced seafood. Don't miss the signature New Orleans gumbo, complemented by a seafood tasting starter of soft-shell crab, local prawns and oyster shooters. Die-hard bug aficionados need look no further than the towering seafood medley.

See Salt CAFE $$
(08-9949 1400; www.seesalt.com.au; 1 Thew St, Shopping Centre; meals $8-22; 6.30am-3.30pm daily, 6pm-8.30pm Thu-Sun) Repackaged and relocated Ningaloo Health retains the same wholesome daylight menu while expanding to dinners later in the week. Kick start your morning with chilli eggs or a bowl of Vietnamese *pho* (beef and rice-noodle soup). The more timid can dive into a berry pancake stack, Bircher muesli or a detox juice.

See Salt also offers light lunches, salads, smoothies, take-away picnic hampers (great for a day trip to Cape Range National Park) and excellent coffee.

★ BBqFather BARBECUE, ITALIAN $$
(Pinocchio; ☎08-9949 4905; www.thebbqfather.com.au; Murat Rd, Exmouth Ningaloo Caravan Park & Resort; mains $18-40; ⏰6-9pm Mon-Sat Feb-Oct) This popular, licensed alfresco *ristorante* has changed its name and gone BBQ crazy, serving up huge, succulent, smoky slabs of beef, pork and veal ribs. After receiving a reality check from the locals, their much loved pizzas and home-made pastas are also back on the menu. The servings are as legendary as ever.

5 Kennedy St MODERN AUSTRALIAN $$$
(☎08-9949 4507; www.5kennedyst.com.au; 5 Kennedy St; mains from $30; ⏰noon-late Tue-Thu, 9am-late Fri-Sun) On the old Whalers site, Exmouth's newest restaurant offers sophisticated dishes using the best of local and sustainable ingredients. The menu is divided by dish size and ranges from bite-size snacks to 1kg slabs of meat and bone.

Shopping

Exmouth Shopping Centre SHOPPING CENTRE
(Maidstone Cres) The shopping centre includes a dive shop, gift shop, surf and camping stores, and two supermarkets. A Sunday craft market runs from April to October.

Ningaloo Kite & Board OUTDOOR EQUIPMENT
(Exmouth Camper Hire; ☎08-9949 4050; www.exmouthcamperhire.com.au; 16 Nimitz St; ⏰call first) New and second-hand kites, full beginners' kits and lots of local info from these experts who also rent out fully-stocked camper vans.

Reef Beef FOOD
(☎0408 951 775; 11 Pelias St; ⏰9am-5pm Mon-Fri, 9am-noon Sat) Their blurb says it all – delicious beef jerky. Best road-trip snack ever.

Information

For information on environmental projects around the cape, check out the Cape Conservation Group's website (www.ccg.org.au).

Internet access is available at the **library** (☎08-9949 1462; 22 Maidstone Cres; ⏰8.30am-4pm Mon-Thu, 8.30am-noon Sat; @) and at Potshot Hotel (p182).

Department of Parks & Wildlife (DPaW; ☎08-9947 8000; www.dpaw.wa.gov.au; 20 Nimitz St; ⏰8am-5pm Mon-Fri) Supplies maps, brochures and permits for Ningaloo, Cape Range and Muiron Islands, including excellent wildlife guides. Can advise on turtle volunteering.

Tours N Travel Ningaloo (Europcar; ☎0437 106 183; cnr Pellew St & Murat Rd; internet per hr $5; ⏰8.30am-7pm; @) Internet access, second-hand books and the local Europcar agent.

Visitor Centre (☎08-9949 1176; www.visit-ningaloo.com.au; Murat Rd; ⏰9am-5pm) Tour bookings, bus tickets, accommodation service, Yardie Creek boat tickets and parks information.

Getting There & Away

Exmouth's Learmonth Airport is 37km south of town.

Qantas (☎13 13 13; www.qantas.com.au) Daily flights between Perth and Learmonth.

Airport Shuttle Bus (☎08-9949 4623; $25) Meets all flights; reservations are required when heading to the airport.

Integrity (☎1800 226 339; www.integrity-coachlines.com.au) Coaches run from the visitors centre to Perth ($240, 17 hours), Coral Bay ($47, 90 minutes) and Broome ($240, 18 hours) three times a week; there are weekly services to Karijini ($167, 10 hours).

Red Earth Safaris (☎1800 501 968; www.redearthsafaris.com.au; $200) Weekly Perth express departing Exmouth from the Potshot Resort at 7am on Sunday ($200, 30 hours). Includes meals and an overnight stop.

Getting Around

Budget, Avis and Europcar have agents around town, with car hire starting at $80 per day.

Allens (☎08-9949 2403; rear 24 Nimitz St; per day from $60) Older cars with 150 free kilometres.

Exmouth Boat & Kayak Hire (☎0438 230 269; www.exmouthboathire.com; 7 Patterson Way; kayaks per day $50) Tinnies (small dinghies) or something larger (including a skipper!) can be hired from $100 per day.

Exmouth Camper Hire (☎08-9949 4050; www.exmouthcamperhire.com.au; 16 Nimitz St; 4 days from $660) Camper vans with everything you need to spend time in Cape Range National Park, including solar panels.

Scooters2go (☎08-9949 4488; www.facebook.com/pages/Exmouth-Scooters2go/155067980518 8747; cnr Murat Rd & Pellew St; per day/week $80/$175) You only need a car licence for these 50 & 125cc scooters, which are much cheaper by the week. Best to ring first.

Around Exmouth

Head north past **Harold E Holt Naval Base** (HEH) to an intersection before the VLF antenna array. Continue straight on for Bundegi Beach or turn left onto Yardie Creek Rd for the magnificent beaches and bays of the western cape and Ningaloo Reef.

The Cape Range National Park entrance station is at the 40km mark and the road south is navigable by all vehicles as far as **Yardie Creek**. Experienced 4WD-ers can attempt crossing the sandy creek at low tide, before continuing along a rough coastal track all the way to Coral Bay (p178). Check road conditions first at Milyering visitor centre (p185).

Sights & Activities

Bundegi Beach BEACH

(P) In the shadow of the VLF antenna array, and within cycling range of Exmouth (it's 14km north), the calm, sheltered waters of Bundegi Beach and accompanying reef provide pleasant swimming, snorkelling, diving, kayaking and fishing.

North West Cape

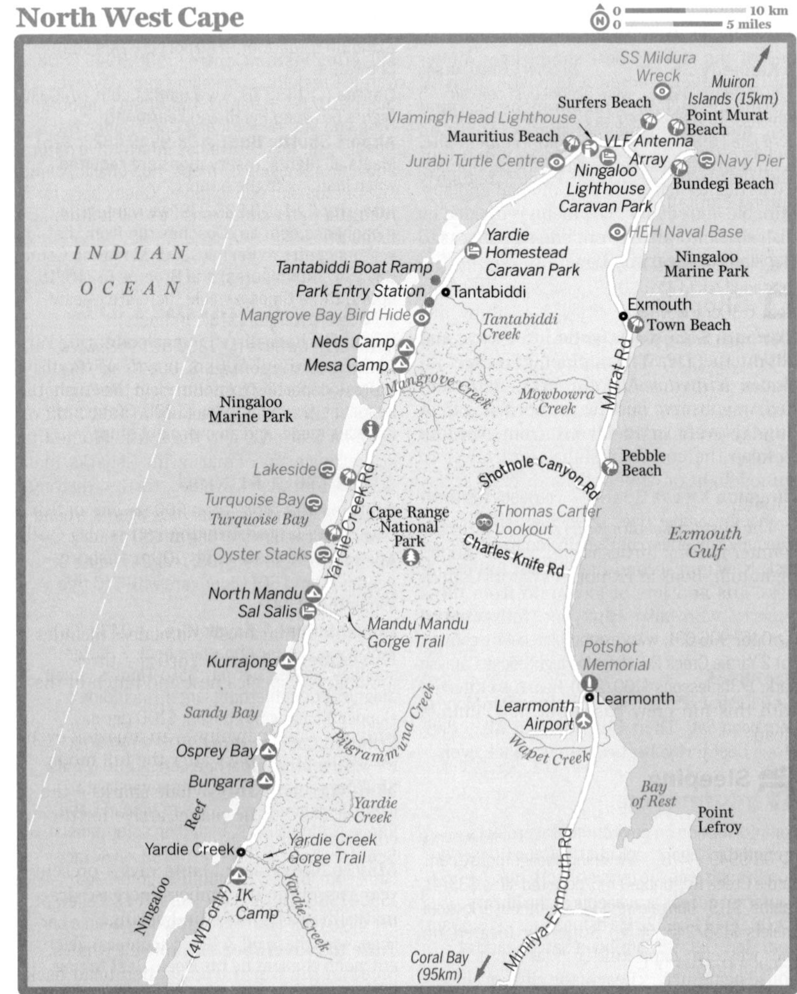

SS Mildura Wreck SHIPWRECK
(Mildura Wreck Rd) Follow the signpost from Yardie Creek Rd to find the 1907 cattle ship that ran aground on the reef.

Vlamingh Head Lighthouse LIGHTHOUSE
It's hard to miss this hilltop lighthouse built in 1912. Spectacular views of the entire cape make it a great place for watching whales and sunsets.

Mauritius Beach BEACH
(Yardie Ck Rd, 21km NW; P) Clothing-optional beach near Vlamingh Head Lighthouse.

★ **Navy Pier** DIVING
(Point Murat; dives $155) Point Murat, named after Napoleon's brother-in-law, is home to one of the world's best shore dives, under the Navy Pier. There's a fantastic array of marine life including nudibranchs, scorpion fish, moray eels and reef sharks. As it's on Defence territory, you'll need to join a tour and the exclusive licence rotates regularly among Exmouth dive shops.

Jurabi Turtle Centre WILDLIFE INTERACTION
(JTC; ☎08-9947 8000; Yardie Creek Rd; 2hr night tour adult/child $20/10; ⏱open 24hr; night tours from 6.30pm Nov-Mar) FREE Visit by day (free entry) to study turtle life cycles, and obtain the DPaW pamphlet *Marine Turtles in Ningaloo Marine Park*. Return at night to observe nesting turtles and hatchlings (November to March), remembering to keep the correct distance and never to shine a light or camera flash directly at any animal.

The best and ecologically safest way to encounter nesting turtles is on a DPaW guided night tour. Book at Exmouth Visitors Centre.

Exmouth Kite Centre KITESURFING
(☎0467 906 091; www.exmouthkitecentre.com.au; Lot 2 Yardie Creek Rd, Ningaloo Lighthouse Caravan Park; 1/3hr lessons $100/270) Learn to kitesurf with this fun crew based out at Vlamingh Head.

Sleeping

Ningaloo Lighthouse Caravan Park CARAVAN PARK $
(☎08-9949 1478; www.ningaloolighthouse.com; Yardie Creek Rd; unpowered/powered sites $33/41, cabins $115, bungalows $135, lighthouse/lookout chalets $155/245;) Superbly located on the western cape under Vlamingh lighthouse near Surfers Beach, the clifftop chalets have fantastic views. There's plenty of shady tent sites for lesser mortals and a cafe during peak season (May to September).

Yardie Homestead Caravan Park CARAVAN PARK $
(☎08-9949 1389; www.yardie.com.au; Yardie Creek Rd; unpowered/powered sites $32/38, cabins $130, chalets $180; P) Located just outside Cape Range National Park, this former sheep station caters mainly for anglers, though travellers are also welcome and there are some nice grassy tent sites. There's a range of cabins (most require a security bond) plus a pool, shop and camp kitchen.

Information

Milyering Visitor Centre (☎08-9949 2808; Yardie Creek Rd; snorkelling gear day/overnight $10/15; ⏱9am-3.45pm) Serving both Ningaloo Marine Park and Cape Range National Park, this centre has informative natural and cultural displays, maps, tide charts, camp site photos and publications. Check here for road and water conditions. It's 53km from Exmouth.

Ningaloo Marine Park

World Heritage–listed Ningaloo Marine Park protects the full 300km length of exquisite Ningaloo Reef, from Bundegi Reef on the eastern tip of the peninsula to Red Bluff on Quobba Station far to the south. Home to a staggering array of marine life – sharks, manta rays, humpback whales, turtles, dugongs, dolphins and more than 500 species of fish – Australia's largest fringing reef is also easily accessible, in places only 100m offshore.

When to Go

Year-round marine awesomeness includes:
November to March Turtles – three endangered species nest and hatch in the dunes.

March Coral spawning – an amazing event occurring seven days after the full moon.

Mid-March to July Whale sharks – the biggest fish on the planet arrive for the coral spawning.

May to November Manta rays – present year round; their numbers increase dramatically over winter and spring.

June to November Humpback whales – breed in the warm tropics then head back south to feed in the Antarctic.

Wildlife

Over 220 species of hard coral have been recorded in Ningaloo, ranging from bulbous brain corals found on bommies, to delicate branching staghorns and the slow-growing massive coral. While less colourful than soft corals (which are normally found in deeper water on the outer reef), the hard corals have incredible formations. Spawning, where branches of hermaphroditic coral simultaneously eject eggs and sperm into the water, occurs after full and new moons between February and May, but the peak action is usually six to 10 days after the March full moon.

It's this spawning that attracts the park's biggest drawcard, the solitary speckled whale shark *(Rhiniodon typus)*. Ningaloo is one of the few places in the world where these gentle giants arrive like clockwork each year to feed on plankton and small fish, making it a mecca for marine biologists and visitors alike. The largest fish in the world, the whale shark can weigh up to 21 tonnes, although most weigh between 13 and 15 tonnes, and reach up to 18m long. They can live for 70 years.

Upload your whale-shark pics to Ecocean (www.whaleshark.org), which will identify and track your whale shark, or geo-tag your other critters with Coastal Walkabout (www.coastalwalkabout.org). To learn more about Ningaloo's denizens, grab a copy of DPaW's *The Marine Life of Ningaloo Marine Park & Coral Bay.*

Activities

Most travellers visit Ningaloo Marine Park to **snorkel**. ALWAYS stop first at Milyering visitor centre (p185) for maps and info on the best spots and conditions. Check the tide chart and know your limits, as currents can be dangerous, the area is remote, and there's no phone coverage or lifeguards. While not common, unseasonal conditions can bring dangerous smacks of irukandji jellyfish. The park office also rents snorkelling equipment.

★ Turquoise Bay SNORKELLING
(Yardie Creek Rd, 65km from Exmouth) The **Bay Snorkel Area** is suitable for all skill levels with myriad fish and corals just off the beach to the right of the Bay car park. The **Drift** attracts stronger swimmers where the current carries you over coral bommies. Don't miss the exit point or you'll be carried out through the gap in the reef.

The Drift Snorkel Area is 300m south along the beach from the Drift car park; swim out for about 40m then float face down in the current. Get out before the sandy point where the current strengthens, then run back along the beach and start all over!

Lakeside SNORKELLING
(Yardie Creek Rd, 54km from Exmouth) Walk 500m south along the beach from the car park then snorkel out with the current before returning close to your original point.

Oyster Stacks SNORKELLING
(Yardie Creek Rd, 69km from Exmouth) These spectacular bommies are just metres offshore, but you need a tide of at least 1.2m and sharp rocks make entry/exit difficult. If you tire, don't stand on the bommies; look for some sand.

★ Ningaloo Kayak Trail KAYAKING
Still in its infancy, this fantastic new Parks & Wildlife initiative will see a string of specialist kayak-only moorings stretch from Bundegi Beach to Coral Bay, interspersed with designated remote beach camp sites. The moorings allow kayakers to tether their craft while snorkelling, and the camp sites allow for extended trips. Contact DPaW (p183) in Exmouth for more information, or enter Ningaloo Marine Park Kayak Moorings into your internet search engine for a downloadable brochure outlining the trail.

Lighthouse Bay DIVING
(Yardie Creek Rd) There's great scuba diving at Lighthouse Bay at sites such as the Labyrinth, Blizzard Ridge and Mandu Wall. Check out the DPaW book *Dive and Snorkel Sites in Western Australia* for other ideas.

Reef Search VOLUNTEERING
(Reef Check; www.reefcheckaustralia.org) Add a new dimension to your snorkelling or diving by collecting marine data in your own time, or volunteering for reef monitoring (courses available).

Cape Range National Park

The jagged limestone peaks and gorges of rugged 510-sq-km **Cape Range National Park** (per car $12) offer relief from the otherwise flat, arid expanse of North West Cape, and are rich in wildlife, including the rare black-flanked rock wallaby, five types of

SURFING THE CAPE

The big swells arrive on North West Cape between July and October and there's plenty of breaks and lots of rocks.

Surfers Beach (Dunes; Mildura Wreck Rd, 17km northwest of Exmouth) Ruggedly beautiful, surfers flock to the western cape during winter, while in the summer months windsurfing and kiteboarding are popular. The first car park provides the best access to the reef break.

Lighthouse Bombie (Yardie Creek Rd, 19km northwest of Exmouth) Off Vlamingh Head, the bombie is a big paddle out. Only for more experienced surfers.

Wobiri Access (Yardie Creek Rd, 23km northwest of Exmouth) On the western cape some 23km from Exmouth, gentle waves are suitable for beginners and surf classes are sometimes held.

Muiron Islands Serious surfers should grab a few mates and charter a boat to the Muiron Islands, just off Point Murat, where there are countless breaks and no one to ride them. You can camp on South Muiron with a permit from Exmouth DPaW (p183). There's also excellent snorkelling and diving. Your charter fee should include all meals, accommodation (onboard or camping) and fishing and snorkelling gear. Charters may be arranged from the Exmouth visitor centre (p183).

bat and over 200 species of bird. Spectacular deep canyons cut dramatically into the range, before emptying out onto the windblown coastal dunes and turquoise waters of Ningaloo Reef.

The main park access is via Yardie Creek Rd. Several areas in the east are accessible from unsealed roads off Minilya–Exmouth Rd, south of Exmouth. The park was hit by bad floods in 2014 and several camp sites and attractions are now closed: some permanently, others are being redeveloped. Check Parkstay (http://parkstay.dpaw.wa.gov.au) for the latest update.

Sights & Activities

Charles Knife Canyon GORGE

(Charles Knife Rd, Eastern Cape, 23km south of Exmouth) On the east coast, an incredibly scenic and at times dramatic road ascends a knife-edge ridge via rickety corners, necessitating frequent stops to make the most of the breathtaking views. A rough track continues to **Thomas Carter lookout**, where (in the cooler months) you can walk the 8km **Badjirrajirra loop trail** through spinifex and rocky gullies; there's no shade or water. Under no circumstances attempt this during summer.

Mangrove Bay Bird Hide BIRD SANCTUARY

(Western Cape, 8km from Cape Range National Park entrance station; P) FREE Spot migratory birds among the mangroves, or just wander out along the tidal flats.

Mandu Mandu Gorge GORGE

(20km south of Milyering; P) A pleasant but dry 3km return walk onto the gorge rim.

Yardie Creek Gorge GORGE

(36km south of Milyering; P) Excellent views above a water-filled gorge on this easy 2km return walk.

Yardie Creek Boat Tours BOAT TOUR

(☎08-9949 2920; www.yardiecreekboattours.com.au; adult/child/family $35/15/80; ⏰11am & 12.30pm seasonally, closed Feb) A relaxing one-hour cruise up the short, sheer Yardie Creek Gorge where you might spot rare black-flanked rock wallabies.

Sleeping

Cape Range Camp Sites CAMPGROUND $

(per person $10) A string of sandy camp sites line the coast within the Cape Range National Park. Facilities and shade are minimal, though most have toilets and some shelter from prevailing winds. Some can be booked online using Parkstay (http://parkstay.dpaw.wa.gov.au), others are allocated on arrival at the park entrance station (not the visitor centre!). If you like quiet, ask for 'generator free'.

Most camps have resident caretakers during peak season. The two furthest sites are the other side of Yardie Creek, you'll need a high-clearance 4WD to access them.

Sal Salis LUXURY CAMPGROUND $$$
(☎1300 790 561; www.salsalis.com; wilderness tent s/d 2 nights from $1126/1500; ⏰Mar-Dec) Want to watch that flaming crimson Indian Ocean sunset from between 500-threadcount pure cotton sheets? Pass the chablis! For those who want their camp without the cramp, there's a minimum two-night stay, three gourmet meals a day, a free bar (!) and the same things to do as the couple over the dune in the pop-up camper.

THE PILBARA

Dampier to Roebourne

Most travellers skip the mining-services section of the coast from Dampier to Roeburn as there's little to see, unless you like huge industrial facilities. However, there are several interesting sights, good transport, well-stocked supermarkets and useful repair shops.

Tours

Ngurrangga Tours CULTURAL TOUR
(☎0423 424 093; www.facebook.com/Ngurrangga Tours; adult/child from $110/55; ⏰Feb-Nov) Ngarluma man, Clinton Walker's cultural tours are gathering rave reviews from travellers across the Pilbara. His half-day Murujuga National Park tour explores rock art petroglyphs on the Burrup Peninsula near Dampier, while longer day tours explore the culturally significant areas of Gregory's Gorge (adult $220, child $110) and Millstream (adult $220, child $110), the latter also available as an overnight option (adult $440, child $220).

Festivals

Red Earth Arts Festival ARTS
(www.reaf.com.au; ⏰Sep) An annual celebration of music, theatre and visual arts spread across the Pilbara coast.

Dampier

Dampier, spread around King Bay, is the region's main port and is home to heavy industry. Offshore, the coral waters and pristine island reserves of the **Dampier Archipelago** support a wealth of marine life and endangered marsupials.

Hearson Cove (P) has a pleasant beach providing Staircase to the Moon (p1029) viewing and access to Murujuga rock art.

Murujuga National Park FREE is home to the world's largest concentration of petroglyphs, stretched out along the unwanted rocky hills of the heavily industrialized Burrup Peninsula. The most accessible are at Deep Gorge, near Hearson Cove and devastatingly, some sites have been vandalised. You'll need a 4WD to explore north of Withnell Bay.

Karratha

Most travellers in Karratha bank, restock, repair stuff and get out of town before their wallet ignites.

If you have time, the **Jaburara Heritage Trail** (Yaburara) leaves from behind the visitor centre. This series of trails (the longest of which is 3.5km one way) winds through significant traditional sites, detailing the displacement and eventual extinction of the Jaburara people. Bring plenty of water and start early.

Sleeping & Eating

Accommodation prospects, previously dire, are gradually improving. Search online for last-minute deals or try the visitor centre. Weekends are usually cheaper than midweek. Point Samson and Millstream are nicer alternatives.

The shopping centre has most things you'll need, including ATMs, take-away food and supermarkets.

Pilbara Holiday Park CARAVAN PARK $
(☎08-9185 1855; www.aspenparks.com.au; Rosemary Rd; powered sites $42, motel/studio d $190/200; ❄@≋) This park is neat and well run with good facilities.

Soul CAFE $$
(☎0422 667 649; Warambie Rd, Pelago Centre; ⏰6am-4pm) City-style sophisticated breakfasts and quick lunches.

Information

Karratha Visitor Centre (☎08-9144 4600; www.karrathavisitorcentre.com.au; Karratha Rd; ⏰8.30am-5pm Mon-Fri, 9am-2pm Sat & Sun, shorter hrs Oct-Mar; @) has good local info, supplies Rail Access road permits, books tours (including to mining infrastructure) and may find you a room.

OFF THE BEATEN TRACK

MT AUGUSTUS (BURRINGURRAH) NATIONAL PARK

Mt Augustus (Burringurrah), in Wajarri country, is a huge monocline (1105m), twice as large as Uluru and a good deal more remote, which rises 717m above the surrounding plains. There are a number of walking trails and Aboriginal rock-art sites to explore, including the superb summit trail (12km return, six hours).

In a 2WD it's a rough 450km from Carnarvon via Gascoyne Junction or 350km from Meekatharra. With a 4WD there are at least three other routes including a handy back door to Karijini via Dooley Downs and Tom Price. All of these routes see little traffic, so be prepared for the worst. There's no camping in the park.

At the closest accommodation to Mt Augustus, **Mt Augustus Tourist Park** (☎08-9943 0527; www.mtaugustustouristpark.com; unpowered/powered sites $22/33, donga d $88, units $176; P ❄), dusty camp sites, wallabies and tumbleweeds are all you'll see here.

ℹ Getting There & Away

Karratha is well connected. Virgin (p178), Qantas (p178) and Alliance (p178) all fly daily to Perth. Airnorth (p178) flies to Broome, Darwin and Port Hedland twice weekly.

Integrity (☎1800 226 339; www.integrity-coachlines.com.au) Departs from the visitor centre for Perth ($282, 24 hours), Port Hedland ($89, three hours) and Broome ($187, 10 hours) twice a week.

Roebourne

Sitting on Ngaluma country, 40km east of Karratha, Roebourne is the oldest (1866) Pilbara town still functioning. It's home to a large Aboriginal community; Yindjibarndi is the dominant language group. There are some beautiful old buildings and a thriving Indigenous art scene (www.roebourneart.com.au). The **Yinjaa-Barni** (☎08-9182 1959; www.yinjaa-barni.com.au; Lot 3 Roe St; ⏲vary) Indigenous-run gallery showcases gifted Millstream artists.

Housed in the old gaol, the **visitor centre** (Old Gaol; ☎08-9182 1060; www.roebourne.org.au; Queen St; ⏲9am-4pm Mon-Fri, 9am-3pm Sat & Sun, shorter hrs Nov-Apr) has an interesting museum, a courtyard minerals display and a guide to Roebourne's significant buildings.

Cossack

The scenic ghost town of Cossack, at the mouth of the Harding River, was previously the district's main port but was usurped by Point Samson and then eventually abandoned. Many of the historic bluestone buildings date from the late 1800s.

The small, self-guided **Social History Museum** (adult/child $2/1; ⏲9am-4pm) in Cossack's old courthouse celebrates the town's halcyon days, while the Japanese section of the tiny **Pioneer Cemetery** bears witness to Cossack's pearling past.

At the road-end, **Reader Head Lookout** (P) has great views over the river mouth, beach and Staircase to the Moon (p1029). Usually empty, **Settlers Beach** is great for a dip.

The informative (and shadeless!) 6km **Cossack Heritage Trail** links all the major sites (grab the brochure from Roebourne visitor centre (p189)).

There are five basic rooms at **Cossack Budget Accommodation** (☎08-9182 1190; www.karratha.wa.gov.au/cossack; d without/with air-con $100/120; ❄), housed in the atmospheric old police barracks. BYO food.

Point Samson

Point Samson is a small, industrial-free seaside village that's home to great seafood and clean beaches, making it the nicest place to stay in the area. There's good **snorkelling** off Point Samson, and the picturesque curved beach of Honeymoon Cove.

The tiny **Samson Beach Caravan Park** (☎08-9187 1414; Samson Rd; powered sites $42) is set in lovely, leafy surrounds, close to the water and tavern. Bookings are essential during school holidays. Over at **Cove** (☎08-9187 0199; www.thecoveholidayvillage.com.au; Macleod St; sites $49, 1-/2-bedroom units $240/310) it's a bit 'van city', but the modern, clean facilities complement a great location and it's an easy walk to all the attractions.

Samson Beach Chalets (☎08-9187 0202; www.samsonbeach.com.au; Samson Rd; chalets $280-650; P ❄ 📶 ≋) offers beautifully appointed self-contained chalets (various sizes) just a short walk from the beach. There's a shady pool, free wi-fi and in-house movies. While **Samson Beach Bistro** (☎08-9187 1435; mains $11-44; ⊙11am-3pm & 5-8.30pm), underneath the pub, serves great seafood on a shady deck overlooking the ocean.

Millstream Chichester National Park

Amongst the arid, spinifex-covered plateaus and basalt ranges between Karijini and the coast, the tranquil **Millstream Chichester National Park** (per vehicle $12) waterholes of the Fortescue River form cool, lush oases. In the park's north are the stunning breakaways and eroded mesas of the Chichester Range. A lifeline for local flora and fauna, the park is one of the most important Indigenous sites in WA. Once the station homestead, the unstaffed **visitor centre** houses historical, ecological and cultural displays.

Sights & Activities

Jirndarwurrunha Pool CULTURAL SITE
(Millstream) A short stroll from the Millstream Chichester National Park visitor centre, beautiful lily and palm-fringed Jirndarwurrunha is strongly significant to the traditional Yindjibarndi owners. Swimming is not permitted.

Deep Reach Pool SWIMMING HOLE
(Nhangganggunha; Millstream; P) Shady picnic tables and barbecues back onto a perfect swimming hole believed to be the resting place of the Warlu (creation serpent).

Mt Herbert LOOKOUT
(Roebourne-Wittenoom Rd, Chichester Range; P) A 10-minute climb from the car park on the road to Roebourne reveals a fantastic view of the ragged Chichester Range.

Python Pool SWIMMING HOLE
(Chichester Range; P) This plunge pool is normally fine for swimming, though check for algal bloom before sliding in.

Murlamunyjunha Trail WALKING
This palm-lined 7km walking trail (two hours return) featuring interpretive plaques by the traditional Yindjibarndi owners, links Crossing Pool and Milliyanha Campground.

Chichester Range Camel Trail HIKING
Fit hikers might attempt the 8km Camel Trail linking Mt Herbert and Python Pool via McKenzie Spring. Allow three hours one way.

Sleeping

Milliyanha Campground CAMPGROUND
(Millstream; sites per person $10; P) A nicely shaded, circular camp site near the visitors centre with a kitchen in the middle. If full, try the sparse Stargazers camp site.

Karijini National Park

The narrow, breathtaking gorges, hidden pools and spectacular waterfalls of Karijini National Park (per car $12) form one of WA's most impressive attractions. Adventurers and nature lovers flock to the rocky, red ranges and deep, dark chasms, home to abundant wildlife and over 800 different plant species.

Kangaroos, snappy gums and wild flowers dot the spinifex plains, rock wallabies cling to sheer cliffs and endangered olive pythons lurk in giant figs above quiet pools. The park also contains WA's three highest peaks: Mt Meharry, Mt Bruce and Mt Frederick.

Banyjima Dr, the park's main thoroughfare, connects with Karijini Dr at two entrance stations. The **eastern** access is closest to the visitor centre and Dales Gorge. Take extra care driving as tourist roll overs are common. Avoid driving at night.

Choose walks wisely, dress appropriately and never enter a restricted area without a certified guide. Avoid the gorges during and after rain, as flash flooding does occur.

Sights & Activities

Exploring Karijini's gorges is a magical experience, but obey all signs and keep out of restricted areas.

Dales Gorge GORGE
(19km from the East Entrance; P) A short, sharp descent from near Dales Campground leads to **Fortescue Falls**, behind which a leafy stroll upstream reveals beautiful **Fern Pool** (Jubura); head 1km downstream from Fortescue Falls to picturesque **Circular Pool**; ascend to **Three Ways Lookout** and return along the cliff top.

Karijini National Park

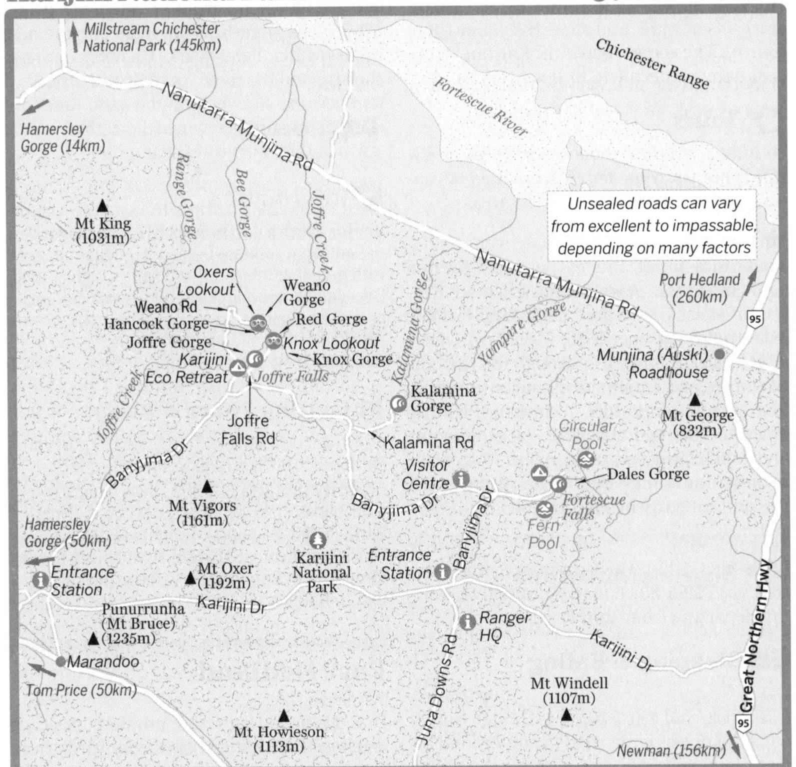

Kalamina Gorge GORGE
(Kalamina Gorge Rd; P) Wide, easy gorge with a small, tranquil pool and falls.

Joffre Gorge GORGE
(Joffre Falls Rd; P) **Joffre Falls** (when not trickling) are spectacular but the frigid pools below are perennially shaded. There's a walking track to the falls from the Karijini Eco Retreat (p192).

Knox Gorge GORGE
(Joffre Falls Rd) Descend from **Knox Lookout** to several nice, sunny swimming holes, fringed by native figs.

Weano Gorge GORGE
(Weano Rd; P) The upper gorge is dry, but the steep track winding down from the car park to the lower gorge narrows until you reach the perfect, surreal bowl of **Handrail Pool**.

Oxers Lookout LOOKOUT
(Weano Rd; P) The final 13km to the breathtaking Oxers Lookout can be rough, but it's worth it for the magnificent views of the junction of the Red, Weano, Joffre and Hancock Gorges some 130m below.

Hancock Gorge GORGE
(Weano Rd; P) A steep descent (partly on ladders) brings you to the sunny **Amphitheatre**. Follow the slippery **Spider Walk** to sublime **Kermits Pool**.

Hamersley Gorge GORGE
(off Nanutarra-Wittenoom Rd; P) Away in Karijini's northwest corner, this idyllic swimming hole and waterfall makes a pleasant stopover if you're heading north towards the coast or Millstream.

Punurrunha WALKING
(Mt Bruce) Gorged out? Go and grab some altitude on WA's second-highest mountain

(1235m), a superb ridge walk with fantastic views all the way to the summit. Start early, carry lots of water and allow five hours (9km return). The access road is off Karijini Dr opposite the western end of Banyjima Dr.

Tours

To fully appreciate the awesomeness of Karijini's gorges, consider an accredited adventure tour through the restricted areas.

★ West Oz Active Adventure Tours ADVENTURE TOUR
(☎0438 913 713; www.westozactive.com.au; Karijini Eco Retreat; 1-/3-/5-day tours $245/$745/1450, 3-day tour ex Tom Price $335; ⏲Apr-Nov) Offers action-packed day trips through the restricted gorges and combines hiking, swimming, floating on inner tubes, climbing, sliding off waterfalls and abseiling. All equipment and lunch provided. Also offers longer all-inclusive multi-day tours with airport pick ups and Integrity bus rendezvous.

Lestok Tours BUS TOUR
(☎08-9188 1112; www.lestoktours.com.au; day adult/child $165/80) Full-day outings to Karijini departing from Tom Price.

Sleeping & Eating

Dales Gorge CAMPGROUND $
(sites adult/child $10/2.20; P) Though somewhat dusty, this large DPaW campground offers shady, spacious sites with nearby toilets and picnic tables. Forget tent pegs – you'll be using rocks as anchors.

★ Karijini Eco Retreat RESORT $$$
(☎08-9425 5591; www.karijiniecoretreat.com.au; Weano Rd; sites $40, tent d low/high season $190/315; P) This 100% Indigenous-owned retreat is a model for sustainable tourism, and the attached bar and **restaurant** (mains $28-39) has fantastic food, including the best barra within light years. Campers get hot showers and the same rocks (to use instead of tent pegs) as elsewhere in the park. Rates are cheaper in summer when the retreat winds down and temperatures soar.

Information

Visitor Centre (☎08-9189 8121; Banyjima Dr; ⏲9am-4pm Feb-late Dec) Indigenous-managed with excellent interpretive displays highlighting Banyjima, Yinhawangka and Kurrama culture, as well as displays on park wildlife, good maps and walks information, a public phone and really great air-con.

Getting There & Away

Bring your own vehicle. The closest airports are Paraburdoo (101km) and Newman (201km).

Integrity (☎1800 226 339; www.integrity-coachlines.com.au) Weekly service to/from Perth ($293, 25 hours), Broome ($198, 12 hours) and Exmouth ($146, eight hours) passes through Tom Price, where you can pick up a tour to Karijini.

Port Hedland

POP 14,000

Port Hedland ain't the prettiest place. A high-visibility dystopia of railway yards, iron-ore stockpiles, salt mountains, furnaces and a massive deep-water port confront the passing traveller. Yet under that red-dust lurks a colourful 130-year history of mining booms and busts, cyclones, pearling and WWII action. Several pleasant hours may be spent exploring Hedland's thriving art and cafe (real coffee!) scene, historic CBD and scenic foreshore.

TOM PRICE & NEWMAN

Bookending Karijini National Park are the neat, company-built mining towns of **Tom Price** and **Newman**. Newman, to the east on the Great Northern Hwy, is larger though more distant, with better transport and accommodation. Both have good (ie air-conditioned) supermarkets, petrol stations and visitor centres, where you can book mine tours if huge holes are your thing. The local libraries have internet access, and Newman's caravan parks are OK for a tent.

Newman Visitor Centre (☎08-9175 2888; www.newman.org.au; Fortescue Ave; mine tour adult/child $30/15; ⏲8am-5pm Mar-Oct, shorter hrs Nov-Feb) Has a mud map of local sights and six short-term chalets ($150) to stay in.

Tom Price Visitor Centre (☎08-9188 5488; www.tomprice.org.au; Central Rd; mine tour adult/child $30/15; ⏲8.30am-5pm Mon-Fri, 8.30am-12.30pm Sat & Sun, shorter hrs Nov-Apr) Can supply Rail Access Rd permits and book tours.

OFF THE BEATEN TRACK

MARBLE BAR

Marble Bar, a long way off everybody's beaten track, burnt itself into the Australian psyche as the country's hottest town when, back in 1921, the mercury didn't dip below 37.8°C (100°F) for 161 consecutive days. The town is (mistakenly) named after a bar of jasper beside a pool on the Coongan River, 5km southwest.

Most days there's not much to do. You can pore over the minerals at the **Comet Gold Mine** (08-9176 1015; Hillside Rd; admission $3; 9am-4pm; P), 8km out of town on the Hillside Rd, or you can prop at the bar and have a yarn with Foxie at the **Ironclad Hotel** (08-9176 1066; 15 Francis St; vary). This classic outback pub offers comfy motel rooms, decent meals and a welcome to budget travellers.

But come the first weekend in July, the town swells to 10 times its normal size for a weekend of drinking, gambling, fashion crime, country music, nudie runs and horse racing known as the **Marble Bar Cup**. The **caravan park** (08-9176 1569; 64 Contest St; sites unpowered/powered $20/30) overflows and the Ironclad is besieged as punters from far and wide come for a bit of an outback knees-up.

The **shire office** (08-9176 1008) runs a weekly bus service to Port Hedland and Newman (via Nullagine) and provides tourist information. If you're heading south, the easiest route back to bitumen is the lonely but beautiful Hillside Rd.

Sights & Activities

Collect the excellent *Port Hedland, A Discoverer's Journal* from the visitor centre and take a self-guided tour around the CBD and foreshore.

Between November and February flatback turtles nest on nearby beaches. Check at the visitor centre for volunteer options.

Goode St, near Pretty Pool, is handy to observe Port Hedland's Staircase to the Moon.

★ Courthouse Gallery GALLERY
(08-9173 1064; www.courthousegallery.com.au; 16 Edgar St; 9am-4.30pm Mon-Fri, 9am-2pm Sat & Sun) More than a gallery, this leafy arts HQ is the centre of all goodness in Hedland. Inside are stunning local contemporary and Indigenous exhibitions, while the shady surrounds host sporadic craft markets. If something is happening, these folks will know about it.

Spinifex Hill Studios GALLERY
(0457 422 875; www.spinifexhillstudio.com.au; 18 Hedditch St, South Hedland; 9am-5pm Mon-Fri) Great new initiative showcasing Indigenous artists from Hedland and across the Pilbara. Call before visiting.

Marapikurrinya Park PARK
(end of Wedge St) Watch ridiculously large tankers pass by. After dark, nearby **Finucane Lookout** provides a smouldering view into BHP Billiton's Hot Briquetted Iron plant.

Pretty Pool FISHING
A popular fishing and picnicking spot (beware of stonefish and backpackers), 7km east of the town centre.

Tours

BHP Billiton GUIDED TOUR
(adult/child $45/30; vary) Popular iron-ore plant tour departing from the visitor centre.

Local History BUS TOUR
(90min $25; Apr-Sep) Run by a local historian these informative tours delve into Hedland's chequered past. Book at the visitor centre.

Sleeping & Eating

Finding a room in Hedland isn't easy or cheap. Try the visitor centre, otherwise head for 80 Mile Beach or Point Samson.

There are supermarkets, cafes and take aways at both the **Boulevard** (cnr Wilson & McGregor Sts) and **South Hedland** (Throssell Rd) shopping centres.

Cooke Point Caravan Park CARAVAN PARK $$
(08-9173 1271; www.aspenparks.com.au; cnr Athol & Taylor Sts; powered sites $54, d without bathroom $130, unit d from $204;) You might be able to snag a dusty van or tent site here, but the other options are usually full. There's a nice view over the mangroves and the amenities are well maintained.

★ **Silver Star** CAFE $$
(☎ 0411 143 663; Edgar St; breakfast $10-20, lunch $18-24; ⏲ 7am-3pm) Possibly the coolest cafe in the Pilbara, this 1930s American Silver Star railcar serves up decent coffee, brekkies and sophisticated lunches in the original observation lounge and outside on a shady deck.

Information

There are ATMs along Wedge St and in the Boulevard shopping centre (p193). The **library** (☎ 08-9158 9378; Dempster St; ⏲ 9am-5pm Mon-Fri, 10am-1pm Sat; @) has internet access.

Visitor Centre (☎ 08-9173 1711; www.visitport hedland.com; 13 Wedge St; ⏲ 9am-5pm Mon-Fri, 9am-2pm Sat-Sun; @ 📶) This amazing centre sells travel books, publishes shipping times, arranges iron-ore plant tours, and helps with accommodation and turtle monitoring (November to February).

Seafarers Centre (☎ 08-9173 1315; www.phseafarers.org; cnr Wedge & Wilson Sts; ⏲ 9am-11pm; @ 📶) High speed wi-fi and internet. Also sells Integrity bus tickets, Aboriginal artefacts and currency exchange.

Getting There & Around

Virgin and **Qantas** both fly to Perth daily, and on Tuesday Qantas also flies direct to Brisbane and Melbourne. Virgin has handy weekend flights to Bali and Broome. Airnorth (p178) heads to Broome (Tuesday and Friday) with a Darwin connection.

The airport is 13km from town; a **taxi** (☎ 08-9172 1010) will cost around $40.

Integrity (☎ 1800 226 339; www.integrity-coachlines.com.au) has coaches for Perth ($293, 28 to 31 hours) and Broome ($129, six hours) three times weekly. There's also a quicker inland route to Perth ($274, 22 hours) via Newman each week. Departs from the visitor centre and South Hedland shopping centre.

Broome & the Kimberley

Includes ➡

Best Cafes

- ➡ Whale Song Cafe (p219)
- ➡ Jila Gallery (p199)
- ➡ Wild Mango (p208)
- ➡ Rusty Shed (p206)
- ➡ Cygnet Bay Pearl Farm (p220)

Best Off the Beaten Track Locations

- ➡ Middle Lagoon (p219)
- ➡ Mornington Wilderness Camp (p202)
- ➡ Mitchell Falls National Park (p201)
- ➡ Duncan Road (p204)
- ➡ Kalumburu (p203)

Why Go?

Australia's last frontier is a wild land of remote, spectacular scenery spread over huge distances, with a severe climate, a sparse population and minimal infrastructure. Larger than 75% of the world's countries, the Kimberley is hemmed by impenetrable coastline and unforgiving deserts. In between lie vast boab-studded spinifex plains, palm-fringed gorges, desolate mountains and magnificent waterfalls. Travelling here is a true adventure, and each dry season a steady flow of explorers search for the real outback along the legendary Gibb River Road.

Aboriginal culture runs deep across the region, from the Dampier Peninsula, where neat communities welcome travellers to Country, to distant Mitchell Plateau, where ancient Wandjina and Gwion Gwion stand vigil over sacred waterholes.

Swashbuckling Broome and practical Kununurra bookend the region. Both are great places to unwind, find a job and meet other travellers.

When to Go

Broome

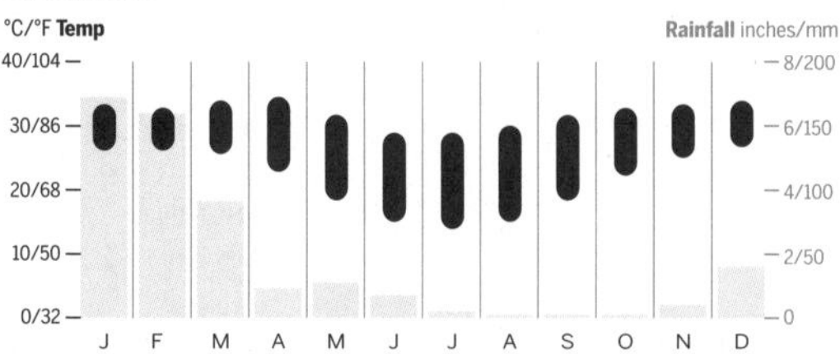

Apr Fly over thundering Mitchell and King George Falls.

May Broome's at its greenest right before the tourist tide.

Sep & Oct Hit Purnululu and the Gibb River Road as the season winds down.

Broome & the Kimberley Highlights

1 Taking a camel ride at sunset along Broome's **Cable Beach** (p211).

2 Learning about traditional culture with Aboriginal communities on the pristine **Dampier Peninsula** (p218).

3 Tackling the notorious **Gibb River Road** (p200) in a 4WD adventure.

4 Flying over the stunning **Mitchell and King George Falls** (p206) after the Wet.

5 Riding the wild **Horizontal Waterfalls** (p199).

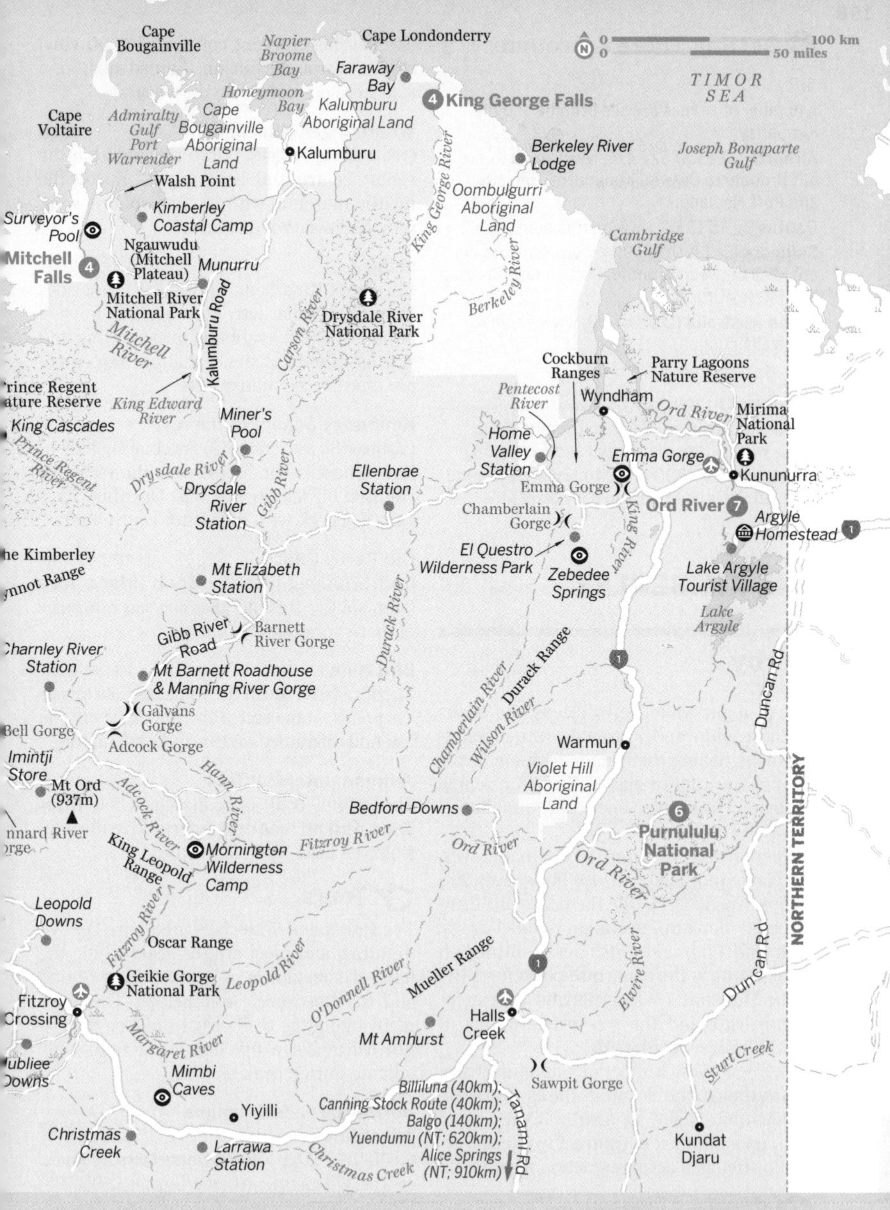

6 Losing yourself among the ancient domes of **Purnululu National Park** (p208).

7 Canoeing the mighty **Ord River** (p206) in a three-day self-guided epic.

8 Immersing yourself in Indigenous art at **Aboriginal art cooperatives** (p207).

9 Trekking through the bowels of the earth at **Tunnel Creek National Park** (p203).

10 Following the **Lurujarri Dreaming Trail** (p215) to James Price Point and beyond.

Getting There & Around

AIR

A number of airlines service Broome and the Kimberley.

Airnorth (1800 627 474; www.airnorth.com.au) Broome to Darwin, Kununurra, Karratha and Port Hedland.

Qantas (13 13 13; www.qantas.com.au)

Skippers (1300 729 924; www.skippers.com.au) Flies between Broome, Derby, Halls Creek and Fitzroy Crossing.

Virgin Australia (13 67 89; www.virgin-australia.com.au)

BUS

Integrity (1300 226 339; www.integrity-coachlines.com.au) Perth to Broome three times weekly (one via Karijini and Exmouth).

Greyhound (1300 473 946; www.greyhound.com.au) Broome to Darwin daily (except Sunday).

THE KIMBERLEY

Derby

POP 3300

Late at night while Derby sleeps, the boabs cut loose and wander around town, marauding mobs flailing their many limbs in battle against an army of giant, killer croc-people emerging from the encircling mudflats… If only.

There *are* crocs hiding in the mangroves, but you're more likely to see birds, over 200 different varieties, while the boabs are firmly rooted along the two main parallel drags, Loch and Clarendon Sts. Derby, sitting on King Sound, is the departure point for tours to the Horizontal Waterfalls and Buccaneer Archipelago, and the western terminus of the Gibb River Road (GRR).

Derby is West Kimberley's administrative centre, though the closure of the asylum seeker detention facility at nearby RAAF Curtin has seen an outflux of contract workers, freeing up stretched accommodation resources.

Sights & Activities

The visitor centre's excellent town map lists every conceivable attraction.

★Norval Gallery GALLERY

(Loch St; vary) Kimberley art legends Mark and Mary Norval have set up an exciting gallery-cafe in an old tin shed on the edge of town. Featuring striking artwork, exquisite jewellery, decent coffee and 5000 vinyl records (brought out on themed nights), a visit here is a delight to the senses.

Wharefinger Museum MUSEUM

(admission by donation) Grab the key from the visitor centre and have a peek inside the nearby museum, with its atmospheric shipping and aviation displays.

Jetty LANDMARK

Check out King Sound's colossal 11.5m tides from the circular jetty, 1km north of town, a popular fishing, crabbing, bird-spotting and staring-into-the-distance haunt. Yep, there are crocs in the mangroves.

Kimberley School of the Air SCHOOL

(Marmion St; admission $10) Fascinating look at how school is conducted over the radio for children on remote stations. Opening times vary, so check with the visitor centre first.

Old Derby Gaol HISTORIC BUILDING

(Loch St) Along with the **Boab Prison Tree** (7km south), this old gaol is a sad reminder of man's inhumanity to man.

Bird Hide BIRDWATCHING

There's a bird hide in the wetlands (aka sewerage ponds) at the end of Conway St, where you can find migratory waders and local raptors.

Joonjoo Botanical Trail WALKING

This 2.3km trail, opposite the Gibb River Road turn off, has neat interpretive displays from the local Nyikina people.

Tours

The Horizontal Waterfalls (p199) are Derby's top draw and most cruises also include the natural splendours of remote King Sound and the Buccaneer Archipelago. There are many operators to choose from (see the visitor centre for a full list). Most tours only operate during peak season.

Horizontal Falls Seaplane Adventures SCENIC FLIGHTS

(08-9192 1172; www.horizontalfallsadventures.com.au; 6hr tours from Derby/Broome $695/795) Flights to Horizontal Falls include a speedboat ride through the falls. There's also an overnight-stay option (ex-Derby) for $845.

North West Bush Pilots SCENIC FLIGHTS

(08-9193 2680; www.northwestbushpilots.com.au; flights from $352) Horizontal Waterfalls, Buccaneer Archipelago and Walcott Inlet – you can look but not touch.

Windjana Tours CULTURAL TOUR
(08-9193 1550; www.windjanatours.com.au; $195; Tue, Thu & Sun May-Aug) Bunuba man, Dillon Andrews, leads informative full-day cultural tours to Windjana Gorge and Tunnel Creek National Parks.

Uptuyu CULTURAL TOUR
(0400 878 898; www.uptuyu.com.au; Oongkalkada Wilderness Camp, Udialla Springs, 50km from Great Northern Hwy; per day from $450) Down in Nyikina country on the Fitzroy River, Neville and Jo run 'designer' cultural tours taking in wetlands, rock art, fishing and Indigenous communities along the Fitzroy and further afield.

Festivals & Events

Boab Festival MUSIC, CULTURE
(www.derbyboabfestival.org.au; Jul) Derby goes off with concerts, mud footy, horse and mud-crab races, poetry readings, art exhibitions and street parades. Try to catch the Long Table dinner out on the mudflats.

Sleeping & Eating

With the closure of the Curtin Detention Centre, accommodation is now easier to find. Try the visitor centre, but if you're heading to/from the Gibb River Road, consider Birdwood Downs Station (p201) instead.

There are several takeaways and cafes along Loch and Clarendon Sts.

Kimberley Entrance Caravan Park CARAVAN PARK $
(08-9193 1055; www.kimberleyentrancecaravanpark.com; 2 Rowan St; unpowered/powered sites $32/38) Not all sites are shaded, though there's always room. Expect lots of insects this close to the mudflats.

Derby Lodge MOTEL $$
(08-9193 2924; www.derbylodge.com.au; 15-19 Clarendon St; r/apt $160/210;) Choose between neat, clean motel rooms or self-contained apartments with cooking facilities.

Spinifex Hotel RESORT $$
(08-9191 1233; www.spinifexhotel.com.au; 6 Clarendon St; dongas/motel r $160/250, mains $24-39;) Rising phoenix-like from the ashes of the old Spini, this sleek new resort has corporate-class rooms (some with kitchenettes) and an on-site restaurant. Peak season brings outdoor live music.

Sampey Meats BUTCHER $
(08-9193 2444; 59 Rowan St; 7am-5pm Mon-Fri, to noon Sat) Homemade jerkies, biltong and vacuum-sealed roasts, all ready for the Gibb.

★ **Jila Gallery** ITALIAN $$
(08-9193 2560; www.facebook.com/Jilagallery; 18 Clarendon St; pizzas $20-28, mains $24-34; 10.30am-2pm & 6pm-late Tue-Fri, 6pm-late Sat) Easily the best food in Derby with great wood-fired pizzas, perfect seafood risotto, wonderful cakes and shady, alfresco dining.

Information

The supermarkets and ATMs are on Loch and Clarendon Sts.

Derby Visitor Centre (08-9191 1426; www.derbytourism.com.au; 30 Loch St; 8.30am-5pm Mon-Fri, 9am-3pm Sat & Sun dry season) is a helpful centre with the low-down on road conditions, accommodation, transport and tour bookings.

Getting There & Away

Derby has two airports. Flights for Perth arrive and depart from Curtin Airport (DCN), 40km

HORIZONTAL WATERFALLS

One of the most intriguing features of the Kimberley coastline is the phenomenon known as 'horizontal waterfalls'. Despite the name, the falls are simply tides gushing through narrow coastal gorges in the Buccaneer Archipelago, north of Derby. What creates such a spectacle are the huge tides, often varying up to 11m. The water flow reaches an astonishing 30 knots as it's forced through two narrow gaps 20m and 10m wide – resulting in a 'waterfall' reaching 4m in height.

Many tours leave Derby (and some Broome) each Dry, by air, sea or a combination of both. It's become de rigueur to 'ride' the tide change through the gorge on a high-powered speedboat, but this is risky at best, and accidents have occurred. Scenic flights are the quickest and cheapest option, and some seaplanes will land and transfer passengers to a waiting speedboat for the adrenalin hit. If you prefer to be stirred, not shaken, then consider seeing the falls as part of a longer cruise through the archipelago. Book tours at the Derby and Broome visitor centres.

away. A **shuttle** (☎08-9193 2568; per person $35) runs to/from Curtin into town; book the day before. Charter and sightseeing flights use the closer Derby Aerodrome (DRB), just past the Gibb turn-off.

All buses depart from the visitor centre.

Derby Bus Service (☎08-9193 1550; www.derbybus.com.au; one way/return $50/90; ⏲Mon, Wed & Fri) Leaves early for Broome (2½ hours), stopping at Willare Roadhouse (and basically anywhere else you ask them to along the way), returning the same day.

Greyhound (☎1300 473 946; www.greyhound.com.au) Broome ($52, 2½ hours), Darwin ($241, 23 hours) and Kununurra ($123, 11 hours) daily (except Sundays).

Skippers (☎1300 729 924; www.skippers.com.au) Flights to Broome, Fitzroy Crossing and Halls Creek several times weekly.

Virgin Australia (☎13 67 89; www.virgin-australia.com) Five flights to Perth from Curtin Airport weekly.

Getting Around

Taxi (☎13 10 08)

Gibb River Road

Cutting a brown swath through the scorched heart of the Kimberley, the legendary **Gibb River Road** ('the Gibb' or GRR) provides one of Australia's wildest outback experiences. Stretching some 660km between **Derby** and **Kununurra**, the largely unpaved Gibb River Road is an endless sea of red dirt, big open skies and dramatic terrain. Rough, sometimes deeply corrugated side roads lead to remote gorges, shady pools, distant waterfalls and million-acre cattle stations. Rain can close the road any time, and it's closed during the Wet. This is true wilderness with minimal services, so good planning and self-sufficiency are vital.

Several pastoral stations offer overnight accommodation from mid-April to late October; advance bookings are essential during the peak period of June to August. Hema Maps' *Kimberley Atlas & Guide* provides the best coverage, while visitor centres sell *The Gibb River & Kalumburu Road Guide* ($5).

A high-clearance 4WD (eg Toyota Land Cruiser) is mandatory, with two spare tyres, tools, emergency water (20L minimum) and several days' food in case of breakdown. Britz (p218) in Broome is a reputable hire outfit. Fuel is limited and expensive, most mobile phones won't work, and temperatures can be life-threatening. Broome and Kununurra are best for supplies.

For just a sniff of outback adventure, try the 'tourist loop' along the Gibb from Derby onto Fairfield–Leopold Downs Rd to Windjana Gorge (p203) and Tunnel Creek (p203) National Parks, then exit onto the Great Northern Hwy near **Fitzroy Crossing**.

Tours

Adventure Tours 4WD TOUR
(☎03-8102 7800; www.adventuretours.com.au; from $1950) Nine-day Gibb River Road camping tours catering for a younger crowd.

Kimberley Wild Expeditions 4WD TOUR
(☎1300 738 870; www.kimberleywild.com.au) Consistent award winner. Tours from Broome range from one ($229) to 14 days ($3995) on the Gibb River Road.

Kimberley Adventure Tours 4WD TOUR
(☎1800 083 368; www.kimberleyadventures.com.au; 3-/9-day tour $550/$1995) Small group camping tours from Broome up the Gibb, with the nine-day tour continuing to Purnululu and Darwin.

Wundargoodie Aboriginal Safaris CULTURAL TOURS
(☎08-9161 1145; www.wundargoodie.com.au; tag-along per vehicle $250, women-only 11-day tour $3500; ⏲Apr-Sep) These insightful Indigenous-run 4WD tagalong tours (ie, you bring your own vehicle) showcase local culture and rock art in the remote West Kimberley. The women-only tour is all-inclusive, camping at special sites and sharing experiences with Aboriginal women from various communities.

Information

Online, check out www.gibbriverroad.net and www.kimberleyaustralia.com or visit the **Derby** and **Kununurra** visitor centre websites.

For maps, take Hema's *Kimberley Atlas & Guide* ($40) or *Regional Map – The Kimberley* ($15).

Mainroads Western Australia (MRWA; ☎13 81 38; www.mainroads.wa.gov.au; ⏲24hr) Highway and Gibb River Road conditions.

Parks & Wildlife (DPaW; www.dpaw.wa.gov.au) Park permits, camping fees and information. A Holiday Pass ($44) works out cheaper if you will be visiting more than three parks in one month.

Shire of Derby/West Kimberley (☎08-9191 0999; www.sdwk.wa.gov.au) Side-road conditions.

Shire of Wyndham/East Kimberley (☎08-9168 4100; www.swek.wa.gov.au) Kalumburu/Mitchell Falls road conditions.

WORTH A TRIP

MITCHELL FALLS & DRYSDALE RIVER

Drysdale River

In the Dry, Kalumburu Rd is normally navigable as far as **Drysdale River Station** (08-9161 4326; www.drysdaleriver.com.au; sites $10-15, d $170-250; 8am-5pm Apr-Dec), 59km from the Gibb River Road, where there's fuel, meals and accommodation, and you can check ongoing road conditions. Scenic flights to Mitchell Falls operate from April to September (from $200 per person).

Mitchell Falls National Park

The **Ngauwudu** (Mitchell Plateau) turn off is 160km from the Gibb River Road, and within 6km a deep, rocky ford crosses the **King Edward River**, formidable early in the season.

On the shady banks of the King Edward river, many people prefer to camp at **Munurru Campground** (adult/child $10/2.20) rather than in Mitchell River National Park and then visit Mitchell Falls as a day trip. There's excellent Aboriginal rock art nearby.

From the Kalumburu Rd it's a rough 87km, past lookouts and forests of *livistona* palms to the dusty campground of **Mitchell River National Park** (entry per vehicle $12, camping adult/child $10/2.20). Leave early if walking to **Punamii-unpuu** (Mitchell Falls; 8.6km return). The easy trail meanders through spinifex, woodlands and gorge country, dotted with Wandjina and Gwion Gwion rock-art sites, secluded waterholes, lizards, wallabies and brolga.

The falls are stunning, whether trickling in the Dry, or raging in the Wet (when only visible from the air). You can swim in the long pool above the falls, but swimming in the lower pools is strictly forbidden because of their cultural importance to the Wunambal people. Most people will complete the walk in three hours.

Derby to Fairfield-Leopold Downs Rd Junction

The first 100-odd kilometres of the Gibb River Road are now sealed.

Mowanjum Art & Culture Centre GALLERY
(08-9191 1008; www.mowanjumarts.com; Gibb River Rd, Derby; 9am-5pm daily during dry season, closed Sat & Sun during wet season, closed Jan; P) Just 4km along the Gibb River Road from Derby, Mowanjum artists recreate Wandjina and Gwion Gwion images in this incredible gallery shaped like their artwork.

Birdwood Downs Station PASTORAL STATION
(08-9191 1275; www.birdwooddowns.com; camping $14, savannah huts per person with/without meals $139/81) About 20km from Derby, 2000-hectare Birdwood Downs offers rustic savannah huts, butterflies and dusty camping. WWOOFers are welcome and it's also the home of the **Kimberley School of Horsemanship**, with lessons, riding camps and trail rides (90-minute sunset ride $99).

May River CAMPGROUND $
Forty kilometres from Derby, a rough track heads left 12km to several bush camp sites on the May River.

King Leopold Ranges

Continuing along the Gibb River Road from Derby, the **Windjana Gorge** turn off at 119km is your last chance to head back to the Great Northern Hwy. The scenery improves after crossing the Lennard River into Napier Downs Station as the **King Leopold** ranges loom straight ahead. Just after **Inglis Gap** is the Mt Hart turn off and another 7km brings the narrow **Lennard River Gorge** (P).

Mt Hart Homestead CAMPGROUND
(08-9191 4645; sites per person $18, r per person incl dinner & breakfast $210; dry season;) Below Inglis Gap a rough 50km track leads to the remote Mt Hart Homestead with grassy camp sites, pleasant gorges, and swimming and fishing holes.

Imintji to Galvans Gorge

Despite its name **March Fly Glen**, 204km from Derby, is a pleasant, shady picnic area ringed by pandanus. Don't miss stunning **Bell Gorge** (per car $12; P), 29km down a rough track, with a picturesque waterfall and popular plunge pool. Refuel (diesel only), grab an ice cream and check your email at

Imintji Store (08-9191 7471; 8am-5pm dry season, shorter hrs wet season;).

Silent Grove CAMPGROUND
(adult/child $12/2.20; P) 19km from the Gibb, this sheltered, somewhat dusty Department of Parks & Wildlife campground in the King Leopold Ranges is popular with groups.

★**Mornington Wilderness Camp** WILDLIFE RESERVE
(08-9191 7406; www.awc.org.au; entry fee per vehicle $25; dry season) Part of the Australian Wildlife Conservancy, the superb Mornington Wilderness Camp is as remote as it gets, lying on the Fitzroy River an incredibly scenic 95km drive across the savannah from the Gibb's 247km mark. Nearly 400,000 hectares are devoted to conserving the Kimberley's endangered fauna and there's excellent canoeing, birdwatching and bush walking. Choose from shady camp sites (per adult $18.50, child $8) or spacious raised tents with verandahs (including full board single $320, double $570). The bar and restaurant offer full dinner ($60), BBQ packs ($19) and the best cheese platter ($25) this side of Margaret River.

Charnley River Station CAMPGROUND $
(08-9191 4646; www.awc.org.au; sites per person $20, day visit $20) Now under the management of the Australian Wildlife Conservancy, this historic station, 44km north of the Gibb, offers shady, grassy camp sites. Check out beautiful Grevillea and Dillie gorges, and Donkey Pool. There's also incredible rock art and bird life.

Over the Range Repairs MECHANIC
(08-9191 7887; 8am-5pm dry season) Between Adcock and Galvans gorges, Nev and Leonie are your best – if not only – hope of mechanical salvation on the whole Gibb.

Galvans Gorge GORGE
(P) A waterfall, lovely swimming hole, rock wallabies and Wandjina art all less than 1km easy stroll from the road.

Mt Barnett to Mt Elizabeth

Fuel up at **Mt Barnett Roadhouse** (08-9191 7007; 8am-5pm), 300km from Derby, and get your camping permit if choosing to stay at nearby Manning River Gorge.

Manning River Gorge CAMPGROUND $
(7km behind Mt Barnett Roadhouse; per person $20;) This dusty campground is often full of travellers waiting for fuel, but at least there's a good swimming hole and even hot showers.

Barnett River Gorge CAMPGROUND
(29km east of Mt Barnett Roadhouse) FREE Bush camp sites several kilometres off the Gibb down a sandy track.

Mt Elizabeth Station PASTORAL STATION
(08-9191 4644; www.mountelizabethstation.com; sites per person $20, s/d incl breakfast & dinner $185/370; Dry) Further up the Gibb (around 338km from Derby) is the turn off to Mt Elizabeth Station, one of the few remaining private leaseholders in the Kimberley. Peter Lacy's 200,000-hectare property is a good base for exploration to nearby gorges, waterfalls and Indigenous rock art. Wallabies frequent the camp site, and the home-style, three-course dinners ($45) hit the spot.

Kalumburu Rd to Home Valley

At 406km from Derby you reach the **Kalumburu** turn off. Head right on the Gibb River Road, and continue through spectacular country, crossing the mighty Durack River then climbing though the **Pentecost Ranges** to 579km where there's panoramic views of the Cockburn Ranges, Cambridge Gulf and Pentecost River.

Ellenbrae Station PASTORAL STATION $
(08-9161 4325; www.ellenbraestation.com.au; 70km east Kalumburu turn off; sites per person $15, bungalow d $155) Atmospheric Ellenbrae Station serves up fresh scones, rather dusty camp sites and quirky bungalows.

★**Home Valley Station** PASTORAL STATION $
(08-9161 4322; www.homevalley.com.au; sites adult/child $17/5, eco-tents sleeping 4 $190, homestead d from $250; P) The privations of the Gibb are left behind after pulling into amazing Home Valley Station, an Indigenous hospitality training resort with a superb range of luxurious accommodation. There are excellent grassy camp sites and motel-style rooms, a fantastic open bistro, tyre repairs and activities including trail rides, fishing and cattle mustering.

Pentecost River to Wyndham/Kununurra

At 589km from Derby you'll cross the infamous **Pentecost River** – take care as water levels are unpredictable and saltwater crocs lurk nearby. The last section of the Gibb Riv-

OFF THE BEATEN TRACK

KALUMBURU

Kalumburu is a picturesque mission nestled beneath giant mango trees and coconut palms with two shops and **fuel** (7am-11am & 1.30-4pm Mon-Fri, 8am-noon Sat). There's some interesting rock art nearby, and the odd WWII bomber wreck. You can stay at the **Kalumburu Mission** (08-9161 4333; kalumburumission@bigpond.com; sites per person $20, donga s/d $125/175), which has a small **museum** (admission $10; 11am-1pm), or obtain a permit from the KAC office to camp at **Honeymoon Bay** (08-9161 4378; sites $20) or **McGowan Island** (08-9161 4748; www.mcgowanisland.com.au; sites $20), 20km further out on the coast – the end of the road.

The road to Kalumburu deteriorates quickly after the Mitchell Plateau turn off and eventually becomes very rocky. You'll need a permit from the **DAA** (1300 651 077; www.daa.wa.gov.au) to visit Kalumburu and a visitors pass (valid for seven days) on entry from the **Kalumburu Aboriginal Community** (KAC; 08-9161 4300; www.kalumburu.org; visitors pass per car $50). Alcohol is banned at Kalumburu.

er Road is sealed. The Emma Gorge turn off is 10km past El Questro; 630km from Derby you cross King River and at 647km you finally hit the highway – turn left for Wyndham (48km) and right to Kununurra (53km).

El Questro Wilderness Park RESORT $
(08-9169 1777; www.elquestro.com.au; permit adult per day/week $12/20; dry season;) This vast 400,000-hectare former cattle station turned international resort incorporates scenic gorges (Amelia, El Questro) and Zebedee thermal springs (mornings only). **Boat tours** (adult/child $63/32; 3pm) explore **Chamberlain Gorge** or you can hire your own ($100). There are shady camp sites and air-con bungalows at **El Questro Station Township** (sites per person $20-28, bungalows d from $329;) and also an outdoor bar and upmarket **steakhouse** (mains $32 to $45). There are a million activities to choose from, but you'll pay for most of them.

Emma Gorge GORGE
(40min walk from the resort car park; P) Emma Gorge features a sublime plunge pool and waterfall, one of the prettiest in the whole Kimberley. The attached **resort** (safari cabin d from $289; Dry;) has an open-air bistro and expensive, stuffy cabins.

Devonian Reef National Parks

Three national parks with three stunning gorges were once part of a western 'great barrier reef' in the Devonian era, 350 million years ago. Windjana Gorge and Tunnel Creek National Parks are accessed via Fairfield–Leopold Downs Rd (linking the Great Northern Hwy with the Gibb River Road), while Geikie Gorge National Park is 22km northeast of Fitzroy Crossing.

Windjana Gorge NATIONAL PARK
(entry per car $12, camping adult/child $12/2.20; Dry; P) The walls of the gorge soar 100m above the Lennard River, which surges in the Wet but is a series of pools in the Dry. Scores of freshwater crocodiles lurk along the banks. Bring plenty of water for the 7km return walk from the campground.

★**Tunnel Creek** NATIONAL PARK
(per car $12, no camping; Dry; P) Sick of the sun? Then cool down underground at Tunnel Creek, which cuts through a spur of the Napier Range for almost 1km. It was the hideout of Jandamarra, an Indigenous guerilla fighter, in the 1800s. In the Dry, the full length is walkable by wading partly through knee-deep water; watch out for bats and bring good footwear and a strong torch.

Geikie Gorge NATIONAL PARK
(Darngku; Apr-Dec; P) Don't miss this magnificent gorge near Fitzroy Crossing. The self-guided trails are sandy and hot, so take one of the informative boat cruises run by either **Department of Parks & Wildlife** (08-9191 5121; 1hr tour adult/child $30/7.50; cruises from 8am May-Oct) or local Bunuba guides.

Tours

Bungoolee Tours CULTURAL TOUR
(08-9191 5355; www.bungoolee.com.au; 2hr tour adult/child $60/15; 9am & 2pm Mon, Wed & Fri during dry season) Bunuba lawman Dillon Andrews runs informative two-hour Tunnel Creek tours explaining the story of Jandamarra, as well as tag-along 4WD tours

on Leopold Downs Station. Overnighting is possible at simple Biridu camp site. Book through Fitzroy Crossing visitors centre.

Darngku Heritage Tours CRUISES
(☎0417 907 609; www.darngku.com.au; adult/child 2hr tour $70/60, 3hr tour $90/75, half-day tour $175/$138; ⊙Apr-Dec) Local Bunuba guides introduce Indigenous culture and bush tucker on these amazingly informative cruises through Geikie (Darngku) Gorge. A shorter one-hour cruise operates during the shoulder season (April and October to December).

Fitzroy Crossing to Halls Creek

Fitzroy Crossing

Gooniyandi, Bunuba, Walmatjarri and Wangkajungka people populate the small settlement of Fitzroy Crossing where the Great Northern Hwy crosses the mighty **Fitzroy River**. There's little reason to stay other than it's a good access point for the Devonian Reef national parks. Check out **Mangkaja Arts** (☎08-9191 5833; www.mangkaja.com; 8 Bell Rd, Fitzroy Crossing; ⊙noon-4pm Mon-Fri) with its unique acrylics, and the exquisite glass and ceramics at **Dr Sawfish** (☎0419 908 586; www.drsawfish.com; ⊙8am-4pm Mon-Fri, shorter hrs Sat & Sun), which is next to the tyre guy, whom you'll probably need. Camping and rooms are available at the atmospheric **Crossing Inn** (☎08-9191 5080; www.crossinginn.com.au; Skuthorpe Rd; unpowered/powered sites $30/38, r from $195; ❄@) and across the river at the upmarket **Fitzroy River Lodge** (☎08-9191 5141; www.fitzroyriverlodge.com.au; Great Northern Hwy; camping per person $15, tent d $160, motel d $220; ❄@🛜≋), which also offers decent counter meals ($22 to $36). There's a new, well-stocked supermarket, and the **visitor centre** (☎08-9191 5355; www.sdwk.wa.gov.au; ⊙8.30am-4pm Mon-Fri) and coach stop is just off the highway.

Mimbi Caves

★**Mimbi Caves** CAVES
(Mt Pierre Station) One of the Kimberley's best-kept secrets, this vast subterranean labyrinth, 90km south-east of Fitzroy Crossing, on Gooniyandi land, houses a significant collection of Aboriginal rock art and some of the most impressive fish fossils in the southern hemisphere. Indigenous-owned **Girloorloo Tours** (www.mimbicaves.com.au; 3hr tour adult/child $80/40; ⊙10am Tue-Sat Apr-Sep) runs trips including an introduction to local Dreaming stories, bush tucker and traditional medicines. Book through Fitzroy Crossing or Halls Creek visitor centres.

Larrawa Station

Larrawa Station CAMPGROUND $
(☎08-9191 7025; www.larrawabushcamp.com; Great Northern Hwy; sites $20, s with/without meals $120/70; @) Halfway between Fitzroy Crossing and Halls Creek, Larrawa makes a good overnight stop, with hot showers, basic camsites, a couple of shearers rooms,

OFF THE BEATEN TRACK

DUNCAN ROAD

Snaking its way east from Halls Creek before eventually turning north and playing hide and seek with the NT border, Duncan Rd is the Kimberley's 'other' great outback driving experience. Unsealed for its entire length (445km), it receives only a trickle of the travellers the Gibb River Road does, but those who make the effort are rewarded with stunning scenery, beautiful gorges, tranquil billabongs and breathtakingly lonely camp sites.

Technically no harder than the Gibb, all creek crossings are concrete lined and croc free. It also makes a nice loop if you've come down the Great Northern Hwy to Purnululu and want to return to Kununurra and/or NT. There are no services on the entire Duncan, so carry fuel for at least 500km. Enquire at Halls Creek or Kununurra visitor centres about road conditions.

The only accommodation on Duncan Rd is **Zebra Rock Mine** (Wetland Safaris; ☎0400 767 650; ruth.a.duncan@gmail.com; Duncan Rd, NT; sites per adult $10, sunset tour $90; ⊙Apr-Sep), which is 10km from the Victoria Hwy, and technically in NT. Travellers love the rustic vibe, and the sunset birdwatching tour is not to be missed. There's also a small cafe and gift shop.

WORTH A TRIP

PARRY LAGOONS NATURE RESERVE

This beautiful RAMSAR-listed wetland, 25km from Wyndham, teems in the Wet with migratory birds arriving from as far away as Siberia. There's a bird hide and boardwalk at **Marlgu Billabong** and an excellent view from **Telegraph Hill**.

The tranquil **Parry Creek Farm** (08-9161 1139; www.parrycreekfarm.com.au; Parry Creek Rd; unpowered/powered sites $34/37, r $125, cabins $230;), 25km from Wyndham and surrounded by Parry Lagoons Nature Reserve, has grassy camp sites that attract hordes of wildlife. Comfy rooms and air-con cabins are connected by a raised boardwalk overlooking a billabong for easy bird spotting. The licensed cafe serves excellent baked barramundi, wood-fired pizzas and other gourmet delights.

The Grotto (Great Northern Hwy) Just off the highway, 33km from Wyndham, steep steps lead down to a deep, peaceful pool in a small gorge, perfect for a quiet dip.

and meals (when available). There's also a three-room cottage.

Yiyilli

Laarri Gallery GALLERY
(08-9191 7195; www.laarrigallery.com; Yiyilli; 8am-4pm school days) This tiny not-for-profit gallery in the back of the community school has interesting contemporary-style art detailing local history. It's 120km west of Halls Creek and 5km from the Great Northern Hwy. Phone ahead.

Halls Creek

On the edge of the Great Sandy Desert, Halls Creek is a small town with communities of Kija, Jaru and Gooniyandi people. The excellent **visitor centre** (08-9168 6262; www.hallscreektourism.com.au; Great Northern Hwy; 7am-5pm) can book tours to the Bungles and tickets for Mimbi Caves. Check your email next door at the **Community Resource Centre** (inside the library, Shire Building; internet per hr $5; 8am-4pm Mon-Fri;). Across the highway, **Yarliyil Gallery** (08-9168 6723; www.yarliyil.com.au; Great Northern Hwy; 9am-5pm Mon-Fri) is definitely worth a look.

Kimberley Hotel (08-9168 6101; www.kimberleyhotel.com.au; Roberta Ave; r from $172, restaurant mains $22-46;) is your best lunch option and you can find a bed there or at **Best Western** (08-9168 9600; www.bestwestern.com.au; d $260;). There's a caravan park, but you're better off heading out of town.

Skippers (p198) flies from Fitzroy Crossing and Halls Creek to Broome and Greyhound (p198) passes through daily.

Wyndham

POP 900

A gold-rush town that has fallen on leaner times, Wyndham is scenically nestled between rugged hills and Cambridge Gulf, some 100km northwest of Kununurra. Sunsets are superb from the spectacular **Five Rivers Lookout** on Mt Bastion (325m) overlooking the King, Pentecost, Durack, Forrest and Ord Rivers entering Cambridge Gulf.

A giant 20m croc greets visitors entering town. The historic port precinct is 5km further and contains a small **museum** (08-9161 1857; Old Courthouse, Port Precinct; 10am-3pm daily during dry season) and pioneer graveyard.

Greyhound (p198) drops passengers 56km away at the Victoria Hwy junction; you'll need to arrange a pick up or **taxi** (0408 898 638) into town prior to arrival. Internet is available at the **Community Resource Centre** (CRC; 08-9161 1002; www.wyndham.crc.net.au; 990 Koojarra Rd; per hr $5; 8am-4pm Mon-Fri;).

Sleeping & Eating

Wyndham Caravan Park CARAVAN PARK $
(08-9161 1064; Baker St; unpowered/powered sites $25/35, donga d $70;) Laid-back park with shady, grassy camp sites.

Rusty Wheelbarrow B&B $$
(0408 902 887; www.facebook.com/pages/The-Rusty-Wheelbarrow-Bed-Breakfast; 1293 Great Northern Hwy; d $160;) Wyndham's newest accommodation is set on a 10-acre block 5km from town. Beautiful, elevated rooms, all with en suites, open onto a common airy 'breezeway'. Both continental and cooked breakfasts are available, there's

plenty of fresh fruit and you can even purchase a 'BBQ pack' should you feel like dining in.

★ **Rusty Shed** CAFE $
(08-9161 2427; www.facebook.com/TheRustyShedCafe; O'Donnell St, Port Precinct; mains $7-17; 8am-3pm Tue-Sun, dinner from 5.30pm Sun during dry season) This local favourite has great coffee, sophisticated breakfasts and delicious cakes and pastries. Opens for roast dinners on selected Sundays, sometimes with guest musicians.

Five Rivers Cafe CAFE $
(08-9161 2271; www.facebook.com/FiveRivers-Cafe; 12 Great Northern Hwy; meals $6-16; 7.30am-2pm Mon-Fri, 8am-1pm Sat, 8am-1pm & 5-8pm Sun) Enjoy an honest barra burger under the mango tree at this early opener. Excellent coffee, smoothies and breakfasts, as well as pizza on Sunday nights.

Kununurra

POP 6000

Kununurra, on Miriwoong country, is a relaxed town set in an oasis of lush farmland and tropical fruit and sandalwood plantations, thanks to the Ord River irrigation scheme. With good transport and communications, excellent services and well-stocked supermarkets, it's every traveller's favourite slice of civilisation between Broome and Darwin.

Kununurra is also the departure point for most of the tours in the East Kimberley, and with all that fruit, there's plenty of seasonal work. Note the Northern Territory is in the Australian Central time zone, which is 90 minutes ahead of Australian Western Standard Time.

Sights & Activities

Across the highway from the township, **Lily Creek Lagoon** is a mini-wetlands with amazing bird-life, boating and freshwater crocs. **Lake Kununurra** (Diversion Dam) has pleasant picnic spots and great fishing. Groups could consider hiring their own 'barbie' boat from **Kununurra Self Drive Hire Boats** (0409 291 959; Casuarina Way, near Lakeside Resort; from $174).

Don't miss the excellent **Waringarri Aboriginal Arts Centre** (08-9168 2212; www.waringarriarts.com.au; 16 Speargrass Rd; 8.30am-4.30pm Mon-Fri, 10am-2pm Sat dry season, weekdays only wet season; P), opposite the road to **Kelly's Knob**, a popular sunset viewpoint.

Mirima National Park NATIONAL PARK
(per car $12; P) Like a mini-Bungle Bungles, the eroded gorges of Hidden Valley are home to brittle red peaks, spinifex, boab trees and abundant wildlife. Several walking trails lead to lookouts, and early morning or dusk are the best times for sighting fauna.

Kununurra Historical Society Museum MUSEUM
(www.kununurra.org.au/khs/museum; Coolibah Dr; admission by gold-coin donation; 10am-3pm) Old photographs and newspaper articles document Kununurra's history, including the story of a wartime Wirraway aircraft crash and the subsequent recovery mission. The museum is opposite the country club exit.

Go Wild ADVENTURE SPORTS
(1300 663 369; www.gowild.com.au; 3-day canoe trips $220) Self-guided multi-day canoe trips from Lake Argyle along the Ord River, overnighting at riverside camp sites. Canoes, camping equipment and transport are provided; BYO food and sleeping bag. They also run group caving ($220), abseiling (from $150) and bushwalking (from $40) trips.

Tours

North West Airboats ADVENTURE TOUR
(0419 805 2780; www.northwestairboats.com; 45min trip $100) Possibly the biggest adrenalin hit you'll get in Kununurra: tie a huge fan to the back of a boat, connect it to a V8 and let it rip. Tours explore the rarely glimpsed lower Ord where salties frolic.

Kimberley Sunset Cruises CRUISE
(08-9169 1995; www.kimberleysunsetcruises.com.au; adult/child $85/35) Popular sunset 'BBQ Dinner' cruises on Lily Creek Lagoon and the Ord River. BYO drinks.

Triple J Tours CRUISE
(08-9168 2682; www.triplejtours.com.au; adult/child $180/140) Triple J cruises the 55km Ord River between Kununurra and Lake Argyle Dam.

Kingfisher Tours SCENIC FLIGHTS
(08-9168 1333; www.kingfishertours.net; per person from $290) Various flights around the Bungles, Cambridge Gulf, Kalumburu and majestic Mitchell and King George Falls.

THE KIMBERLEY'S ART SCENE

The Indigenous art of the Kimberley is unique. Encompassing powerful and strongly guarded Wandjina, prolific and puzzling Gwion Gwion (Bradshaws), bright tropical coastal x-rays, subtle and sombre bush ochres and topographical dots of the western desert, every work sings a story about Country.

To experience it firsthand, visit some of these Aboriginal-owned cooperatives; most are accessible by 2WD.

Mowanjum Art & Culture Centre (p201) This incredible gallery, shaped like a Wandjina image, features work by Mowanjum artists.

Waringarri Aboriginal Arts Centre (p206) This excellent Kununurra gallery-studio hosts local artists working with ochres in a unique abstract style. It also represents artists from Kalumburu.

Warmun Arts (☎08-9168 7496; www.warmunart.com; Great Northern Hwy, Warmun; ⏲9am-4pm Mon-Fri) Between Kununurra and Halls Creek, Warmun artists create beautiful works using ochres to explore Gija identity. Phone first from Warmun Roadhouse for a verbal permit.

Laarri Gallery (p205) This tiny not-for-profit gallery, located in the back of the Yiyilli community school, depicts local history through interesting contemporary-style art. It's 120km west of Halls Creek and 5km from the Great Northern Hwy.

Mangkaja Arts (p204) A Fitzroy Crossing gallery where desert and river tribes interact, producing unique acrylics, prints and baskets.

Yaruman Artists Centre (☎08-9168 8208; Kundat Djaru) Sitting on the edge of the Tanami, 162km from Halls Creek, Yaruman has acrylic works featuring the many local soaks (waterholes). The weekly mail run from Kununurra stops here (Ringer Soak).

Yarliyil Gallery (p205) Great Halls Creek gallery showcasing talented local artists as well as some of the Ringer Soak mob.

Warlayirti Artists Centre (☎08-9168 8960; www.balgoart.org.au; Balgo; ⏲9am-5pm Mon-Fri) This centre, 255km down the Tanami Track, is a conduit for artists around the area and features bright acrylic dot-style works as well as lithographs and glass. Phone first to arrange an entry permit.

Festivals & Events

Ord Valley Muster CULTURAL

(www.ordvalleymuster.com; ⏲May) For 10 days each May, Kununurra hits overdrive with a collection of sporting, charity and cultural events culminating in a large outdoor concert under the full moon on the banks of the Ord River.

Sleeping

There's a great variety of accommodation to choose from, and the more it costs, the more of a discount you'll get in the Wet. Watch out for mozzies if you're camping near the lake.

★ **Wunan House** B&B $

(☎08-9168 2436; www.wunanhouse.com; 167 Coolibah Dr; r from $90; P❄📶) Indigenous owned and run, this immaculate B&B offers light, airy rooms, all with en suites and TVs. There's free wi-fi, off-street parking and an ample Continental breakfast.

Hidden Valley Tourist Park CARAVAN PARK $

(☎08-9168 1790; www.hiddenvalleytouristpark.com; 110 Weaber Plains Rd; unpowered/powered sites $28/38, cabin d $125; @📶🏊) Under the looming crags of Mirima National Park, this excellent little park has nice grassy sites and is popular with seasonal workers. The self-contained cabins are good value.

Kimberley Croc Backpackers HOSTEL $

(☎1300 136 702; www.kimberleycroc.com.au; 120 Konkerberry Dr; dm $27-33, d $89-125; ❄@📶🏊) This slick, modern YHA close to the action has a large pool, barbecue area and excellent kitchen facilities. It also runs the nearby **Kimberley Croc Lodge** (☎08-9168 1411; www.kimberleycroclodge.com.au; 2 River Fig

Ave; dm per week $160; P❄📶≋) for seasonal workers.

Freshwater APARTMENT **$$**
(☎08-9169 2010; www.freshwaterapartments.net.au; 19 Victoria Hwy; studio/1-/2-/3-bedroom apts $224/249/329/399; P❄📶≋) Exquisite, fully self-contained units with exotic open-roofed showers.

Eating

The big resorts all have restaurants offering similar fare. There are two well-stocked supermarkets and several take aways. Most places keep shorter hours during the Wet, and you'll struggle to find lunch after 2pm.

★ **Wild Mango** CAFE **$**
(☎08-9169 2810; 20 Messmate Way; breakfasts $9-23, lunches $6-13; ⏰7.30am-4pm Mon-Fri, 8am-1pm Sat & Sun) 🌿 The hippest, healthiest feed in town with curry wraps, mouth-watering pancakes, chai smoothies, real coffee and homemade gelato. The entrance is in Konkerberry Dr.

Ivanhoe Cafe CAFE **$$**
(☎0427 692 775; Ivanhoe Rd; mains $12.50-24; ⏰8am-4pm Apr-Sep) Grab a table under the leafy mango trees and tuck into tasty wraps, salads and burgers, all made from fresh, local produce. Don't miss their signature mango smoothie.

★ **PumpHouse** MODERN AUSTRALIAN **$$$**
(☎08-9169 3222; www.thepumphouserestaurant.com; Lakeview Dr; lunches $19-36, dinners $32-45; ⏰4.30pm-late Tue-Thu, 11.30am-late Fri, 8am-late Sat & Sun; 📶) Idyllically situated on Lake Kununurra, the PumpHouse creates succulent dishes featuring quality local ingredients. Watch the catfish swarm should a morsel slip off the verandah. Or just have a beer and watch the sunset. There's an excellent wine list and free wi-fi.

Shopping

Artlandish ARTS
(☎08-9168 1881; www.artlandish.com; cnr Papuana St & Konkerberry Dr; ⏰9am-4.30pm Mon-Fri, 9am-1pm Sat) Stunning collection of Kimberley ochres and Western Desert acrylics to suit all price ranges.

Bush Camp Surplus OUTDOOR EQUIPMENT
(☎08-9168 1476; cnr Papuana St & Konkerberry Dr; ⏰8.30am-5pm Mon-Fri, 8.30am-noon Sat) The biggest range of camping gear between Broome and Darwin.

Information

ATMs are near the supermarkets. Most cafes don't offer free wi-fi.

Community Resource Centre (CRC; ☎08-9169 1868; Banksia St; per hr $6; ⏰9am-4pm Mon-Fri; @📶) Internet, printing and after hours self-service wi-fi.

Parks & Wildlife Office (☎08-9168 4200; Lot 248 Ivanhoe Rd; ⏰8am-4.30pm Mon-Fri) Parks information and permits.

Visitor Centre (☎1800 586 868; www.visitkununurra.com; Coolibah Dr; ⏰8am-4.30pm daily, shorter hr Oct-Mar) Check here for accommodation, tours, seasonal work and road conditions.

Getting There & Away

Airnorth (TL; ☎1800 627 474; www.airnorth.com.au) Flights to Broome and Darwin daily; Perth on Saturday.

Greyhound (☎1300 473 946; www.greyhound.com.au) Greyhound buses stop at the BP Roadhouse. There are six weekly services to Broome ($146, 13 hours) via Halls Creek ($91, four hours), Fitzroy Crossing ($106, seven hours) and Derby ($125, 10 hours), and six weekly services to Darwin ($128, 11 hours) via Katherine ($95, six hours).

Virgin Australia (☎13 67 89; www.virgin-australia.com.au) Flights to Perth several times weekly.

Getting Around

Avis (☎08-9168 1999), **Budget** (☎08-9168 2033) and **Thrifty** (☎1800 626 515) all have offices at the airport.

BP Roadhouse (Messmate Way) Petrol, long-distance bus stop, and 24hr laundromat.

Ordco (Weaber Plain Rd; ⏰24hr) Local co-op selling the cheapest diesel in Kununurra.

Taxi (☎13 10 08)

Purnululu National Park & Bungle Bungle Range

Looking like a packet of half-melted Jaffas, World Heritage **Purnululu National Park** (per car $12; ⏰Apr-Nov) is home to the incredible ochre and black striped 'beehive' domes of the Bungle Bungle Range.

The distinctive rounded rock towers are made of sandstone and conglomerates moulded by rainfall over millions of years. Their stripes are the result of oxidised iron compounds and algae. To the local Kidja people, *purnululu* means sandstone, with

Purnululu National Park

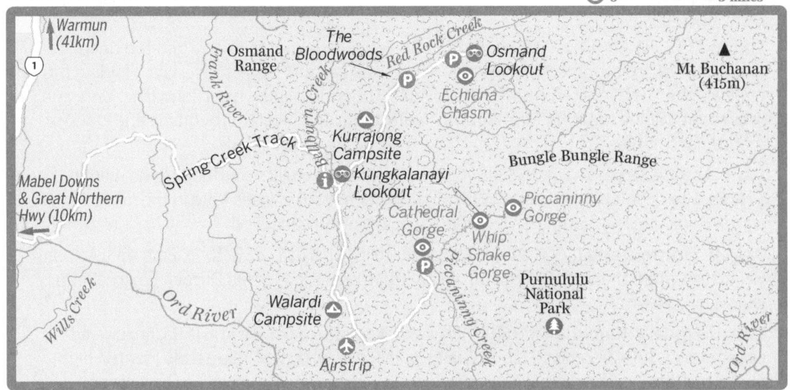

Bungle Bungle possibly a corruption of 'bundle bundle', a common grass.

Over 3000 sq km of ancient country contains a wide array of wildlife, including over 130 bird species. Whitefellas only 'discovered' the range during the mid-1980s. Rangers are based here from April to November and the park is closed outside this time.

You'll need a high clearance 4WD for the 52km twisting, rough road from the highway to the visitor centre near Three Ways junction; allow 2½ hours. There are five deep creek crossings, and the turn off is 53km south of Warmun. **Kurrajong** (sites per person $12; May-Sep) and **Walardi** (sites per person $12; Apr-Nov) camps have fresh water and toilets. Book camp sites online via **DPAW** (http://parkstay.dpaw.wa.gov.au/).

Sights & Activities

Kungkalanayi Lookout LOOKOUT
Sunsets are spectacular from this hill near Three Ways.

Echidna Chasm GORGE
(return 2km, 1hr) Look for tiny bats high on the walls above this palm-fringed, narrow gorge in the northern park. The trail leaves from the Echidna Chasm car park and is marked on the park map available from the rangers office.

Cathedral Gorge GORGE
Aptly named, this immense and inspiring circular cavern is an easy 2km (return) stroll from the southern car park .

Whip Snake Gorge GORGE
(return 10km, 4hrs) An energetic half-day outing from the southern car park to a shady gorge filled with ferns, figs and brittle gums. There's a small terminal pool.

Piccaninny Gorge GORGE
(return 30km, 2-3 days) A 30km return overnight trek from the southern car park to a remote and pristine gorge, best suited for experienced hikers.

Tours

Most Kimberley tour operators include Purnululu in multi-day tours. You can also pick up tours at Warmun Roadhouse, Halls Creek and Mabel Downs. Helicopters will get you closer than fixed-wing flights.

East Kimberley SCENIC FLIGHTS
(08-9168 2213; www.eastkimberleytours.com.au; 1-/2-/3-day tours $720/1593/1831, safari tents from $225) Several fly/drive tours of the Bungle Bungles departing Kununurra. Also offers accommodation inside the park.

Helispirit HELICOPTER
(1800 180 085; www.helispirit.com.au; 18/30/48min flights $225/299/495) Scenic chopper flights over the Bungles from Bellbird and Warmun. They also have flights over Mitchell Falls, Kununurra and Lake Argyle.

Bungle Bungle Expeditions BUS, HELICOPTER
(08-9169 1995; www.bunglebungleexpeditions.com.au; bus day/overnight $285/695, helicopter from $290) Various bus, helicopter and fixed-wing tours of the Bungles from the caravan park on Mabel Downs, near the highway.

WORTH A TRIP

LAKE ARGYLE

Enormous Lake Argyle, where barren red ridges plunge spectacularly into the deep blue water of the dammed Ord River, is Australia's second-largest reservoir. Holding the equivalent of 18 Sydney Harbours, it provides Kununurra with year-round irrigation, and important wildlife habitats for migratory waterbirds, freshwater crocodiles and isolated marsupial colonies.

Lake Argyle Cruises (08-9168 7687; www.lakeargylecruises.com; adult/child morning $70/45, afternoon $155/90, sunset $90/55) Popular sunset cruises take in the lake's highlights. Book ahead as under-subscribed trips are often cancelled.

Argyle Homestead (08-9167 8088; adult/child/family $4/2.50/10; 8am-4pm Apr-Sep) Relocated when the waters rose, this former home of the famous Durack pastoral family is now a museum.

Lake Argyle Village (08-9168 7777; www.lakeargyle.com; Lake Argyle Rd; unpowered/powered sites $30/37, cabins $125-219, units from $359;) Superbly located high above the lake, Lake Argyle Village offers grassy camp sites, a variety of cabins, and hearty meals from its licensed bistro. Don't miss a swim in the stunning infinity pool.

Sleeping

Mabel Downs CAMPGROUND
(Bungle Bungle Caravan Park; 08-9168 7220; www.bunglebunglecaravanpark.com.au; tent sites/powered sites $35/50, safari tents with/without enste $225/120, dinner $25;) Situated just 1km from the highway (outside Purnululu), don't expect much privacy. Tents are jammed between choppers and ridiculously long trailers. Various tours are available.

PORT HEDLAND TO BROOME

The Big Empty stretches from Port Hedland to Broome, as the Great Northern Highway skirts the Great Sandy Desert. It's 609km of willy-willies and dust and not much else. There are only two roadhouses, Pardoo (148km) and Sandfire (288km), so keep the tank full. The coast, wild and unspoilt, is never far away.

Sleeping

Places along the Great Northern Highway can be packed from May to September.

Eighty Mile Beach Caravan Park CARAVAN PARK $
(08-9176 5941; www.eightymilebeach.com.au; unpowered/powered sites $35/41, cabins $190;) Popular with fishermen, this shady, laid-back park 250km from Port Hedland backs onto a beautiful white-sand beach. Turtles nest from November to March.

Port Smith Caravan Park CARAVAN PARK $
(08-9192 4983; www.portsmithcaravanpark.com.au; unpowered/powered sites $30/40, dongas d $80, cabins $180) There's loads of wildlife at this park on a tidal lagoon, 487km from Port Hedland.

Barn Hill Station PASTORAL STATION $
(08-9192 4975; www.barnhill.com.au; unpowered sites $22, powered sites $27-35, cabins from $100) Barn Hill, 490km from Port Hedland, is a working cattle station with its own 'mini-Pinnacles'. It's especially popular among adventurous grey nomads (but all are welcome!).

Eco Beach RESORT $$$
(08-9193 8015; www.ecobeach.com.au; Great Northern Hwy, Thangoo Station; safari tent from $225, villa d from $345;) This award-winning luxury eco-resort is set on secluded coastline 120km southwest of Broome. There's a choice of safari tents (no air-con) or villas, a top-notch restaurant and a host of tours and activities. From Broome, you can reach the resort by light aircraft ($60), helicopter ($270) or your own vehicle.

BROOME

POP 16,000

Like a paste jewel set in a tiara of natural splendours, Broome clings to a narrow strip of red pindan on the Kimberley's far-western edge, at the base of the pristine Dampier Peninsula. Surrounded by the aquamarine waters of the Indian Ocean and the creeks, mangroves and mudflats of Roebuck Bay, this Yawuru country is a good 2000km from the nearest capital city.

The history of Broome is centred around its pearling industry and Broome's cemeteries are a stark reminder of this heritage, which claimed the lives of many Japanese, Chinese, Malay and Aboriginal divers. Broome's pearls, now produced on modern sea farms, are still exported around the world.

Cable Beach, with its luxury resorts, hauls in the tourists during high (dry) season (April to October), with romantic notions of camels, surf and sunsets. Magnificent, sure, but there's a lot more to Broome than postcards, and tourists are sometimes surprised when they scratch the surface and find pindan just below.

Broome's centre is Chinatown, on the shores of Roebuck Bay, while Cable Beach and its resorts are 6km west on the Indian Ocean. The airport stretches between the two; the port and Gantheaume Point are 7km south.

High season is a great time to find casual work in hospitality or out on the pearl farms. In low (wet) season, it feels like you're swimming in a warm, moist glove, and while many places close or restrict their hours, others offer amazingly good deals as prices plummet.

Each evening, the whole town pauses, collective drinks in mid-air, while the sun slips slowly seawards.

Sights & Activities

Cable Beach Area

★Cable Beach BEACH

(Map p214) Western Australia's most famous landmark offers turquoise waters and beautiful white sand curving away to the sunset. Clothing is optional north of the rocks, while south, walking trails lead through the red dunes of **Minyirr Park**, a spiritual place for the Yawuru people. Cable Beach is synonymous with camels, and an evening ride along the sand is a highlight for many visitors. Locals in their 4WDs swarm north of the rocks for sunset drinks.

Gantheaume Point & Dinosaur Prints LOOKOUT

FREE Beautiful at dawn or sunset when the pindan cliffs turn scarlet, this peaceful lookout holds a 135-million-year-old secret. Nearby lies one of the world's most varied collections of **dinosaur footprints**, impossible to find except at very low tides. (Hint: head off to the right of the cliffs but beware: rocks can be slippery.)

Reddell Beach BEACH

For a blistering sunset without tourists, camels or 4WDs, pull into any of the turnoffs along Kavite Rd between Gantheaume Point and the port and watch the pindan cliffs turn into molten lava.

Chinatown

Sun Pictures HISTORIC BUILDING

(Map p212; ☎08-9192 1077; www.sunpictures.com.au; 27 Carnarvon St; adult/child $17/12) Sink back in a canvas deck chair in the world's oldest operating picture gardens. Opened in 1916 to entertain the ever increasing local community (with few means of 'clean' entertainment), the cinema started showing silent movies, then progressed to reels with sound. These days, it still shows evening movies. The history of the Sun building is the history of Broome itself – different racial groups were assigned to different seats, floods were frequent and, planes flew

DON'T MISS

WWII FLYING BOAT WRECKS

On a very low tide it's possible to walk out across the mudflats from Town Beach to the **wrecks** (Map p212) of Catalina and Dornier flying boats attacked by Japanese 'Zeroes' during WWII. The planes had been evacuating refugees from Java and many still had passengers aboard. Over 60 people and 15 flying boats (mostly Dutch and British) were lost. Only six wrecks are visible, with the rest in deep water.

Start walking an hour before low tide, and head roughly southeast for 1.5km (about 30 minutes). Wear appropriate footwear – the mud is sticky and can hide sharp objects, not all of them inanimate. Watch out for marine hazards such as jellyfish and check with the visitor centre for tide times. The **museum** (p213) also has a handy brochure. Or just take the **hovercraft** (☎08-9193 5025; www.broomehovercraft.com.au; 1hr adult/child $119/85, sunset/flying boat $172/109).

Broome

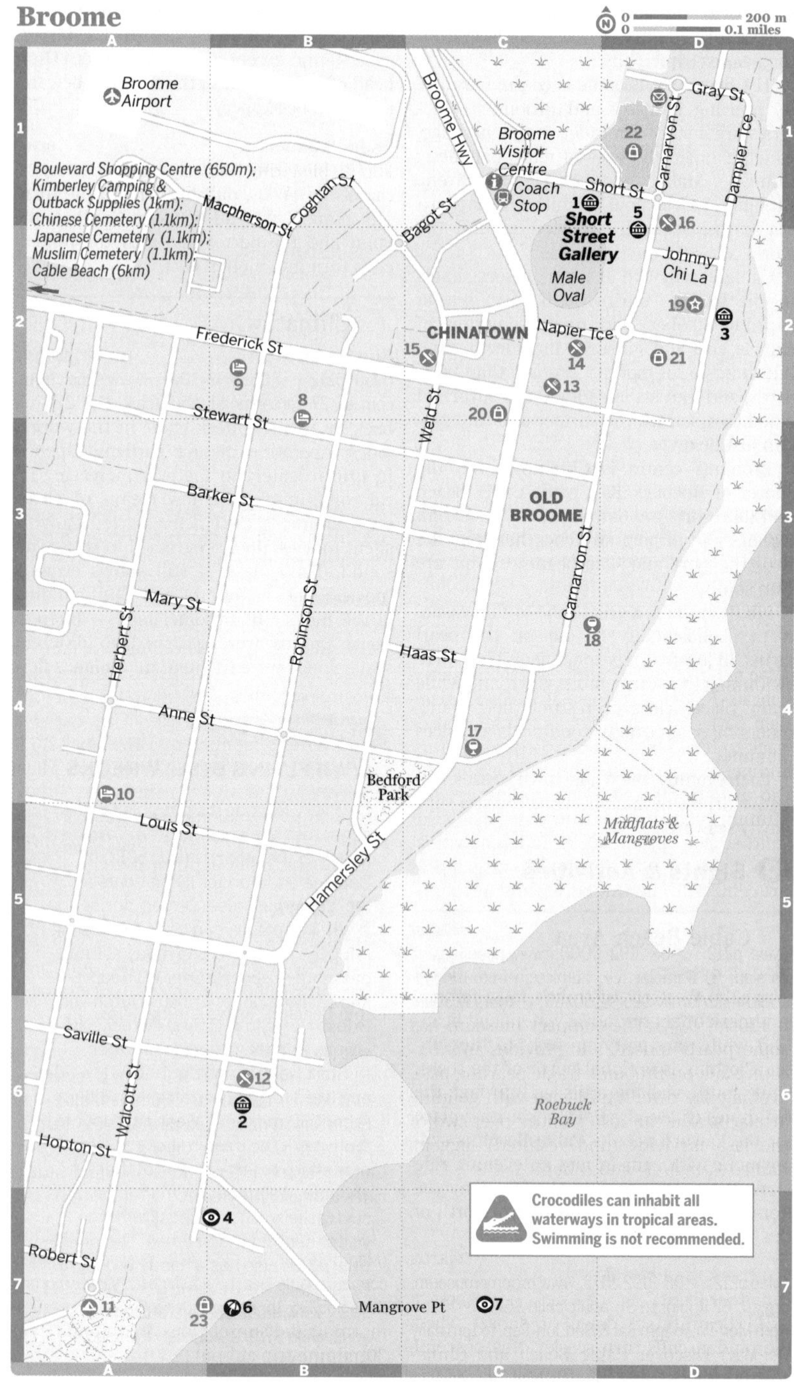
0 200 m
0 0.1 miles
A
B
C
D
1
2
3
4
5
6
7
Broome Airport
Boulevard Shopping Centre (650m); Kimberley Camping & Outback Supplies (1km); Chinese Cemetery (1.1km); Japanese Cemetery (1.1km); Muslim Cemetery (1.1km); Cable Beach (6km)
Macpherson St
Coghlan St
Bagot St
Broome Hwy
Broome Visitor Centre
Coach Stop
Short St
Gray St
Carnarvon St
Dampier Tce
1
Short Street Gallery
5
16
22
Johnny Chi La
Male Oval
19
3
CHINATOWN
Napier Tce
14
21
13
15
Frederick St
9
8
Stewart St
Weld St
20
Barker St
OLD BROOME
Carnarvon St
Mary St
Herbert St
Robinson St
18
Haas St
Anne St
17
Bedford Park
10
Louis St
Mudflats & Mangroves
Hamersley St
Saville St
12
2
Walcott St
Roebuck Bay
Hopton St
Crocodiles can inhabit all waterways in tropical areas. Swimming is not recommended.
4
Robert St
11
23
6
Mangrove Pt
7

Broome

Top Sights
1 Short Street Gallery C1

Sights
2 Broome Museum B6
3 Pearl Luggers D2
4 Pioneer Cemetery B7
5 Sun Pictures D2
6 Town Beach B7
7 WWII Flying Boat Wrecks C7

Sleeping
8 Broome Town B&B B2
9 Kimberley Klub B2
10 McAlpine House A4
11 Roebuck Bay Caravan Park A7

Eating
12 18 Degrees B6
13 Aarli C2
14 Azuki C2
15 Good Cartel C2
16 Yuen Wing D1

Drinking & Nightlife
17 Matso's Broome Brewery C4
18 Tides Garden Bar C4

Entertainment
19 Roebuck Bay Hotel D2

Shopping
20 Courthouse Markets C2
21 Kimberley Bookshop D2
22 Paspaley Shopping Centre D1
23 Town Beach Markets A7

directly overhead (as they do today; the cinema is located under the approach flight path). To hear about this and more, don't miss the evocative 15-minute **audio history** (1pm daily from April to October; $5).

★ **Short Street Gallery** GALLERY
(Map p212; ☎08-9192 6118; www.shortstgallery.com.au; 7 Short St; ⏰10am-3pm Mon-Fri, 11am-3pm Sat) This original building houses back-to-back exhibitions of contemporary Indigenous artworks. The stock room studio at 3 Hopton St, Old Broome holds a stunning collection of canvasses of all sizes (and some sculptures) by Indigenous artists. It's an agent for Yulparija artists plus art centres in the Kimberley and beyond.

Pearl Luggers MUSEUM
(Map p212; ☎08-9192 0000; www.pearlluggers.com.au; 31 Dampier Tce; admission free, 1hr tour adult/child/family $25/12.50/60; ⏰tours 11.30am & 3.30pm) FREE The compact museum has some 'pearls' indeed, and provides an interesting talk on Broome's tragic pearling past, evoking the diver experience with genuine artefacts. You can also wander over two of the last surviving (and restored) luggers, named *Sam Male* and *DMcD*.

Old Broome

Broome Museum MUSEUM
(Map p212; ☎08-9192 2075; www.broomemuseum.org.au; 67 Robinson St; adult/child $5/1; ⏰10am-4pm Mon-Fri, to 1pm Sat & Sun Jun-Sep, to 1pm daily Oct-May) Discover Cable Beach and Chinatown's origins through exhibits devoted to the area's pearling history and WWII bombing in this quirky museum, occupying the former Customs House.

Cemeteries
A number of cemeteries testify to Broome's multicultural past. The most striking is the **Japanese Cemetery** with 919 graves (mostly pearl divers). Next to this, the **Chinese burial ground** (Frederick St) has over 90 graves and monuments. The small **Muslim Cemetery** (Frederick St) honours Malay pearl-divers and Afghan cameleers.

A couple of kilometres southeast, the small **Pioneer Cemetery** (Map p212) overlooks Roebuck Bay at Town Beach.

Tours

Camel Tours
It's a feisty business, but at last count there were three camel-tour operators running at Cable Beach offering similar trips.

Broome Camel Safaris CAMEL TOUR
(Map p214; ☎0419 916 101; www.broomecamelsafaris.com.au; Cable Beach; 30min afternoon rides $25, 1hr sunset rides adult/child $70/55) Run by Alison, known as 'the Camel Lady', Broome Camel Safaris offers afternoon and sunset rides along Cable Beach.

Red Sun Camels CAMEL TOUR
(Map p214; ☎1800 184 488; www.redsuncamels.com.au; Cable Beach; adult/child 40min morning rides $55/35, 1hr sunset rides $75/55) As well as morning and sunset rides, Red Sun offers a 30-minute trip at 4pm ($30).

Cable Beach

Cable Beach

Top Sights
1 Cable Beach A2

Activities, Courses & Tours
2 Broome Camel Safaris B1
3 Red Sun Camels B1

Sleeping
4 Beaches of Broome C2
5 Broome Beach Resort C3

Eating
6 Cable Beach General Store & Cafe B3

Drinking & Nightlife
7 Sunset Bar & Grill B1

Entertainment
8 Diver's Tavern B3

Sundowner Camel Tours CAMEL TOUR
(08-9195 2200; www.sundownercameltours.com.au; Cable Beach; adult/child 40min morning rides $55/45, 30min afternoon rides $40/25, 1hr sunset rides $75/55) In addition to morning, afternoon and sunset rides, Sundowner also has a 'lapsitters' for the little 'uns ($10).

Not Camels

There's seemingly a million tours to choose from, from walking tours of Broome to scenic flights; visit the visitor centre for the full selection.

Broome Adventure Company KAYAKING
(0419 895 367; www.broomeadventure.com.au; 3hr trip adult/child $75/60) Glide past turtles on these eco-certified coastal kayaking trips.

Astro Tours ASTRONOMY TOUR
(0417 949 958; www.astrotours.net; adult/child $80/50) Fascinating after-dark two-hour stargazing tours with big telescopes and great commentary, held just outside Broome. Self-drive and save $15.

Kimberley Birdwatching BIRDWATCHING
(08-9192 1246; www.kimberleybirdwatching.com.au; 3/6/10/12hr tours $90/150/250/300) Join ornithologist George Swann on his informative Broome nature tours. Overnight trips are also available.

Broome Historical Walking Tours WALKING TOUR
(0408 541 102; www.broomehistoricalwalkingtours.com; adult/child $35/20) This fabulous 1½ hour walking tour examines the Broome

of yesteryear through site visits and photographs – from WWII back to the pearling days – with raconteur Wil telling some fabulous stories.

Lurujarri Dreaming Trail GUIDED TOUR
(Frans 0423 817 925; www.goolarabooloo.org.au; changing dates) This 82km song cycle follows the coast north from Gantheaume Point (Minyirr) to Coulomb Point (Minarriny). The Goolarabooloo organise a yearly guided nine-day trip (adult/student $1600/900), staying at traditional camp sites.

Festivals & Events

Broome hosts many festivals, the timing of which may vary from year to year. Check with the visitor centre (p217) or see www.visitbroome.com.au.

Broome Race Round SPORTS
(www.broometurfclub.com.au; Jul/Aug) Locals and tourists frock up and party hard for the Kimberley Cup, Ladies Day and Broome Cup horse races.

Shinju Matsuri Festival of the Pearl CULTURAL
(www.shinjumatsuri.com.au; Aug/Sep) Broome's homage to the pearl includes a week of parades, food, art, concerts, fireworks and dragon-boat races.

A Taste of Broome FOOD
(www.goolarri.com) Indigenous and multicultural flavours feature at this ticket-only event held monthly during high season. Alongside cuisine there are also music and dance events.

Sleeping

Accommodation is plentiful, but either book ahead or be flexible. Prices rocket during the high season and plummet in low season. If you're travelling in a group, consider renting an apartment.

Beaches of Broome HOSTEL $
(Map p214; 1300 881 031; www.beachesofbroome.com.au; 4 Sanctuary Rd, Cable Beach; dm $32-45, motel d without/with bathroom $140/180;) Beaches of Broome wins the hostel vote for clean, air-conditioned rooms, shady common areas, poolside bar and self-catering kitchen. Dorms come in a variety of sizes, while its motel-style rooms are well appointed. Scooter and bike hire available, and continental breakfast is included.

Kimberley Klub HOSTEL $
(Map p212; 08-9192 3233; www.kimberleyklub.com; 62 Frederick St; dm $25-33, d $99-120;) Handy to the airport, this popular, laid-back and slightly worn backpackers is a great place to meet other travellers.

Roebuck Bay Caravan Park CARAVAN PARK $
(Map p212; 08-9192 1366; www.roebuckbaycp.com.au; 91 Walcott St; unpowered sites $32, powered sites $37-50, on-site van d $90) Right next to Town Beach, this shady, popular park by the waterside has several camp site options.

★ **McAlpine House** B&B $$$
(Map p212; 08-9192 0588; www.pinctada.com.au; 55 Herbert St; d $185-420; P) A former pearl master's cottage (built in 1910), Lord McAlpine made this stunning house his Broome residence during the eighties, renovating it to its former glory. Rooms vary in size (some are squeezy), but a library, airy eating patio, pool and verandahs add to its charm. A canopy of trees, from mangos to frangipanis, provide cool relief from the heat.

Broome Town B&B B&B $$$
(Map p212; 08-9192 2006; www.broometown.com.au; 15 Stewart St, Old Broome; r $285; P) This delightful, boutique-style B&B has four spacious rooms with jarrah floors and lots of tropical charm. It epitomises Broome-style

STAIRCASE TO THE MOON

The reflections of a rising full moon rippling over exposed mudflats at low tide create the optical illusion of a **golden stairway** (Mar-Oct) leading to the moon. Between March and October Broome buzzes around the full moon, with everyone eager to see the spectacle. At **Town Beach** (Map p212) there's a lively **evening market** (Map p212) with food stalls, and people bring fold-up chairs, although the small headland at the end of Hamersley St has a better view. While Roebuck Bay parties like nowhere else, this phenomenon happens across the Kimberley and Pilbara coasts – anywhere with some east-facing mudflats. Other good viewing spots are One Arm Point at Cape Leveque, Cooke Point in Port Hedland, Sunrise Beach at Onslow, Hearson Cove near Dampier and the lookout at Cossack. Most visitor centres publish the dates on their websites.

architecture: high-pitched roofs and wooden louvres. Continental breakfast is served the communal pool area.

Broome Beach Resort APARTMENT $$$
(Map p214; ☎08-9158 3300; www.broomebeach-resort.com; 4 Murray Rd, Cable Beach; 1-/2-/3-bedroom apt $295/325/365;) Great for families and groups, these large, modest apartments surround a central pool and are within easy walking distance of Cable Beach.

Eating

Be prepared for 'Broome prices' (exorbitant), 'Broome time' (when it should be open but it's closed) and surcharges: credit cards, public holidays, bad karma. Service can fluctuate wildly – some excellent, others appalling – as most staff are just passing through. Most places close in low season.

You'll find cafes along Carnarvon St in Chinatown, while many resorts have in-house restaurants, though often you're just paying for the view.

Supermarkets are housed in several major shopping centres, including **Broome Boulevard** (106 Frederick St) and the central **Paspaley Shopping Centre** (Map p212; Carnarvon St & Short St). **Yuen Wing** (Map p212; ☎08-9192 1267; 19 Carnarvon St; 8.30am-5.30pm Mon-Fri, to 2pm Sat & Sun) grocery your best bet for spices, noodles and all things Asian.

Good Cartel CAFE $
(Map p212; ☎0406 353 942; 3 Weld St; snacks $7-15; 5.30am-2pm Mon-Fri, 6.30am-2pm Sat, 7am-2pm Sun) What started as a pop-up cafe is now *the* place in town to grab a great coffee, plus Mexican-themed snacks. Its popcorn tin seats pay homage to its location – behind the (new) Sun Pictures Cinema.

Cable Beach General Store & Cafe CAFE $
(Map p214; ☎08-9192 5572; www.cablebeachstore.com.au; cnr Cable Beach & Murray Rds; snacks $10-20; 6am-8.30pm daily;) Cable Beach unplugged – a typical Aussie corner shop with egg breakfasts, barra burgers, pies, internet and no hidden charges. You can even play a round of minigolf.

Azuki JAPANESE $$
(Map p212; ☎08-9193 7211; 1/15 Napier Tce; sushi $13.50-15, mains $22.50-38; 11am-2.30pm & 5.30-8.30pm Mon-Fri) Enjoy the exquisite subtlety of authentic Japanese cuisine at this tiny BYO restaurant, from the fresh sushi rolls to the wonderfully tasty bento boxes. The downside: it's closed on weekends.

Aarli TAPAS $$
(Map p212; ☎08-9192 5529; www.theaarli.com.au; 2/6 Hamersley St, cnr Frederick St; mains $24-38; 8am-late) 'Consistent' is how locals describe Aarli. Indeed, it cooks up some of the most inventive and tasty titbits in Broome, using local produce where possible. The Med-Asian fusion tapas are excellent, and the breakfasts are good, too. Depending on who makes it, coffee isn't bad either.

18 Degrees INTERNATIONAL $$
(Map p212; ☎08-9192 7915; www.18degrees.com.au; Shop 4, 63 Robinson St, Seaview Centre; mains $20-33) Broome's new and very contemporary spot whips up some great share plates, delicious mains (for example, barramundi parcels and lamb tenderloin) and boasts a wine and cocktail list as large as a crocodile smile.

Wharf Restaurant SEAFOOD $$$
(☎08-9192 5800; 401 Port Dr; mains $25.50-55; 11am-11pm) Settle back for a long, lazy seafood lunch with waterside ambience and the chance of a whale sighting. OK, it's pricey, but the wine's cold, the sea stunning and the chilli blue swimmer crab sensational. Just wait until after 2pm before ordering oysters (then they're half price!)

Drinking & Entertainment

Avoid wandering around late at night, alone and off your dial; it's not as safe as it may seem.

Tides Garden Bar BAR
(Map p212; ☎08-9192 1303; www.mangrove-hotel.com.au; 47 Carnarvon St; 11am-10pm) The Mangrove Resort's casual outdoor bar is perfect for a few early bevvies while contemplating Roebuck Bay. Decent bistro meals ($35 to $39) and live music (Wednesday to Sunday) complement excellent Staircase to the Moon viewing.

Sunset Bar & Grill BAR
(Map p214; ☎08-9192 0470; www.cablebeachclub.com; Cable Beach Club Resort, Cable Beach Rd; breakfast 5-10.30am, bar 4-9pm, dinner 5.30-9pm) Arrive around 4.45pm, grab a front-row seat, order a drink and watch the show – backpackers, package tourists, locals, camels and a searing Indian Ocean sunset shaded by imported coconut palms.

Matso's Broome Brewery PUB
(Map p212; ☎08-9193 5811; www.matsos.com.au; 60 Hamersley St; ⏰7am-midnight) Get a Pearler's Pale ale (or another home brew) into you at this popular spot; grab a bite (mains $20 to $42) and kick back to live music on the verandah.

Roebuck Bay Hotel LIVE MUSIC
(Map p212; ☎08-9192 1221; www.roebuckbayhotel.com.au; 45 Dampier Tce; ⏰11am-late) Party central, where Broome's 'old timers' come to play, the Roey's labyrinthine bars offer sports, live music, DJs, cocktails and – love it or hate it – wet T-shirts.

Diver's Tavern LIVE MUSIC
(Map p214; ☎08-9193 6066; www.diverstavern.com.au; Cable Beach Rd; ⏰11am-midnight) Diver's pumps most nights. Locals bands sometimes jam on Wednesday, but always on Sunday.

Shopping

The old tin shanties of Short St and Dampier Tce are chock-full of Indigenous art, jewellery (including pearl items, of course) and cheap, tacky souvenirs.

Kimberley Bookshop BOOKS
(Map p212; ☎08-9192 1944; www.kimberleybookshop.com.au; 4 Napier Tce; ⏰10am-5pm Mon-Fri, 10am-2pm Sat) Extensive range of books on Broome and the Kimberley.

Kimberley Camping & Outback Supplies OUTDOOR EQUIPMENT
(☎08-9193 5909; www.kimberleycamping.com.au; cnr Frederick St & Cable Beach Rd) Camp ovens and everything else you need for a successful expedition.

Courthouse Markets MARKET
(Map p212; Hamersley St; ⏰Sat morning year-round, Sat & Sun Apr-Oct) Local arts, crafts, music and general hippie gear.

Information

The Broome Tourism website (www.visitbroome.com.au) has a good gig guide and what's on page. Environs Kimberley (www.environskimberley.org.au) covers the latest environmental issues as well as projects across the Kimberley.

INTERNET ACCESS

Broome Community Resource Centre (CRC; ☎08-9193 7153; 40 Dampier Tce; per hr $5; ⏰8.30am-4.30pm Mon-Fri; @ wi-fi) Cheap printing, wi-fi and internet ($3 per hour).

Galactica DMZ Internet Café (☎08-9192 5897; 4/2 Hamersley St; per hr $5; ⏰9am-6pm Mon-Thu, 9am-8pm Fri & Sat; @ wi-fi) The usual geek stuff; behind McDonalds.

TOURIST INFORMATION

Broome Visitor Centre (Map p212; ☎08-9195 2200; www.visitbroome.com.au; Male Oval, Hamersley St; ⏰8.30am-5pm Mon-Fri, to 4.30pm Sat & Sun, shorter hrs during low season) Books accommodation and tours. Great for info on road conditions, Staircase to the Moon viewing, dinosaur footprints, WWII wrecks and tide times. Also sells books published by Indigenous publishing company Magabala Books. It's on the roundabout entering town.

Getting There & Away

If you're not on a long-haul road trip, by far the quickest and most convenient way to reach Broome is to fly in direct. Broome International Airport is located close to the centre (though in most instances, you'll need to grab a taxi from there.)

Bus services run between Perth and Derby. Many tours, especially to the Dampier Peninsula, run out of Broome.

AIR

Virgin Airlines (☎13 67 89; www.virgin-australia.com) Flies daily to Perth.

Qantas (☎13 13 13; www.qantas.com.au) Qantas has seasonal direct flights to and from eastern capital cities.

Airnorth (☎08-8920 4001; www.airnorth.com.au) Airnorth flies daily to Darwin (except Tuesday) and Kununurra, and to Karratha and Port Hedland twice weekly.

Skippers (☎1300 729 924; www.skippers.com.au) Flies to Fitzroy Crossing, Halls Creek and Port Hedland three times weekly.

BUS

Derby Bus Service (p200).

Integrity (☎08-9274 7464; www.integrity-coachlines.com.au; one way/return $340/646) Integrity Busline runs twice weekly between Broome and Perth and vice-versa.

Getting Around

Broome is a very spread out town and distances can be deceiving. If you're staying in Old Broome or Chinatown, the local bus is a handy way to get to beaches and attractions. Those staying in Cable Beach or wanting to explore the surrounding areas are best served by having their own set of wheels.

Town Bus Service (☎08-9193 6585; www.broomebus.com.au; adult $4, day pass $10)

The town bus links Chinatown with Cable Beach every hour (from 7.10am to 7.10pm mid-October to April, 8.40am to 6.40pm from May to mid-October). Under 16s ride free with an adult; unders 16s riding independently are charged $2.

Broome Cycles (☎08-9192 1871; www.broomecycles.com.au; 2 Hamersley St; per day/week $24/84, deposit $50; ⏰8.30am-5pm Mon-Fri, to 2pm Sat) Located in Chinatown with an additional branch at Cable Beach (☎0409 192 289; Old Crocodile Park car park, Cable Beach; ⏰9am-noon May-Oct) operating during the high season.

Broome Broome (☎08-9192 2210; www.broomebroome.com.au; 3/15 Napier Tce; per day cars/4WDs/scooters from $65/155/35) Local operator Broome Broome offers an unlimited kilometre option plus alternative insurance conditions to nationwide companies.

Britz (☎08-9192 2647; www.britz.com; 10 Livingston St) Britz hires campervans (per day from $50 to $300) and rugged 4WDs (per day $160 to $280), the latter essential for Gibb River Road.

Broome Taxis (☎13 10 08) One of several taxi services in town.

Chinatown Taxis (☎1800 811 772) Reliable service about town.

AROUND BROOME

Malcolm Douglas Wilderness Park WILDLIFE RESERVE
(☎08-9193 6580; www.malcolmdouglas.com.au; Broome Hwy; adult/child/family $35/20/90; ⏰2-5pm daily) Visitors enter through the jaws of a giant crocodile at this 30-hectare animal refuge 16km northeast of Broome. The park is home to dozens of crocs (there are feedings and informative talks at 3pm), as well as kangaroos, cassowaries, emus, dingos, jabirus and numerous other birds.

Broome Bird Observatory NATURE RESERVE
(☎08-9193 5600; www.broomebirdobservatory.com; Crab Creek Rd; admission by donation, camping per person $15, unit with shared bathroom s/d/f $50/85/100, chalets $165; ⏰8am-4pm Mar-Nov) On Roebuck Bay, this amazing bird observatory in a beautiful bush setting near an accessible beach 25km from Broome is a vital staging post for thousands of migratory birds (around 40 species), some travelling over 12,000km. Tours range from one-hour introductory 'walk and talks' ($20) or 2½-hour driving tours ($70) to a five-day all-inclusive course ($1290). You can even stay here in a unit or a self-contained chalet.

Dampier Peninsula

Stretching north from Broome, the red pindan of the Dampier Peninsula ends abruptly above deserted beaches, secluded mangrove bays and cliffs burnished crimson by the setting sun. This remote and stunning country is home to thriving Indigenous settlements of the Ngumbarl, Jabirr Jabirr, Nyul Nyul, Nimanburu, Bardi Jawi and Goolarabooloo peoples. Access is by 4WD, along the largely unsealed 215km-long Cape Leveque Rd.

On Cape Leveque Rd, turn left after 14km onto Manari Rd, and head north along the spectacular coast. There are bush camping sites (no facilities) at Barred Creek, Quandong Point, James Price Point and Coulomb Point, where there is a nature reserve.

If you wish to visit Aboriginal communities, accessed from Cape Leveque Rd, you must *always* book ahead (directly with your community hosts or through the Broome Visitor Centre); check if permits and/or payments are required. Look for the excellent booklet *Ardi – Dampier Peninsula Travellers Guide* ($5). You should be self-sufficient, though limited supplies are available. Many communities (or outstations) offer accommodation – formal or camping – plus fishing, kayaking and crabbing opportunities.

☞ Tours

★Chomley's Tours GUIDED TOUR
(☎08-9192 6195; www.chomleystours.com.au; 1-/2-day tours $280/520) Chomley's offers several excellent day and overnight tours of the Peninsula (including mudcrabbing and other activities), plus one-way transfers. Reduced rates for children.

Beagle Bay

Beagle Bay Church CHURCH
(☎08-9192 4913; admission by donation) Around 110km from Broome, Beagle Bay is notable for the extraordinarily beautiful mother-of-pearl altar at Beagle Bay church, built by Pallottine monks in 1918. There's no accommodation, but fuel is available (weekdays only). Book ahead and proceed directly to the church.

Middle Lagoon & Around

Middle Lagoon COMMUNITY
(☎08-9192 4002; www.middlelagoon.com.au; unpowered/powered sites $30/40, beach shelter d $50, cabins d $140-240) Middle Lagoon, 180km from Broome and surrounded by empty beaches, is superb for swimming, snorkelling, fishing and well, doing nothing. There's plenty of shade and bird life, and the cabins are great value.

Mercedes Cove CABINS $$$
(☎08-91924687; www.mercedescove.com.au; Pender Bay; eco tents/air-con cabins $150/300) Near Middle Lagoon and with its own secluded beach, Mercedes Cove offers isolation, with several appealing meshed huts ('eco tents') and air-con cabins with gorgeous views. It's very well-run (read attention to detail) and you can almost roll into the sea from your camp site – it's a 20m stroll down down a gently sloping sandy path.

Gnylmarung Retreat CAMPGROUND $
(☎0429 411 241; www.gnylmarung.org.au; sites per person $20, bungalows from $90) This small, low-key community near Middle Lagoon offers a limited number of secluded camp sites and basic bungalows, and is popular with fishers.

Pender Bay

★ **Whale Song Cafe** CAFE $$
(☎08-9192 4000; Munget; light meals $7-25; ⏲9am-3pm Jun-Aug) This exquisitely located eco-cafe overlooking Pender Bay serves fabulous organic mango smoothies, homemade gourmet pizzas and the best coffee on the peninsula. There's a tiny bush campground (camp sites per person $20) with stunning views, funky outdoor shower and not a caravan in sight. Telstra mobile reception available.

Goombaragin CAMPGROUND $$
(☎0429 505 347; www.goombaragin.com.au; Pender Bay; camp site per person $18, nature tent with shared bathroom $75, eco tent with bathroom $175, bungalow with bathroom $220;) This friendly spot has a couple of secluded camp sites, plus slightly worn safari tents, a fixed 'nature' tent (BYO food) and a comfortable bungalow. The location is superb – set on a bluff overlooking scarlet-hued (pindan) cliffs and the beach below.

Lombadina & Around

Lombadina COMMUNITY
(☎08-9192 4936; www.lombadina.com; entry per car $10, r with shared bathroom $170; ⏲office 8am-noon, 1-4pm Mon-Fri, weekends by prior arrangement) Between Middle Lagoon and Cape Leveque, Lombadina is located 200km from Broome. This beautiful tree-fringed village offers various tours (minimum of three people required) including fishing, whale watching, 4WD, mudcrabbing, kayaking and walking, which can be booked through the office. Accommodation is in backpacker-style rooms and self-contained cabins ($220 to $240), but there's no camping. Fuel is available on weekdays and there are lovely articles for sale at the Arts Centre (open weekdays).

Chile Creek COMMUNITY $$
(☎08-9192 4141; www.chilecreek.com; sites per adult/child $16.50/10, bush bungalows with shared bathroom $95, 4-person safari tents $185) Tiny Chile Creek, 10km from Lombadina down a very sandy track, offers basic bush camp sites and en-suite safari tents (minimum two-night stay), all just a short stroll to the creek, or 2km from the Indian Ocean. Good for birders.

Cape Leveque & Around

Cape Leveque (Kooljaman) CAMPGROUND
Cape Leveque is spectacular, with gorgeous white beaches and stunning red cliffs. Eco-tourism award-winner **Kooljaman** (☎08-9192 4970; www.kooljaman.com.au; entry per adult $5, unpowered/powered sites d $38/43, dome tents $65, cabins with/without bathroom d $170/145, safari tents d $275;) offers grassy camp sites, driftwood beach shelters, hilltop safari tents, and budget tents. There's a minimum two-night stay, and the place is packed from June to October. The BYO **restaurant** (☎08-9192 4970; mains $29-38, BBQ packs $22-26; ⏲8am-4pm & 6pm-10pm, Apr-Oct, lunch Nov-Mar) opens for lunch and dinner, or you can order a BBQ pack.

Brian Lee Tagalong Tours GUIDED TOUR
(☎08-9192 4970; www.brianleetagalong.com.au; Kooljaman; adult/child ½ day from $75/35, full day $125/75) Be sure to hook up with one of Kimberley's characters, Brian, whose trips are considered tops for fishing lovers and keen crabbers. Own car required.

Bundy's Tours CULTURAL TOUR
(☎08-9192 4970; www.bundysculturaltours.com.au; Kooljaman; adult $45-75, child $25-35) Bardi custodian Bundy offers a tour through local eyes, providing a wonderful insight into traditional customs, including bush tucker, fish poisoning and spear making.

★ **Cygnet Bay Pearl Farm** PEARL FARM
(☎08-9192 4283; www.cygnetbaypearls.com.au; Cygnet Bay) Overlooking stunning Cygnet Bay, this pearl farm-cum-tourist venture provides fascinating explanations of the pearling process (adult/child $27/10) and is home to the region's best restaurant (mains $17 to $50). Accommodation choices include camping ($90 per double), safari tents ($230 per double) or more luxurious pearlers' shacks (from $290 per double). Boat trips to the giant tides cost $155.

Ardyaloon (One Arm Point) COMMUNITY
(per person $10; ⏰8.30am-4.30pm Mon-Fri) The community of Ardyaloon (One Arm Point) has a well-stocked store, fuel, great fishing and swimming with views of the Buccaneer Archipelago. Entry to the community (which includes hatchery visit) is payable at the trochus hatchery. Note: there's no camping in Ardyaloon.

Gambanan CAMPGROUND $
(☎0427 786 345; near One Arm Point; per adult $20, under 12 free; ⏰end May-Sep) Offers little bling but this small outstation on the water, between Cape Leveque and Ardyaloon, has unpowered sites, a remote location and plenty of bush tucker trees.

Understand West Coast Australia

West Coast Australia Today

Welcome to a city, state and economy in flux, where the unbridled mining-led confidence and growth of the last decade has been replaced with a more clear-eyed view of future prospects and the need for a more diversified economy. The resources sector is still huge, but challenges lie ahead as Western Australia (WA) struggles with the implications of building an economy not so heavily dependent on getting stuff out of the ground and selling it.

Best on Film

Gallipoli (1981) Young men from rural WA enlist to fight as Anzac soldiers in the ill-fated Gallipoli campaign.
Rabbit-Proof Fence (2002) Three Aboriginal girls trek through the WA desert to be reunited with their families.
Japanese Story (2003) A touching film set in the Pilbara that's equal parts romance and thriller.
Tracks (2013) Recreating Robyn Davidson's epic 1975 journey by foot from Alice Springs to the Indian Ocean.

Best in Print

Cloudstreet (Tim Winton, 1991) A chronicle of post-WWII working-class families sharing a house in Perth.
Sand (John Kinsella and Robert Drewe, 2010) Poetry and prose exploring the role of sand in the Australian psyche.
That Deadman Dance (Kim Scott, 2011) Novel exploring the 19th-century interactions between settlers, whalers and the Indigenous Noongar people of Albany.
Eyrie (Tim Winton, 2014) WA's best-known author usurps his usual focus on wide open spaces in this blackly comedic novel set in a Fremantle apartment block.

A Newly Cautious Economy

Fuelled by mega-construction projects of mines, ports, railways and roads designed to harness the state's mineral wealth, for more than a decade WA has enjoyed the country's fastest growing economy. In late 2014, that record came to an end as the property-led economy of New South Wales knocked WA off the number one spot, and resources growth in the Northern Territory also increased its economic impetus. Two key reasons account for WA's economic cooling: the mining sector has moved from a capital- and labour-intensive construction phase to an export phase, and China's rapacious demand for iron ore has eased. Indian demand remains strong and the Chinese economy will no doubt fire up again, but a diminishing confidence in the Western Australian economy and a weakening of the Australian dollar indicate the growing need to diversify.

In the state capital of Perth, city-altering construction projects – including new urban developments, a new hospital and a football stadium – continue unabated, but with the revelation that WA state debt has ballooned beyond $20 billion, there is a real chance that future generations may eventually pay for the city's current impetuous growth through cuts in facilities and services.

Past, Present & Future

The year 2014 marked a very important anniversary in Australian history: the centennial commemorations of when Australian soldiers and nurses travelled from afar to take part in WWI. Up to 65% of Australian servicemen were killed or wounded in 'The Great War' – one of the highest national casualty rates for the war – and poignant memorials are now dotted in sleepy farming and fishing towns across WA. Many of the servicemen and women left Australian shores by boat from WA's King George Sound, and the recently opened National

Anzac Centre in the southwestern city of Albany is a fitting tribute to their journey and sacrifice. Many New Zealand troops also departed from Albany, and the new museum is an essential destination for visitors of all nationalities.

In the 21st century, Australian air-force personnel are once again fighting in the Middle East as part of a coalition intervention in Syria and Iraq, but the increasingly cosmopolitan, ethnic make-up of Perth is a powerful antidote to the divisive hate that might otherwise arise. Immigrants from the Philippines, Korea, India and Thailand are Perth's fastest growing groups, giving the city an increasingly multicultural ambience and reinforcing it's almost as far to Sydney or Melbourne as Singapore or Jakarta.

Tourism Bounces Back

Battling the impact of a strong Australian dollar, the last few years have been tough for the Western Australian tourism industry. Now that Australia's currency has eased, the state's tourism operators are enjoying more success. International visitors have increased by 7.5%, new flights are maximising Perth's proximity to Asia, and Singaporean, Malaysian and Chinese travellers are three of the top five highest-spending nationalities visiting WA. Other key trends include the expansion of tourism in the spectacular Kimberley region, and the growth in Indigenous tourism offerings.

Fuelled by both international visitors and Australia's ever-expanding armada of 'grey nomads' – retired Australian baby boomers exploring their own country in campervans or caravans – accommodation in the Kimberley and along the famed Gibb River Road is becoming more comfortable. Local Indigenous people have identified the best way to preserve their culture is to share it with tourists, and recently launched operators run tours to millennia-old petroglyphs (rock carvings) and subterranean caves. In Perth and the state's southwest, local food, wine and craft beer are increasingly seen as opportunities to engage with visitors, and farmers markets, cooking classes and culinary festivals are all growing in popularity. In an Australian state getting used to a reduced share of overall income from the mining sector, such diversification in tourism is very important.

POPULATION: **2.57 MILLION**

POPULATION GROWTH: **2.4%**

AREA: **2,529,875 SQ KM**

GDP: **$2.56 BILLION**

GDP GROWTH: **2.8%**

UNEMPLOYMENT: **5.2%**

if Perth were 100 people

65 would be born in Australia
11 would be born in the UK
3 would be born in New Zealand
21 would be born elsewhere

belief systems

(% of population)

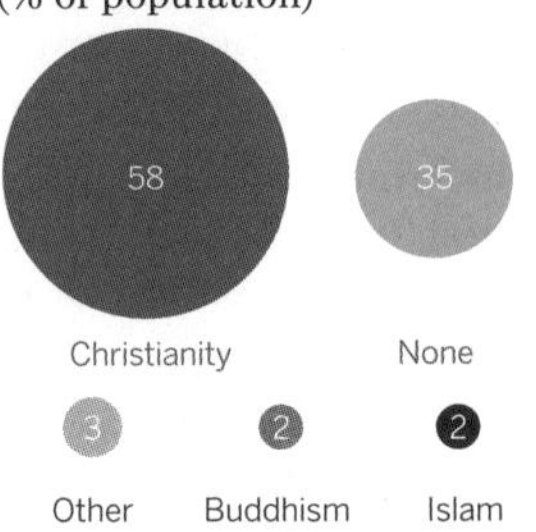

population per sq km

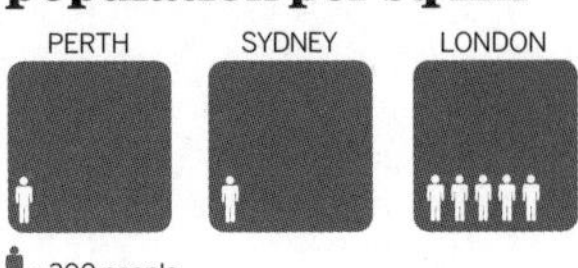

≈ 300 people

History

Michael Cathcart

The story of Western Australia's history is one of hardship, boom, bust, and boom again. Human history started some 40,000 years ago, when the first people are thought to have arrived – although some argue that this could have occurred as long as 65,000 years ago.

Michael Cathcart teaches history at the Australian Centre, University of Melbourne. He is well known as a broadcaster on ABC Radio National and has presented history programs on ABC TV.

Dirk Hartog is considered the first European explorer to land on the shores of Western Australia (WA) – as a record of his journey he displayed a pewter plate on an island in Shark Bay in 1616, now known as Dirk Hartog Island.

The British set up a military base in Albany, in the south of the state, in 1826. Perth was then founded in 1829, when Captain James Stirling declared all surrounding land property of King George IV.

In 1829 immigrants led by Stirling arrived in the territory of the Noongar people, sparking controversy between the two groups. Conflict with the Indigenous population continued, notably in the Battle of Pinjarra (1834), when some 25 Aboriginal people and one European were killed.

WA began its economic transformation with the discovery of gold in the 1880s and the inception of the nickel boom in the early 1960s, albeit thwarted by the two world wars and the Depression. Riches from the mines at Mt Newman, Tom Price and Kalgoorlie, among several others, dovetailed into the economic bubble of the 1980s, which burst when WA Inc (as the dealings among select businessmen and state politicians came to be known) was discovered to have lost $600 million in public money. Ever enterprising, it was not long, however, before the state was soon back on its feet, enjoying untrammelled economic mining growth and development.

Recently the Chinese economy's appetite for Australian iron ore has cooled, causing the Australian economy and dollar to stumble, but mining and the resource sector remain an inextricable part of WA.

TIMELINE

40,000 BC

First humans arrive on the shores of Australia.

4000 BC

Aboriginal communities from northwestern Australia trade and interact with Macassan fishermen from Sulawesi.

1616

Dutch explorer Dirk Hartog lands on an island in Shark Bay, marking his visit with a pewter plate on which he inscribed a record of his visit.

First Arrivals

People first arrived on the northern shores of Australia at least 40,000 years ago. As they began building shelters, cooking food and telling each other tales, they left behind signs of their activities. They left layers of carbon – the residue of their ancient fires – deep in the soil. Piles of shells and fish bones mark the places where these people hunted and ate. And on rock walls across WA they left paintings and etchings, some thousands of years old, which tell their stories of the Dreaming, that spiritual dimension where the earth and its people were created, and the law was laid down.

Contrary to popular belief, these Aboriginal people, especially those who lived in the north, were not entirely isolated from the rest of the world. Until 6000 years ago, they were able to travel and trade across a bridge of land that connected Australia to New Guinea. Even after white occupation, the Aboriginal people of the northern coasts regularly hosted Macassan fishermen from Sulawesi, with whom they traded and socialised.

When European sailors first stumbled on the coast of 'Terra Australis', the entire continent was occupied by hundreds of Aboriginal groups, living in their own territories and maintaining their own distinctive languages and traditions. The fertile Swan Valley around Perth, for example, is the customary homeland of about a dozen groups of Noongar people, each speaking a distinctive dialect.

Today Western Australia (WA), the largest state in the country, is also the most sparsely populated, being home to less than 10% of the population.

The prehistory of Australia is filled with tantalising mysteries. In the Kimberley, scholars and amateur sleuths are fascinated by the so-called Bradshaw paintings. These enigmatic and mystical stick figures are thousands of years old. Because they look nothing like the artwork of any other Aboriginal group, the identity of the culture that created them is the subject of fierce debate.

Meanwhile there are historians who claim the Aboriginal peoples' first contact with the wider world occurred when a Chinese admiral, Zheng He, visited Australia in the 15th century. Others say that Portuguese navigators mapped the continent in the 16th century.

Early Dutch Exploration

Most authorities believe that the first man to travel any great distance to see Aboriginal Australia was a Dutchman named Willem Janszoon. In 1606 he sailed the speedy little ship *Duyfken* out of the Dutch settlement at Batavia (modern Jakarta) to scout for the Dutch East India Company, and found Cape York (the pointy bit at the top of Australia), which he thought was an extension of New Guinea.

1629

Debauchery, rape and murder break out while the *Batavia* is shipwrecked at the Houtman Abrolhos Islands. All crew but two are subsequently executed at senior merchant Francisco Pelsaert's behest.

1644

Dutchman Abel Tasman charts the western and southern coasts of Australia.

1697

Willem de Vlamingh replaces Hartog's plate with his own.

1826

The British army establishes a military post in Albany, on the southern coast.

Ten years later, another Dutch ship, the *Eendracht,* rode the mighty trade winds across the Atlantic, bound for the 'spice islands' of modern Indonesia. But the captain, Dirk Hartog, misjudged his position, and stumbled onto the island (near Gladstone) that now bears his name. Hartog inscribed the details of his visit onto a pewter plate and nailed it to a post. In 1697, the island was visited by a second Dutch explorer, named Willem de Vlamingh, who swapped Hartog's plate for one of his own.

Other Dutch mariners were not so lucky. Several ships were wrecked on the uncharted western coast of the Aboriginal continent. The most infamous of these is the *Batavia.* After the ship foundered in the waters off modern Geraldton in 1629, the captain, Francisco Pelsaert, sailed a boat to the Dutch East India Company's base at Batavia. While his back was turned, some crewmen unleashed a nightmare of debauchery, rape and murder on the men, women and children who had been on the ship. When Pelsaert returned with a rescue vessel, he executed the murderers, sparing only two youths whom he marooned on the beach of the continent they knew as New Holland. Some experts believe the legacy of these boys can be found in the sandy hair and the Dutch-sounding words of some local Aboriginal peoples. The remains of the *Batavia* and other wrecks are now displayed at the Western Australian Museum in Geraldton and in the Fremantle Shipwreck Galleries, where you can also see de Vlamingh's battered old plate.

The Dutch were businessmen, scouring the world for commodities. Nothing they saw on the dry coasts of this so-called 'New Holland' convinced them that the land or its native people offered any promise of profit. When another Dutchman named Abel Tasman charted the western and southern coasts of Australia in 1644, he was mapping not a commercial opportunity but a maritime hazard.

The British Claim the West Coast

Many of the first ships to bring convicts to WA were whalers. Human cargo would be unloaded and then the ships continued whaling.

Today the dominant version of Australian history is written as though Sydney is the only wellspring of Australia's identity. But when you live in WA, history looks very different. In Sydney, white history traditionally begins with Captain James Cook's epic voyage of 1770, in which he mapped the east coast. But Cook creates little excitement in Albany, Perth or Geraldton – places he never saw.

Cook's voyage revealed that the eastern coastline was fertile, and he was particularly taken with the diversity of plant life at the place he called 'Botany Bay'. Acting on Cook's discovery, the British government decided to establish a convict colony there. The result was the settlement of Sydney in 1788 – out of which grew the great sheep industry of Australia.

1829

Led by Captain James Stirling, a boatload of free immigrants land in the territory of the Noongar people.

1829

Governor Stirling declares all surrounding Aboriginal lands to be the property of King George IV. Perth is founded.

1834

The Battle of Pinjarra occurs after Stirling leads a punitive expedition against the Noongar. It is thought that 25 Aboriginal people are shot, with Stirling's camp suffering one fatality.

1840–41

An Aboriginal man called Wylie and explorer Edward Eyre make a staggering journey across the Nullarbor Plain to Albany.

By the early 19th century, it was clear that the Dutch had no inclination to settle WA. Meanwhile, the British were growing alarmed by the activities of the French in the region. So on Christmas Day 1826, the British army warned them off by establishing a lonely military outpost at Albany, on the strategically important southwestern tip of the country.

The Founding of Perth

The challenge to Aboriginal supremacy in the west began in 1829, when a boatload of free immigrants arrived with all their possessions in the territory of the Noongar people. This group was led by Captain James Stirling – a swashbuckling and entrepreneurial naval officer – who had investigated the coastal region two years earlier. Stirling had convinced British authorities to appoint him governor of the new settlement, and promptly declared all the surrounding Aboriginal lands to be the property of King George IV. Such was the foundation of Perth.

Stirling's glowing reports had fired the ambitions of English adventurers and investors, and by the end of the year, 25 ships had reached the colony's port at Fremantle. Unlike their predecessors in Sydney, these settlers were determined to build their fortunes without calling on government assistance and without the shame of using convict labour.

The founding of Perth is most famously depicted in George Pitt Morison's painting *The Foundation of Perth* (1829). It is often erroneously credited as an authentic record of the ceremony rather than a historical reconstruction.

Frontier Conflict

As a cluster of shops, houses and hotels rose on the banks of the Swan River, settlers established sheep and cattle runs in the surrounding country. This led to conflict with Aboriginal people, following a pattern which was tragically common throughout the Australian colonies. The Aboriginal people speared sheep and cattle – sometimes for food, sometimes as an act of defiance. In the reprisals that resulted, people on both sides were killed, and by 1832 it was clear that Aboriginal people were organising a violent resistance. Governor Stirling declared that he would retaliate with such 'acts of decisive severity as will appal them as people for a time and reduce their tribe to weakness'.

In October 1834 Stirling showed he was a man of his word. He led a punitive expedition against the Noongar, who were under the leadership of the warrior Calyute. In the Battle of Pinjarra, the governor's forces shot, according to one report, around 25 people and suffered one fatality themselves. This display of official terror had the desired effect. The Noongar ended their resistance and the violence of the frontier moved further out.

The Deployment of Convicts

Aboriginal resistance was not the only threat to the survival of this most isolated outpost of the British Empire. The arid countryside, the loneliness

1850

Shiploads of male convicts start to arrive in Fremantle. They go on to build key historical buildings such as Fremantle prison, Government House and Perth Town Hall.

1860s

With no democracy, a network of city merchants and squatters exercises control over the colony.

1880s–90s

Gold changes everything. The first discoveries are in the Kimberley and the Pilbara, followed by massive finds in Coolgardie and Kalgoorlie.

1890

The state's first trade unions are formed by three men. Unions exert a substantial influence for the following century.

and the cost of transport also took their toll. When tough men of capital could make a fortune in the east, there were few good reasons to struggle against the frustrations of the west, and most of the early settlers left. Two decades on, there were just 5000 Europeans holding out on the western edge of the continent. Some of the capitalists who had stayed began to rethink their aversion to using cheap prison labour.

Built by convicts, the Fremantle Arts Centre was once a lunatic asylum and then a poorhouse, or 'women's home'. Today this Gothic building is a thriving arts centre that's well worth a visit.

In 1850 – just as the practice of sending British convicts to eastern Australia ended – shiploads of male convicts started to arrive in Fremantle harbour.

Exploration & Gold

Meanwhile, several explorers undertook journeys into the remote Aboriginal territories, drawn in by dreams of mighty rivers and rolling plains of grass 'further out'. Mostly their thirsty ordeals ended in disappointment. But the pastoralists did expand through much of the southwestern corner of WA, while others took up runs on the rivers of the northwest and in the Kimberley.

Perhaps the most staggering journey of exploration was undertaken by an Aboriginal man called Wylie and the explorer Edward Eyre, who travelled from South Australia, across the vast, dry Nullarbor Plain, to Albany.

By the 1880s, the entire European population of this sleepy western third of Australia was not much more than 40,000 people. In the absence of democracy, a network of city merchants and large squatters exercised political and economic control over the colony.

The great agent of change was gold. The first discoveries were made in the 1880s in the Kimberley and the Pilbara, followed by huge finds in the 1890s at Coolgardie and Kalgoorlie, in hot, dry country 600km inland from Perth. So many people were lured by the promise of gold that the population of the colony doubled and redoubled in a single decade. But the easy gold was soon exhausted, and most independent prospectors gave way to mining companies who had the capital to sink deep shafts. Soon the miners were working not for nuggets of gold but for wages. Toiling in hot, dangerous conditions, these men banded together to form trade unions, which remained a potent force in the life of WA throughout the following century.

The Great Pipeline to Kalgoorlie

The year 1890 also saw the introduction of representative government, a full generation after democracy had arrived in the east. The first elected premier was a tough, capable bushman named John Forrest, who borrowed courageously in order to finance vast public works to encourage immigrants and private investors. He was blessed with the services of

1890

Representative government is formed. Bushman John Forrest is the first elected premier.

1893

Inception of the Education Act, which allows white parents to bar Aboriginal children from schools. What follows is a policy of removal of 'half-caste' children from their parents.

1901

Western Australia (WA) and the other colonies are federated to form the nation of Australia.

1902

Following false accusations of incompetence and corruption, CY O'Connor, engineer of the great pipeline from Perth to Kalgoorlie, takes his own life at a Fremantle beach.

a brilliant civil engineer, CY O'Connor. O'Connor oversaw the improvement of the Fremantle harbour, and built and ran the state's rail system. But O'Connor's greatest feat was the construction of a system of steam-powered pumping stations along a mighty pipeline to drive water uphill, from Mundaring Weir near Perth to the thirsty goldfields around distant Kalgoorlie.

By the time Forrest opened the pipeline, O'Connor was dead. His political enemies had defamed him in the press and in parliament, falsely accusing him of incompetence and corruption. On 10 March 1902, O'Connor rode into the surf near Fremantle and shot himself. Today, the site of his anguish is commemorated by a haunting statue of him on horseback, which rises out of the waves at South Beach.

Ironically, just as the water began to flow, the mining industry went into decline. But the 'Golden Pipeline' continues to supply water to the mining city of Kalgoorlie, where gold is once again being mined, on a Herculean-scale unimaginable a century ago. Today you can visit the No 1 Pump Station at Mundaring Weir and follow the Golden Pipeline Heritage Trail as a motorist from Perth to Kalgoorlie, where you can visit the rather astonishing Super Pit.

The Stolen Generations

At the turn of the century, the lives of many Aboriginal people became more wretched. The colony's 1893 Education Act empowered the parents of white schoolchildren to bar any Aboriginal child from attending their school, and it was not long before Aboriginal children were completely excluded from state-run classrooms. The following decade, the government embarked on a policy of removing so-called 'half-caste' children from their parents, placing them with white families or in government institutions. The objective of the policy was explicit. Full-blood Aboriginal people were to be segregated, in the belief that they were doomed to extinction, while half-caste children were expected to marry whites, thereby breeding Aboriginal people out of existence. These policies inflicted great suffering and sorrow on the many Aboriginal peoples who were recognised in the 1990s as 'the stolen generations'.

Kim Scott's *Benang* (1999), which won the Miles Franklin Award in 2000, is a confronting but rewarding read about the assimilation policies of the 20th century and the devastating effect they had on Aboriginal Australia.

Wars & the Depression

On 1 January 1901, WA and the other colonies federated to form the nation of Australia. This was not a declaration of independence. This new Australia was a dominion within the British Empire. It was as citizens of the empire that thousands of Australian men volunteered to fight in the Australian Imperial Force when WWI broke out in 1914. They fought in Turkey, Sinai and Europe – notably on the Somme. More than 200,000 of them were killed or wounded over the terrible four years of the war.

1914
Over 200,000 are killed or wounded in WWI.

1933
Two-thirds of the voting population votes to secede from the rest of the country. Although never enacted, secession remains topical.

1939
WWII begins. Several towns in WA's north, including Broome, are bombed during the war. Fremantle is turned into an Allied naval base, and a US submarine-refuelling base is established at Exmouth.

1952
The British explode their first nuclear bomb on WA's Monte Bello Islands.

Today, in cities and towns across the state you will see war memorials that commemorate their service.

Though mining, for the time being, had ceased to be an economic force, farmers were developing the lucrative Western Australian wheat belt, which they cultivated with the horse-drawn stump-jump plough, one of the icons of Australian frontier farming. At the same time, a growing demand for wool and beef and the expansion of dairy farming added to the state's economic growth.

Largely set in Western Australia, *Gallipoli* (1981, directed by Peter Weir, screenplay by David Williamson) is an iconic Australian film exploring naivety, social pressure to enlist and, ultimately, the utter futility of this campaign.

Nevertheless, many people were struggling to earn a living – especially those ex-soldiers who were unable to shake off the horrors they had endured in the trenches. In 1929, the lives of these 'battlers' grew even more miserable when the cold winds of the Great Depression blew through the towns and farms of the state. So alienated did West Australians feel from the centres of power and politics in the east that, in 1933, two-thirds of them voted to secede from the rest of Australia. Although the decision was never enacted, it expressed a profound sense of isolation from the east that is still a major factor in the culture and attitudes of the state today.

In 1939, Australians were once again fighting a war alongside the British, this time against Hitler in WWII. But the military situation changed radically in December 1941 when the Japanese bombed the American fleet at Hawaii's Pearl Harbor. The Japanese swept through Southeast Asia and, within weeks, were threatening Australia. Over the next two years they bombed several towns in the north of the state, including Broome, which was almost abandoned.

It was not the British but the Americans who came to Australia's aid. As thousands of Australian soldiers were taken prisoner and suffered in the torturous Japanese prisoner-of-war camps, West Australians opened their arms to US servicemen. Fremantle was transformed into an Allied naval base for operations in the Indian Ocean, while a US submarine-refuelling base was established at Exmouth. In New Guinea and the Pacific, Americans and Australians fought together until the tide of war eventually turned in their favour.

Postwar Prosperity

When World War II ended, the story of modern WA began to unfold. Under the banner of 'postwar reconstruction', the federal government set about transforming Australia with a policy of assisted immigration, designed to populate Australia more densely as a defence against the 'hordes' of Asia. Many members of this new work force found jobs in the mines, where men and machines turned over thousands of tonnes of earth in search of the precious lode. On city stock exchanges, the names of such Western Australian mines as Tom Price, Mt Newman

1963

Development of the gargantuan Ord River Irrigation Scheme to fertilise the desert.

1967

Australia's Indigenous people are recognised as Australian citizens and granted the right to vote.

1970

The *Indian Pacific* train completes its first transcontinental journey from Sydney to Perth.

1979

The *Skylab* space station crashes in the state's remote southeastern sector. Remnants are now at the Esperance Museum.

WESTERN AUSTRALIA IN BLACK & WHITE

Like other Indigenous Australians in the rest of the country, the 70,000 or so who live in Western Australia (WA) are the state's most disadvantaged group. Many live in deplorable conditions; outbreaks of preventable diseases are common, and infant-mortality rates are higher than in many developing countries. Indigenous employment in the resources sector is slowly increasing, but the mining boom has not alleviated Indigenous social and economic disadvantage to any large degree.

In 1993, the federal government recognised that Aboriginal people with an ongoing association with their traditional lands were the rightful owners, unless those lands had been sold to someone else.

Despite this recognition, the issue of racial relations in WA remains a problematic one, and racial intolerance is still evident in many parts of the state.

and Goldsworthy became symbols of development, modernisation and wealth. Now, rather than being a wasteland that history had forgotten, the west was becoming synonymous with ambition, and a new spirit of capitalist pioneering. As union membership flourished, labour and capital entered into a pact to turn the country to profit. In the Kimberley, the government built the gigantic Ord River Irrigation Scheme, which boasted that it could bring fertility to the desert – and which convinced many West Australians that engineering and not the environment contained the secret of life.

There was so much country it hardly seemed to matter that salt was starting to poison the wheat belt or that mines scoured the land. In 1952 the British exploded their first nuclear bomb on the state's Monte Bello Islands. And when opponents of the test alleged that nuclear clouds were drifting over Australia, the government scoffed. The land was big – and anyway, it needed a strong, nuclear-armed ally for protection in the Cold War world.

This spirit of reckless capitalism reached its climax in the 1980s when the state became known as 'WA Inc' – a reference to the state in operation as a giant corporation in which government, business and unions had lost sight of any value other than speculation and profit. The embodiment of this brash spirit was an English migrant named Alan Bond, who became so rich he could buy anything he pleased. In 1983 he funded a sleek new racing yacht called *Australia II* in its challenge for the millionaire's yachting prize, the America's Cup. Equipped with a secret – and now legendary – winged keel, the boat became the first non-American yacht to win the race. It seemed as though everyone in

The wealth of Alan Bond, once bankrupt and convicted of corporate fraud, was estimated at $265 million by *Business Review Weekly* in 2008.

1980s

The state becomes known as WA Inc, a reference to its image as a giant corporation intent on speculation and profit.

1983

'Bondie' (Alan Bond) funds the racing yacht *Australia II*, which wins the America's Cup with its secret winged keel. Bond is later jailed for corporate fraud.

1987

Sleepy Fremantle is transformed for Australia's first defence of America's Cup. Australia loses 5-0 to the United States.

1990s

Aboriginal rock art, featuring distinctive stick-like images, is found in the Kimberley. Known as the Bradshaw paintings, these could be among the earliest figurative paintings ever executed.

Australia was cheering on the day Bond held aloft the shining silver trophy.

But in the 1990s, legal authorities began to investigate the dealings of Alan Bond, and of many other players in WA Inc. Bond found himself in court and spent four years in jail after pleading guilty to Australia's biggest corporate fraud. Following his release in 2000, by 2008 Bond had resurrected his estimated wealth to $265 million through African mining investments, and died in 2015 at the age of 77 after a colourful life.

When *Australia II* won the America's Cup in 1983, Australian prime minister Bob Hawke opined, 'Any boss who sacks a worker for not turning up today is a bum'.

The 21st Century

Throughout the early 21st century, WA's mining boom made the state one of the most dynamic parts of the country. The populations of Perth and key mining areas such as the Pilbara grew faster than those of east-coast Australia; of the state's total population of 2.55 million, many were originally born overseas. There are substantial South African and British communities in Perth, and many New Zealanders and Irish immigrants are working in the mining and resources sector.

From late 2014, however, signs became evident that the vital Chinese economy fuelling the mining boom was slowing down, causing a weakening in the Australian currency, lessening employment opportunities and reducing the stock-market value of the resources sector. As well, the construction phase of WA's resources industry was largely complete, with roads, ports and railways all in place to segue the state economy more strongly to an export phase.

With the weakening of the Australian dollar, some relief emerged for the growing tourism sector, and a general easing of salaries in the resources sector eased the pressure for those Perth and WA residents not earning a mine-worker's salary.

Going ahead, WA is still firmly focused on the benefits of the resources sector, and a renewed focus on liquified natural gas (LNG), uranium and other minerals remains vitally important. Agricultural exports to nearby mega-Asian economies such as Indonesia and Vietnam are also growing in importance.

The chill winds blowing through Australia's economy in early 2015 cannot be ignored, but WA's energy and resilience will continue to be vital drivers for the nation's eventual economic re-emergence and strengthening.

It's not a matter of if, but when, a Western Australian AFL (Australian Rules) club wins the Grand Final. The Fremantle Dockers made the finals series for three years running from 2012 to 2014.

1990s

The stolen generations are formally recognised.

1995

The Fremantle Dockers join the Australian Football League.

1998

One of Australia's most infamous trade union battles is waged in Fremantle between the Maritime Union and Patrick Corporation (a stevedore company).

2000s

Economic growth due to the mining boom, albeit with a reduction in vital Chinese demand from late 2014.

Local Produce & Wineries

Regional produce and local wines are the highlights of Western Australia (WA), and leisurely, outdoor eating is best experienced in the vineyard restaurants of the Margaret River, the Porongurups, Denmark and the Swan Valley. Select spots up north – Geraldton, Kalbarri, Carnarvon, Kununurra and Broome – include a few local gems.

Regional Produce

Regional produce includes marron (small freshwater crayfish unique to the southwest), crayfish (rock lobster, from up north), McHenry Hohnen beef (Margaret River) and barramundi (the Kimberley). Much of WA's best produce is also available at supermarkets and delicatessens. Look out for Browne's iced coffee and yoghurts, Harvey Fresh products – especially its fresh orange juice – and excellent chilli mussels.

Perth's leading chefs celebrate the region's produce by showcasing Manjimup truffles, Mt Barker chicken and Shark Bay scallops. Top-end spots in the central city include Restaurant Amusé (p64), Print Hall (p65) and Balthazar (p64), while Mt Lawley has Must Winebar (p67) and St Michael 6003 (p67). Excellent midrange cafes and restaurants include Brika (p66) and Pleased to Meet You (p66) in Northbridge, Duende (p68) and Sayers (p68) in Leederville, and Cantina 663 (p66) and El Público (p66) in Mt Lawley. In Fremantle, Bread in Common (p83) and Canvas (p83) are both very good. Regional dining highlights include the Studio Bistro (p123) near Yallingup, Pepper & Salt (p139) in Denmark, and Piari & Co (p118) in Dunsborough.

Organic & Sustainable

Perth's City Farm Organic Growers Market (p65)

Margaret River Farmers Market (p126)

Greenhouse (p64)

Cullen Wines (p124)

The Raw Kitchen (p83)

Then There's Beer

WA's leading working-class beers are Emu Bitter (EB) and Swan Draught. They're both pretty bland, so focus instead on exploring the craft-beer scene. In Fremantle and the southwest in particular, local microbreweries abound, and the Swan Valley is also a top spot.

In Fremantle, visit the Sail & Anchor (p84) and Monk (p85) for blackboards full of ever-changing brews. Freo also has the iconic Little Creatures (p84), now owned by a multinational company but still tasting great with its hoppy Pale Ale.

In the Swan Valley, the best craft breweries are Homestead Brewery (p101) at Mandoon Estate, Feral Brewing Company (p101) and Mash (p101). Mash also has locations in Bunbury and Rockingham, and its hoppy Copycat APA was dubbed Australia's best beer in 2014.

Continuing south, the Margaret River region is a definite craft-beer hot spot,and Denmark's Boston Brewery (p139) and Pemberton's Jarrah Jacks (p133) are worth visiting. To the east, good beers and ciders are crafted at the Cidery (p130) in Bridgetown.

Up north, the only craft brewery you'll find is Matso's (p217) in Broome. EB and Swan are surprisingly difficult to find, and east-coast beers such as Carlton, XXXX and Tooheys dominate the mainstream market.

Best for Vegetarians

Perth/Fremantle restaurants: The Raw Kitchen (p83) and Veggie Mama (p66)

Perth/Fremantle delicatessens: Kakulas Bros (p65) and Kakulas Sister (p83)

Regional WA: Samudra (p118), Maleeya's Thai Cafe (p145)

Local Produce & Wineries

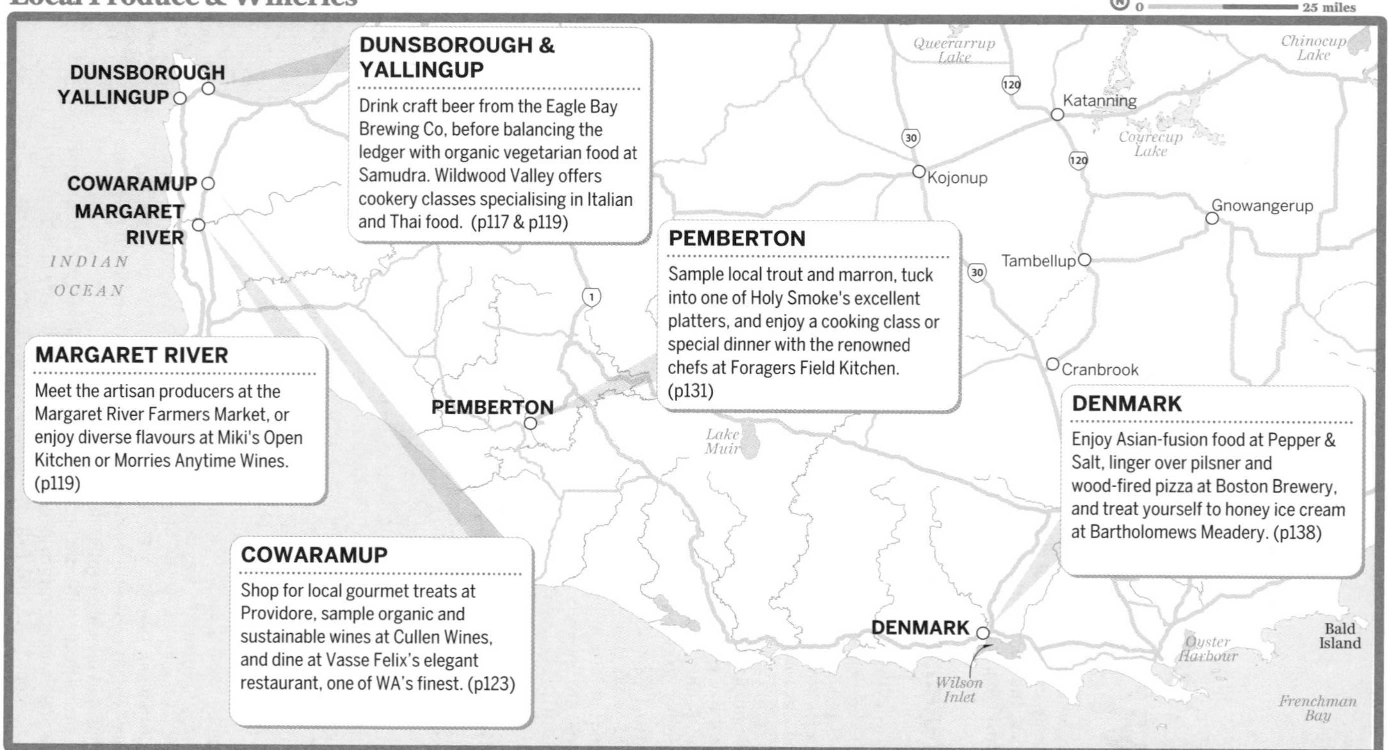

Australian beer has a higher alcohol content than British or American beer. Standard beer is around 5% alcohol (midstrength is around 3.5%, light 2% to 3%).

Wine & the Cellar Door

Wine is a big deal in WA, with the focus firmly on the quality end of the market. The Margaret River region produces only 3% of Australia's grapes but accounts for over 20% of the country's premium wines.

The first wineries began in the southwest in the 1960s, and Vasse Felix was a notable early player. Because the southwest has always focused on low-yield, quality output, it wasn't as influenced by the problems of oversupply that beset the Australian wine industry in 2005 and 2006. Fortuitous combinations of rain and warm weather also produced consistently excellent Margaret River vintages from 2007 to 2011.

Aside from Margaret River, other key wine areas are the Swan Valley, the Great Southern (Frankland, the Porongurups, Denmark, Mt Barker), Pemberton, and the Peel and Geographe regions. These all uphold WA's reputation as a world-class wine producer.

Margaret River

WA's best wineries are in Margaret River, 250km (3½ hours' drive) southwest of Perth. The climate is defined by cooling ocean breezes, producing Margaret River's distinctively elegant and rich wines.

Margaret River also produces many blends of semillon and sauvignon blanc grapes. These very popular fruity wines are not Margaret River's very best, but they are often the most affordable. Cape Mentelle, Cullen Wines and Lenton Brae all make good examples. Cullen Wines is also renowned for its organic and sustainable approach to wine making.

Smaller cellar doors to explore around Margaret River include the following:

Ashbrook (p124) A friendly family-owned operation.

Thompson Estate (p124) With a spectacular award-winning tasting room.

Stella Bella (p128) Excellent wines and wonderfully designed labels.

Swan Valley

The Swan Valley may once have aspired to take on mighty Margaret River, but now the region's true merit lies in its proximity to Perth and its small clutch of winery-restaurants – not the wines per se. It's hotter than down south, so leisurely outdoor-dining opportunities are better. You can also travel from Perth along the Swan River to the Sandalford winery (p101).

Eating Out

Tipping is not required

BYO – bringing your own beer or wine to the restaurant – is a widely accepted and budget-friendly practice.

For information and tasting notes about Western Australian wines, and to shop online for reds and whites, visit www.mrwines.com.

MARGARET RIVER'S FOUNDING FIVE

Five top wineries compose the cornerstone of Margaret River.

Cape Mentelle Makes consistently excellent cabernet sauvignon as well as a wonderful example of sauvignon blanc semillon.

Cullen Wines (p124) Still in the family, producing superb chardonnay and excellent cabernet merlot while adhering to sustainable wine-making principles.

Leeuwin Estate (p128) Stylish cellar door, a highly regarded restaurant, and responsible for putting chardonnay on the map in Australia with its Art Series.

Moss Wood Makes a heady semillon, a notable cabernet sauvignon and a surprising pinot noir.

Vasse Felix (p123) Must-see winery with a renowned restaurant.

Houghton Wines (p101) is the area's best winery, and the Houghton Classic White, a blend of white-wine grapes that drinks like a mix of tropical, zesty fruits, is the Swan Valley's most ubiquitous wine. Others of note include Lamont's (p101) and Sandalford. Best for lunch are River-Bank Estate (p101) and Lamont's (tapas only).

Wine for Dudes (p119) has excellent wine tours led by a winemaker. It also visits craft breweries around Margaret River.

Peel & Geographe Regions

Because the Peel region starts about 70km south of Perth, it's often hot, dry and rugged. Much like the Swan Valley, wine here is not generally considered to be of great significance. Millbrook Winery (p97), relatively close to Perth, is excellent for lunch, with a verandah right beside the vines.

Further south, in the slightly cooler Geographe region, are wineries of varying quality, and many people come to visit Capel Vale (p116). This winery has a 30-year history of wine-making excellence, particularly with chardonnay, shiraz and, more recently, merlot.

Great Southern & Pemberton

In central Perth, Lalla Rookh (p69) is a classy wine bar with an excellent selection of Western Australian wines.

The Great Southern region will never challenge Margaret River's preeminence among wine-touring regions – Margaret River is so spectacularly beautiful – but it nevertheless produces good-quality wines. Wine tourism here is not as developed, and that can be a good thing. Shiraz, cabernet sauvignon, riesling and sauvignon blanc do especially well.

The region stretches from the southeast town of Frankland, further southeast to Albany, and then west again to Denmark. Mt Barker, in the middle, is 350km southeast of Perth. The Great Southern's wines are full of flavour and power, and have a sense of elegance – try the peppery shirazes.

In Frankland, **Alkoomi** (www.alkoomiwines.com.au; 225 Stirling Tce; 11am-5pm Mon-Sat) is a family-run business, and produces cabernet sauvignon and riesling. Ferngrove produces an honest chardonnay, an excellent shiraz and a cabernet sauvignon shiraz blend called 'the Stirlings'. Frankland Estate is one of the key wineries that has helped revitalise riesling.

There are more wineries southwest of Frankland, in Mt Barker, and among the nearby Porongurup range. Riesling and shiraz are consistently great performers here; also try the lean, long-flavoured cabernet sauvignon. Two of the best are Forest Hill (p138) – try its cabernet sauvignon, and Plantagenet Wines (p144), the area's best winery.

Further south, in Denmark and Albany, are some of Australia's most esteemed wine names. Howard Park (p138), the area's stand out, has superb cabernet sauvignon, riesling and chardonnay. West Cape Howe (p144) is a straightforward winery that's excellent value, while Wignal's Wines is noted for its pinot noir.

Travelling east of Margaret River in the direction of the Great Southern wine region, you'll hit the Pemberton–Manjimup area (280km due south of Perth). Pemberton is a beautiful, undulating area home to forests of the area's famous karri trees, and its cool-ish climate produces cooler wine styles – pinot noir, merlot and chardonnay, in particular. Excellent producers in Pemberton are Salitage (p131) and Smithbrook Wines. Salitage is a large, stylish winery and the wines back it up; try one of the winery tours. Smithbrook Wines has excellent merlot.

Best Margaret River Winery Restaurants

- *Cullen Wines (p124)*
- *Knee Deep in Margaret River (p124)*
- *Leeuwin Estate (p128)*
- *Vasse Felix (p123)*
- *Watershed Premium Wines (p128)*

Mining & the Environment

If you fly into Perth, you'll notice one thing straight away. The fly-in, fly-out (FIFO) lifestyle is not only ubiquitous but now the norm. Large clutches of workers nonchalantly board their flights to remote mines and oil and gas plants every few hours. Some will be wearing their fluorescent orange or yellow 'high-vis' vests, required attire on site, and an understated badge of honour at the airport.

A few years ago, many construction workers were also part of this airborne ebb and flow, but now that massive infrastructure projects are largely completed in the state's north, the focus is mainly on mining workers. Contraction of the Chinese economy throughout 2014 has slowed Australia's exports of iron ore, causing the Aussie dollar to devalue and the Australian economy to weaken, but mining is still the biggest game out west.

The 'four weeks on, one week off' fly-in, fly-out schedule on the mines is referred to as the 'divorce roster'.

Teens just out of school have been bypassing the traditional employment rite of passage of an apprenticeship to earn annual incomes topping six figures. Irish and New Zealand workers have flocked to Western Australia (WA) to join in the resources-led bonanza, and Perth restaurant owners and wheat-belt farmers have found it hard to lure workers away from the well-paid appeal of the mines.

And against this backdrop of growth and opportunity, albeit tempered by a slowing of Chinese demand for Australia's iron ore, the boom's effect on the environment remains a source of concern for many in WA and across the country.

Life on the Mines

The source of the state's affluence remains outside many travellers' field of view. Take the Pilbara gold-mining town of Telfer, for instance, considered the most remote town in WA. Life here is altogether different to that in the leafy western suburbs of Perth. For Telfer is less traditional country town (with main street, two quiet pubs, maybe a community town hall) and more giant mine plus attendant camp, purpose-built for its hundreds of workers.

Tim Flannery's *The Future Eaters* is a highly readable overview of evolution in Australasia, covering the last 120 million years of history, with thoughts on how the environment has shaped Australasia's human cultures.

The Birth of the Mobile Workforce

In an effort to accommodate a workforce that periodically grows and shrinks, Telfer has been dismantled and rebuilt a few times by mining companies over the years. But in the mid-1990s it was discovered that it was cheaper to simply fly the entire work force in and out rather than continually build and reconstruct permanent accommodation. Under the new plan, those flown in would work for a sustained period of time (say four weeks), then have a week or two off back home – in Perth, New Zealand, or even Bali. The company would then be able to draw from a broader, more skilled labour force, and workers would no longer need to contemplate the unattractive lifestyle of living in the middle of nowhere. As this business model was adopted across the state, the FIFO work culture was born.

Setting Up Camp

The FIFO lifestyle is perhaps nowhere more apparent than in Karratha, once a sleepy, nondescript town but today harbouring a FIFO population, relatively expensive food and accommodation shortages. The recent slowing of WA's resources sector has now brought Karratha's accommodation prices to a more realistic level, and there's a better sense of community here as a few more families commit to the town long term.

Mt Augustus (1105m), on the central west coast, is the largest rock in the world, twice the size and three times as old as Uluru (Ayers Rock) in the Northern Territory.

Woodside, a major oil and gas producer, has set up camp here, exploring for gas off the north coast. The pace of expansion has been so speedy, that there wasn't time to build brick-and-tile homes for the workers. And so today in Karratha, bolted onto the original small town centre, are a number of suburbs composed of 'dongas' – makeshift, moveable, one-man accommodation units. A typical donga in Gap Ridge, the main suburb, has a single bed, a TV, a shower and a toilet carved into a shipping-container–like box-home. Meals are taken in the 'wet mess', much like a mess hall.

Karratha locals have for some time been voicing concerns that a FIFO population parties in their town without regard for the community. Places like Gap Ridge are home to a young, moneyed, male population, and this has created a pattern of influx and change in Karratha that is echoed in other mining towns across the state. Many labourers are away from home and family, and have considerable funds to sink into beer and good times.

Such social shifts have not gone unnoticed by politicians, including Western Australian premier Colin Barnett. One initiative rolled out since the peak of the boom is 'Royalties for Regions' – putting money back into regional areas such as Karratha, which had not been able to easily build much-needed infrastructure despite the boom. Mobile-phone coverage is now being expanded on the remote highways.

Work Hard, Play Hard

Drinking has long been part of Australian culture, but FIFO workers off the clock focus particularly keenly on playing hard. Throughout the global financial crisis ('GFC' in Australian parlance), letting off steam over a few beers simply continued apace for many. But by late 2014, the Chinese economy had slowed considerably, and falling iron-ore and nickel prices had started to reduce the number of nights out on the town. Jobs had been shed, and share prices for resource companies had fallen. And it is perhaps those who hold the mantra 'work hard, play hard' most closely to their hearts who have been found to be the most vulnerable to shakes in the economy. Many young workers have limited education and have been earning big sums from a young age. For some, the upkeep of their lifestyle (jet skis, cars, houses) has always been contingent on a mining salary that did not waver. Now that the economy has inevitably slowed, some workers are struggling to unearth a Plan B.

In *The Weather Makers*, Tim Flannery argues lucidly and passionately that there is an immediate need to address the implications of a global change in climate that is damaging all life on earth and endangering our very survival. An accessible read.

You're In or You're Out

Aboriginal Australian employment is very low within the mining industry. Some argue that training programs for Aboriginal Australians – attempts to settle Australia's most disadvantaged into the Western working life – have not proved effective. Mining magnate Andrew 'Twiggy' Forrest, who Forbes labelled Australia's richest man in 2010, in 2008 boldly promised support for 50,000 jobs for Aboriginal Australians. This government-backed program is also one of the most high-profile attempts by a key mining figure to not only change employment patterns but also speak frankly about the lack of opportunity afforded to Aboriginal communities across the state. Just how the 50,000 jobs will be taken up in the long term is yet to be determined, and that will be the tricky bit. By late 2012, four years after the program was developed, some 10,000 positions had been taken up.

In 2014, Andrew Forrest also released *Creating Parity,* an Australian government-sponsored review of Indigenous jobs and training. From September 2014, public submissions were invited on the report's recommendations, but some ideas – such as a cashless 'Healthy Welfare Card' promoted to aid family budgeting and minimise access to drugs and alcohol – came under criticism from Indigenous and welfare rights advocacy groups.

It is now more widely acknowledged that the gap between the resource-boom-driven 'haves' and 'have-nots' is real and ever increasing, with signs of economic strain creeping up the social strata. The tension between income and cost of living – strongly driven by the high cost of housing – has become so tight that some middle-class workers employed on good salaries struggle to pay the rent. Foreign financial investment is gargantuan, and it will likely be here for some years to come. But patterns of recent job losses are causing many to wonder aloud if the good times have indeed passed.

Field Guide to the Birds of Australia is full colour, splendidly detailed, accessible and portable. This endlessly fascinating reference, Graham Pizzey and Frank Knight's claim to fame, is in its 8th edition.

Recent Environmental Flashpoints

James Price Point

James Price Point is an expanse of wilderness along the Kimberley coast 60km north of Broome. A multinational consortium and the WA state government was proposing a liquefied natural gas (LNG) station here – the biggest in the world. In 2013, eight years after first proposing the development, Woodside Petroleum Ltd announced that the refineries were not economically viable, a significant victory for environmental groups seeking to protect the largely pristine Kimberley coastline.

Aside from its dinosaur fossils, the proposed area is a playground for dolphins, dugongs and breeding bilbies. Humpback whales breed and calve along the coastline, and the rainforest backing the coast harbours a multitude of plant species. Not least, this is traditional Aboriginal land. Negotiating a native title deed this size would have marked a historic achievement.

James Price Point had become a leading symbol of tensions between the growing financial fortunes of the state and the less easily quantified value of an untouched landscape. Not only were business interests, traditional land owners, politicians and environmentalists in fierce disagreement with each other, but divisions within these groups continue

Head to Ningaloo Reef from April to June to swim alongside many-metres-long, remarkably docile whale sharks.

NINGALOO'S CLOSE SCRAPE

Some locals still sport 'Save Ningaloo' bumper stickers on their cars. No one seems to pay much attention to the faded stickers these days, but they're a reminder of one of the most high-profile and fiercely contested environmental campaigns Western Australia has seen. 'Save Ningaloo', with its thousands of protesters, successfully blocked development of a massive marina resort (slated for 2003) on a loggerhead-turtle nesting ground. Comprising 280km of coral reef, and visited by species such as manta rays, whale sharks, dugongs, humpback whales and turtles, Ningaloo is one of the last healthy major reef systems in the world.

The area has nevertheless remained a site of interest for property developers and the resources sector. In late 2012 BHP Billiton submitted a proposal to the state government to explore for liquefied natural gas (LNG) some 5km from Ningaloo's perimeter. Regardless of whether exploration goes ahead, the condition of this World Heritage–listed reef remains precarious and controversial.

to run deep despite the amendment of the project to utilise floating offshore LNG rigs. For locals in nearby Broome, 'whose side you're on' is often common knowledge, and this lack of anonymity is a further source of strain.

Whether the 2013 abandonment of onshore plans for James Price Point is the final word remains uncertain. In late 2014 the Western Australian government was again assessing potential environmental impacts at the site, and Premier Colin Barnett continued to spruik the economic benefits of an LNG hub in the area. Given the recent decline in income from iron ore exports to China, the pressure on James Price Point looks set to continue.

Keep your eyes peeled for the banded anteater, also known as the numbat. Tiny, light-footed and incredibly shy, the numbat is a solitary creature who will venture outside its neatly delineated territory only to find a mate. Singular dietary requirement: termites.

Elsewhere on the Land

WA's environmental flashpoints are by no means limited to the extended controversy surrounding proposed onshore LNG processing plants at James Price Point. Other controversial sites slated for mining include the Burrup Peninsula on the Dampier Archipelago, which is the location of a multitude of petroglyphs (rock art), archaeological wonders thought to date from the last ice age. Although disruption to the works began in the 1960s, in 2007 Woodside Petroleum Ltd had several petroglyphs gingerly removed and fenced off in a separate area to better facilitate development. Some argue that the works are not discrete: that the disruption of one petroglyph compromises the entire site. Elsewhere in the state, uranium mines are under consideration.

Meanwhile, ground water has been utilised freely for decades; alternative water sources, using desalination plants, have been in place for some time. Old-growth forests, with their 1000-year-old karri trees, were logged until the 1990s; today scientists cite lowered rainfall in the southwest as the result of deforestation.

And, much like other major cities in Australia, Perth is subject to suburban sprawl. Because the mining boom has driven much property development, the city now tails out across 100km, densely studded with so-called affordable housing. The environmental effects of the lifestyle out here are not immediately apparent, but may nevertheless prove significant. Many housing estates are divorced from public-transport routes, so people must always drive for their litre of milk, and the roads are becoming increasingly congested. Many have long been calling for more high-density housing in and near the city of Perth.

Balancing Economy & Environment

Going ahead, the balancing act between the economy and environmental issues remains at the very heart of WA society and politics, and the stakes have never been higher. Now that the Chinese economy's appetite for iron ore has weakened, developers and the Western Australian government will be even more focused on harnessing other rich veins of WA's resources sector. Inevitably, there will be more conflict between industrial interests and environmental advocates. For many West Australians, the benefits of a prosperous resources economy has definitely provided them with access to a rewarding and cosmopolitan lifestyle.

For detailed directions on where and how to surround yourself with wildflowers, see the Wildflower Society of Western Australia's website (www.members.ozemail.com.au/~wildflowers).

The boom has spawned mining magnates whose influence extends well beyond resources into politics and the media, and they are continuing to eye new areas of pristine wilderness to continue to harness the benefits of new mines and gas plants.

The Western Australian – and therefore Australia's – resources boom may be slowing slightly, but the ongoing tension between economic growth and environmental protection will continue to define Australia's most sprawling state for the foreseeable future.

How It All Began

Really, mining is old news – this is a frontier land founded on mining money. Although in the 1800s WA was once quietly focused on acquiring more modest fortunes from wheat, meat and wool, in 1892 gold was discovered in Coolgardie, and in 1893 it was uncovered again in Kalgoorlie. And so the transformation to riches began. Today, gold mining is still going strong, albeit with incrementally diminishing returns. In Kalgoorlie you can visit the Super Pit, an open-pit gold mine the size of 35 football fields sunk 360m into the ground. Copper, nickel, oil and gas are also steady sources of income for the state, with uranium mining (slated for Wiluna, in the midwest) a current aspiration.

Boomtown 2050, by landscape architect Richard Weller, is a nicely packaged book about how a rapidly growing town like Perth could be developed – sustainably.

But iron ore is today's multi-billion-dollar blockbuster industry. Karara mine in the midwest, for example, sits on just under $100 billion worth of iron ore. All this magnetite dug up out of the ground, later to become iron ore, is expected to generate $3 billion per year in export revenue for the next 30 years. Most of it will go to China, but the demand for it in recent years has been slowing, sending a chill through the entire Australian economy.

Of course, foreign investment remains big business. And while such major investment has now been criticised for exposing the state to the capricious fortunes of the Chinese economy, the boom would never have occurred without it. For an iron-ore mine, for example, about $1 billion must be available up front just to develop the extraction machinery. These biscuits are just too big for the Australian economy alone.

Indigenous Art in Western Australia

Experiencing the Indigenous art of Western Australia (WA) creates an indelible link for travellers to this land of red dirt and desert expanses. Ancient rock art echoes across the centuries, traditional designs and motifs inspire modern artists, and Indigenous tour operators inform with stories of spirituality, bush tucker and Country.

Indigenous Art

Rock Art

Some Aboriginal rock paintings are believed to date back between 18,000 and 60,000 years and provide a record of changing environments and lifestyles over the millennia. For the local Indigenous people, rock-art sites are a major source of traditional knowledge – they are historical archives in place of a written form.

The earliest hand or grass prints were followed by a naturalistic style, with large outlines of people or animals filled in with colour. Then came the dynamic style, in which motion was often depicted (a dotted line, for example, to show a spear's path through the air). In this era the first mythological beings appeared, with human bodies and animal heads. Following this were simple human silhouettes, and then the more recent X-ray style, displaying the internal organs and bones of animals.

Art of the Kimberley

The art of the Kimberley is perhaps best known for its images of the Wandjina, a group of ancestral beings who came from the sky and sea and were associated with fertility. They controlled the elements and were responsible for the formation of the country's natural features.

Wandjina images are found painted on rock as well as on more recent contemporary media; some of the rock images are more than 7m long. They generally appear in human form, with large black eyes, a nose but no mouth, a halo around the head (representative of both hair and clouds) and a black oval shape on the chest.

Each Wandjina traditionally has its own custodian family, and to ensure good relations between the Wandjina and the people, the images have to be retouched annually.

BEST NORTHERN WA GALLERIES

- Short Street Gallery, Broome (p213)
- Mowanjum Art & Culture Centre, Gibb River Road (p201)
- Waringarri Aboriginal Arts Centre, Kununurra (p206)
- Artlandish, Kununurra (p208)

BEST SOUTHERN WA GALLERIES

- Art Gallery of Western Australia, Perth (p49)
- Indigenart, Perth (p74)
- Japingka, Fremantle (p85)
- Tunbridge Gallery, Margaret River (p126)
- Kepa Kurl Art Gallery, Esperance (p148)

One of the other significant styles of painting found in the Kimberley is that of the Gwion Gwion figures (also named the Bradshaw images after the first non-Indigenous person who saw them). The Gwion Gwion figures are generally small and seem to depict ethereal beings engaged in ceremony or dance. It is believed that they pre-date the Wandjina paintings, though little is known of their significance or meaning.

Western Desert Painting

Western Desert painting, also known as dot painting, is probably the most well known of Indigenous painting styles. It partly evolved from 'ground paintings', which formed the centrepiece of dances and songs. These were made from pulped plant material, with designs made on the ground. While dot paintings may look random and abstract, they depict Dreaming stories and can be read in many ways, including as aerial landscape maps. Many paintings feature the tracks of birds, animals and humans, often identifying the land's ancestral beings. Subjects may be depicted by the imprint they leave in the sand – a simple arc depicts a person (as that is the print left by someone sitting cross-legged), a coolamon (wooden carrying dish) is shown by an oval shape, a digging stick by a single line, and a campfire by a circle. Men or women are identified by the objects associated with them: digging sticks and coolamons for women, spears and boomerangs for men. Concentric circles usually depict Dreaming sites, or places where ancestors paused in their journeys.

While these symbols are widely used, their meaning in each painting is known only by the artist and the people closely associated with them – either by clan or by the Dreaming – since different clans apply different interpretations to each painting. In this way sacred stories can be publicly portrayed, as the deeper meaning is not revealed to uninitiated viewers.

The Western Desert Mob (www.westerndesertmob.com.au) is a coalition of artists cooperatives of the Ngaanyatjarra lands of Western Australia. Mediums include *punu*, the traditional art of woodcarving.

Buying Indigenous Art Ethically

By buying authentic items you are supporting Indigenous culture and helping to ensure that traditional and contemporary expertise and designs continue to be of economic and cultural benefit to Indigenous individuals and communities. Unfortunately, some of the so-called Indigenous art sold as souvenirs is ripped off – either appropriated designs illegally taken from Indigenous people or just plain fake – and sometimes made overseas by underpaid workers. Artworks should have a certificate of authenticity. Note that haggling is not part of Aboriginal culture.

The best place to buy art is either directly from the communities that have art collectives, or from galleries and outlets that are owned and operated, or supported, by Indigenous communities. You can then be sure that the items are genuine and that the money you spend goes to the right people. However, some Indigenous artists continue to be paid small

WHERE TO SEE ROCK ART

- Mulkas Cave, near Wave Rock and Hyden
- Around Esperance with Kepa Kurl (p148)
- Burrup Peninsula in the Pilbara with Ngurrangga Tours (p188)
- Some of the Wandjina and Gwion Gwion images hidden across the Kimberley are accessible from stations on the Gibb River Road, including Mt Elizabeth Station (p202)
- Mitchell Plateau in the Kimberley – Mitchell Falls (Punamii-unpuu) and Munurru Campground (p201)

sums for their work, only to find it being sold for much higher prices in commercial galleries in cities.

To negate this, it's vital to do some research. The **Australian Commercial Galleries Association** (www.acga.com.au) lists galleries considered to observe ethical practices. Another excellent organisation is **Solid Arts** (www.solidarts.com.au); its online portal offers support for Indigenous artists and outlines ethical considerations to keep in mind when purchasing Indigenous art.

Survival Guide

Directory A–Z

Accommodation

Accommodation in Western Australia (WA) ranges from camping grounds to high-end hotels. Perth's accommodation is generally more expensive, although Margaret River, Broome, the Coral Coast and Pilbara mining towns come very close.

Over summer (December to February) and around school and public holidays, prices are at their highest. Outside these times discounts and lower walk-in rates can be found. One exception is the far north, where the wet season (November to March) is the low season and prices can drop by as much as 50%. Listed prices include all state and federal taxes.

Accommodation in the Pilbara can be hard to find, due to the fly-in, fly-out (FIFO) mining phenomenon. Camping is often the best option.

B&Bs

Bed and breakfast (B&B) options range from rooms in heritage buildings to a bedroom in a family home. A full cooked breakfast is not the norm. Tariffs for couples are typically in the $150 to $250 range but can be much higher for exclusive properties.

For online information:

- www.australianbedandbreakfast.com.au
- www.babs.com.au
- www.ozbedandbreakfast.com.

Camping & Caravan Parks

For many travellers, touring with a tent or campervan is the consummate WA experience. In the outback and up north you often won't even need a tent. Check with visitor centres before heading out to confirm locations of free roadside stops. Many stops have been phased out immediately north of Perth but are more frequent further away from the city.

Designated camp sites in national parks cost $7.50/2.20 per adult/child with no or basic facilities. Sites with showers (including unpowered caravan sites) cost $10/2.20. You'll also need to pay entrance fees ($12 per car) for many national parks, but only when you enter the park. If you're exploring several parks, pick up a four-week national-park holiday pass ($44). Some national-park camp sites can be pre-booked online. See www.parks.dpaw.wa.gov.au/stay.

At WA's ubiquitous holiday parks, prices are from around $30 to $50 for two people, ranging from unpowered tent sites to powered caravan sites. Many caravan parks are phasing out unpowered sites because they are less profitable. Most holiday parks offer private accommodation from simple chalets to flasher motel units.

Pick up the free *Caravanning, Camping and Motorhoming in WA* at visitor centres or see www.caravanwa.com.au.

Dongas

Commonly found in the outback, especially in mining towns, the donga is basically a prefabricated tin room (usually air-conditioned) with a single bed, TV and small fridge.

Farmstays & Station Stays

The Gascoyne and Pilbara areas are popular spots for station stays, and at some you may be asked to pitch in. Accommodation is either in the main homestead (B&B style, with dinner on request) or in adjacent self-contained cottages. Other farms provide

BOOK YOUR STAY ONLINE

For more accommodation reviews by Lonely Planet authors, check out http://lonelyplanet.com/hotels. You'll find independent reviews, as well as recommendations on the best places to stay. Best of all, you can book online.

SLEEPING PRICE RANGES

Price ranges per night for a double room:

$ Less than $150

$$ $150 to $250

$$$ More than $250

budget options in outbuildings or former shearers' quarters. Search for 'Farmstay' online at www.tacawa.com.au.

Hostels

Prices for dorm beds range from $25 to $35, while private rooms range from $70 to $90. Hostel staff can sometimes help in securing seasonal work.

Some hostels – especially in Perth – are popular as short-term accommodation for fly-in, fly-out (FIFO) workers but this also changes the traditional travellers' vibe.

A **Youth Hostel Association** (YHA; www.yha.com.au) or Hostelling International annual membership ($42) gives a 10% discount at participating hostels. Sign up at the first YHA you stay in.

VIP Backpackers (www.vipbackpackers.com) also offers discounts in participating WA hostels. For $47 you'll receive a 12-month membership, with discounts on accommodation and some transport, tours and activities. Join online, or at VIP hostels.

Hotels & Motels

Full-service hotels are rare outside of Perth, and coastal properties tend to be resort style, with stand-alone cottages or apartments. Rates vary widely, but there are benefits in booking early directly with the properties, or last-minute on accommodation-booking websites.

In rural areas book ahead, as motels are used by government workers and tour groups.

Pubs

You can sometimes rent a single room at a country pub for not much more than a hostel dorm. If you're a light sleeper, never book a room above the bar. Some pubs also have separate motel-style accommodation.

Rental Accommodation

The ubiquitous holiday flat resembles a motel unit but has cooking, and often laundry, facilities. They're often rented on a weekly basis, and nightly prices are higher for shorter stays. For listings of holiday homes, see www.stayz.com.au.

Self-contained accommodations, many of which have full kitchens, are a good option for saving money by not eating out. Check out our listings flagged as 'cottage', 'chalet' and 'apartment'.

In cities a good alternative is a serviced apartment. Number Six has apartments around Perth, Fremantle and Margaret River, or hop online and check out the offerings on www.airbnb.com.au.

Customs Regulations

For comprehensive information, contact the **Australian Customs Service** (☎02-9313 3010; www.customs.gov.au).

On arrival, declare all goods of animal or plant origin, as it's vital to protect Australia's unique environment and agricultural industries. If you fail to declare quarantine items on arrival, you risk an on-the-spot fine of over $200 or even prosecution and imprisonment. For more information contact the Australian **Department of Agriculture** (www.agriculture.gov.au/biosecurity).

Duty-free allowances:

- Alcohol – 2.25L
- Cigarettes – 50
- Other goods – up to $900 value; or items for personal use that you will be taking with you when you leave.

Discount Cards

The most common card for discounts on accommodation, transport and some attractions in WA is the International Student Identity Card (ISIC), issued to full-time students aged 12 years and over. See the website of the **International Student Travel Confederation** (ISTC; www.istc.org) for details.

The ISTC also has an International Youth Travel Card (IYTC or Go25), issued to people between 12 and 26 years of age who are not full-time students. Benefits are equivalent to the ISIC.

Electricity

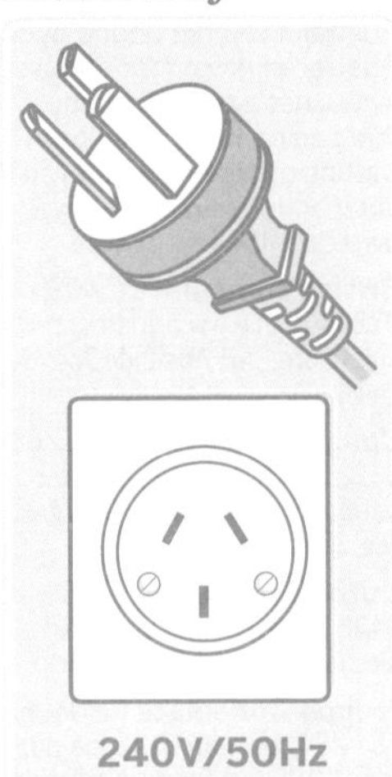

Embassies & Consulates

The principal diplomatic representations to Australia are in Canberra, but many countries are represented in Perth by consular staff.

PRACTICALITIES

- **Newspapers** Key papers are the *West Australian* or the *Australian*, a national broadsheet, from Monday to Saturday, and the *Sunday Times* on Sunday.
- **TV** Networks include the commercial-free ABC, multicultural SBS, and commercial TV stations Seven, Nine and Ten.
- **Radio** Tune in to the ABC on the radio – pick a program and frequency from www.abc.net.au/radio.
- **DVDs** Discs sold in Australia can be watched on players accepting region 4 DVDs (the same as Mexico, South America, Central America, New Zealand, the Pacific and the Caribbean). The USA and Canada are region 1 countries, and Europe and Japan are region 2.
- **Weights & measures** The metric system is used.
- **Smoking** Banned on public transport and planes, in cars carrying children, between the flags at patrolled beaches, within 10m of a playground and in government buildings. It's also banned within bars and clubs but permitted in some al fresco or courtyard areas.

Remember that while in Australia you are bound by Australian laws. Your embassy will not be sympathetic if you end up in jail after committing a crime locally, even if such actions are legal in your own country.

British Consulate (☎08-9224 4700; www.british-consulate.org; 251 Adelaide Tce, Level 12)

Canadian Consulate (☎08-9322 7930; www.canadainternational.gc.ca; 267 St Georges Tce, 3rd floor)

Dutch Consulate (☎08-9486 1579; http://australia.nlembassy.org; 1139 Hay St)

French Consulate (☎0406 654 254; www.ambafrance-au.org; 4/105 Broadway, Nedlands)

German Consulate (☎08-9221 2941; www.canberra.diplo.de; 2 The Esplanade, Level 18, Exchange Plaza)

Irish Embassy (☎02-6214 0000; www.embassyofireland.au.com; 20 Arkana St, Yarralumla, ACT)

New Zealand High Commission (☎08-6270 4211; www.nzembassy.com; Commonwealth Ave, Canberra, ACT)

USA Consulate (☎08-9202 1224; http://perth.usconsulate.gov; 16 St Georges Tce, 4th fl)

EATING PRICE RANGES

Price ranges refer to the price of a main course:

$ Less than $15

$$ $15–32

$$$ More than $32

Gay & Lesbian Travellers

In general Australians are open-minded about homosexuality and, in WA, gay and lesbian people are protected by anti-discrimination legislation and share an equal age of consent with heterosexuals (16 years).

Perth has the state's only gay and lesbian venues and its small scene is centred around Northbridge. It's very unlikely you'll experience any real problems, although the further away from the main centres, the more likely you are to experience overt homophobia.

Useful resources:

Gay & Lesbian Tourism Australia (www.galta.com.au) Lists WA members offering accommodation and tours.

Q Pages (www.qpages.com.au) Gay and lesbian business directory and what's-on listings.

Living Proud (Map p56; ☎08-9486 9855, counselling 1800 184 527; www.livingproud.org.au; 2 Delhi St, City West Lotteries House) Information and counselling line.

Health

Australia is a healthy country for travellers. Malaria and yellow fever are unknown, cholera and typhoid are unheard of, and animal diseases such as rabies and foot-and-mouth disease have yet to be recorded. The standard of hospitals and health care is high.

Few travellers should experience anything worse than an upset stomach or a bad hangover.

Before You Go

Pack medications in their original, clearly labelled, containers. A signed and dated letter from your physician describing your medical conditions and medications, including generic names, is also a good idea. If carrying syringes or needles, be sure to have a physician's letter documenting their medical necessity.

Insurance

If your health insurance doesn't cover you for medical expenses abroad, consider getting extra insurance – check www.lonelyplanet.com for more information. Find out in advance if your insurance plan will make payments directly to providers or reimburse you later for overseas health expenditures.

Availability & Cost of Health Care

Health insurance is essential for all travellers. While health care in Australia is of a high standard and not overly expensive by international standards, considerable costs can build up and repatriation is extremely expensive.

Australia's health-care system is a mixture of privately-run medical clinics and hospitals alongside a government-funded system of public hospitals. The Medicare system covers Australian residents for some health-care costs. Visitors from countries with which Australia has a reciprocal health-care agreement (New Zealand, the UK, the Netherlands, Sweden, Finland, Norway, Italy, Malta, Ireland, Slovenia and Belgium) are eligible for benefits to the extent specified under the Medicare program. If you are from one of these countries check the details before departure. In general the agreements provide for any episode of ill health that requires prompt medical attention. For further details see www.humanservices.gov.au and search for 'reciprocal'.

Over-the-counter medications are widely available at pharmacies. These include painkillers, antihistamines for allergies and skin-care products.

Some medications readily available over the counter in other countries are only available in Australia by prescription. These include the oral contraceptive pill, most medications for asthma and all antibiotics. If you take medication on a regular basis, bring an adequate supply and ensure you know the generic name, as brand names may differ.

Infectious Diseases

BAT LYSSAVIRUS

This disease is related to rabies and some deaths have occurred after bites. The risk is greatest for animal handlers and vets. Rabies vaccine is effective, but the risk to travellers is very low.

DENGUE FEVER

Also known as 'breakbone fever', because of the severe muscular pains that accompany the fever, this viral disease is spread by a species of mosquito that feeds primarily during the day. Most people recover in a few days, but more severe forms of the disease can occur, particularly in residents who are exposed to another strain of the virus (there are four types) in a subsequent season.

GIARDIASIS

Giardiasis is widespread in the waterways around Australia. Drinking untreated water from streams and lakes is not recommended. Water filters, and boiling or treating water with iodine, are effective in preventing the disease. Symptoms consist of intermittent bad-smelling diarrhoea, abdominal bloating and wind. Effective treatment is available (tinidazole or metronidazole).

MENINGOCOCCAL DISEASE

This disease occurs worldwide and is a risk with prolonged, dormitory-style accommodation. A vaccine exists for some types of this disease, namely meningococcal A, C, Y and W. No vaccine is presently available for the viral type of meningitis.

ROSS RIVER FEVER

The Ross River virus is widespread throughout Australia and is spread by mosquitoes living in marshy areas. In addition to fever the disease causes headache, joint and muscular pains and a rash, before resolving after five to seven days.

SEXUALLY TRANSMITTED DISEASES

STDs occur at rates similar to those in most other Western countries. Always use a condom with any new sexual partner. Condoms are readily available in chemists and through vending machines in many public places including toilets.

VIRAL ENCEPHALITIS

Also known as the Murray Valley encephalitis virus, this is spread by mosquitoes and is most common in northern Australia, especially during the wet season (November to April). This potentially serious disease is normally accompanied by headache, muscle pains and light sensitivity. Residual neurological damage can occur and no specific treatment is available. However, the risk to most travellers is low.

REQUIRED VACCINATIONS

Proof of yellow-fever vaccination is required from travellers entering Australia within six days of having stayed overnight or longer in a yellow-fever-infected country. For a full list of these countries see the websites of the **World Health Organization** (www.who.int/wer) or the **Centers for Disease Control & Prevention** (www.cdc.gov/travel).

Insurance

Sign up for a travel-insurance policy covering theft, loss and medical problems.

Some policies exclude designated 'dangerous activities' such as scuba diving, parasailing, or even bushwalking. Ensure your policy fully covers you for activities

GST REFUNDS

The goods and services tax (GST) is a flat 10% tax on all goods and services with the exception of basic food items (milk, bread, fruits and vegetables etc). By law the tax is included in the quoted or shelf price of goods, so all prices we list are GST inclusive.

If you purchase goods with a minimum value of $300 from any one supplier (on the same invoice) no more than 60 days before you leave Australia, you are entitled under the Tourist Refund Scheme (TRS) to a refund of any GST paid. The scheme only applies to goods you take with you as hand luggage or wear on the plane or ship when leaving. You can collect your refund at the airport up to 30 minutes before departure. At Perth Airport, the refund counter is just after passport control. Using a recently launched app speeds up the process. For more information, contact the **Australian Customs Service** (www.customs.gov.au).

of your choice. Check you're covered for ambulances and emergency medical evacuations by air.

Third-party personal-injury insurance (p261) is included in vehicle registration cost, and comprehensive insurance is usually included when hiring a vehicle, though consider reducing your excess to offset costs in the event of an accident.

Worldwide travel insurance is available at www.lonelyplanet.com/travel-insurance. You can buy, extend and claim online anytime – even if you're already on the road.

Internet Access

Internet cafes are found across WA but are becoming much less common with the growth of smartphones and other internet-enabled mobile devices. Many backpacker hostels and public libraries offer wi-fi connections. In smaller towns visit Community Resource Centres. The cost ranges from around $5 an hour in Perth to $10 an hour in locations that are more remote.

The best bets for free wi-fi connections are public libraries and cafes. Wi-fi is becoming more prevalent in accommodation; it's sometimes free in hostels but is often charged for in caravan parks and hotels.

Legal Matters

Police have the power to stop your car and see your licence (you're required to carry it), check your vehicle for road-worthiness, and compel you to take a breath test for alcohol.

First-time offenders in possession of small amounts of illegal drugs are likely to receive a fine rather than go to jail, but a conviction may affect your visa status. If you remain in Australia after your visa expires, you will officially be classified as an 'overstayer' and could face detention and expulsion, and be prevented from returning to Australia for a period of up to three years.

Maps

Tourist-information offices usually have serviceable town maps. For more detailed information, the **Royal Automobile Club of WA** (www.rac.com.au) has road maps available (including downloadable route maps). UBD publishes a handy *South West & Great Southern* book.

Hema Maps (www.hemamaps.com.au) Best for the north, especially the dirt roads.

Landgate (www.landgate.wa.gov.au) Statewide maps as well as topographical maps for bushwalking.

Money

All prices are given in Australian dollars, unless otherwise stated.

ATMs

Bank branches with 24-hour ATMs can be found statewide. In the smallest towns there's usually an ATM in the local pub. Most ATMs accept cards from other banks and are linked to international networks.

Cash

The Australian dollar is made up of 100 cents; there are 5c, 10c, 20c, 50c, $1 and $2 coins, and $5, $10, $20, $50 and $100 notes.

Cash amounts equal to or in excess of the equivalent of A$10,000 (in any currency) must be declared on arrival or departure in Australia.

Changing foreign currency or travellers cheques is usually no problem at banks throughout WA.

Credit & Debit Cards

Visa and MasterCard are widely accepted and a credit card is essential (in lieu of a large deposit) for car hire. With debit cards, any card connected to the international banking network (Cirrus, Maestro, Plus and Eurocard) will work. Diners Club and Amex are not as widely accepted.

Photography

Purchase memory cards and batteries in larger cities and towns as they're cheaper than in the remote areas. Most photo labs have self-service machines from which you can make your own prints and burn CDs and DVDs.

SCHOOL HOLIDAYS

The Christmas season is part of the summer school holidays (mid-December to late January), when transport and accommodation are often booked out, and there are long, restless queues at tourist attractions. There are three shorter school-holiday periods during the year that change slightly from year to year. Generally, they fall in mid-April, mid-July and late September to mid-October.

Public Holidays

New Year's Day 1 January

Australia Day 26 January

Labour Day First Monday in March

Easter (Good Friday and Easter Monday) March/April

Anzac Day 25 April

Foundation Day First Monday in June

Queen's Birthday Last Monday in September

Christmas Day 25 December

Boxing Day 26 December

Safe Travel

Environmental Hazards

HEAT EXHAUSTION & HEATSTROKE

Heat exhaustion occurs when fluid intake does not keep up with fluid loss. Symptoms include dizziness, fainting, fatigue, nausea or vomiting. On observation the skin is usually pale, cool and clammy. Treatment consists of rest in a cool, shady place and fluid replacement with water or diluted sports drinks.

Heatstroke is a severe form of heat illness that occurs after fluid depletion or extreme heat challenge from heavy exercise. This is a true medical emergency: heating of the brain leads to disorientation, hallucinations and seizures. Prevention is by maintaining an adequate fluid intake to ensure the continued passage of clear and copious urine, especially during physical exertion.

HYPOTHERMIA

Hypothermia is a significant risk, especially during the winter months in southern parts of Australia. Early signs include the inability to perform fine movements (such as doing up buttons), shivering and a bad case of the 'umbles' (fumbles, mumbles, grumbles, stumbles).

The key elements of treatment include changing the environment to one where heat loss is minimised, changing out of any wet clothing, adding dry clothes with windproof and waterproof layers, adding insulation and providing fuel (water and carbohydrate) to allow shivering, which builds the internal temperature.

In severe hypothermia, shivering actually stops – this is a medical emergency requiring rapid evacuation in addition to the above measures.

Animal Hazards

Australia is home to some seriously dangerous creatures. On land there are poisonous snakes and spiders, while the sea harbours deadly box jellyfish and white pointer sharks. The saltwater crocodile spans both environments.

In reality you're unlikely to see these creatures in the wild, much less be attacked by one. Far more likely is a hangover after a big night, or getting sunburnt after not wearing sunscreen.

BOX JELLYFISH & OTHER MARINE DANGERS

There have been fatal encounters between swimmers and box jellyfish on the northern coast. Also known as the sea wasp or 'stinger', they have venomous tentacles that can grow up to 3m long. You can be stung any time, but from November to March you should stay out of the water unless you're wearing a 'stinger suit' (available from sporting shops).

If you are stung, first aid consists of washing the skin with vinegar to prevent further discharge of remaining stinging cells, followed by rapid transfer to a hospital; antivenene is widely available.

Marine spikes from sea urchins, stonefish, scorpion

TAP WATER & OTHER WATER SOURCES

Tap water is universally safe to drink in Western Australia. Increasing numbers of streams, rivers and lakes, however, are being contaminated by bugs that cause diarrhoea, making water purification essential. The simplest way to purify water is to boil it thoroughly. Consider purchasing a water filter; it's very important when buying a filter to read the specifications, so that you know exactly what it removes from the water and what it doesn't. Simple filtering will not remove all dangerous organisms, so if you cannot boil water it should be treated chemically. Chlorine tablets will kill many pathogens, but not some parasites such as giardia and amoebic cysts. Iodine is more effective in purifying water and is available in tablet form. Follow the directions carefully and remember that too much iodine can be harmful.

A BIT OF PERSPECTIVE

Despite the recent increase in fatal shark attacks in Western Australia, statistically it's still very unlikely that visitors will be attacked. Blue-ringed octopus deaths are even rarer – only two in the last century – and there's only ever been one confirmed death from a cone shell. Jellyfish kill about two people annually, but you're still 100 times more likely to drown.

On land, snakes kill one or two people per year (about the same as bee stings, or less than one-thousandth of those killed on the roads). There hasn't been a recorded death from a tick bite for over 50 years, nor from spider bites in the last 20.

fish, catfish and stingrays can cause severe local pain. If this occurs, immediately immerse the affected area in water that's as hot as can be tolerated. Keep topping up with hot water until the pain subsides and medical care can be reached. The stonefish is found only in tropical Australia; antivenene is available.

CROCODILES

In northwest WA, saltwater crocodiles can be a real danger. They live around the coast, and are also found in estuaries, creeks and rivers, sometimes a long way inland. Observe safety signs or ask locals whether an inviting waterhole or river is croc-free before plunging in. The last fatality in WA caused by a saltwater crocodile was in 1987, and attacks occurred in 2006 and 2012.

INSECTS

For four to six months of the year you'll have to cope with flies and mosquitoes. Flies are more prevalent in the outback, where a humble fly net is effective. Repellents may also deter them.

Mozzies are a problem in summer, especially near wetlands in tropical areas, and some species are carriers of viral infections. Keep your arms and legs covered after sunset and use repellent.

The biting midge (sandfly) lives in WA's northern coastal areas. Locals often appear immune, but it's almost a rite of passage for those heading north to be covered in bites. Cover up at dusk.

Ticks and leeches are also common. For protection, wear loose-fitting clothing with long sleeves. Apply 30% DEET on exposed skin, repeated every three to four hours, and impregnate clothing with permethrin.

SHARKS

From 2012 to 2014, there were seven fatal shark attacks in WA, and most involved surfers at more remote beaches. Around popular coastal and city beaches, shark-spotting methods include nets, spotter planes, jet skis and surf lifesavers, and the WA government has also launched a $20-million program to track, identify and mitigate (ie kill) sharks that are considered to pose an imminent threat. A shark cull also continues to be discussed, a controversial proposal given that great white sharks are a protected species.

SNAKES

There are many venomous snakes in the Australian bush, the most common being the brown and tiger snakes. Unless you're interfering with one, or accidentally stand on it, it's extremely unlikely you'll be bitten.

Australian snakes have a reputation that is justified in terms of the potency of their venom, but unjustified in terms of the actual risk to travellers and locals. They are endowed with only small fangs, making it easy to prevent bites to the lower limbs (where 80% of bites occur) by wearing protective clothing (such as gaiters) around the ankles when bushwalking.

The bite marks are small and preventing the spread of toxic venom can be achieved by applying pressure to the wound and immobilising the area with a splint or sling before seeking medical attention. Application of an elastic bandage (you can improvise with a T-shirt) wrapped firmly, but so not tightly that circulation is cut off, around the entire limb – along with immobilisation – is a life-saving first-aid measure.

SPIDERS

The redback is the most common poisonous spider in WA. It's small and black with a distinctive red stripe on its body. Bites cause increasing pain at the site followed by profuse sweating and generalised symptoms. First aid includes application of ice or cold packs to the bite and transfer to hospital. White-tailed (brown recluse) spider bites may cause an ulcer that is very difficult to heal. Clean the wound thoroughly and seek medical assistance.

Hospitals have antivenene on hand for all common snake and spider bites, but it helps to know which type you've been bitten by.

Other Hazards

BUSHFIRES

Bushfires are a regular occurrence in WA and in hot, dry and windy weather, be extremely careful with any naked flame. Even cigarette butts thrown out of car windows can start fires. On a total fire ban day it's forbidden even to use a camping stove in the open.

Bushwalkers should seek local advice before setting

out. When a total fire ban is in place, delay your trip until the weather improves. If you're out in the bush and you see smoke, even a long distance away, take heed – bushfires move fast and change direction with the wind. Go to the nearest open space, downhill if possible. A forested ridge is the most dangerous place to be during a bushfire.

CRIME

WA is a relatively safe place to visit, but you should still take reasonable precautions. Don't leave hotel rooms or cars unlocked, and don't leave valuables unattended and visible in cars.

In recent years there has been a spate of glassings (stabbings with broken glass) at Perth venues. If you see trouble brewing it's best to walk away. Take due caution on the streets after dark, especially around hot spots such as Northbridge. There have also been reports of drinks spiked with drugs in Perth pubs and clubs. Authorities advise women to refuse drinks offered by strangers in bars and to drink bottled alcohol rather than that in a glass.

DRIVING

Australian drivers are generally a courteous bunch, but rural 'petrolheads', inner-city speedsters and drink drivers can pose risks. Open-road dangers can include wildlife, such as kangaroos (mainly at dusk and dawn); fatigue, caused by travelling long distances without the necessary breaks; and excessive speed. Driving on dirt roads can also be tricky for the uninitiated.

OUTBACK TRAVEL

If you're keen to explore outback WA, it's important not to embark on your trip without careful planning and preparation. Travellers regularly encounter difficulties in the harsh outback conditions, and trips occasionally prove fatal.

SWIMMING

Popular beaches are patrolled by surf life-savers and flags mark out patrolled areas. Even so, WA's surf beaches can be dangerous places to swim in if you aren't used to the often heavy surf. Undertows (or 'rips') are the main problem. If you find yourself being carried out by a rip, just keep afloat; don't panic or try to swim against the rip, which will exhaust you. In most cases the current will stop within a couple of hundred metres of the shore and you can then swim parallel to the shore for a short way to get out of the rip and swim back to land.

On the south coast, freak 'king waves' from the Southern Ocean can sometimes break on the shore with little or no warning, dragging people out to sea. In populated areas there are warning signs; in other areas be extremely careful.

People have been paralysed by diving into waves in shallow water and hitting a sandbar; check the depth of the water before you leap.

Telephone

The two main telecommunications companies are **Telstra** (☎13 22 00; www.telstra.com.au) and **Optus** (☎1800 780 219; www.optus.com.au). Both are also major players in the mobile (cell) market, along with **Vodafone** (☎1300 650 410; www.vodafone.com.au) and **Virgin** (☎1300 555 100; www.virginmobile.com.au).

Local calls from private land lines cost 15c to 30c, while local calls from public phones cost 50c; both allow for unlimited talk time. Calls to mobile phones attract higher rates and are timed.

Although the whole of WA shares a single area code (☎08), once you call outside of the immediate area or town, it is likely that you are making a long-distance call. STD calls (Subscriber Trunk Dialling – a long-distance call within Australia) can be made from public phones and are cheaper during off-peak hours, generally between 7pm and 7am.

Phonecards can be purchased at newsagents and post offices for a fixed dollar value (usually $10, $20, $30 etc) and can be used with any public or private phone by dialling a toll-free access number and then entering the PIN number on the card. Call rates vary, so shop around. Some public phones also accept credit cards.

Mobile Phones

Australia's GSM and 3G/4G mobile networks service more than 90% of the population but leave vast tracts of the country uncovered, including much of inland WA. Perth and the larger centres get good reception, but outside these centres coverage is haphazard or non-existent, especially in the north. Of the mobile telcos, Telstra has the best coverage for both voice and internet services. Telstra's data plans are expensive though, and Optus is usually a better-value alternative for most WA travellers if you're sticking to main tourist areas. For travel to more remote areas in the north of the state, Telstra have superior service around Indigenous communities.

Australia's digital network is compatible with GSM 900 and 1800 (used in Europe), but is generally not compatible with the US or Japanese systems. All the main service providers offer prepaid mobile services for short-term access.

Phone Codes

☎**0011** International calling prefix (the equivalent of 00 in most other countries).

☎**61** Country code for Australia.

☎**08** Area code for all of WA. If calling from overseas, drop the initial zero.

☎**04** All numbers starting with 04 (such as 0410, 0412) are mobile phone numbers. If calling from overseas, drop the initial zero.

190 Usually recorded information calls, charged at anything from 35c to $5 or more per minute (more from mobiles and public phones).

1800 Toll-free numbers; can be called free of charge from anywhere in the country, though they may not be accessible from certain areas or from mobile phones.

1800-REVERSE (738 3773) or 12 550 Dial to make a reverse-charge (collect) call from any public or private phone.

13 or 1300 Charged at the rate of a local call. The numbers can usually be dialled Australia-wide, but may be applicable only to a specific state or STD district.

Note: Telephone numbers beginning with 1800, 13 or 1300 cannot be dialled from outside Australia.

Tourist Information

For general statewide information, try the **WA Visitor Centre** (Map p54; 1800 812 808, 08-9483 1111; www.bestofwa.com.au; 55 William St, Perth; 9am-5.30pm Mon-Fri, to 4.30pm Sat, 11am-4.30pm Sun), **Tourism Western Australia** (www.westernaustralia.com) or the **Department of Parks & Wildlife** (www.parks.dpaw.wa.gov.au).

Around WA, tourist offices with friendly staff (often volunteers) provide local knowledge including info on road conditions.

Travellers with Disabilities

Disability awareness in WA is excellent. Legislation requires that new accommodation meets accessibility standards, and discrimination by tourism operators is illegal. Many of the state's key attractions provide access for those with limited mobility and an increasing number are addressing the needs of visitors with visual or aural impairments. Contact attractions in advance to confirm the facilities.

Useful online resources:

National Public Toilet Map (www.toiletmap.gov.au) Lists more than 14,000 public toilets around Australia, including those with wheelchair access.

People with Disabilities WA (www.pwdwa.org) Website detailing WA's major disability services.

Tourism WA (www.westernaustralia.com) Website highlighting all accessible listings (accommodation, restaurants, tours etc).

Useful organisations:

VisAbility (08-9311 8202, 1800 847 466; www.visability.com.au) Support for people living with blindness and vision impairment.

National Information Communication & Awareness Network (Nican; 02-6241 1220, TTY 1800 806 769; www.nican.com.au) Australia-wide directory providing information on access, accommodation, sports and recreational activities, transport and specialist tour operators.

WA Deaf Society (08-9441 2677, TTY 08-9441 2655; www.wadeaf.org.au)

Visas

All visitors to Australia need a visa – only New Zealand nationals are exempt, and even they receive a 'special category' visa on arrival. Visa application forms are available from Australian diplomatic missions overseas, travel agents or the website of the **Department of Immigration and Citizenship** (www.immi.gov.au).

eVisitor

Many European passport holders are eligible for an eVisitor visa, which is free and allows visitors to stay in Australia for up to three months. eVisitors must be applied for online and they are electronically stored and linked to individual passport numbers, so no stamp in your passport is required. It's advisable to apply at least 14 days prior to the proposed date of travel to Australia. Applications are made on the Department of Immigration and Citizenship website (www.immi.gov.au).

Electronic Travel Authority (ETA)

Passport holders from eight countries that aren't part of the eVisitor scheme – Brunei, Canada, Hong Kong, Japan, Malaysia, Singapore, South Korea and the USA – can apply for either a visitor or business ETA. ETAs are valid for 12 months, and allow stays of up to three months on each visit. Apply online at www.eta.immi.gov.au.

Tourist Visas

Short-term tourist visas have largely been replaced by the eVisitor and ETA. However, if you are from a country not covered by either, or you want to stay longer than three months, you'll need to apply for a visa. Tourist visas cost from $130 and allow single or multiple entry for stays of three, six or 12 months and are valid for use within 12 months of issue.

Visa Extensions

If you want to stay in Australia for longer than your visa allows, you'll need to apply for a new visa (usually a tourist visa 676) through the Department of Immigration and Citizenship at www.immi.gov.au/visitors/tourist. Apply at least two or three weeks before your visa expires.

Work & Holiday Visas (462)

Nationals from Argentina, Bangladesh, Chile, Indonesia, Malaysia, Poland, Thailand, Turkey, Uruguay and the USA between the ages of 18 and 30 can apply for a work and holiday visa prior to entry to Australia. It allows the holder to enter Australia within three months of issue, stay for up to 12 months, leave and re-enter Australia

RESPONSIBLE INDIGENOUS TRAVEL

There are a range of protocols for visiting Indigenous lands, but it's always courteous to make contact prior to your visit. In many cases you must acquire a permit to enter, so check with local Indigenous Land Councils and police stations before visiting.

Some Indigenous sites are registered under heritage legislation and have conditions attached, or may be visited only with permission from their traditional custodians or in their company. Don't touch artworks, as the skin's natural oils can cause deterioration. Dust also causes problems – move thoughtfully at rock-art sites and leave your vehicle some distance away. Respect the wishes of Indigenous custodians by reading signs carefully, keeping to dedicated camping areas and staying on marked tracks. Remember that rock art and engravings are manifestations of sacred beliefs and laws.

When interacting with Indigenous Australians, you'll generally find them polite and willing to share their culture with you – but it must be on their terms. Show respect for privacy and remember that your time constraints and priorities may not always be shared. In some areas, English is not a first language, but in others many people speak English fluently. Body language and etiquette often vary: the terms 'thank you', or 'hello' and 'goodbye', may not be used in some areas, or direct eye contact may be avoided. So take note of local practices: take them as they come and follow the cues. Some Aboriginal communities are 'dry'. There may be rules relating to the purchase and consumption of alcohol, or it may be forbidden altogether.

any number of times within that 12 months, undertake temporary employment to supplement a trip, and study for up to four months.

Working Holiday Maker (WHM) Visas (417)

Young visitors (those aged 18 to 30) from Belgium, Canada, Cyprus, Denmark, Estonia, Finland, France, Germany, Hong Kong, Ireland, Italy, Japan, Korea, Malta, the Netherlands, Norway, Sweden, Taiwan and the UK are eligible for a WHM visa, allowing visits of up to one year for casual employment.

The emphasis of this visa is on casual and not full-time employment, so you're only supposed to work for any one employer for a maximum of six months. A first WHM visa must be obtained prior to entry to Australia and can be applied for at Australian diplomatic missions abroad or online (www.immi.gov.au/visitors/working-holiday). You can't change to a WHM visa once you're in Australia, so apply up to 12 months before your departure to Australia.

Volunteering

Lonely Planet's *Volunteer: A Traveller's Guide to Making a Difference Around the World* provides useful information about volunteering.

Online resources:

Go Volunteer (www.govolunteer.com.au) National website listing volunteer opportunities.

i-to-i (www.i-to-i.com) Conservation-based volunteer holidays in Australia.

Responsible Travel (www.responsibletravel.com) Volunteer travel opportunities.

Transitions Abroad (www.transitionsabroad.com) Listings of volunteer opportunities.

Volunteering Australia (www.volunteeringaustralia.org) Support, advice and volunteer training.

Useful organisations:

Conservation Volunteers Australia (CVA; ☎1800 032 501, 03-5330 2600; www.conservationvolunteers.com.au) A nonprofit organisation focusing on practical conservation projects such as tree planting, walking-track construction, and flora and fauna surveys. Most projects are either for a weekend or a week and all food, transport and accommodation is supplied in return for a contribution to help cover costs.

Department of Parks & Wildlife (www.dpaw.wa.gov.au) Current and future opportunities at national parks all over WA. Online, click on the Community & Education tab and then Volunteer Programs. Opportunities vary enormously, from turtle tagging at Ningaloo Marine Park to feral-animal control at Shark Bay. Working with the dolphins at Monkey Mia is a popular option (contact: monkeymiavolunteers@westnet.com.au).

Willing Workers on Organic Farms (WWOOF; ☎03-5155 0218; www.wwoof.com.au) WWOOFing is where you do a few hours work each day on a farm in return for bed and board. Most hosts are concerned to some extent with alternative lifestyles, and have a minimum stay of two nights. Join online for $70. You'll get a membership number and a booklet listing participating enterprises ($5 overseas postage).

Earthwatch Institute (☎03-9016-7590; www.earthwatch.org) Offers volunteer 'expeditions' focusing on conservation and wildlife.

Women Travellers

WA is generally a safe place for women travellers, although the usual sensible precautions apply. Avoid walking alone late at night in major cities and towns, and always keep enough money aside for a taxi home. The same applies to outback and rural towns with unlit, semi-deserted streets between you and your temporary home. Lone women should be wary of staying in basic pub accommodation unless it appears safe and well managed.

Lone hitching is risky for everyone, but women especially should consider taking a male companion.

Work

If you come to Australia on a tourist visa then you're not allowed to work for pay – working for approved volunteer organisations in exchange for board is OK. If you're caught breaching your visa conditions, you can be expelled from the country and banned for up to three years.

Seasonal Work

WA is experiencing a labour shortage and a wealth of opportunities exist for travellers (both Australian and foreign) for paid work year-round.

In Perth, plenty of temporary work is available in tourism and hospitality, administration, IT, nursing, childcare, factories and labouring. Outside Perth, travellers can easily get jobs in tourism and hospitality, plus a variety of seasonal work. Some places have specialised needs; in Broome, for example, there is lucrative work in pearling, on farms and boats.

INDUSTRY	TIME	REGION
grapes	Feb-Mar	Denmark, Margaret River, Mt Barker, Manjimup
apples/ pears	Feb-Apr	Donnybrook, Manjimup
prawn trawlers	Mar-Jun	Carnarvon
bananas	Apr-Dec	Kununurra
bananas	year-round	Carnarvon
veggies	May-Nov	Kununurra, Carnarvon
tourism	May-Dec	Kununurra
flowers	Sep-Nov	Midlands
lobsters	Nov-May	Esperance

Information

Backpacker accommodation, magazines and newspapers are good resources for local work opportunities.

Useful websites:

Australian Jobsearch (www.jobsearch.gov.au) Government site offering a job database.

Career One (www.careerone.com.au) General employment site; good for metropolitan areas.

Department of Human Services (www.humanservices.gov.au) The Australian government employment service has information and advice on looking for work, training and assistance.

Gumtree (http://perth.gumtree.com.au) Great classified site with jobs, accommodation and items for sale.

Harvest Trail (http://jobsearch.gov.au/HarvestTrail) Specialised recruitment search for the agricultural industry, including a 'crop list' detailing what you can pick and pack, when and where.

Jobfinder (www.jobfinder.com.au) Online job listings.

Job Shop (www.thejobshop.com.au) WA-based recruitment agency specialising in jobs for WA as well as the Northern Territory.

MyCareer (www.mycareer.com.au) Website for general employment; good for metropolitan areas.

Seek (www.seek.com.au) General employment site, good for metropolitan areas.

Travellers at Work (www.taw.com.au) Excellent site for working travellers in Australia.

Transport

GETTING THERE & AWAY

Unless you're coming by land from other states in Australia, chances are you'll be touching down in Perth. And, as you'll be told at some point no doubt, the capital of Western Australia (WA) is actually closer to Jakarta than Sydney.

Flights, tours and rail tickets can be booked online at www.lonelyplanet.com/bookings.

Entering the Country

Global instability has resulted in increased security in Australian airports, in both domestic and international terminals. Customs procedures may be a little more time-consuming but are still straightforward.

Air

If you're coming to Australia from Europe, Asia or Africa you'll find it quicker to fly directly to **Perth Airport** (www.perthairport.com; George Wiencke Dr), rather than via the east coast cities. If you do fly to the east coast first, there are frequent connecting flights to Perth from major cities. Port Hedland and Broome both welcome interstate flights, and there are weekend flights between Port Hedland and Bali.

Airlines Flying to/from WA

Most airlines fly into Perth, unless otherwise specified; listed phone numbers are for calls made within Australia.

Air Asia (D7; ☎1300 760 330; www.airasia.com) Budget flights from Kuala Lumpur and Denpasar (Bali).

Air Mauritius (MK; ☎1800 247 628; www.airmauritius.com) Flies from Mauritius.

Air New Zealand (NZ; ☎13 24 76; www.airnewzealand.com.au) Flies from Auckland year-round and from Christchurch from December to April.

Airnorth (TL; ☎1800 627 474; www.airnorth.com.au) Destinations include Perth, Broome, Darwin, Kununurra, Karratha and Port Hedland.

Cathay Pacific (CX; ☎13 17 47; www.cathaypacific.com) Flies from Hong Kong.

China Southern Airlines (CZ;☎1300 889 628; www.csair.com) To/from Guangzhou.

Emirates (EK; ☎1300 303 777; www.emirates.com) Flies from Dubai.

Etihad (EY; ☎1300 532 215; www.etihad.com) Flights from Abu Dhabi.

Garuda Indonesia (GA; ☎08-9214 5101; www.garuda-indonesia.com) Flies from Denpasar and Jakarta.

CLIMATE CHANGE & TRAVEL

Every form of transport that relies on carbon-based fuel generates CO_2, the main cause of human-induced climate change. Modern travel is dependent on aeroplanes, which might use less fuel per kilometre per person than most cars but travel much greater distances. The altitude at which aircraft emit gases (including CO_2) and particles also contributes to their climate change impact. Many websites offer 'carbon calculators' that allow people to estimate the carbon emissions generated by their journey and, for those who wish to do so, to offset the impact of the greenhouse gases emitted with contributions to portfolios of climate-friendly initiatives throughout the world. Lonely Planet offsets the carbon footprint of all staff and author travel.

Jetstar (JQ; ☎13 15 38; www.jetstar.com) Runs cheapies from Sydney, Melbourne, Cairns, Adelaide and the Gold Coast. International routes include Jakarta and Denpasar.

Malaysia Airlines (MH; ☎13 26 27, 08-9263 7043; www.malaysiaairlines.com) Flies from Kuala Lumpur.

Qantas (QF; ☎13 13 13; www.qantas.com.au) Flies between Perth and all Australian state capitals (excluding Hobart), as well as Broome, Geraldton, Exmouth, Cairns, Alice Springs and Uluru (Ayers Rock). Also flies from Kalgoorlie to Adelaide and Perth, and from Melbourne to Broome year-round, and from Sydney and Brisbane to Broome during school holidays.

Qatar Airways (QR; ☎1300 340 600; www.qatarairways.com) Flies from Doha.

Scoot (TZ;☎02-8520 1888; www.flyscoot.com) Low-cost flights to/from Singapore.

Singapore Airlines (SQ; ☎13 10 11; www.singaporeair.com.au) Flies from Singapore.

South African Airways (SA; ☎1300 435 972; www.flysaa.com) Flies from Johannesburg.

Thai Airways International (TG; ☎1300 651 960; www.thaiairways.com) Flies from Bangkok.

Tiger Airways (TR; ☎03-9335 3033; www.tigerairways.com) From Melbourne, Sydney and Singapore.

Virgin Australia (VA;☎13 67 89; www.virginaustralia.com) Links Perth to Busselton, Albany, Esperance, Geraldton, Exmouth, Port Hedland and Kalgoorlie. Also has flights to Sydney, Melbourne, Darwin and Brisbane, and weekend flights between Port Hedland and Bali.

Land

The nearest state capital to Perth is Adelaide, 2560km away by the shortest road route. To Melbourne it's at least 3280km, Darwin is around 4040km and Sydney is 3940km. Despite the vast distances, sealed roads cross the Nullarbor Plain from the eastern states to Perth, and then up the Indian Ocean coast and through the Kimberley to Darwin.

Bus

The only interstate bus is the daily **Greyhound** (☎1300 473 946; www.greyhound.com.au) service between Darwin and Broome (from $263, 26 hours), via Kununurra, Fitzroy Crossing and Derby.

Car, Motorcycle & Bicycle

Driving to Perth from any other state is a *very* long journey, but it's a great way to see the country. Be aware that there are strict quarantine restrictions on fruit and vegetables when crossing the border into WA.

Hitching

Hitching is never entirely safe and we don't recommend it. Travellers who hitch should understand that they are taking a small but serious risk. Hitching to or from WA across the Nullarbor is definitely not advisable, as waits of several days are not uncommon.

People looking for travelling companions for driving to WA from Sydney, Melbourne, Adelaide or Darwin frequently leave notices in backpacker hostels, or you can look for car-sharing options online:

- www.coseats.com
- www.gumtree.com.au
- www.shareyourride.net/carpool/Australia

Train

The only interstate rail link is the famous *Indian Pacific*, run by **Great Southern Rail** (☎13 21 47; www.greatsouthernrail.com.au), which travels 4352km to Perth from Kalgoorlie (10 hours), Adelaide (two days), Broken Hill (2¼ days) and Sydney (three days). From Port Augusta to Kalgoorlie the seemingly endless crossing of the virtually uninhabited centre takes well over 24 hours, including the 'long straight' on the Nullarbor – at 478km this is the longest straight stretch of train line in the world. You can take 'whistle-stop' tours of some towns on the way.

Flexible one-way adult fares for the full journey start from $939 (reclining seat) and $1929 (sleeper cabin including meals). Substantial discounts are available off the seat-only price for backpackers, students, children and pensioners, and advance purchase at least six months before travel secures the best prices for sleeper cabins. Across December and January, cheaper low-season fares are often available.

Cars can be transported between Perth and Sydney, Melbourne and Adelaide – a good alternative to driving across the Nullarbor Plain in both directions. Note that service is usually around 25% cheaper *from* Perth, than *to* Perth.

GETTING AROUND

The distances between key WA towns are vast, especially in the north.

Air

Unless you have unlimited time, consider internal flights.

Airlines Flying Within WA

Airnorth (TL; ☎1800 627 474; www.airnorth.com.au) Routes include Perth–Kununurra, Karratha–Port Hedland, Karratha–Broome, Port Hedland–Broome and Broome–Kununurra.

Cobham (☎1800 105 503; www.cobham.com.au) Flies between Perth and Exmouth and Karratha.

Qantas (QF; ☎13 13 13; www.qantas.com.au) WA destinations include Kalgoorlie, Paraburdoo,

Newman, Exmouth, Karratha, Port Hedland and Broome.

Skippers Aviation (☎1300 729 924; www.skippers.com.au) Flies following routes in both directions: Perth–Leonora–Laverton, Perth–Wiluna–Leinster, Perth–Mt Magnet–Meekatharra, Perth–Carnarvon, Perth–Geraldton–Carnarvon and Perth–Kalbarri–Monkey Mia. Mostly used by those in the mining industry. Also flies Broome–Fitzroy Crossing–Halls Creek.

Alliance Airlines (☎1300 780 970; www.allianceairlines.com.au) Mine-industry services linking Broome and Karratha, but can also be booked by the public.

Virgin Australia (VA; ☎13 67 89; www.virginaustralia.com) Links Perth to Busselton, Albany, Esperance, Geraldton, Exmouth, Port Hedland and Kalgoorlie.

Bicycle

Bicycle helmets are compulsory in WA, as are white front lights and red rear lights for riding at night.

If you're coming specifically to cycle, bring your own bike. Check with your airline for costs. Within WA you can load your bike onto a bus to skip the boring bits of the country. Book ahead so that you and your bike can travel on the same vehicle.

Suffering dehydration is a real risk in WA and can be life-threatening. It can get very hot in summer, so take things slowly until you're used to the heat. A prudent plan is to start riding every day at sunrise, relax in the shade – bring your own shelter – during the heat of the day and then ride a few more hours in the afternoon. Always wear a hat and plenty of sunscreen, and drink *lots* of water.

Outback travel needs to be planned thoroughly, with the availability of drinking water the main concern. Those isolated water sources (bores, tanks, creeks) shown on your map may be dry or undrinkable, so you can't always depend on them. Also don't count on getting water from private mine sites as many are closed to the public. Bring necessary spare parts and bike-repair knowledge. Check with locals (start at the visitor centres) if you're heading into remote areas, and always let someone know where you're headed before setting off.

Useful contacts for information on touring around WA, including suggested routes, road conditions and cycling maps:

Bicycle Transportation Alliance (☎0400 047 349; www.btawa.org.au) Advocacy group for cyclists with good tips and safe-riding advice.

Cycle Touring Association of WA (www.ctawa.asn.au) Supporting cycle touring around WA.

Bus

WA's bus network could hardly be called comprehensive, but it offers access to substantially more destinations than the railways. All long-distance buses are modern and well-equipped with air-con, toilets and films.

Greyhound (☎1300 473 946; www.greyhound.com.au) Following a recent rationalisation of routes and services, Greyhound's only WA service is now from Broome to Darwin, via Derby, Fitzroy Crossing and Halls Creek.

Integrity Coach Lines (☎1800 226 339; www.integritycoachlines.com.au) Buses between Perth and Port Hedland via the Great Northern Hwy, and also from Perth to Lancelin, Cervantes, Geraldton, Exmouth, Karratha and Broome. Hop-on, hop-off tickets valid for 12 months with unlimited stops are available (Perth–Exmouth $245, Perth–Broome $365). This includes connecting shuttle services west to the coast for Kalbarri and Shark Bay. Also run handy services linking Exmouth and Karijini.

South West Coach Lines (☎08-9261 7600; www.transdevsw.com.au) From Perth to all the major towns in the southwest – your best choice for Margaret River.

Transwa (☎1300 662 205; www.transwa.wa.gov.au) The state government's transport service, operating mainly in the southern half of the state. Main routes include Perth–Augusta, Perth–Pemberton, Perth–Albany (three different routes), Perth–Esperance (two routes), Albany–Esperance, Kalgoorlie–Esperance, Perth–Geraldton (three routes) and Geraldton–Meekatharra.

Car & Motorcycle

Providing the freedom to explore off the beaten track, travelling with your own vehicle is the best transport option in WA. With several people travelling together, costs can be contained and, if you don't have major mechanical problems, there are many benefits.

The climate is good for motorcycles for much of the year, and many small trails into the bush lead to perfect camping spots. Bringing your own motorcycle into Australia requires valid registration in the country of origin and a Carnet de Passages en Douanes, allowing the holder to import their vehicle without paying customs duty or taxes. Apply to the motoring organisation/association in your home country. You'll also need a rider's licence and a helmet. A fuel range of 350km will cover fuel stops up the centre and on Hwy 1 around the continent. The long, open roads are really made for large-capacity machines above 750cc.

The **Royal Automobile Club of WA** (www.rac.com.au) has useful advice on statewide motoring, including road safety, local regulations and buying/selling a car. It also offers car insurance to members, and membership can secure discounts on car rentals and motel accommodation.

Also popular are car-share websites, especially for securing a lift to Broome, Perth, Denmark and Darwin:

- www.coseats.com
- www.gumtree.com.au
- www.shareyourride.net/carpool/Australia

Driving Licence

You can use your home country's driving licence in WA for up to three months, as long as it carries your photo for identification and is in English. Alternatively, arrange an International Driving Permit (IDP) from your home country's automobile association and carry it along with your licence.

Fuel

Fuel (predominantly unleaded and diesel) is available from service stations. Liquefied petroleum gas (LPG) is not always stocked at more remote roadhouses – if your car runs on gas it's safer to have dual fuel capacity.

Prices vary wildly in WA, even between stations in Perth. For up-to-date fuel prices, visit the government fuel-watch website (www.fuelwatch.wa.gov.au).

Distances between fill-ups can be long in the outback, but there are only a handful of tracks where you'll require a long-range fuel tank or need to use jerry cans. However, if you are doing some back-road explorations, always calculate your fuel consumption, plan accordingly and carry a spare jerry can or two. Keep in mind that most small-town service stations are only open from 6am to 7pm and roadhouses aren't always open 24 hours. On main roads there'll be a small town or roadhouse roughly every 150km to 200km.

Always carry two spare tyres and at least 20L of water.

Hire

Competition between car-rental companies in Australia is fierce, so rates vary and special deals come and go. The main thing to remember when assessing your options is distance – if you want to travel widely, you need to weigh up the price difference between an unlimited-kilometres deal and one that offers a set number of kilometres free with a fee per kilometre over that set number.

Local firms are always cheaper than the big operators – sometimes half the price – but cheap car hire often comes with restrictions on how far you can take the vehicle away from the rental centre.

Some, but not all, rental companies offer one-way hires, so research this option before you arrive. It's worth investigating and combining with an internal flight if you're travelling to somewhere like Exmouth, Broome or Esperance. A significant premium is usually charged. There are sometimes good deals for taking a car or campervan from, say, Broome back to Perth, but you'll need to contact local rental companies closer to the time of rental.

You must be at least 21 years old to hire from most firms – if you're under 25 you may only be able to hire a small car or have to pay a surcharge. A credit card will be essential.

Renting a 4WD enables you to safely tackle routes off the beaten track and get out to more remote natural wonders. Note that many 'normal' rental cars aren't allowed off main roads, so

4WD DRIVING TIPS

We don't need to see more 4WDs on tow trucks; the victims of a dirt-road roll over, a poorly judged river crossing, or coming to grief when meeting the native fauna on the road. Here are some tips to help keep you from riding upfront in a tow truck:

- Before heading off-road, check the road conditions at www.mainroads.wa.gov.au.
- Recheck road conditions at each visitor centre you come across – they change quickly.
- Let people know where you're going, what route you're taking and how long you'll be gone.
- Don't drive at night: it's safer to stop in the mid-afternoon to avoid wildlife.
- Avoid sudden changes in direction – 4WDs have a much higher centre of gravity than cars.
- On sand tracks, reduce tyre pressure to 140kpa (20psi) and don't forget to re-inflate your tyres once you're back on the tarmac.
- When driving on corrugated tracks, note that while there is a 'sweet spot' speed where you feel the corrugations less, it's often too fast to negotiate a corner – and roll overs often happen because of this.
- When crossing rivers and creeks, always walk across first to check the depth – unless you're in saltwater crocodile territory, of course!

always check insurance conditions carefully, especially the excess, as they can be onerous. Even for a 4WD, the insurance offered by most companies does not cover damage caused when travelling 'off-road', which basically means anything that is not a maintained bitumen or dirt road.

Avis (☎13 63 33; www.avis.com.au)

Backpacker Car Rentals (☎08-9430 8869; www.backpackercarrentals.com.au; 235 Hampton Rd, South Fremantle) Good-value local agency.

Bayswater Car Rental (☎08-9325 1000; www.bayswatercarrental.com.au) Local company with four branches in Perth and Fremantle.

Britz Rentals (☎1800 331 454; www.britz.com.au) Hires fully equipped 4WDs fitted out as campervans, popular on the roads of northern WA. Britz has offices in all the state capitals, as well as Perth and Broome, so one-way rentals are possible.

Budget (☎1300 362 848; www.budget.com.au) Wide range of cars.

Campabout Oz (☎08-9301 2765; www.campaboutoz.com.au) Campervans, 4WDs and motorbikes.

Hertz (☎13 30 39; www.hertz.com.au)

Mighty Cars & Campers (☎1800 670 232; www.mightycampers.com.au)

Thrifty (☎1300 367 227; www.thrifty.com.au) Excellent service.

Insurance

In Australia, third-party personal-injury insurance is always included in the vehicle registration cost. This ensures that every registered vehicle carries at least minimum insurance. You'd be wise to extend that minimum to at least third-party property insurance as well – minor collisions with other vehicles can be surprisingly expensive.

If you're bringing your own car from within Australia, take out the most comprehensive roadside assistance plan you can. It's not a matter of if your car will break down, but when. Having the top cover will offset your recovery costs considerably.

For hire cars, establish exactly what your liability is in the event of an accident. Rather than risk paying out thousands of dollars if you do have an accident, you can take out your own comprehensive insurance on the car, or (the usual option) pay an additional daily amount to the rental company for an 'insurance excess reduction' policy. This brings the amount of excess you must pay in the event of an accident down from between $2000 and $5000 to a few hundred dollars. However, check your travel insurance policy as well as any insurance you have through your credit card before forking out the cash to reduce your excess, as excess reduction may be covered by a policy you already have. Alternatively, companies such as Tripcover and RAC offer excess-reduction policies that often cost much less than those offered by car-hire companies.

Be aware that if you're travelling on dirt roads you may not be covered by insurance. Because of potential accidents with wildlife, some companies' insurance may preclude driving after dusk at night. Also, most companies' insurance won't cover the cost of damage to glass (including the windscreen) or tyres. Always read the small print.

Purchase

If you're planning a stay of several months that involves lots of driving, buying a second-hand car will be much cheaper than renting. But remember that reliability is all-important. Breaking down in the outback is very inconvenient (and potentially dangerous) – the nearest mechanic can be a very expensive tow-truck ride away!

You'll probably get any car cheaper by buying privately through the newspaper (try Saturday's *West Australian*) rather than through a car dealer. Buying through a dealer can include a guarantee, but this is not much use if you're buying a car in Perth for a trip to Broome. Online, see www.carpoint.com.au and www.drive.com.au to buy a car.

There are local regulations to comply with when buying or selling a car. In WA a vehicle has to have a compulsory safety check and obtain a road-worthiness certificate (RWC) before it can be registered in the new owner's name – usually the seller will indicate whether the car already has a RWC. Stamp duty has to be paid when you buy a car; as this is based on the purchase price, it's not unknown for the buyer and the seller to agree privately to understate the price.

To avoid buying a lemon, you might consider forking out some extra money for a vehicle appraisal before purchase. The RAC offers this kind of check in Perth and other large WA centres from around $214/238 for members/nonmembers; it also offers extensive advice on buying and selling cars on its website.

The beginning of winter (June) is a good time to start looking for a used motorbike. Local newspapers and the bike-related press have classified advertisement sections.

Fremantle has a number of secondhand-car yards, including a cluster in North Fremantle on the Stirling Hwy, while in Perth there's the **Traveller's Auto Barn** (☎1800 674 374; www.travellers-autobarn.com.au; 16 Adrian Street, Welshpool). See the website for directions from the city or the airport. It also hires cars and campervans.

Road Conditions

WA is not criss-crossed by multi-lane highways; there's not enough traffic and the distances are too great to justify them. All the main routes are well surfaced and have two lanes, but not far off the beaten track you'll find yourself on unsealed roads. Anybody seeing the state in reasonable detail can expect some dirt-road travelling. A 2WD car can cope with the major ones, but for serious exploration, plan on a 4WD.

Driving on unsealed roads requires special care – a car will perform differently when braking and turning on dirt. Under no circumstances exceed 80km/h on dirt roads; if you go faster you won't have enough time to respond to a sharp turn, stock on the road, or an unmarked gate or cattle grid. Take it easy and take time to see the sights.

It's important to note that when it rains, some roads flood. Flooding is a real problem up north because of cyclonic storms. Exercise extreme caution at wet times, especially at the frequent yellow 'Floodway' signs. If you come to a stretch of water and you're not sure of the depth or what could lie beneath it, pull up at the side of the road and walk through it (excluding known saltwater-crocodile areas, such as the Pentecost River crossing on the Gibb River Road!). Even on major highways, if it has been raining you can sometimes be driving through 30cm or more of water for hundreds of metres at a time.

Mainroads (☎13 81 38; www.mainroads.wa.gov.au) provides statewide road-condition reports, updated daily (and more frequently if necessary).

Road Hazards

Travelling by car within WA means sometimes having to pass road trains. These articulated trucks and their loads (consisting of two or more trailers) can be up to 53.5m long, 2.5m wide and travel at around 100km/h. Overtaking them is tricky – once you commit to passing there's no going back. Exercise caution and pick your time, but don't get timid mid-manoeuvre. Also, remember that it is much harder for the truck driver to control their giant-sized vehicle than it is for you to control your car.

WA's enormous distances can lead to dangerous levels of driver fatigue. Stop and rest every two hours or so – do some exercise, change drivers or have a coffee. The major routes have rest areas and many roadhouses offer free coffee for drivers; ask for maps from the RAC that indicate rest stops.

Cattle, emus and kangaroos are common hazards on country roads, and a collision is likely to kill the animal and cause serious damage to your vehicle. Kangaroos are most active around dawn and dusk, and they travel in groups. If possible plan your travel to avoid these times of the day. If you see a roo hopping across the road in front of you, slow right down – its friends are probably just behind it.

It's important to keep a safe distance behind the vehicle in front, in case it hits an animal or has to slow down suddenly. If an animal runs out in front of you, brake if you can, but don't swerve unless it is safe to do so. You're likely to come out of a collision with an emu better than a collision with a tree or another vehicle.

Road Rules

Driving in WA holds few surprises, other than those that hop out in front of your vehicle. Cars are driven on the left-hand side of the road (as in the rest of Australia). An important road rule is 'give way to the right' – if an intersection is unmarked, you must give way to vehicles entering the intersection from your right.

The speed limit in urban areas is generally 60km/h, unless signposted otherwise. The state speed limit is 110km/h, applicable to all roads in non-built-up areas, unless otherwise indicated. The police have radar speed traps and speed cameras, often in carefully concealed locations.

Oncoming drivers who flash their lights at you may be giving you a warning of a speed camera ahead – or they may be telling you that your headlights are not on. It's polite to wave back if someone does this. Don't get caught flashing your lights yourself, as it's illegal.

Seat belts are compulsory, and not using them incurs a fine. Children must be strapped into an approved safety seat. Talking and texting on a mobile phone while driving is illegal.

Drink-driving is a serious problem in WA, especially in country areas, and random breath tests are used to reduce the road toll. If you're caught driving with a blood-alcohol level of more than 0.05%, expect a hefty fine, a court appearance and the loss of your licence.

Local Transport

Perth has an efficient, fully integrated public-transport system called **Transperth** (☎13 62 13; www.transperth.wa.gov.au) covering public buses, trains and ferries in a large area that reaches south to include Fremantle, Rockingham and Mandurah. Larger regional centres, including Bunbury, Busselton and Albany, have limited local bus services.

Taxis are available in most of the larger towns.

Tours

The **WA Visitor Centre** (Map p54; ☎1800 812 808, 08-9483 1111; www.bestofwa.com.au; 55 William St; ⏲9am-5.30pm

Mon-Fri, 9.30am-4.30pm Sat, 11am-4.30pm Sun) in Perth has a wide selection of brochures and suggestions for tours all over the state. Prices given are rates per person in twin share; there's usually an extra supplement for single accommodation. Students and YHA members often get a discount.

The hop-on, hop-off bus options are a popular way for travellers to get around in a fun, relaxed atmosphere. Some adventure tours include serious 4WD safaris, taking travellers to places that they simply couldn't get to on their own without large amounts of expensive equipment.

AAT Kings Australian Tours (☎1300 228 456; www.aatkings.com.au) A long-established and professional outfit offering a wide range of fully escorted bus trips and 4WD adventures. Tours in WA range from a six-day Perth to Monkey Mia trip to an 11-day Untamed Kimberley adventure.

Adventure Tours (☎1300 654 604; www.adventuretours.com.au) WA trips up to 14 days, often with a focus on adventure and Indigenous culture. Accommodation may include hostels and camping, and tour options include Perth to Broome ($1995, 14 days).

Outback Spirit (☎1800 688 222; www.outbackspirittours.com.au) Luxury all-terrain explorations including a Western Wildflowers Discovery tour ($6495, 15 days) and Pilbara, Karijini and Ningaloo Reef ($6995, 13 days).

Red Earth Safaris (☎1800 501 968; www.redearthsafaris.com.au) Operates a six-day Perth to Exmouth minibus tour ($785) with a two-day return trip ($200). Also available is a two-day/one-night return trip from Perth to Cervantes and the Pinnacles ($225). This also incorporates the Swan Valley and the monastery town of New Norcia.

Train

The state's internal rail network, operated by **Transwa** (☎1300 662 205; www.transwa.wa.gov.au), is limited to the *Prospector* (Perth to Kalgoorlie), the *AvonLink* (Perth to Northam) and the *Australind* (Perth to Bunbury). Transperth's local train network reaches as far south as Mandurah.

Behind the Scenes

SEND US YOUR FEEDBACK

We love to hear from travellers – your comments keep us on our toes and help make our books better. Our well-travelled team reads every word on what you loved or loathed about this book. Although we cannot reply individually to postal submissions, we always guarantee that your feedback goes straight to the appropriate authors, in time for the next edition. Each person who sends us information is thanked in the next edition – the most useful submissions are rewarded with a selection of digital PDF chapters.

Visit **lonelyplanet.com/contact** to submit your updates and suggestions or to ask for help. Our award-winning website also features inspirational travel stories, news and discussions.

Note: We may edit, reproduce and incorporate your comments in Lonely Planet products such as guidebooks, websites and digital products, so let us know if you don't want your comments reproduced or your name acknowledged. For a copy of our privacy policy visit lonelyplanet.com/privacy.

OUR READERS

Many thanks to the travellers who used the last edition and wrote to us with helpful hints, useful advice and interesting anecdotes:

David Connolly, Fiona Grahame, Helen Carter, Jessica Dwyer, Katerina Lianou, Kevin Callaghan, Martijn Mennen, Petra O'Neill

AUTHOR THANKS

Brett Atkinson

Thanks to the helpful folk at visitor information centres and national parks offices throughout Western Australia. Special thanks to Jayde and Michelle in Perth, and to the Homestead team in the Swan Valley for the tasty behind the scenes tour. At Lonely Planet, cheers to Tasmin Waby, my fellow scribes, and the hardworking editors and cartographers. Final thanks to Carol for holding the fort across the ditch in New Zealand so we could eventually escape to Burma.

Kate Armstrong

Sincere thanks to Roger Chomley and Gunilla for sharing a special part of the world; Neville Poelina, Wil Thomas, Liz Jack and Robyn Maher for their generosity of spirits. To my experienced friend Don who gave me necessary flight bravado and sea legs. Tasmin Waby, this opportunity is greatly appreciated. Finally, thanks to fellow authors Steve and Brett and the Lonely Planet team.

Steve Waters

Thanks to the hire-car folks at Broome airport, the CP people for the late-checkout in Exmouth, the tyre repair guys at Drysdale & Paraburdoo, Leonie and Nev for beer and sunsets, Trace & Heath, Brodie, Abbidene, Meika and Kaeghan for Wedge Love, Honest Ed's Steak and Car Cleaning Service, Roz and Megan for caretaking, Hamish for putting up with the same playlist forever, and Seb and Tasmin for guiding me through the twittersphere.

ACKNOWLEDGMENTS

Climate map data adapted from Peel MC, Finlayson BL & McMahon TA (2007) 'Updated World Map of the Köppen-Geiger Climate Classification', Hydrology and Earth System Sciences, 11, 163344.

Cover photograph: Esperance beach/John W Banagan/Getty.

THIS BOOK

This 8th edition of Lonely Planet's *West Coast Australia* guidebook was researched and written by Brett Atkinson, Kate Armstrong and Steve Waters. The previous edition was researched and written by Brett Atkinson and Steve Waters. This guidebook was produced by the following:

Destination Editor Tasmin Waby

Product Editors Katie O'Connell, Alison Ridgway

Regional Senior Cartographer Julie Sheridan

Book Designer Jessica Rose

Assisting Editors Carolyn Boicos, Kate Evans, Kate James, Catherine Naghten, Lauren O'Connell, Kathryn Rowan, Vicky Smith, Gabrielle Stefanos

Assisting Cartographer James Leversha

Cover Researcher Naomi Parker

Thanks to Jo Cooke, Anna Harris, Claire Naylor, Karyn Noble, Di Schallmeiner, Ellie Simpson, Lauren Wellicome

Index

Map Pages **000**
Photo Pages 000

Map Pages **000**
Photo Pages 000

Map Legend

Sights
- Beach
- Bird Sanctuary
- Buddhist
- Castle/Palace
- Christian
- Confucian
- Hindu
- Islamic
- Jain
- Jewish
- Monument
- Museum/Gallery/Historic Building
- Ruin
- Sento Hot Baths/Onsen
- Shinto
- Sikh
- Taoist
- Winery/Vineyard
- Zoo/Wildlife Sanctuary
- Other Sight

Activities, Courses & Tours
- Bodysurfing
- Diving/Snorkelling
- Canoeing/Kayaking
- Course/Tour
- Skiing
- Snorkelling
- Surfing
- Swimming/Pool
- Walking
- Windsurfing
- Other Activity

Sleeping
- Sleeping
- Camping

Eating
- Eating

Drinking & Nightlife
- Drinking & Nightlife
- Cafe

Entertainment
- Entertainment

Shopping
- Shopping

Information
- Bank
- Embassy/Consulate
- Hospital/Medical
- Internet
- Police
- Post Office
- Telephone
- Toilet
- Tourist Information
- Other Information

Geographic
- Beach
- Hut/Shelter
- Lighthouse
- Lookout
- Mountain/Volcano
- Oasis
- Park
- Pass
- Picnic Area
- Waterfall

Population
- Capital (National)
- Capital (State/Province)
- City/Large Town
- Town/Village

Transport
- Airport
- Border crossing
- Bus
- Cable car/Funicular
- Cycling
- Ferry
- Metro station
- Monorail
- Parking
- Petrol station
- Subway station
- Taxi
- Train station/Railway
- Tram
- Underground station
- Other Transport

Note: Not all symbols displayed above appear on the maps in this book

Routes
- Tollway
- Freeway
- Primary
- Secondary
- Tertiary
- Lane
- Unsealed road
- Road under construction
- Plaza/Mall
- Steps
- Tunnel
- Pedestrian overpass
- Walking Tour
- Walking Tour detour
- Path/Walking Trail

Boundaries
- International
- State/Province
- Disputed
- Regional/Suburb
- Marine Park
- Cliff
- Wall

Hydrography
- River, Creek
- Intermittent River
- Canal
- Water
- Dry/Salt/Intermittent Lake
- Reef

Areas
- Airport/Runway
- Beach/Desert
- Cemetery (Christian)
- Cemetery (Other)
- Glacier
- Mudflat
- Park/Forest
- Sight (Building)
- Sportsground
- Swamp/Mangrove

OUR STORY

A beat-up old car, a few dollars in the pocket and a sense of adventure. In 1972 that's all Tony and Maureen Wheeler needed for the trip of a lifetime – across Europe and Asia overland to Australia. It took several months, and at the end – broke but inspired – they sat at their kitchen table writing and stapling together their first travel guide, *Across Asia on the Cheap*. Within a week they'd sold 1500 copies. Lonely Planet was born.

Today, Lonely Planet has offices in Franklin, London, Melbourne, Oakland, Beijing and Delhi, with more than 600 staff and writers. We share Tony's belief that 'a great guidebook should do three things: inform, educate and amuse'.

OUR WRITERS

Brett Atkinson

Perth & Fremantle, Around Perth, Margaret River & the Southwest Coast, Southern WA, Monkey Mia & the Central West For this edition, Brett flew across the gorges of WA's Karijini National Park, met the dolphins of Monkey Mia, and uncovered more excellent Australian craft breweries around Margaret River and the Swan Valley. Ever-changing Perth seems more exciting each time he returns, especially hip and funky Northbridge. Brett is based in Auckland, New Zealand and has covered around 50 countries as a guidebook author and travel and food writer. See www.brett-atkinson.net for his most recent work and upcoming travels. Brett also wrote the Plan Your Trip, Understand (other than History) and Survival Guide chapters.

Kate Armstrong

Broome & the Kimberley Hailing from the cold southeast, Kate couldn't wait to head northwest, hitting the road in a rattling 4WD, her first time north of Perth. She's written over 30 Lonely Planet guidebooks – covering Greece, Portugal, South Africa and Mexico – but this time round, she shocked herself: she fell in love; with her own country. For this edition, she cruised Broome and up and down the Dampier Peninsula, falling for its pearls: the extraordinary red pindan soils, the fishing and swimming, and the local Aussie down-to-earthliness.

Steve Waters

Coral Coast & the Pilbara, Broome & the Kimberley This was Steve's sixth trip to the north of WA and while some things hadn't changed (huge distances, heat, blowing a tyre on the Kalumburu Rd), others were totally different (Cape Range National Park after the floods, volunteering for the Mornington Bird Census, trying to find the same restaurant in Exmouth). Then there was the added novelty of coming to grips with social media :) Steve's written online articles on WA and co-authored previous editions of *Australia*, *Indonesia*, *Great Adventures* and *Best in Travel*, and come the next Dry will probably be heading north once again.

Read more about Steve at:
http://auth.lonelyplanet.com/profiles/stevewaters

Contributing Authors

Michael Cathcart Michael teaches history at the Australian Centre, University of Melbourne. He is well known as a broadcaster on ABC Radio National and has presented history programs on ABC TV. Michael wrote the History chapter.

Published by Lonely Planet Publications Pty Ltd
ABN 36 005 607 983
8th edition – November 2015
ISBN 978 1 74321 556 2

10 9 8 7 6 5 4 3 2 1
Printed in China